How to Start Your Own Business...and Succeed

How to Start Your Own Business ...and Succeed

REVISED EDITION

ARTHUR H. KURILOFF

JOHN M. HEMPHILL, JR.

McGraw-Hill Book Company

New York St. Louis San Francisco Auckland Bogotá Hamburg Johannesburg London Madrid
Mexico Montreal New Delhi Panama Paris São Paulo Singapore Sydney Tokyo Toronto

Library of Congress Cataloging in Publication Data

Kuriloff, Arthur H
    How to start your own business . . . and succeed.

    1. Business—Handbooks, manuals, etc. 2. Small
business—Handbooks, manuals, etc. 3. Entrepreneur—
Handbooks, manuals, etc. I. Hemphill, John Mearl,
date   joint author. II. Title.
HF5356.K88   1980   658.1'141   80-13059
ISBN 0-07-035650-5

HOW TO START YOUR OWN BUSINESS . . . AND SUCCEED

This book was set in Melior by Holmes Composition Service.
The editor was Donald W. Burden; the production supervisor
was Richard A. Ausburn.
Edwards Brothers Incorporated was printer and binder.

For those adventurous persons who want to start their own business
. . . and succeed

_____

Contents

Preface

This book has its origins in four sources:

1. Each of us has started and operated several small successful businesses. We define a small business as one in which the entrepreneur-owner can walk around and know everyone on the payroll by first name—at the most several dozen people.

We learned from the mistakes we made in our first ventures and we try to continue to learn as we teach and consult. Each of us keeps his hand in by running a small business today.

2. Over the past eight years, experience in teaching entrepreneurship and small business management in the Graduate School of Management at UCLA and the Graduate School of Business and Economics at California State University, Los Angeles, shows that a growing number of students want to start their own business after leaving school. They prefer the adventure of their own enterprise to the "security" that comes with working for a large corporation.

3. Many people of all ages, including early and late retirees, are hungry for information about starting their own business. We've seen a steady growth in attendance in recent years in university sponsored small business seminars for the general public. The number of women who attend our seminars has increased over the past eight years; the percentage has jumped from about 10 to over 50 percent.

4. We have done consulting assignments for nearly two hundred small businesses in the past decade. We've witnessed about every known pitfall small businesspersons can fall into—plus some that they seem to have invented. We've rescued a good number from disaster; others cried for help too late.

These experiences sharpened our perceptions of the need for a practical step-by-step guidebook for prospective small business owners, one that would show beginners how to avoid the pitfalls in starting a small business and what positive actions to take to improve their chances for success.

We've designed this book as a guide and workbook beginners can use to gain understanding and skill in the basics needed to start and operate a small business successfully. We've tried to give appropriate answers to many questions we're asked in our seminars. The following examples are typical:

- Is this a good time to start a business?

- Is it better to buy a going business or to start a new one?

- Should I form a corporation when I start my business?

- How shall I price my product (or service)?

The answers we give come sometimes from experience, sometimes from research, and sometimes from a combination of the two. We've attempted, without off-putting academic gobbledygook or the patter of the snake-oil pitchman, to give you the straight goods. This book should give you a firm basis for starting . . . and succeeding in your own business.

ACKNOWLEDGMENTS

To those who have contributed in their special ways to help us in the preparation of this book we give grateful thanks and ackowledgment:

Freddie Pacht Kuriloff, for invaluable aid as editor of our manuscript; members of the McGraw-Hill family for encouragement and assistance: Robert G. Manley, Philip A. Cecchettini, Bernard Scheier, Donald W. Burden, Suzanne Knott, Mary Miller, and Bruce Kortebein; Virginia Hemphill, wife, critic, and partner in creating this book; and Marjorie Larkin, Ruth Sheridan, and Rebecca Aguilar, for a first rate job of preparing the typescript.

We also appreciate the assistance of Roy Aaron, Attorney at Law; Donald G. Malcolm, Dean, School of Business and Economics, California State University, Los Angeles; Douglas Markley, Entrepreneur; David Menkin, Entrepreneur; Edward Poll, Attorney at Law; Irvine Robbins, Entrepreneur; Keith Smith, Professor of Finance, Graduate School of Management, UCLA; Hans Schollhammer, Professor of Management, Graduate School of Management, UCLA; and Jack Vineberg, Certified Public Accountant.

Arthur H. Kuriloff

John M. Hemphill, Jr.

How to Start Your Own Business...and Succeed

Chapter 1

Stars in Your Eyes?

YOU MUST KNOW THE BUSINESS

YOU MUST HAVE MANAGEMENT SKILLS

DEVELOPING YOUR BUSINESS PLAN

WORKSHEETS

f you want to start your own business, and you have stars in your eyes—good. But make sure they don't blind you, that you know where you're going.

Remember the famous chat Alice had with the Cheshire Cat in *Alice in Wonderland?*

Alice: "Would you tell me, please, which way I ought to go from here?"
Cat: "That depends a good deal on where you want to get to."
Alice: "I don't much care where. . . ."
Cat: "Then it doesn't much matter which way you go."
Alice: ". . . so long as I get *somewhere.*"
Cat: "Oh, you're sure to do that, if you only walk long enough."

There are some critical lessons for the beginning enterpriser in this brief conversation. Not knowing "where you want to get to" shows a lack of planning that can be disastrous. And if you haven't thought it through and figured out how to get where you want to go, getting "somewhere" may be very costly. You'll get somewhere, to be sure, but it may be a not-too-happy where: folding up your venture—perhaps, at best, selling it at a loss—or, at worst, bankruptcy.

Most new businesses fail because their owners don't have balanced business experience.[1] Balanced experience requires three basic strengths:

1. **Technical competence** in the business you have chosen, which means that you should have the know-how to get out the product or render the service in good style

2. **Marketing competence,** which means that you should know how to find your special niche in the market, how to identify your customers, and how to sell enough of what you offer at a price that will return an adequate profit for your efforts

3. **Financial competence,** which means that you should know how to plan for and get the money you'll need to start and keep your business running without getting into cash troubles

You'll have to know many other things about starting and running a business, but these three are fundamental. They make the foundation upon which you can build success.

YOU MUST KNOW THE BUSINESS   1 A, 2 A (3)*

You should have experience in the business you want to start before all else. It's hard

---

*You'll find reference numbers like this after major headings in all chapters throughout the book. These reference numbers identify specific items in the Outline for Developing Your Basic Business Plan (Prospectus) given in Appendix A at the back of the book. For example, this particular reference, 1 A, 2 A (3) says that the information given under the heading YOU MUST KNOW THE BUSINESS fits in the Outline at point 1A (Description of your proposed business) and at point 2A (3) (Describe your qualifications to run the business).

enough to get a venture going, with a thousand matters to absorb your attention, without trying to learn how to produce the product or render the service at the same time. If you don't have this essential know-how, you'd be well-advised to find a job in that business. Work in it for a year or so. Keep your eyes and ears open. Learn everything you can about the product or service. In other words, acquire the technical competence you'll need to start your own company. You can use your spare time for the planning you must do to tilt the odds for success in your favor before you set up your own business. And you'll get paid while you learn.

YOU MUST HAVE MANAGEMENT SKILLS 2 A (3)

This book is designed to help you gain the management skills you'll need before you start your business. We emphasize marketing and financial planning, as these have been shown to be essential for success in small business. The text is keyed to helping you develop your fundamental business plan—the carefully drawn road map—you must have to show you where you want to go and how to get there in the shortest time with the least cost.

The business plan is the critical tool you'll need to raise capital or borrow money. In developing the plan for your business you'll gain a firm grasp of the requirements you'll have to meet to start and run your business. By carefully following the procedures recommended in this text, you'll acquire such detailed knowledge about your proposed venture that even the most sophisticated investor won't be able to ask you a question you can't answer. You'll show confidence in what you want to do. And by showing confidence and knowledge, you'll build the confidence of your prospective investors in your ability to carry through your project successfully.

DEVELOPING YOUR BUSINESS PLAN (Appendix A)

The text is designed to help you develop your business plan. In Appendix A you will find an outline for your business plan. This plan will be the road map for your

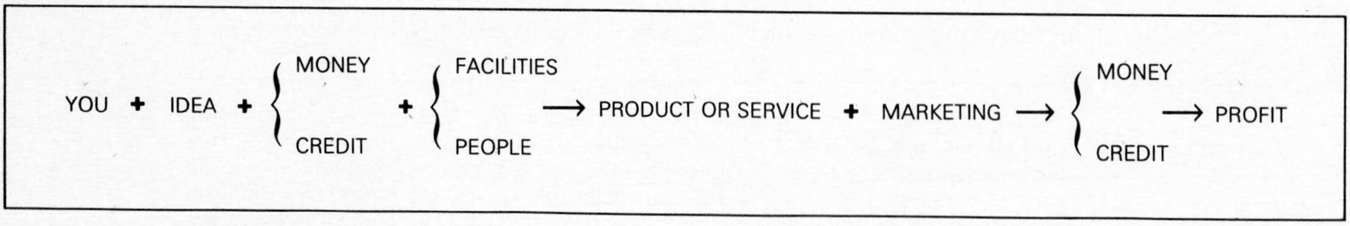

YOU + IDEA + { MONEY / CREDIT } + { FACILITIES / PEOPLE } → PRODUCT OR SERVICE + MARKETING → { MONEY / CREDIT } → PROFIT

Figure 1-1

4

business; it has been tried and tested over the years. We know many entrepreneurs who have raised money successfully on the basis of plans developed from this outline and have used the plans to achieve a successful business. The basic theme of your business plan, or prospectus as it's often called, is shown in Figure 1-1. We'll look at the characteristics of successful entrepreneurs so you can see how well yours match, and what you can do to strengthen them. We'll outline ways of going after capital and presenting your business plan to prospective investors and bankers. We'll describe ways of using credit, of turning out the product or service, and of building the organization of people you'll want as you grow. We'll consider the marketing requirements of your product or service. If you manage these business processes well, with a bit of luck, you'll be able to convert your product or service into profit large enough to repay you for all the time, energy, and money you will have put into your venture.

WORKSHEETS

At the end of each chapter in this book, you will find a worksheet. Each chapter and worksheet is aimed at helping you understand and write a specific part of the plan for your prospective business. Major headings in each chapter are keyed by code number and letter to their appropriate place in the outline (see footnote, page 3). We urge you to study each chapter carefully. Collect the data required to fill out each worksheet for your business (sources of information are given throughout the text). When you've finished all the worksheets, you'll have the substance of a basic plan for your business. You'll write up and polish this plan, then use it to convince investors and other credit sources to put money in your business.

An outline of the main points in each chapter appears on the divider page at the front of the chapter; these will aid you in finding points you want to check. A list of suggested readings appears at the end of each chapter; these have been chosen to give you sources of information on subjects that you may want to explore in detail.

Highlights of business plans for retail, service, and manufacturing businesses are located in Appendix B. They are offered as guides to give you direction in preparing your own plan. *You should, of course, work up the data for your own business;* you should *not* rely on the specifics given in these examples. Each business is unique, and you must develop the specific information that fits your business in order to have a sound plan, or prospectus, that will get you where you want to go at the least cost in time and money.

NOTE ABOUT OPINION SURVEY

Before you begin Chapter 2, please take the time to fill out the Opinion Survey that follows. This survey is designed to help you pinpoint what you now believe about those persons known as entrepreneurs, who are able to start a business and drive it through to success. When you have finished studying Chapter 2, we want you to review your opinions about entrepreneurs. Perhaps some of your ideas as shown in the survey will have changed; perhaps they will have been reinforced. Either way, you'll have set the basis for gaining an understanding of yourself as a potential entrepreneur. And you'll be prepared to take advantage of the suggestions given in Chapter 2 for strengthening your entrepreneurial drive.

OPINION SURVEY

	True	Don't know	False	
1. The most noticeable trait of entrepreneurs is their high need for power.	✓		✓	F
2. The here-and-now is more important to the entrepreneur than tomorrow.			✓	F
3. People who start their own business are gamblers.	✓		✓	F
4. Entrepreneurs are inclined to rely on tested and proven ways of solving problems.	✓			F
5. When entrepreneurs need advice they rely on their close friends.			✓	DK
6. Most of the time, entrepreneurs "fly by the seat of their pants."		✓	✓	F
7. Entrepreneurs feel very uncomfortable unless they know how they're doing.	✓			T
8. Entrepreneurs value money above other kinds of rewards.			✓	F
9. Entrepreneurs set impossibly high goals to stimulate themselves to high accomplishment.			✓	F
10. Entrepreneurs tend to avoid routine tasks.			✓	F
11. The payoff in owning your own business is being your own boss.	✓			F

CHAPTER 1/FOOTNOTES

[1]*The Business Failure Record*, Dun & Bradstreet, Inc., New York. This is a yearly publication prepared by the Business Economics Department of this firm. Year after year it reports lack of balanced managerial experience as a prime cause of the failure of new businesses.

Chapter 2

So You Want to Start Your Own Business

THE ENTREPRENEURIAL CHARACTERISTICS

REINFORCING ACHIEVEMENT MOTIVATION

REWARDS AND PENALTIES OF OWNING YOUR OWN BUSINESS

The third time really was a charm," said Sam Brunelle, "I failed twice before I made this business go."

Sam is the owner of a profitable small business that makes prototype components for electronics manufacturers. Located just off Route 128 outside of Boston, Sam's company has supplied small runs of components for pilot production to middle- and large-sized companies around the country for the past ten years.

"Yes," said Sam, "I learned the hard way. After I closed up my second shop, I looked back to see what had happened. What had I done wrong?

"It dawned on me that I was playing in a different game as the owner of a business than I had been as a tool-and-die maker. Being a good machinist didn't give me the license to run a business. So I set out to learn all I could before trying again—which I was bound and determined to do."

That Sam had learned what was needed to be a successful entrepreneur is clear. His small business employs sixty people, did almost $2 million in gross sales last year at a profit of 20 percent before taxes—close to $400,000. Sam's bulldog determination, willingness to admit his deficiency, and refusal to give up the idea of becoming his own boss show his entrepreneurial qualities.

If you want to start and succeed in your own business, you should first of all ask yourself, "Do I have what Sam has—do I have what it takes?" Not everyone does. The personal characteristics of the prospective enterpriser are not found in everyone. Entrepreneurs are special people. They have special strengths upon which to draw for their adventure into business.

We know a great deal about the characteristics of successful entrepreneurs, primarily as a result of research done by Harvard's David C. McClelland and his associates over the past twenty-five years. McClelland's findings suggest that all human beings have psychological needs that may be described in three general classes: the *need for affiliation,* the *need for power,* and the *need for achievement.* We all have some of each of these needs. But in every person, one is the most powerful and impels us into specific kinds of work or activity. Nurses and social workers, for example, show a high need for affiliation. They want to work closely with others, to be helpful, and to experience the rewards of the helping relationship. Effective salespersons and politicians show a high need for power. They find their reward in manipulating the behavior of others and in controlling the means for making others respond to their sales pitch. The need we're interested in, the one shown by successful small businesspersons, is the *need for achievement* (often referred to as n Ach).

To find out if you have what it takes to be a winner in starting your own business, you should check your characteristics against those found in successful entrepreneurs. Think as honestly as you can about your behavior and activities in the past as you go through the descriptions that follow. Decide whether your characteristics match at least reasonably well. If they do, you have things going for you, and you can strengthen your n Ach as outlined later. If there is a wide gap, you probably have a high need for affiliation or a high need for power and would be better off working for someone else. By choosing this course, you would avoid the possibility of facing a sea of troubles—of losing your money, your time, and your happy frame of mind.

Prime among the qualities of the high n Ach personality is a commitment to excellence. Successful entrepreneurs value excellence; they demand high performance from themselves and will not be satisfied with less. They aim at accomplishment of worthwhile and challenging tasks. Although they daydream about achievement, they're not content to let it go at dreaming as most people do. Their visions seem to stimulate an inner drive for making their dreams come true. They find a special joy in winning; for them achievement is an end in itself.

> Do you have a burning desire to be a winner?

Commitment to the Task

Once committed to a course of action, high n Ach persons become absorbed in it. They don't let go. They can't forget or forgive themselves for an unfinished project. The burden of failure would bother them too much and too long. Knowing that big achievements don't come easily or quickly, they don't wait for the lucky break. They dig in for the long haul and stay with a project until it's successfully completed.

> Do you have this quality of stick-to-itiveness?

Choosing Moderate Risk

Despite a commonly accepted notion, entrepreneurs are *not* gamblers. They choose moderate risk rather than the wild speculative gamble. Some people prefer the wild risk; some prefer a conservative approach that minimizes their exposure to loss. High n Ach people take a middle course. They want a moderate risk, large enough to be exciting, but with reasonable hope for gain.

Achievement-oriented persons willingly assume responsibility for a project or task they believe they can manage successfully through their own competencies. They know their own skills. Their attitude is therefore one of aggressive realism. Their commitment to a task rests on considered judgment of their ability to influence the outcome successfully.

> Do you prefer a middle course when you have studied a risky problem objectively and think you can solve it through your own knowledge and skill?

10

Seizing Opportunities

Entrepreneurial persons are quick to see and seize opportunities. They show an innovative turn of mind and convert opportunities they observe into active programs for achievement. Because they are intensely realistic, they anticipate and plan carefully how to get where they want to go. They favor logical predictions based upon fact. In realizing an opportunity, they're not overwhelmed by obstacles but, rather, are challenged to figure out ways to get around them. They often come up with innovative ways to overcome obstacles.

> Are you alert to opportunities; do you seize and convert them to your advantage?

Objectivity

High n Ach people are more realistic than others about themselves and the ends they seek. They're utterly unsentimental about undertakings close to their hearts. They're not likely to let personal likes and dislikes stand in their way. When they require assistance, they select experts rather than friends or relatives to help them. They take a businesslike attitude toward their business.

> Do you choose the tough, businesslike way to solve problems rather than giving in to personal likes and dislikes in finding help?

Need for Feedback

Entrepreneurs seek immediate feedback on their performance. They want prompt accurate data on the results they're getting. It doesn't seem to make any difference whether the information they get is good or bad; they are stimulated by it to pour more energy into accomplishing the task.

> Do you find it important to know how you're doing when you're working on a project?

Optimism in Novel Situations

High n Ach persons tend to be optimistic in unfamiliar situations. The odds may not be clear, but the circumstances may be appealing. Entrepreneurial persons may, in such situations, see no reason why they can't win out through their own abilities.

They plow ahead undeterred by lack of guidelines and frequently make more of whatever opportunities there are than more cautious persons who wait for the odds to become better.

As they begin to understand the situation and its elements, high n Ach persons revert to their more usual habits and begin to calculate their chances very closely. Thus, they present the paradoxical picture of boldness in the face of the unknown and prudence in the face of the familiar. They move from the ill-defined to the sharply defined and often win out by applying their special knowledge and skills.

> Do you welcome tackling and solving an unfamiliar but interesting problem?

Attitude Toward Money

Persons with high n Ach tend to respect money, but they're not greedy. They don't see money as something to hoard. Rather, they see money as counters in a game. When their operations are profitable, they view the profit as an indicator that they are winning the game.

Profit, or its lack, gives entrepreneurs the feedback signal they want. When business is profitable, it tells them that their activities are sound and should be strengthened or enlarged. When profits begin to slide off, it tells them they'd better identify and solve the problems causing the decline.

> Do you see money as an end in itself, or do you see it as a valuable asset that tells you how you're doing?

Proactive Management

Most conventional managers let things happen. Then they race around "putting out brush fires," trying to straighten things out. They practice reactive management. Not so the successful entrepreneur. Although high n Ach persons are careful to keep an eye on the present, they keep a significant part of their thinking directed toward the future. They plan their business worlds the way they would like them to be. They then work hard to bring their plans to actuality. This quality of working out ways to make a desired objective come true is the essence of *proactive* management. Proactive management is the basis for successful management of the small business.

> Do you like to think ahead and plan your future—and then work to make it come true?

12

REINFORCING ACHIEVEMENT MOTIVATION

In general, people with a high n Ach—those who strive for and become successful in business—are more energetic, more persistent, more realistic, and more action-minded than people with other kinds of motivational patterns. To judge yourself you must ask the question: How well do I fit the pattern of the high n Ach personality as outlined above? If there's a reasonable fit and you want to strengthen your need for achievement, you may want to adopt the procedures suggested by McClelland and his associates. These are outlined in the following paragraphs.

Thinking Like an Achiever

You can increase your achieving motivation by learning to think like an achiever. Direct your fantasies toward the accomplishment of worthwhile goals. Incorporate standards of excellence in considering what you want to do. Think of newer and better things to do and newer and better ways of doing the things you must do. By paying attention to the act of thinking in this way, you'll stimulate your n Ach.

Adopting the Language of Achievement

You can help to strengthen your achieving motivation by adopting the language of achievement and using it all the time. It's often said that we create our personal worlds by the words we choose to describe them; there appears to be a great deal of truth in this statement. You should try to use positive language to support your positive thinking, without, of course, being brash about it. A strong continuing effort to think and talk constructively cannot but help you strengthen your n Ach.

Planning for Achievement

Entrepreneurs show a high level of future orientation. You can reinforce your desire to achieve by planning your goals in writing. Set down on paper what you wish to accomplish in the next year, the next month, the next week. Check how you're doing in meeting your stated goals from week to week. In this way you'll be following the course of successful enterprisers. You'll see how effective your activities are; you'll be stimulated to take corrective and more effective actions from the feedback you get; and you'll be enhancing your n Ach.

Behaving in a Positive Fashion

Successful entrepreneurs seize opportunities for improvement and gain by creative positive action. Innovation and creativity underlie a major part of successful enterprising activity. Those who don't think very well of themselves are poorly equipped to take the risky step of venturing into the unknown, which creativity and innovation imply. You should therefore learn to have confidence in yourself, and this can flow only from a positive self-image.

Many psychologists say that we are what we do. To improve your self-image, you should practice new behavior aimed at building your personal effectiveness. For most of us, this is a long, hard road. Recognizing the need for endurance in reaching the goal of an improved self-image, you should dig in for the long haul and practice the new behavioral pattern persistently.

That n Ach may be heightened by these procedures has been shown by McClelland and his associates. McClelland summarizes the results of several n Ach development programs as follows:

> The courses have been given: to executives in a large American firm, in several Mexican firms, to underachieving high school boys, and to businessmen in India from Bombay and from a small city—Kakinada in the state of Andhra Pradesh. In every instance save one (the Mexican case), it was possible to demonstrate statistically, some two years later, that men who took the course had done better (made more money, got promoted faster) than comparable men who did not take the course or who took some other management course.[1]

To sum up the foregoing suggestions, you can reinforce your n Ach by:

- Learning to think like an achiever

- Adopting the language of achievement

- Planning and assessing your level of achievement by timely feedback on your performance

- Behaving in a confident, positive fashion

REWARDS AND PENALTIES OF OWNING YOUR OWN BUSINESS

We asked a group of twenty highly successful entrepreneurs from many different kinds of business what they had experienced as the rewards and penalties of owning their own enterprises. After a lively discussion, they came to consensus on the following major points:

- You enjoy the satisfaction of being your own boss, for the most part. You have the power to do things in your own way. If you have foibles—and most entrepreneurs do—you can cater to them in the way you choose to manage. This freedom is exhilarating.

- You can experience the rewards of ownership in tangible and intangible ways. You can secure your own future by putting aside a substantial retirement fund, and you can sell your business when it's profitable to do so. You create jobs for others, and you can help them to grow, which is a satisfying experience.

■ You can share your prosperity by paying dividends if you're a corporation or a percentage of the profits to your partners if you're a partnership.

■ You command the respect and deference of others. You will undoubtedly be called upon to serve your community in some way, and you'll get satisfaction out of this public service.

These are some of the more significant rewards attending the creation of a successful business. However, as in most cases in life, it is not possible to achieve benefits without some costs. Following are the more important penalties the successful entrepreneurs agreed upon:

■ You are *not* your own boss in some major respects. Your customers and the various government agencies you must report to are your bosses. Your customers are likely to be finicky and demanding. If you don't continually check their needs and make sure you're satisfying them, you'll suffer a declining business. And meeting more and more legal demands becomes more onerous with time; yet you must pay your taxes and fulfill the requirements of federal, state, and city legislation to stay in business.

■ The scope of your operations is limited by your limited resources. You must often abandon a dream for taking on a major project because you don't have sufficient money or other resources. You must therefore content yourself with a scope of operation you can manage—and sometimes this will frustrate you.

■ You work long and hard. When you start your own business, you'll find that it's a ten-to-twelve-hour day and a seven-day week. The business will not only absorb your energies, it will also demand your time. Your social life and your family life will suffer. You should make sure that your wife or husband shares your desire to venture into business with you—and accepts the fact that there'll be many lonely hours without your presence.

These, then, are some major pros and cons as seen by enterprisers who have been there. As a prospective entrepreneur, you should weigh them. Those with a high need for achievement will undoubtedly find that the rewards far outweigh the penalties. In this book we suggest ways to achieve the rewards and minimize the penalties by taking the proper steps in starting and running your own business.

CHAPTER 2/FOOTNOTE

[1]David C. McClelland, "That Urge to Achieve," *Think* (November/December 1966), IBM.

Your Personal Assessment

This worksheet will help you decide where to improve your personal skills in order to strengthen your drive toward achievement. Follow the instructions as honestly as you can. Have your wife or husband, or someone who knows you very well, check your answers. In this way, you will be sure that your answers are sound.

1. STICK-TO-ITIVENESS

Look back on your career. Think carefully about an event in the course of your work that you really like to remember. What was there about the situation that you like to recall? Was there a special challenge? Tough problems that you had to solve? Did you stick to the task in spite of discouraging setbacks? And did you achieve the result you wanted?

On a sheet of paper, write the event you've been recalling. State the major problem or problems and how you solved them. State how you felt while working out the answers and how you felt when you accomplished the task successfully.

Now answer these questions by putting a checkmark on the scale at the point that best tallies with your answer.

DO I HAVE A BURNING DESIRE TO BE A WINNER?

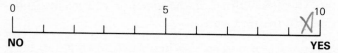

DO I HAVE THE STICK-TO-ITIVENESS TO BE A WINNER?

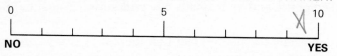

Repeat the process for other events of a similar kind.

Every new business faces difficulties that can be overcome only by long, hard effort. If your answers are to the left of 5 on the scale, you should reappraise your attitude and reorient your thinking before trying your own business. If your answers are to the right of 5 on the scale, you more than likely have the stick-to-itiveness to be successful in launching your own business.

2. RISK TAKING

Would you choose to invest at your bank in certificates of deposit at a 6 percent return or in an oil stock at a possible return of 15 percent? Or would you prefer to invest in the

16

stock market, after careful and continued study of trends and projections, with a fairly good chance of making 10 percent through your effort?

Successful entrepreneurs usually choose the middle course in which the possibility for gain is reasonable and the outcome depends to a great extent on the skill and knowledge they can bring to the situation.

Look back on your own approaches to decisions you've made. Describe below a typical decision you made in a matter of some importance to you.

_____

_____

_____

_____

_____

_____

Do you normally choose a middle course in which you can affect the outcome by using your own knowledge and skill?

YES _X_. NO ___.

A *yes* answer is a favorable indicator for your future as an enterpriser. A *no* answer doesn't rule you out; it says you'd be wise to change your ways.

3. SEIZING OPPORTUNITIES

Have you ever taken advantage of your company's offer to pay your tuition if you took a course at night school to gain a skill you could use on the job? If you are self-employed, have you ever grasped the chance to make some extra money through recognizing and seizing an opportunity?

List an example from your experience in the space below:

_____

_____

_____

_____

_____

_____

Do you recognize, seize, and convert opportunities to your advantage?

YES ___. NO ___.

The small new business should be founded on a new and exciting idea for product or service. Profitability comes from entrepreneurial innovation, as many economists have pointed out. But innovation can't stop with the first idea. It must be practiced continually to ensure that the firm keeps a competitive edge. Therefore, as a small business owner, you must stay alert always for ways to improve your product or service and to add new products and services to your line.

Alertness is a characteristic that can be acquired with practice. The person wanting to start a business should practice searching for opportunities. Successful search finds its reward in continuing innovation, which is the foundation for profitability.

4. OBJECTIVITY

Think back to a time when you wanted to do something beyond your skill. Perhaps you wanted a cabinet built for your record player or bookshelves installed in your den. Did you choose your good friend, an amateur home craftsperson, to do the job? The work might be passable but certainly not up to that of the skilled cabinet maker—who might charge a fairly sizeable fee for the work but whose quality of work you could be certain of.

I'd prefer the skilled craftsperson despite my friendship with the amateur:

YES ____. NO ____.

If you answered *no* above, bring yourself up short! Learn to be objective and unsentimental in choosing people to help you solve your business problems. The successful entrepreneur prefers the expert to the amateur when in need of help, as the research clearly shows, and this objectivity pays off handsomely in running the business.

5. NEED FOR FEEDBACK

Have you ever wanted to know how you were doing on the job? Have you tackled the boss to find out? Do you keep track of the mileage you're getting from your car and see to it that the tires are properly inflated and the engine tuned when the mileage shows signs of falling off? Is it your custom to check on matters of this kind and to make improvement when the signs show the need?

YES ____. NO ____.

A *yes* answer bodes well for your new venture. Enterprisers look to feedback signals from what they do and from what things do for or to them. They want to know how they're doing. They'll do more of the right thing and change course to overcome the effects of having done the wrong thing. A *no* answer suggests that need to learn how to get and use feedback for improving your performance.

6. OPTIMISM IN NOVEL SITUATIONS

Have you ever tackled a job that you didn't know too much about but decided to take on because it looked exciting and you thought you could do it? For example, have you tried to convert your attic into a playroom, or put together a loom from a do-it-yourself kit?

18

Although the job proved to be difficult, did you plow ahead, gaining skill as you went, and complete the project?

YES ___. NO ___.

Entrepreneurs sometimes take on projects that interest them even when they are not thoroughly familiar with the details. The novelty may attract them, and they believe they can bring their own special skills to accomplish the job. If you answered *yes* to the question above, you have another indicator of n Ach in your makeup.

7. ATTITUDE TOWARD MONEY

Do you view money as an end in itself, to be accumulated and socked away? Or do you see it as a means for accomplishing goals that you think important?

SCALE OF IMPORTANCE OF MONEY TO YOU:

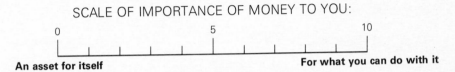

Entrepreneurs tend to see money as a means for doing things they consider worthwhile and also as counters in the business game. They value money but don't revere it. The trick in business is to use it for accomplishment. If your answer on the scale above is less than 5, you'd better start viewing money as a means for doing important things and not as an end in itself.

8. PROACTIVE MANAGEMENT

Are you accustomed to think ahead? Do you set a goal for yourself, such as a new house or a new car? Then do you plan and work consistently to achieve the goal, thinking through your special requirements and setting aside funds for the purchase?

YES ___. NO ___.

To become a successful businessperson, it is important that you learn to plan ahead, yet keep your present circumstances under control. This is the essence of proactive management, and if you said *no* above, you can and should acquire the skill of being proactive. All it takes is practice!

IF YOU WANT TO READ MORE

David C. McClelland, *The Achieving Society*, (paperback), The Free Press, New York, 1967. In this monumental work, McClelland describes the research that went into the development of the concept of the need for achievement and shows how it relates to economic success in business.

David C. McClelland, *Motivating Economic Achievement*, The Free Press, New York, 1969. This book describes McClelland's activities and research in stimulating economic performance in various countries through helping prospective entrepreneurs strengthen their need for achievement.

Chapter 3

So You Need a Bright Idea

Nothing is so futile as a "me-too" business. To set up to make a product just like those on the market is to court disaster; to open a boutique to sell apparel just like someone else's is to enter a hard battle for survival. Your new business cannot hope to compete with a manufacturing operation that is well established and has the momentum of know-how and satisfied customers. Nor can your boutique hope to cut into the business of a nearby respected dress shop with loyal customers.

You should found your business on a bright new idea. You must develop a superior product or service that will attract and hold sufficient customers so you can make a reasonable profit. And this means that you need an innovative concept as the basis for your business. But that's not all—you must practice creativity regularly to ensure the long-term success of your business after you open your doors.

SOURCES OF INNOVATIVE IDEAS   2 A (1), 4 A (4)

Before you proceed with the text in this chapter, list as many ways of identifying innovative ideas for your business as you can in ten minutes. This exercise will prepare you for the creative thinking you'll want to do in Worksheet 2 at the end of the chapter. _____

_____

_____

_____

_____

_____

_____

_____

_____

We have two types of creativity: *external* and *internal*. External creativity means the introduction of new ideas from the outside; internal creativity means discovering from our own thinking new ways of doing things or new things to do.

External Creativity

You can stimulate your external creativity by systematically exercising your curiosity about new developments, new ideas, new forces in the environment, about what goes on around you. As you do this, you'll build a reservoir of information about many things, including facts, impressions, images and pictures, and a great variety of ideas. You'll find an occasional idea that you can grasp and use immediately. But beyond that you'll build a backlog of ideas upon which you can draw when you're involved in internal creativity.

Internal Creativity

You'll experience sudden flashes of insight when you're engaged in internal creativity. In this kind of effort, your thinking will draw upon the reservoir we've just mentioned. Knowledge is transferable. You'll suddenly see new ways to combine ideas from different fields to get a better answer to a problem or to improve an existing product or service. Sometimes these ideas will pop into your head at unexpected moments. Then the reading and observing you've done will pay off as your unconscious produces the answer you've been seeking. Inventions are sometimes born this way. Edwin Land, of Polaroid fame, is said to have expressed it this way: "Invention is the sudden cessation of ignorance."

GUIDELINES FOR GENERATING IDEAS FOR PRODUCT OR SERVICE   **4** A (4)

At a meeting with a group of successful entrepreneurs, our purpose was to find out how they had hit upon the idea for their business. We give here condensed versions of their stories about developing the concept that started them on a successful business venture. We believe you'll find in these episodes guidelines that will trigger your thinking in useful ways for your new business adventure.

Hobby or Personal Interest

Joan Snelling, of Joan's Apparel: "I'd been wanting my own business for years," said Joan. "My hobby ever since high school has been making my own clothes. And I always thought it would be great to have my own dress shop.

"My opportunity came when my Aunt Sue got married and wanted to move to Chicago with her husband. She had a little dress shop at Cardiff-by-the-Sea, which she suggested I buy. I made the deal to buy her shop for a small down payment and a little each month.

"My Aunt's operation had catered to a fairly conservative clientele. But you know Cardiff—lots of teen-agers, surfers, young men and young women. . . . I decided to change the image of the store, to move it to mod fashions for younger women. This concept took hold, and my store began to do fairly well.

"One day a young woman walked in and showed me a sketch of a very smart dress. She asked me if I could run one up for her, which I thought I could do in the alteration room we had at the back of the store.

"The dress turned out well. Soon I had several requests for similar dresses from friends of the young woman who had asked me to make the first one. Before I knew what was happening, I found myself in the apparel manufacturing business. Volume grew to a point where I decided to give up the retail business and concentrate on manufacturing.

"One thing led to another—and the business grew rapidly. I saw it was getting beyond me; I needed help in managing the business. I talked it out with a management consultant and my husband. They agreed that the future of the business looked bright, bright enough for my husband to quit his engineering job and join me. He took over our manufacturing, and I managed our marketing. Together we worried about and solved the financial problems we experienced with the growth of the business.

"The rest of the story is quite simple. We've just sold the business after twelve years and we're retiring. We are going to take the trip around the world in our own boat that we've always wanted, and that's been in our plans from the very first day we started the business."

Develop the basic idea for your business from your hobby or special interest!

Why Isn't There a . . . ?

Ralph Bascom, of Bascom Products, Inc.: "I was trying to clean the bristles of a paint brush full of old hardened paint one day when I had a sudden thought: 'Why isn't there a disposable paint brush?' We have so many convenience items that are disposable, everything from diapers to dresses to paper plates—why not a paint brush that you could use once and throw away when you were through painting?

"I went to work on the idea with a friend. He's in the plastics field, a capable engineer. After several weeks of experimenting we found that we could make an inexpensive practical brush of flexible polyurethane. We could sell a two-inch brush for well under a dollar at retail and still afford the retailer and ourselves a reasonable profit.

"We made up a couple hundred of the brushes. Then we got permission from several hardware and paint stores in our area to demonstrate the brushes. We'd set up an easel, keep cans of several kinds of paint handy, and have small pieces of plywood and hardboard to paint on.

"When customers tried the brushes we could see how well they worked for different people, and also test the customers' reaction. The results were promising enough for us to take the next step.

"We had 5000 brushes made. An industrial artist prepared a design from which we had a number of cardboard counter displays made. With these we were able to persuade a dozen hardware and paint stores to display our brushes on their counters.

"In the meantime we had applied for patent protection on the brush, which we eventually got. In the end we sold the patent to a large company and have been happy to receive steady royalties ever since."

Find the answer to the question. "Why isn't there a . . . ?"

Shortcomings in Existing Products or Services

John Thornley, of Thornley Molded Products: "I'm a technical salesman by background," said John. "For several years I sold electronics components as a manufacturer's representative. In dealing with my customers, I found an extremely desirable niche in the market—at least I thought so, if I could solve the basic problem in filling it.

"In my contacts with many large electronics manufacturing firms, I came to see that they had a real need for short runs of small insulating devices for their new products. They needed insulating bases, encapsulating shells, and molded parts to hold such things as capacitors and resistors. The short runs were needed for pilot production purposes. They'd want 100, 250, or at the most, 500 pieces of a specially designed small base, for example, for an electronic component. They didn't want to take the risk of ordering permanent tooling for their new product until they were sure that the design was sound and warranted full production.

"But there was no place they could go to get a small run at an economical price. The usual supplier could manufacture in huge quantities quite cheaply, but this required a major investment in permanent tooling. I saw that if I could figure out a way to make temporary tooling at low cost, I could get many customers for short-run business. This would save my customers much money as they wouldn't have to machine the item they needed from solid plastic stock.

"It took me almost two years of hard work to figure out how to make the temporary tooling for the short-run production I've talked about. But once I had that, I was able to supply short-run needs of my customers very quickly and economically. As a result, I've built my business to the $10 million mark in yearly sales—and it's returning better than $750,000 profit after taxes this year."

> Observe and capitalize on the shortcomings in the products or services of others!

Extraordinary Uses for Ordinary Things

Lou Rhodes, of the Abbott-Lane Company: "My partner and I started in the specialized wood products business in Oregon before World War II. We learned something about applying baking enamel to pressed wood and metal panels. After processing these were used as decorative wall paneling.

"One day it occurred to us that fir plywood, which was becoming well known in the West, offered a good possibility as decorative wall paneling if we could sand the surface very smooth and coat it with a glossy enamel. Our objective was to make the surface look like colored plate glass. But try as we would, we couldn't stabilize the grain of the plywood, even with the help of a consulting chemist. And then one day we got the idea! Instead of trying to fool Mother Nature, why not work with her? Instead of trying to stabilize the grain, why not accentuate the grain pattern? You see, every piece of fir plywood has a different pattern from every other piece; each piece is unique. Therefore, by using a finishing method that would make the grain pattern stand out clearly, we could offer a beautiful paneling for walls, store interiors, fixtures, and the like.

"We were able to devise equipment for processing the plywood panels, and with our consulting chemist's help, we developed special finishes for getting the contrast we wanted between hard and soft grain. We then offered the finishes in a variety of colors and called our new plywood product EtchedWood.

"We sold our EtchedWood by the carload to well-rated Eastern concerns. Plywood was not very well known east of the Mississippi in those days, so we could command a substantial and profitable price for our product. We believed that it would take competition about eighteen to twenty-four months to begin to hurt us. So we worked at developing another product, which we could have ready to put on the market at the appropriate time."

Find extraordinary uses for ordinary things!

Changes in Social Custom

Nancy Auburn, President of Auburn Associates, Inc.: "I became involved with the women's movement when I was working for my master's degree in business administration. This interest led me to study intensively in the behavioral sciences. I was particularly excited by the newer findings and techniques that were available for helping people to change their attitudes and behaviors.

"Just before I got my degree, I was invited to participate as a resource person in a workshop aimed at helping women to become assertive—not aggressive, you know, but assertive. That is, the workshop was designed to help the women who attended to express honest feelings directly and comfortably, to be straightforward, and to exercise their personal rights without denying the rights of others and without feeling undue anxiety or guilt.

"I enjoyed the experience immensely. It triggered my thinking about what I wanted to do after I got out of school. I thought, 'This is for me. I can help women improve their lives by helping them to gain new skills in interpersonal relationships, by achieving important behavioral changes. Not only that, I'll use my education and my special training in a way that I believe is vital and socially useful.'

"I found a position with an all-woman consulting firm in this field and spent three years with them. This experience has proved of great worth to me. I learned how to run a management consulting firm, which is really a special kind of business. And while I was learning, I improved my personal skills as a behavioral consultant and change agent. The day arrived when I felt ready to move out on my own.

"I started slowly as an individual consultant, getting my first break as a generous gesture from my previous boss, who referred a client to me. Once I got going, I was able to expand my operation as I developed a clientele. I worked for large and small companies, putting on inhouse workshops for their employees; I did workshops through university continuing education programs; I put on programs for government agencies, for hospital personnel, and for not-for-profit organizations. Gradually I increased my staff, adding carefully selected women consultants.

"Our firm now has eight full-time women consultants. This year we will gross very close to five hundred thousand dollars. We expect to continue to grow for several years. And we will try hard to add new ideas, new methods and techniques to our services as we grow."

Look for opportunities in social change!

Necessity, the Mother of Invention

Stan Drexel, president of Drexel Irrigation Products Co.: "I had grown citrus and avocados as an avocation on some seventeen acres in San Diego County for a number of years. It's been customary to irrigate new plantings of citrus or avocados with "spitters." Spitters are small brass fittings screwed on to a cap fitted on a vertical section of pipe that rises about a foot above the ground. The spitter has a small hole in its nozzle end and is designed to emit a fan-shaped spray of water over the area of the tree roots. Water sprays from the nozzle at a rate that permits it to be absorbed by the soil without runoff. When they operate, spitters do a good job.

"However, the water used for irrigating in many Southern California areas is hard and often carries small particles of calcium carbonate or even debris that clogs the spitter. You may turn on the main valve to water a new planting of 100 trees only to find that 98 of them are being properly watered, but that 2 are getting no water at all because of clogged spitters. This means that you have to walk back to the main valve, perhaps 200 yards away, to turn off the valve, then walk back to the clogged spitter, unscrew it with a wrench, clean out the nozzle with a pipe cleaner or wire, screw the nozzle back on, walk back to the main valve, and turn on the water again. To your dismay, you may then find the same or another spitter clogged. So you repeat the process, but not very graciously. In addition, you must keep an eye on the whole planting until the irrigating chore is finished. By any measure, this is a time-consuming nuisance.

"I thought about the problem. I knew enough about water flowing in pipes to know that there are two kinds of pressure that operate. One is the pressure caused by the flow of the water; the other is static pressure that exists in the pipe when the pipe is closed but has a head of water behind it. When a spitter gets clogged, the pressure of flow changes to a static pressure. Now, I thought, if the orifice in the spitter were made of a flexible material it might be possible to have it dilate and eject the clogging particle under the static pressure in the piping system.

"I experimented with materials and designs and finally came up with a soft neoprene material that would withstand sunlight without deterioration and would give the necessary flexibility to eject a clogging particle. I had molds made and tested the product in my own orchard.

"This product was the first in a line of irrigating devices. I formed my company a bit later, after the word got around to my neighbors and other orchardists in the area. We've grown quite well since. Next fiscal year we expect to cross the million dollar mark in sales."

28

Technological Advance

Joe Balzano, President of Pacific Coast Faultfinders, Inc.: "My partner, Ed Brock, and I had come out of the electronics engineering test field. Ed's an engineering type— always poking into new ideas, reading about new discoveries in electronics testing procedures, and so on. One day he came to me—we were working for one of the big aerospace companies—and said, 'Joe, look here, here's a new way to check printed electronic circuit boards. You connect the board you want to test to this gadget and make interface connections with a computer. You get a computer printout that tells you exactly what's wrong with the board. It'll say that capacitor C-6 isn't function-ing, or you have a bad solder joint at P-11. You can find any fault in a board for just a few cents instead of having a technician spend all kinds of time locating the prob-lem'."

Joe continued: "Ed's find started us thinking and talking. We'd wanted to start our own business for a long time. We'd talked about it but had never been able to hit on an idea that suited us—until this one came along.

"We decided that this was it. With Ed's engineering and my sales ability, we'd make a strong combination. So we went to work making an arrangement with the New York company that had developed the advanced device that was the heart of the new testing system.

"We had very little money. But we worked out an interesting deal with the people in the East. After they checked us out and found that we were responsible citizens, they agreed to give us title to one of their machines, which sold for over $50,000 at the time. This was a calculated risk on their part, of course. But we were able to go to the bank and borrow $35,000 against the testing machine. And now we were in business.

"Although we went through the usual struggles for a couple of years, things got easier as we built a list of responsible customers; our customer roster today looks like the blue book of the electronics industry.

"Now what we're concerned with is working out new services to offer our customers as we're expecting to see competitors get into the field before too long."

Spinoff from Your Present Occupation

Robert Stevenson, Partner in Stevenson Associates, manufacturers' representatives: "I'd worked as a purchasing agent for many years, at first in the heavy construction contracting business, in later years in the electronics industry. I'd worked for one firm for ten years. I was the chief of purchasing for a main division of the company. Over the years, I observed what I thought was extremely ruthless treatment of the older employees, particularly the professionals, who were summarily dismissed at the close of a contract or often at the mere whim of top management. I realized one day that I was sixty years old and, because of these circumstances, a likely candidate for getting fired.

"My wife and I talked things over very carefully. We explored my strengths and weaknesses; we talked over all the reasons we could think of for taking on a new business of our own—and those for my not leaving the company. Our children were grown, long since on their own, so there was no obligation there. We decided that the risk of going into business was minimal. This seemed quite clear in view of my background, my knowledge of the vendors in the electronics and electromechanical fields, and the wide friendships I had built in the business during the past ten years.

"So we took the step. I've been able to build relationships with several concerns that supply superior products to the electronics and manufacturing companies in our county. I've gone through several different kinds of deals with other representatives and with vendors, and I've screened out the undesirable and the less desirable ones. Now I've reached the point where I have a sound business. I have three associates who work with me and on whose sales I share commission. The company gives me a comfortable income, and I don't worry about getting fired! I have several streams flowing in to make the river, and if one dries up, I can find another. I'm rid of the anxiety I felt when I worked for my old company."

Think about spinoff from your present occupation!

NEW APPROACHES FOR ESTABLISHED BUSINESS   2 A (4), 3 A B

We stress the need for uniqueness in your business throughout this book. Uniqueness, however, doesn't necessarily have to be within the product or the service itself. It can be in some aspect of the marketing effort, in the environment, or in the quality of service offered.

Consider the Baskin-Robbins Ice Cream Stores as an example. There is certainly nothing inherently unique about the product, although its quality is kept very high. Ice cream has been around for a long time. But what is unique about the Baskin-Robbins business is the approach they've taken in creating a special and attractive image.

Early in their history, when the two founding partners were struggling for survival against mammoth ice cream suppliers in Southern California, they were advised by a tiny new advertising agency (incidentally spun off by young men from a nationally known advertising consulting firm for which they had worked) to do everything in their power to create an image of fun; to make people want to come in to buy their ice cream because it was good fun to visit a store that was clean and white and decorated with pink and brown balloons; and to make it fun, a joyful experience to select from among thirty-one varieties of ice cream (many of which carried deliberately selected zany names).

The success of this venture needs no elaboration here. In answer to a question from the authors of this book, Irvine Robbins recently said that he expected that the firm would do better than $160,000,000 in gross business for the current year. That's an exemplary record for a company in an old business, started with a few hundred dollars in capital, but keyed into the market with a unique image-building approach.

NEED FOR CONTINUING INNOVATION   2 A (4), 4 A (4)

The respected economist Joseph A. Schumpeter gave a special twist to the meaning of entrepreneur—an emphasis any person thinking of starting a business should take to heart. He suggested that the true manager is an innovator as well as an administrator. The innovator introduces new ways of doing things and new things to do—and is the originator of all profit. Your profitability, which comes from the introduction of an attractive new product or service, tends to be temporary. It will vanish as competitors come into the market to ride on your coattails after you are seen to be outstandingly successful.

Fortunately there is a lag between your entry into the market with your new idea and the formation of effective competition. This gives you the time you need to prepare improvements, develop additional features, or add new items to your line. As competition arises and eats into your profitability, you can bring out the new features or items and keep ahead in the competitive race.

You must be aware of another factor that emphasizes the need for continual innovative effort in your business. That is the shortening of the life cycle of product or service in recent years. Three decades ago the profitable life of product or service might well have been ten or fifteen years. Today this time span has shrunk to much less—perhaps three to five years. This shortening of the useful life of product or service comes from the tremendous increase in technical knowledge and available research and from the instantaneous spread of news through modern communication channels. The word gets around in a hurry. Any new idea launched on the market becomes known to potential competitors quickly. The result is a shortening of the time in which marketing countermeasures can be invented and brought to reality.

You must therefore plan for and practice innovative activity continuously to keep your business alive and healthy.

INNOVATION IN AN EXISTING BUSINESS   5, 6

We've stated the need for continuous innovative effort even after your business has been launched and is well under way. A powerful tool to use in thinking about newer and better things to do and newer and better ways of doing older things is a product (or service) market matrix (Figure 3-1).

		MARKET	
		EXISTING	NEW
PRODUCT OR SERVICE	EXISTING	1. EXISTING PRODUCT/SERVICE, EXISTING MARKET	3. MARKET DIVERSIFICATION
	NEW	2. PRODUCT OR SERVICE DIVERSIFICATION	4. NEW PRODUCT OR SERVICE, NEW MARKET

Figure 3-1 Product/Service-Market Matrix

Here's the way you can use this matrix. First, think about your existing product or service and the present customers you are serving. This is indicated in the upper left-hand box, labeled Box 1. Think of all the ways you can increase your business with these customers by upgrading your sales techniques, advertising, merchandising appeal, or image. This kind of thinking can lead to innovative effort that will expand the sales of your present product or service. Changing the decor of your store, training your sales people to be more responsive to customers' request, packaging your product in colorful and attractive boxes—these are some typical ways in which you may be able to increase your present business.

Second, look at the lower left-hand box in the figure, marked Box 2. Here we suggest product or service diversification. This means adding new features to your product or new items to your product line or adding improvements or new services to those you now furnish. The objective here is to increase your sales to your existing customers.

As an instance, if you were making do-it-yourself kits of small items of furniture for home assembly, you might add a what-not shelf, or a shoe shine kit, or an electric wall clock to your existing line to gain additional sales from your present customers. Firms in the mail-order business constantly add and change the items they offer to their customers. Experience has shown them that once a customer has bought from them and been satisfied, that customer is likely to be a steady repeater—if their offerings are refreshed by new additions.

In the case of services, a small firm in the data processing business added to its original service of preparing amortization schedules for banks, savings and loan companies, and real estate agents the following services, one at a time: truth-in-lending tables, accounts payable, monthly statements, name and address maintenance files, interest tables, and precomputed ledger cards. Starting by adding services for its existing list of customers, the firm was able to expand its business fivefold in three years.

Third, examine Box 3 in Figure 3-1. The aim illustrated here is to increase the scope of the existing business by adding new customers for the present product or service. For example, the Menda Scientific Products company discovered that the alcohol dispensers they make (originally intended for medical use in preparing a patient's skin for injection) served admirably for cleaning purposes in soldering operations in electronics. By finding this new use for their product, they expanded their market significantly; they added new customers in a field completely different from what they had originally planned.

In a service-oriented business, a young man who operated a small window-cleaning service found that many of his customers had drapes at their windows. In the course of washing windows, he and his crew saw that more often than not these drapes needed cleaning. He made a deal with a reputable cleaning establishment from whom he learned how to estimate cleaning charges, how to take the drapes down, and how to rehang them after they were cleaned. He was able to add a service that augmented his income considerably.

Fourth, look at Box 4 in Figure 3-1. This box shows the final combination you may use, new products or services for a new market. This is by far the riskiest of the four combinations in the matrix. But it also offers the best chance for the greatest profit.

If you choose this course, you must build on your strengths and assess the risk in carefully calculated entrepreneurial fashion. You'll want to go through all the steps of product or service feasibility testing and market analysis that you'll find in the following chapters. You'll want to make sure of your planning and key your efforts to your resources. Often the new product can come as a spinoff from existing manufacturing operations.

A small company making electrical measuring instruments found it necessary to manufacture its own precision wire-wound resistors because these were not commercially available to the tolerances they required. They opened a new market by adding precision capacitors to their precision wire-wound resistors. The two items, combined to customer specifications, formed a special product known as an R–C network. These commanded a high price and opened a new market for the company.

In the service area, the small data processing firm previously mentioned added a new service that enabled it to open a new market. This was the addition of an addressing and mailing service for firms not having their own facilities for this kind of task.

GENERATING THE UNIQUE IDEA   SUMMARY

We have stressed the need for innovation in starting your new business and for continuing innovation to run it successfully once you have it started. We have suggested that you use both external and internal creativity in your search for unique ideas; and we have given you the following guidelines to use in generating ideas for product or service:

- Develop the basic idea for your business from your hobby or special interest.

- Find the answer to the question "Why isn't there a . . . ?"

- Observe and capitalize on the shortcomings in the products or services of others.

- Find extraordinary uses for ordinary things.

- Look for opportunities in social change.

- Develop new means to solve problems.

- Turn technological advance to your advantage.

- Think about spinoff from your present occupation.

Once you've established your business, you'll want to keep improving your product or service to ward off the encroachment of competition. You'll find the product–service matrix a useful tool in working toward this end. The matrix comprises four boxes that show the possibilities for using your resources to increase your sales. These are:

- Existing product or service—existing market, which covers your traditional market

- New product or service—existing market, which suggests selling more items to your present customers

- Existing product or service—new market, which implies diversifying your market by adding new customers

- New products or service—new market, which means developing new products or services and creating a new market through new customers

Of the four possibilities, you'll find the last, new products or new services—new market, the riskiest. At the same time, it is the choice that offers the chance for the greatest profit. You should study each box in the matrix with great care. From this study, you'll be able to plan courses of action that should produce the beneficial results in growth and profit for which you aim.

Your Bright Idea for Your Business

This worksheet will serve as a memo for you. It gives you a place to record your idea and your thinking about where you can go with it in the future.

Describe your proposed product or service briefly:

_____

_____

_____

_____

_____

_____

_____

_____

Show your idea, if practicable, by sketch, diagram, illustration, or pictures:

Note briefly your thinking about improved versions of your product or service you may want to bring out as "follow-on" improvements or additions.

_____

_____

_____

_____

_____

_____

_____

_____

Although you should start your business with an acceptable product or service, you must be prepared to add improvements, new features, or new products once you are established and have a successful track record. Keep thinking ahead about polishing your image in your market niche. The importance of noting the next steps you see, for adding features or items to your offering, is twofold: It will help you work out a basis for your survival in business, and it will show prospective investors that you understand the need for ensuring the future of your business. You'll show competence—you'll show that you know what you're doing—as a business manager.

IF YOU WANT TO READ MORE

Below is a sampling of a large number of books that deal with innovation and creativity. You'll find references and listings of other publications treating creativity and innovation in them.

James L. Adams, *Conceptual Blockbusting—A Guide to Better Ideas*, W. H. Freeman, San Francisco, 1974. This paperback tells of ways to expand your conceptual ability—your ability to gain new ways of looking at problems and problem situations. Much of the book's emphasis is on creativity.

Tony Buzan, *Use Both Sides of Your Brain*, E. P. Dutton, New York, 1976. This useful and interesting paperback outlines ways to loosen up and free your thinking. It can be helpful in showing you how to produce creative ideas. The language Buzan uses is simple and straightforward.

Edward de Bono, *New Think*, Basic Books, New York, 1967. In this text the author suggests different points of view and different approaches from those you may be accustomed to for coming up with new ideas.

William J. J. Gordon, *Synectics*, Harper & Row, New York, 1961. This book describes a powerful and proven technique for group problem solving. If you work with others in developing ideas for your business, you may find the synectics technique it describes of considerable benefit.

Robert McKim, *Experiences in Visual Thinking*, Brooks/Cole, Monterey, Calif., 1972. This is a well-designed book with many illustrations, puzzles, experiments, and problems. It will help you to stimulate your visual thinking, which can be the basis for generating many ideas for your business.

Chapter 4

Picturing Your Small Business as a Marketing System

ACHIEVING A CUSTOMER ORIENTATION

WHAT BUSINESS ARE YOU REALLY IN?

SEIZING OPPORTUNITIES FOR CHANGE

We stated early in this book that most small businesses fail because of lack of sales. This seems obvious—and simple. It is. It's too simple, because <u>lack of sales should be seen as a *symptom*</u> of a failing business, not the *cause*.

Don't fall into the error of confusing selling with marketing. Making sales is the end result of a carefully planned and effectively carried out marketing strategy. And marketing strategy pulls together all the resources of the business that must be used to perfect a unique idea for product or service and carry it through to profitable sales.

You should therefore picture marketing as a *system* of business activities designed to plan, price, promote, and distribute want-satisfying products or services to existing and potential customers at a profit. This definition emphasizes three critical points:

1. Marketing requires successful relationships and interaction among the business activities that make up the marketing system. Marketing is not a single isolated activity. It is not an assortment of random activities. It *is* a purposeful set of activities, guided by a carefully thought out network of plans, which, in turn, are keyed to a master strategy.

2. Marketing is a managed set of activities. Entrepreneurs must take the responsibility for managing the marketing system of their firms. This includes analyzing, planning, and controlling activities both inside and outside the business.

3. Marketing must be based on a customer orientation. What the customer needs may suggest product or service to fill that need. But only when the need is transformed into a *want* can there be a sale.

As the top executive in your business, you have the responsibility to manage your marketing system. Interestingly enough, your management affects both the inside and the outside of your firm. By doing the right things inside, you can influence your market outside to produce sales. Your customers will see only the outcome of your marketing system. They will see, evaluate, and be influenced to buy your product or service—or not to buy. If they buy, they'll get satisfaction or not get satisfaction from your product or service. It will be your job to develop a marketing system that will convert customer needs into customer wants and sales into customer satisfaction—and profit for you.

ACHIEVING A CUSTOMER ORIENTATION   1 B, **5**

Your philosophy of business will significantly affect how you plan, launch, and manage your firm. What you value guides the formulation of your philosophy. If you think more highly of the product you have nurtured than the needs of your potential customers, your business philosophy will be self-centered. You will be looking inward to serve your own needs. This is a dangerous trap to be avoided. Customers don't care about your needs; they care only about their own. You should understand clearly that satisfying the needs of your customers is the only reason for the existence of your company. This is the essence of the *marketing concept*.

The marketing concept should be the foundation of your business. Embedded in this foundation should be two precepts: (1) All planning, policies, and operations of your business should be oriented toward the customer in some way. (2) Your business objective should be to make sales at enough volume—and a high enough price—to produce adequate profit for the time, energy, and money you've put into the business.

Avoiding Market Myopia

As we've hinted above, it's dangerous to fall in love with your product or service. If you think your business offers the greatest gadget ever devised to do a certain task—and that everyone who sees it will buy it—you're in for a severe shock. The buying public couldn't care less about your product or you. They care about what they need. And only by offering them what they need and by converting need into want can you be successful. So don't fall in love with your product or service. Respect it; consider it worthwhile. But be objective enough to change it, modify its performance, or even discard and replace it with something else if it doesn't suit your customers.

In the early days of industrial expansion, it might well have been true that the world would beat a path to the door of the producer of a better mouse trap. Today this isn't true. Consumers can choose from a limitless array of products and services. Entrepreneurs who believe that consumer appeal will be generated by forcing their own perceptions of a desirable product or service on the market are in for bitter disappointment.

Therefore, offer your potential customers a product or service that will fulfill their needs. Don't become the victim of marketing myopia—short-sightedness that can trap you into bankruptcy, as it did John Galley, whose real-life case follows.

A Case of Marketing Myopia

John Galley, a man who wanted to make his mark in the restaurant business, opened a small restaurant in a Southern California beach community known for its concentration of high-income residents—movie stars, television producers, business executives, professional persons, writers, and artists. One value high in Mr. Galley's philosophy of business was shown in his statement that he wanted to capture the "carriage trade." He rented space for his restaurant at one end of a dilapidated motel on the landward side of the busy, four-lane divided coastal highway.

Mr. Galley adopted a ship's galley motif for his restaurant (no doubt influenced by his own surname and his closeness to the sea). Items on the menu were named for figures famous in the literature of adventure on the high seas: "Captain Hook's Seafood Platter," "Ishmael's New England

Chowder," and the like. Prices were set at a level considerably higher than in competing restaurants along the highway.

Although he'd made elaborate preparation for the grand opening, the response was nothing like what he had expected. Revenue was low during the first few months, which was not unexpected. But after ten months, business hadn't improved. Friends suggested that Mr. Galley reduce prices to be in line with his competitors, who catered to the somewhat casual beach-going and local family trade. He was told by knowledgeable businesspersons in the community that his restaurant would never attract the wealthy patron because of its uninviting location and drab external appearance. Customers considered the food good, but not different enough or excellent enough to justify the high prices. They didn't return.

Mr. Galley was so bound by his own outlook that he persisted in trying to attract the well-known and wealthy. His reaction to his business's performance during its first year was, "Well, sales are low, but I offer the best food in town and I'll charge for it. If I can stay with it, the wealthy people around here are going to discover me."

His response to advice was, "I'm not going to appeal to families with kids. Why should I? What this town needs is a high-class restaurant."

The business went into its second year with few marketing changes. Some special dishes were added to the menu and a brightly lit sign was installed facing the highway. Sales levels remained unprofitable, but Mr. Galley insisted that, "Word'll get around. They'll find my restaurant, you just wait!" Unfortunately, it was John Galley who waited. He waited until he exhausted his savings, until he fell behind in his rent, and until his suppliers withdrew credit. He was forced to close the restaurant after eighteen months.

Soon after the closing, the restaurant was reopened under a new name by a seasoned restaurateur. He changed the marketing approach radically with some obvious steps.

He simplified the menu and reduced prices; he offered reasonably priced luncheon specials to the local businesspersons; he featured family-style dinners. In addition to these product changes, he advertised heavily in the local neighborhood papers and carried out a direct mail advertising campaign in the area. His venture started earning profit after the first six months.

Don't fall victim to marketing myopia!

WHAT BUSINESS ARE YOU REALLY IN?　　1 A, 2 A (4)

Defining your business from the customer's point of view is the first step in avoiding marketing myopia. Think about the kinds of customer satisfaction your product or service gives. What kinds of needs are fulfilled by consuming what you have to sell? In short, look at your business through the eyes of your potential customers.

One of the most successful locksmiths in New York City affords an excellent example of how to define a business. This entrepreneur and his two sons sell, install, and maintain security systems for commercial and residential use. When the father was asked recently why, in the midst of dozens of other similar businesses, he is so successful, he replied, "Because I know what I sell—I sell peace of mind." This entrepreneur isn't just selling locks. He's selling products that meet a basic customer need—security; and he defines his business in these terms.

Colonel Sanders' Kentucky Fried Chicken is another example of how to define a business. The things that are sold besides fried chicken—convenience, food at reasonable prices, family atmosphere, and standardized quality—contribute materially to the success of this business.

The first step in developing the marketing system for your business is to answer the question: What business are you really in?

Forces of Change

At the right of the diagram in Figure 4-1 is an irregular area called THE MARKET. This area may be thought of as the overall market, whether it's a neighborhood, a city, a nation, or a cluster of nations. It's filled with people of all ages, colors,

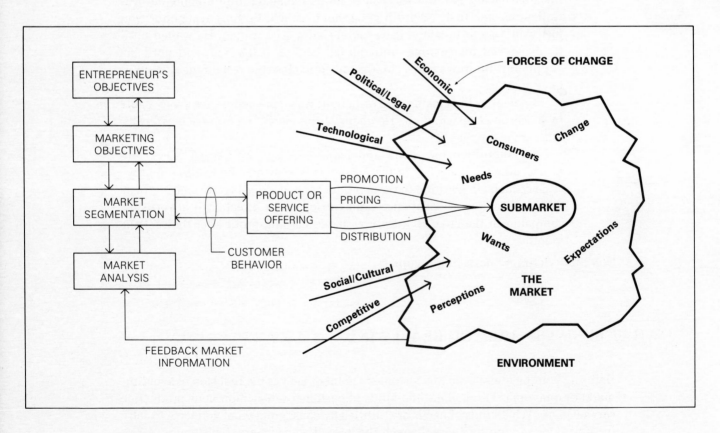

Figure 4-1 The Marketing System of the Small Business

42

backgrounds, and levels of education. The men and women and boys and girls within it have a wide variety of needs, wants, and expectations. They perceive the world in many different ways, depending on their upbringing, conditioning, and education. They have greatly varied expectations about what a new product or service will do for them. And they are continually exposed to the forces of change that modify their needs, wants, perceptions, and expectations.

Within the market area is a small circle labeled SUBMARKET. This is the segment of the market that you're interested in—it's the specific market you'll want to reach. You will concentrate your effort on the ultimate task of making sales within this market segment.

The external forces shown along the left side of the diagram produce changes in the market; these forces are beyond your control. Nevertheless, you must try to analyze each for its effect on the behavior of your customers and on the position of your company in your submarket and sometimes the market.

Economic Forces

Any change in the economy directly affects the amount of money people can spend and the prices they must pay. Inflation and recession have occurred simultaneously in recent times, and the small business failure rate has risen. How does this strange combination of economic forces—"stagflation"—affect consumers? For one thing, they postpone buying some kinds of products and services; for another, they eliminate luxury items from their budget; and they exercise much more care in buying. They look for quality and value in what they buy. Inflation can speed the buying process. People often decide to buy now in anticipation of higher prices to come.

Are there opportunities for your small business in a period of stagflation? Perhaps so. Consumers seek value, particularly in products and services at such a time. They select products that perform well and promise to have a long life and services that offer special rewards. You should be aware that value doesn't necessarily mean low price. *Value* is an illusory term—it's in the mind of the buyer. For example, during 1974, shortly after the Arab oil boycott, luxury car prices declined. The sales of luxury automobiles at lower prices actually increased while sales of medium-priced cars decreased across the board. Purchasers saw increased value in luxury cars at depressed prices, even though these cars burned more gasoline at inflated cost per gallon than the smaller cars.

Value for consumers can lie in personalized, friendly service, trust in the entrepreneur or in the reputation of the business, high quality of the product or service, or status in owning something unique. These are the value considerations you can offer as a businessperson. Your small business, by its inherent characteristics, can readily give personalized service to your customers. In addition, you can build trust and a reputation for excellence by ensuring high quality in what you offer in goods or service.

It's easier for your small business to give these values than it is for the large corporation with its arms-length, automated and computerized approach. Consumers are more skeptical and suspicious of large institutions than ever before—even angered by the power they wield. The rising number of product and store boycotts, the increasing size and activity of consumer action groups, and the recent increase in the number of antitrust suits brought by the U.S. Department of Justice attest to the distrust and frustration consumers experience in the marketplace. You can take advantage of this situation by building loyalty among your customers through personalized service and honest value.

Entrepreneurs must keep on top of not only the overall economic picture and its impact on their segment of the market but also of the regional or local economic picture. Regional variation in economic activity and sensitivity to the business cycle make this analysis necessary. You should therefore look to your local bank and business associations for up-to-the-minute information on the state of, and prospects for, the local economic situation.

Political/Legal Forces

Shopping behavior can be influenced by political change and by political decisions. Sometimes this happens through economic policy, sometimes, more subtly, through the confidence inspired by apt political leadership. Local governments often make policy and decisions that directly affect the consumer market, especially in real estate and housing. Changes in codes and local ordinances may affect the entrepreneur's business. If your business is subject to these kinds of change, it's wise for you to involve yourself in community affairs. You'll know what's going on and can often influence policy to avoid being hurt.

As an example, the manager of a small canning company in Arizona learned that his city was considering a ban on "convenience containers." This was of immediate concern to him because much of his revenue came from canning soft drinks. He had learned of the proposed action through membership in a citizens' advisory committee in the local government. He was able to block the ban by showing the city council studies indicating that adverse effects on employment and on his industry's antilitter program would follow such a decision. This manager was *proactive*—that is, able to foresee and *avoid* misfortune—because he had timely information from participation in community activities.

As the owner of a small business, you will obviously not be able to cover all bases. You'll have to exercise good judgment in selecting the part you should play in community activities. Whatever you decide to do, you'll get side benefits through such activities. You'll develop new business contacts and gain insights for improving your business.

Technological Change

Many small businesses have benefitted from technological change. Technological advance is so widespread and rapid today that it defies cataloging. Any scientific advance may produce an opportunity for your small business. You may be able to devise newer and better ways to do something important to your product or service, or you may find something newer and better to do. As a small example, several kinds of digital readouts are now available. These take the form of displays that show a varying quantity in numerical form: Light emitting diodes and liquid crystal displays are two such kinds of readouts. These may be applied to show the temperature, time, or other desired quantity directly in numbers. They replace a dial and needle display. Users therefore don't have to estimate the position of a needle on a dial; the quantity being measured shows directly in numbers. The product becomes more attractive to the consumer through this kind of readout.

Many businesses have been founded on spinoffs from technological innovation. Plastic pipe, for example, can now be substituted for galvanized iron or copper in residential construction. The strength and resilience of this material has led some entrepreneurs to use it as frames for modern furniture. Plastic pipe is easy to work into various shapes, is pleasing to the eye, makes durable and comfortable furniture, and is inexpensive.

Sometimes "reverse technology"—developing something simpler, less sophisticated—opens business opportunities. Hand-driven clothes washers using plastic wringers have been produced and successfully marketed in developing countries. Home wine-making kits is another example of reverse technology.

Government-sponsored research and development have started many new businesses. The Small Business Administration (SBA) maintains an inventory of inventions, improved materials, and new processes coming from research funded by the federal government. This information is public property and can be tapped free of charge by the entrepreneur. Research and development sponsored by NASA, for example, produced a light, compact energy cell for use on the moon rover. This technological advance resulted in a product developed by one entrepreneur for propelling wheelchairs used by paraplegics.

Although technological change brings opportunities in some areas, it produces obsolescence in others. You should keep abreast of "the state of the art," as it can affect your business for better or for worse. If you're aware, you can avoid the impact of obsoleting forces and take advantage of new product or service ideas that flow from this external force for change.

Social/Cultural Change

The small firm can be extremely vulnerable to the forces of social and cultural change. In most cases, the business *responds* to social or cultural change; in very few instances does the business introduce it. You must train yourself to be aware of what is going on in society—the changes that are taking place in life styles, custom, and social or cultural trends. These can have important consequences for your small business. You can identify new products or services to fit a newly growing need, or avoid the pitfall of obsolescence by withdrawing an existing product or service from the market.

A fascinating example of social and cultural change may be seen in the "Movement," or anticulture, which has had a large impact on business. The Movement can't be neatly defined but may be clearly seen in the behavioral patterns of a good part of the younger segment of the population. These young people have rejected many traditions and much customary behavior. Their life style centers around sensory experiences and their preference is for "natural" food. New enterprises catering to the needs of this segment of the population have sprung up and multiplied. Several examples of enterprises that started in a small way are now found everywhere in businesses such as head shops, health food, organic gardening supplies, and water beds. Music and stereo equipment businesses and industries have enjoyed commercial success, as have "natural" cosmetics, mod clothing, and van autos.

We shouldn't make the mistake, however, of tying social and cultural change to any one age group. Men of all ages have shed traditional styles and colors for multicolored, high-fashion clothing. Variety seems to be the key in the newer mens' fashions.

We can't speak of social change as permeating American society; we would be wrong to characterize the United States as having a culture. We should recognize that the national market includes several subcultures of differing life styles.

One significant change seems widespread and growing, and it offers all kinds of opportunity for the entrepreneur. It is the rise of what might be called "experiential" products or services. These are products or services in which the buyer participates and experiences some personal satisfaction, as opposed to the passive involvement in watching baseball games or television programs. Among the experiential products are games, hobby kits, crafts, how-to books, do-it-yourself kits, organic gardening, all kinds of sporting goods, and fix-it and build-it-yourself items.

Alvin Toffler points out in *Future Shock* that, "As rising affluence and transience ruthlessly undercut the old urge to possess, consumers begin to collect experiences as consciously and passionately as they collected things."[1] The increasing desire for interesting experiences opens many opportunities for small businesses in such fields as recreation, entertainment, and education. One entrepreneur saw an opportunity in the reactions of the passengers who had been stranded for several days on the *Queen Elizabeth II* when her engines failed in the Caribbean Sea. Their experience, they said, was "exciting," "you can't buy an unexpected fascinating time like that," and "it was a great adventure."

The entrepreneur grasped the opportunity to set up a vacation travel service that offers tours that don't spell out for the client exactly what will happen. Clients choose a tour, within the area of their special interest, such as golf, mountain climbing, flowers, opera, or art. The agency makes all arrangements, including a way of reaching clients' families if necessary. Clients don't know what's going to happen; they're intrigued by the possibilities of the unknown. For example, in an opera tour, the cities rather than the operas may be an unknown; in art, the particular museum may be unknown.

Marketing experiential value is more apparent in the service business than in any other. Airlines have discovered, for example, that an important marketing factor is not the sale of transportation alone, but the sale of an experience as well. After all, one airline's planes look like and operate much like another's. Therefore, the airlines now offer carefully designed psychological packages on each major flight. Passengers are given choices in the menu; travel information specialists offer counsel; fashionably dressed flight attendants serve food and drinks; passengers may see color movies and hear stereo music of their choice. Even the decor of the cabins is carefully designed to be attractive.

The Esalen Institute at Big Sur, California sells human awareness and interpersonal experiences, as does the National Training Laboratories at Bethel, Maine. Even traditional universities have discovered that rather than "retail" facts, concepts, and theories in their extension programs for adults, they can be more successful by offering "intellectual growth," "increased personal awareness," or "expanded human potential."

The desire for experiential products or services can have important implications for your business. Whether you're going into manufacturing, retailing, or service, you can probably benefit from this trend. From landscape consulting to body awareness classes, from specialized travel agencies to participative home games, from lessons in cross-country skiing to raising ladybird beetles for insect control, consumers seek the unstandardized, the novel, the unique personal experience. You should therefore search for ways to benefit from people's desire to be personally involved in doing something interesting and exciting.

Yet another trend is worth exploration for new business ideas. This trend may be called "use without ownership." What is involved is the renting or leasing of almost anything. Consumers want to rent tools, mobile homes, cars, furniture, appliances, clothing, and even people: secretaries, maids, cooks, gardeners, baby sitters, and companions.

Increased mobility of consumers has created needs that are being met by new small businesses. About 20 percent of the population of the United States moves every year. These people represent a special market of large size. They have needs for products or services that are convenient and save time and space. Items moved by singles or young couples have been found usually to include expensive stereo equipment, clothing, and a few cherished belongings. The remaining household items were either discarded or returned to the agency from which they were rented.

One small company in a midwestern city took advantage of the increase in intracity moves made by upwardly mobile young people. This enterprising company developed a moving service to give fast, dependable, low-cost, one-day service. It included with its business an apartment decorating and furnishing service, creatively combining the physical task of moving with serving the settling-in and decorating needs that follow.

Competitive Forces

The foundation of capitalism is open and healthy competition among business firms. Competition requires that the firm continually adjust its marketing strategies and tactics. If your new business is successful and enjoys a monopoly in its market area, you should expect, and be prepared for, other firms to enter and try to copy your success.

The chances for a small firm's survival are greatly improved if the entrepreneur exploits the strengths that launched the new business rather than resorting to cut-throat price competition. Large business offers a lesson for small business; instead of competing through price cutting, large companies compete on the basis of brand image, promotional activities, or store location. Your small business should compete by offering uniqueness, personalized service, and value—building on its special strengths.

The threat of competition highlights the need for two critical competitive tools. First, you should be continually alert for new products or services to offer your customers. Customers, especially repeat customers, have a "what've-you-done-for-me-lately" attitude. They look for innovation. Your small company can't hope to out-advertise large firms; advertising wars are as disastrous as price wars and should be avoided. Therefore, you must strive to meet competition with new or refined products or services.

Second, you should plan your market segmentation very carefully. You should use a rifle, not a shotgun, approach to marketing in your business. One of the greatest weaknesses of small business is the failure to define the specific submarket it intends to reach. Most small businesses don't take very much capital to enter. With barriers to entry low, you must build awareness of your store and product or service quickly; your objective should be to develop customer loyalty before competitors enter your market.

Marketing efforts can be tailored for maximum impact to maintain customer loyalty by defining *target* markets. We'll cover this in the next chapter.

SEIZING OPPORTUNITIES OF CHANGE

SUMMARY

As a prospective enterpriser, you should understand the critical impact of external forces on the market and on your submarket. These forces pose both opportunities and threats. As a beginner about to start your own business, you should concentrate on identifying the opportunities; later it will be important for you to recognize the threats as well. Your alertness to change of all kinds will allow you to seize and capitalize on emerging trends. In this way you'll avoid the danger of becoming a me-too business.

CHAPTER 4/FOOTNOTE

[1]Alvin Toffler, *Future Shock*, Random House, New York, 1970, p. 200.

Your Business as a Marketing System

1. Develop a marketing description of your business. Answer the question, from the customer's viewpoint: What business am I really in?

_____

_____

_____

_____

_____

_____

_____

_____

2. For each of the forces of change listed below, give at least _one_ example of how current events, apparent trends, or changing conditions could affect your business. Answer the question: How will my business (or my submarket) be affected by changes in each of these factors?
   a. Economic: How could I offset rising prices by giving extra value through specialized service?

   _____

   _____

   _____

   _____

   _____

   b. Political/Legal: What community, civic, or local business group should I join? My choice of group and why I chose it:

   _____

   _____

   _____

   _____

   _____

   _____

What change in the law is likely to affect my business and how do I plan to cope with it?

_____

_____

_____

_____

_____   _____

c. Technological: What is my action plan for keeping on top of advances in my field of business?

_____

_____

_____

_____

_____

d. Social/Cultural: How can I profit by seizing opportunities opened up by change in fashion, custom, or social trends?

_____

_____

_____

_____

_____

e. Competitive: What is my most threatening competition? How do I plan to meet it?

_____

_____

_____

_____

_____

This worksheet is intended merely as a sample of the kind of thinking you must continue to do as long as you're in business. Change of almost any kind offers opportunities for those who can see and grasp them. Alertness to change can open opportunities to you.

IF YOU WANT TO READ MORE

Lee Adler, "Systems Approach to Marketing," *Harvard Business Review*, May/June, 1967, pp. 105–118. This article gives several benefits stemming from the use of the systems concept in marketing. It presents a practical method for problem solving and identifying opportunities.

"Marketing When Growth Slows," *Business Week*, April 14, 1975. This article describes economic trends and prospects during the 1970s and offers suggestions and examples of how small business can adapt to economic change.

E. Jerome McCarthy, *Basic Marketing*, 5th ed., Richard D. Irwin, Homewood, Ill., 1975, pp. 90–97. This portion of the book presents an excellent discussion of how government and legislation affect small and large business.

Alvin Toffler, *Future Shock*, Bantam Books, New York, 1970. A thorough and interesting description of social change in the United States, this book identifies many opportunities for small business and tells about likely consumer purchasing patterns in the future.

Arnold C. Cooper, "Identifying, Appraising, and Reacting to Major Technological Change," in *Changing Marketing Systems . . . Consumer, Corporate and Government Interfaces*, ed. Reed Meyer, American Marketing Association, Chicago, 1968, pp. 93–97. This chapter recommends that the entrepreneur carry on a continuous program of "threat analysis" to avoid the pitfalls of serious and sudden technological change.

Alfred Gross, "Adapting to Competitive Change," *MSU Business Topics*, Winter, 1970. The author uses as a model a retail firm to illustrate the do's and don'ts of anticipating and reacting to competition.

Chapter 5

Analyzing Your Market and Consumer Behavior

WHY WILL CONSUMERS BUY FROM YOU?

WHO'LL BUY YOUR PRODUCT OR SERVICE?

WHAT, HOW, WHERE, AND WHEN DO CUSTOMERS BUY?

PINPOINTING THE MARKETING QUESTIONS YOU MUST ANSWER

n this chapter we look at those elements of the marketing system shown in heavy lines in Figure 5-1. These include market analysis and segmentation through identifying the unique characteristics of your submarket. We'll suggest ways for you to find out who your customers are and how to reach them.

The most challenging—and rewarding—task the entrepreneur must undertake in preparing for marketing action is to understand consumer behavior and to analyze the market for the business. Your market could be the local community, your city, a region, or it could be national or international in scope. Whatever its size, you must answer six basic questions:

- *Why do consumers buy?* Why will they buy your products or services?

- *Who buys?* What is your target market? What are the characteristics of consumers likely to buy from you?

- *What do they buy?* Which products or services do they typically choose? What brands do they prefer? How do they allocate their income, and how much discretionary income do they have—that is, income above what is needed for necessities?

- *How do they buy?* Do they shop around for your kind of product or service, or do they buy when it's convenient? Do they prefer to pay cash, use personal credit, or a credit card?

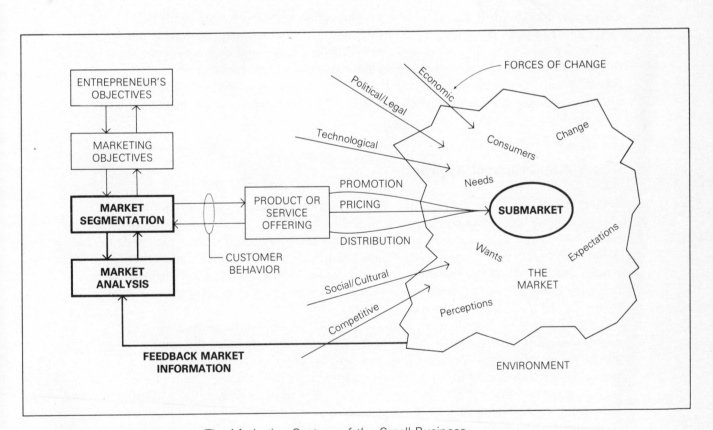

Figure 5-1   The Marketing System of the Small Business

- *Where do they buy?* Do your potential customers prefer to buy from retail stores, through mail order, or from door-to-door sales people? How far will they travel to buy what they want?

- *When do they buy?* Do seasonal influences affect the shopping behavior of your intended customers? How do holiday seasons influence their shopping behavior? How does inflation or recession affect their buying patterns?

These questions may seem difficult to you as a beginning entrepreneur. The problems are how to answer these key questions thoroughly at minimal cost, where to go to acquire the necessary information, and how to use the information you assemble. This chapter will guide you in accomplishing these tasks. After studying it, you'll be ready to take specific steps, with very little out-of-pocket expense, to complete the analysis of your market. From the information you collect, you'll be able to develop a detailed profile of the consumers in the segment of the market you're trying to reach.

WHY WILL CONSUMERS BUY FROM YOU?   **2** A (1), **3** B (4), **8** A (7)

Consumers buy to fulfill a need, to be sure. But action planning for the small business requires a more thorough and practical answer. To explain buyer behavior, we must look to social science and understand a little theory. Remember, theory seeks to explain why certain phenomena occur so that they may be influenced or controlled. Buyer behavior is complex; you must cut through the maze of scientific technicality and select a straightforward approach that will let you manage the marketing of your business venture in a proactive manner.

The Not-So-Practical Approach

Let's first look briefly at the Freudian, or psychodynamic theory, so that you may compare the approach we suggest with this older but still popular explanation of buyer behavior. Freud said that our behavior results from subconscious motives deep within us. These "inner drives," along with our instincts, libido, and other factors, are part of our "personality" and together determine our behavior. Furthermore, the internal state, much of it unconscious, is created largely in early life and is extremely difficult, if not impossible, to change.

According to the Freudian approach, as the individual grows, the inner state or psyche becomes more complex. A part of the psyche, the id, remains the source of strong drives and urges. Another part, the ego, becomes the conscious planning center for finding outlets for inner drives. And a third part, the superego, guides instinctive drives into socially acceptable outlets. The guilt or shame that individuals feel toward some of their urges, especially sexual, causes them to "repress" or "sublimate" these urges.

56

Consumer researchers attempting to reveal inner motives for purchase decisions along Freudian lines have come up with some interesting and often bizarre findings. For example, they have suggested that:

- Men want their cigars to have a strong smell in order to prove their masculinity.

- Women are extremely serious when baking a cake because, unconsciously, they are going through the symbolic act of giving birth.

- Men buy convertibles as substitutes for mistresses.

- Consumers prefer vegetable shortening because animal fats stimulate a sense of sin.

This explanation of buyer behavior has little value for entrepreneurs. The methods for identifying inner drives of consumers are complex and usually very expensive. Because much of the internal state of consumers is assumed to be unconscious, the causes of behavior may not be evident without long-term psychoanalysis. Moreover, this approach can be attacked on scientific as well as practical grounds. Most Freudian notions about behavior can't be tested objectively. Even if they were accurate, the findings have doubtful utility for planning the marketing program for a small business.

A Practical Approach

A more practical explanation of consumer behavior is given by another school of thought. We'll call this the behavioral approach because the focus is on what consumers do, or say they would do, rather than on what internal characteristics "motivate" them.

The basis of this approach is simple: Behavior is determined by its consequences or outcomes. Thus, this theory says that our behavior patterns in the marketplace are based on what we know to be the consequences, or what we anticipate to be the consequences, of our buying decisions.

Attached to any particular behavior pattern or decision, such as eating at a restaurant versus eating at home, are several perceived consequences—both positive (rewarding) and negative (aversive). Consumers evaluate these consequences and select the alternative with the highest **net** rewards. Using the eating-out example, the consumer's decision might be viewed as follows:

CONSEQUENCES

Rewarding (positive)	Aversive (negative)
■ I get a special dish that I really like ■ The atmosphere will be peaceful and relaxing ■ My wife and I get a night out ■ I won't have to shop for dinner or help cook ■ I won't have to clean up later	■ Driving to get there, a tedious chore ■ The dinner, expensive ■ Parking, a nuisance ■ Babysitter expenses

57

The consumer identifies the consequences and makes judgments about their relative importance. In the example, if, after weighing the consequences, the consumer thinks the rewards are greater than the aversive outcomes, the choice will be for eating at a restaurant. After eating, the consumer will make another evaluation that will influence future decisions or behavior related to having dinner out. If the service at the restaurant has been poor and the dinner mediocre, the consumer might choose to have dinner at home the next time.

The behavioral approach says that behavior patterns are learned as a result of the consequences of activities; it maintains that the identification and evaluation of behavior outcomes determine future behavior. Therefore, in starting your own business, you should concentrate on one central issue: What are the consequences, positive and negative, as my customers would perceive them, of buying my product or service?

Steps You Should Take

The practical value of taking the behavioral approach is that **you** can obtain data from potential customers about their perception and evaluation of your products or services. Determining what potential customers believe to be the behavioral consequences of buying from you will tell you a great deal about how to market your new business effectively.

The worksheet at the end of this chapter describes the steps you should complete to answer the question: Why will customers buy from me? The value of this exercise is illustrated in the recent case of Elaine Woodworth, who inherited a large collection of rare antique bric-a-brac from her mother. Ms. Woodworth didn't feel sentimental about the legacy and, being knowledgeable about antiques, decided to open her own antique store using her inheritance as the opening inventory. She also inherited a building in a rather run-down, commercial section of a large city, but wasn't sure the location was good for her store. The area had numerous small boutiques and restaurants, and a few antique stores—most of them selling furniture and fixtures. Parking spaces were hard to find along the four-lane thoroughfare that bisected the area. Off-street parking adjacent to her building was limited to three cars, and close side-street parking was limited to 30 minutes. And the neighborhood was reputed to have a crime problem.

We assisted Ms. Woodworth in her efforts to determine why consumers might or might not shop in her store. First, we asked her to identify what she believed to be the rewarding and the aversive consequences of shopping at her proposed place of business. She believed that most of her potential customers were located across town in a high-income, exclusive neighborhood. The wide assortment of bric-a-brac, she believed, would give her an advantage over other antique stores that typically relegated these items to a small display and emphasized other kinds of antiques such as furniture.

Ms. Woodworth planned to charge lower prices than comparable stores because she would have no rent to pay.

We summarized Ms. Woodworth's assessment as follows:

Rewarding Consequences	Aversive Consequences
■ Wide assortment of bric-a-brac antiques ■ Lower prices than similar stores in fashionable neighborhoods	■ Travel time to get to store ■ Limited parking in the area ■ Shabby area in which to shop, with reputed danger of being held-up or mugged

She concluded from her analysis that her prospects for success appeared to be bleak. Her assessment suggested that to attract customers she would have to maintain a high-cost inventory with a wide assortment of items and sell them at a lower price than competitive stores. Furthermore, she'd have to interest consumers enough to drive across town to get to her store. And somehow, reasonable parking would have to be made available, and the negative image of the area overcome.

We suggested Ms. Woodworth take an additional step with her analysis before deciding whether to sell or rent the building and locate in the high-rent district of her major market. In order to make an informed judgment, data were needed from three different groups: (1) potential customers in the high-income neighborhood, (2) consumers who shopped in the commercial district where her building was located, and (3) proprietors in the immediate area of her building. We recommended the focus-group interview as a way she could collect this data herself.

The focus-group interview brings together about ten to fifteen people representing a cross section of the consumer population to be studied. The interviewer asks direct questions in an objective manner to solicit answers on issues of importance to the study. The interviewer must take care not to bias the group members; they shouldn't be influenced to say what the interviewer wants to hear. This approach usually elicits useful qualitative data and valuable insights.

Ms. Woodworth decided to conduct interviews with each of the three groups she identified. She started with potential customers in the high-income area.

She called acquaintances who she knew were interested in antiques and invited them to a morning coffee at her home. She told her guests that she was planning to start her own business and needed their opinions on some unresolved issues. Twelve people participated in the interview, and the entire session was taped.

Ms. Woodworth told the group about her experience in the antique business; she described the antiques she'd sell and passed around several samples with the price attached to each; she showed them pictures of her building, described in detail the commercial district where it was located, and told them of her remodeling plans. She did **not** tell about her own consumer analysis to avoid biasing them, and she asked them to be candid with her.

First, she asked each person to list the possible rewards or advantages of shopping in her store as compared with shopping in antique stores in their neighborhood. Second, she instructed each person to list the disadvantages or negative aspects they could see in her proposed business. Third, she asked them to rank items on their lists in order of importance to them. Fourth, she divided the twelve into subgroups of four each and asked each subgroup to discuss their findings and to try to reach a combined rank-ordered list of advantages and disadvantages. Fifth, after the small groups had finished, she brought the whole group together and had one member of each subgroup report on that group's discussion. There followed a lively conversation about the problems. Ms. Woodworth reminded the group again to be candid with her. Additional information was volunteered as a result. Ms. Woodworth used probing questions to clarify and expand the discussion. For example, she asked, "What do you mean by that?" "Can you give me an example of what you're saying?" "Why is that the case?"

At the conclusion of the session, she thanked the group and gave the members antique trivets in appreciation of their help.

She then analyzed the data she had collected. In addition to studying the lists of the rewards and the aversive consequences, she listened carefully to the taped recording to pick up anything she might have missed. Ms. Woodworth was astonished at what she called her "naivete" in analyzing consumer behavior. For example, the data revealed that there were **two** major market segments for her business—one composed of devoted bric-a-brac antique enthusiasts who would travel almost any distance to shop for rare items, and another that included casual antique consumers who would shop at irregular intervals and at stores convenient to them. She also discovered that her expertise in antiques was more important to consumers than she'd thought. The addition of her store to several other antique stores in the district might also help to attract customers from the high-income area. Some of the group members had expressed some fear about shopping in the area because of reports of crime. However, they believed the area had "charm" and was unique because of the numerous old buildings and the concentration of boutique-type stores. Most participants, she was surprised to learn, believed her proposed prices were too low; they said that the bric-a-brac buff wouldn't pay much attention to price and that the casual consumer wouldn't have enough experience to recognize whether the price was too high or too low.

Ms. Woodworth summarized the findings from the group interview as follows:

Anticipated Consumer Consequences of Shopping at My Store

Rewarding Consequences	Aversive Consequences
■ Experience and expertise of owner in her specialty of antiques ■ Access to other types of antiques stores in area ■ Wide assortment of bric-a-brac antiques ■ Pleasing store environment in which to shop ■ Status of owning a hard-to-find bric-a-brac antique ■ Interesting and unique area in which to shop	■ Travel time to get to the commercial district where store is located ■ Limited parking in the area ■ Fear of crime in the area

Encouraged by her findings, Ms. Woodworth proceeded to interview consumers shopping in the district. She chose three days she knew to be days of high, moderate, and low business activity. She then conducted ten interviews each day at different locations. Her approach was to introduce herself to shoppers after they had come out of one of the antique stores; she explained that her purpose in the interview was to explore the possibility of opening a specialty store in the area.

Because her interviews had to be limited to a few minutes, her questions were descriptive. For example: Where do you live? Why did you choose this district to shop in? Were you browsing or did you have a special item you've been shopping for? How often do you shop here? Would you shop in a store specializing in bric-a-brac antiques? What problems have you encountered in shopping in this area?

Her findings confirmed the idea that there were two market segments represented in the consumer traffic of the district: (1) antique collectors seeking special items who wouldn't be deterred by distance or parking difficulties, and (2) casual shoppers for antiques who drop in to browse and purchase what might catch their eye. Three-fourths of the consumers lived at least three miles from the district and shopped there about once a month. The rest were first-time shoppers who had driven through the area previously and had become interested enough to stop and shop. Most of these consumers lived within one mile of the district. The parking problem was mentioned often, but reputed crime in the area didn't appear to be a problem with those interviewed.

At this point, Ms. Woodworth began to think that the prospects for her store were looking up because many of the shoppers were already driving some distance to shop in the district, and some were from the high-income neighborhood that interested her. She was further encouraged to find that the district appealed to "drive-through" traffic in spite of reports of crime in the area.

Her next step was to interview proprietors in the area. She wanted to see if there were possible solutions to the parking problem in the district, and whether cooperative efforts in promoting it in other ways would be feasible. She found that a store owners' association had been organized recently and that the membership was working with the city's transportation department to expand the local parking facilities. She met several proprietors who were keenly interested in cooperating to improve the image of the district.

Ms. Woodworth opened her antique store in the building she inherited about eight months after she had finished her consumer interviews. The store is very profitable and continues to specialize in bric-a-brac antiques. Not only is Ms. Woodworth's store successful, but she has also capitalized on her expertise and is now retained by several wealthy buyers to travel around the world in search of rare antiques.

A Concluding Note

You can use approaches taken by Ms. Woodworth in this example to gain insights into the behavior of consumers. You'll increase your chances for successful marketing efforts by emphasizing those things that potential customers perceive as rewarding and lessening or eliminating those factors seen as aversive. You should always remember that the **marketing concept** stresses consumer orientation every step of the way. Had Ms. Woodworth relied on her own intuition or guesswork or even her first tentative analysis, she would never have opened her doors to business in her own building. Never be reluctant to ask good questions of anybody you think can help you.

WHO'LL BUY YOUR PRODUCT OR SERVICE?   **1** B (1), **5** A (1)

Once you've identified your consumers' perceptions of the rewarding features of your business, you must decide which segment of the market you'll need to concentrate your marketing efforts on. **This is one of the most critical decisions you'll make for your new venture.** (In giving assistance to over 150 small businesses experiencing marketing problems, we've found a root cause of troubles is most often improper or ineffective market segmentation.)

Market segmentation means the carving up of the mass market into smaller submarkets. The consumers of each of these markets share unique buying characteristics. Teen-agers, for example, only recently have taken on the characteristics of a distinct market segment. As consumers they behave differently from other age groups.

All successful large and small firms practice some form of market segmentation. Your business can't satisfy everyone, nor can you expect all consumers to want your product or service. Use a rifle, not a shotgun, to target your marketing program. Choice of the markets you intend to reach is what will guide all your later marketing plans and actions. The characteristics of your product or service, your pricing approach, your promotional strategy, and how you distribute your product or service should be tailored to the submarket you've selected.

Requirements for Effective Segmentation of Your Market

We'll describe several ways you can segment your market. Any method you choose must satisfy these three requirements:

- *Market Measurement:* You must be able to identify and measure the characteristics and size of the market segment.

- *Economic Opportunity:* The market segment or segments to which you intend to appeal must be large enough and have enough discretionary income to make it worthwhile; that is, your consumers must have money to spend for whatever they want above their basic living expenses.

- *Market Access:* The market segment must be "reachable." Can you locate your business or place your products within easy reach of intended customers? Can your promotion program reach and influence consumers in the market segment?

You must answer these questions.

62

It's not difficult to meet the first two conditions that your market be measurable to some reasonable degree and that it have money to spend. It's in the third requirement that most entrepreneurs experience marketing problems. They fail in some way to gain access to their intended submarket.

Consider these two cases:

Case 1: Antonio Alverez, the Tortilla Manufacturer

Mr. Alverez started and operated a small manufacturing plant in a large metropolitan area in the Southwest. His plant was located near the center of a community of Mexican-Americans. He made corn and flour tortillas and, along with specialty food products he imported from Mexico, distributed them directly to supermarkets. He had three driver–salespersons who delivered his products by truck. The drivers would stock the shelves and take orders for the next delivery.

Mr. Alverez had been operating his business for about a year when he came to us for help. The problem, he said, was that each quarter his income statement showed a loss even though he was meeting his sales objectives.

An examination of his distribution patterns showed that his accounts were widely scattered. With the exception of two stores a stone's throw from his business, all accounts were over 45 miles from his plant. All were located in above-average income areas. Sales volume in each distant account wasn't enough to cover his distribution costs.

Mr. Alverez didn't have **access** to these markets. Mexican food products in these upper income areas were considered novelties rather than staple food items. Supermarket managers were allocating only a small amount of shelf space to his products, in hard-to-find locations. When we asked him about this situation, Mr. Alverez said: "But look at the size of these markets! Incomes are much higher there than around here and nobody's selling products like mine there." True enough, but Mr. Alverez was assuming that the mere existence of his products would change the eating habits of his customers to include more Mexican food products. He simply didn't have the resources to reach consumers directly to inform and influence them about his products.

Following our recommendations, he phased out his distant accounts within six months. He reorganized his distribution to concentrate on supermarkets catering to Mexican-American consumers. As a result, he improved both sides of his profit situation—total sales increased beyond his projections and total costs declined, primarily because of substantially reduced distribution costs. His business is now in good shape financially.

Case 2: Mr. John Morgan, the Pool Cleaner

Mr. Morgan operated a pool cleaning service. He cleaned residential swimming pools monthly for about 100 customers. He employed two high school students part time; the firm was healthy and growing. He had tinkered with various mechanical pool cleaning devices over the years and had perfected a model that worked much better than existing products. Excited about the prospects for his invention, he contacted dozens of retailers to see if they would carry his product.

He found that none of the dealers wanted his device even though it was technically superior and could be sold at lower cost than competitive models. Their reluctance to stock and sell his product was based on two factors. First, each dealer had "exclusive dealing" arrangements with sellers of pool cleaning devices and accessories—a policy whereby the seller requires dealers to agree to handle only the seller's products. Second, retailers doubted whether Mr. Morgan could produce enough to satisfy demand. They also questioned his ability to furnish adequate warranty protection and service.

Mr. Morgan **couldn't gain distribution access** to a mass consumer market. He then decided to market the device himself to his existing clients. This effort proved successful. Eventually, he sold the patent rights for his invention to a large pool equipment manufacturer for a substantial sum of money.

You can see from these cases the importance and the difficulty of gaining access to submarkets. Several suggestions for overcoming this problem will be presented as we explore marketing strategy in the next chapter.

Segmenting Your Market

Most small businesses segment their market on the basis of demographic variables such as age, income, race, or sex, and geographic concentration of consumers with the desired characteristics. Markets are segmented along these lines for three reasons: (1) Demand for most products or services is related to factors such as age, income, and race. (2) It's relatively easy to measure these characteristics. (3) The data required for measuring are readily available at little or no cost.

Here are the steps you should take to segment your market:

1. Develop a detailed demographic profile of your intended market— average age, income level, racial mix, education level of potential customers. Or use other factors that describe your target market.

2. Identify where high concentrations of these potential customers with the desired characteristics live.

3. Determine how, where, and when they prefer to buy, the types of stores they usually shop in, their preferences about credit or cash. Also find out about their buying habits. Do they shop and compare price and quality; are their purchases scattered during the year or concentrated during holiday seasons; and to what extent do economic conditions affect their buying?

You may want to consider other factors in segmenting your market. For example, within a particular age or income group, wide variations in consumption patterns may be found because of differing life styles or religious beliefs. And the rate of use or frequency of purchase of various products or services may be different within an age or income group. It may be possible to identify nonusers, light users, and heavy users of products or services in the same category as yours. In short, you may want to combine other factors with demographic and geographical variables to identify your market segment thoroughly.

WHAT, HOW, WHERE, AND WHEN DO CUSTOMERS BUY?   **1** B (1), **3** A (1), **8** A (7)

The answers to the questions of what, how, where, and when will help you to understand the shopping behavior of your intended customers. Much information is readily available to help you develop your marketing plans. The problem, as noted earlier, is to understand where to go, what to look for, and how to use the information you collect.

Sources of Information for Segmenting and Understanding Your Market

Here's a list of some major sources of information:

Daily Newspapers
Each major newspaper conducts ongoing marketing research in the area it serves. Information about this research is usually given free of charge to advertisers or potential advertisers. It's not uncommon for the newspaper to conduct comprehensive market surveys to determine what people are buying, how frequently they buy certain items, where they do their buying, and the prices they pay. The information is collected for the metropolitan area and, more important, is usually subdivided and related to small geographical areas. These areas are called "census tracts" and contain an average of about 4000 individuals with roughly the same demographic characteristics.

You can do effective market segmentation by using demographic data for these census tracts. You can pinpoint submarkets with high potential—those having the largest number of people with the characteristics you want—by using newspaper survey information and census tract data. You can gain insights from such information on several important marketing decisions such as store location, placement of products in existing stores, buyer preferences, and even on where to concentrate advertising.

To use census data, you should understand some of the classifications and the rationale used by the U. S. Bureau of the Census. The bureau offers a geographical classification known as a Standard Metropolitan Statistical Area (SMSA), because county and city boundaries may not adequately define a market. Such things as transportation and commercial activities or patterns are taken into account in establishing SMSAs. To qualify as an SMSA, an area must have at least one city with a population of 50,000 or more inhabitants. Then to the area occupied by that city are added those areas in which the residents have commerce with the city. The resulting SMSA, then, will contain "a market" because individuals within that area are likely to have commercial dealings with one another.

Each SMSA is further subdivided into census tracts—small areas with an average of about 4000 individuals who are considered to be fairly homogeneous. This means that census tracts are constructed with the expectation that families within their boundaries will be similar in population characteristics, economic status, and living conditions.

You should keep in mind that the census tract data reveal only demographic information. Market surveys conducted by most larger newspapers, and other institutions we'll mention below, enrich population information with consumer buying data. The **combination and availability of the two types of information** have great potential for use in your marketing planning.

Newspapers will often supply two additional types of market information: detailed maps that show concentrations of commercial activity—the location of supermarkets and shopping centers, for example—and maps that show average driving time from one place to another within a city; and special market reports for a specific kind of business, like beauty salons or auto parts stores.

Weekly Newspapers

Most large cities have weekly newspapers that cater to small sections of the metropolitan area. Weeklies concentrate on local news and attract local business advertisers. You'll find that the marketing staff of large daily newspapers will be one of your richest sources of statistical information; the staff of weeklies will be one of the best sources for informed opinions on commercial activity and trends in the smaller areas they serve. They'll usually be eager to respond to your questions about their market, because you're a potential advertiser in their newspaper.

Government

The federal government is dedicated to the preservation of a strong, healthy, and profitable small business community. Marketing and management assistance free of charge, financial assistance in many circumstances, and other services have been created by specific legislation. Two federal agencies, the U. S. Department of Commerce (USCD) and the U. S. Small Business Administration (SBA) furnish marketing assistance that will be discussed here. Other services offered by the SBA will be described in other chapters as it is the agency created by Congress specifically to help small firms in many ways.

The USCD was established early in this century to develop and promote foreign and domestic commerce. The Bureau of the Census mentioned earlier is part of the USCD, but in addition to census data the Department publishes a wide variety of information. You should visit one of the forty-two field offices, located in major cities, and find out about the services and information they provide. In addition to census data and industry-by-industry sales statistics that you may find helpful, the USCD supplies specific information for small businesses. For example, their publication, *Franchise Company Data,* lists all kinds of franchised operations, firms doing business under those categories, and general information about each firm. Let's say you're interested in fast-food franchises. In this publication you'll find the equity capital required by different companies; what, if any, financial management and training assistance is given; how many franchises are in operation; and how long the companies have been in business.

Entrepreneurs often overlook international market opportunities for their business. The USCD (any field office) is the place to go to find out about such potential. Publications on how to get started in world trade, foreign business regulations, international trade statistics, and information on a country-by-country basis are available. A thorough reading of USCD literature will help you decide on your best potential foreign market. Free seminars are also given by each field office on how to set up foreign marketing ventures.

The SBA, established in 1953, also has field offices in every major city and offers two major types of marketing assistance.

First, the SBA publishes hundreds of pamphlets on specific small business subjects, and each local office conducts a free seminar monthly on various aspects of starting your own business. The SBA publications give practical how-to suggestions on several marketing issues faced by the entrepreneur. For example, if you want to explore the opportunities for selling your product by mail order, the SBA's *Selling by Mail Order* is a bibliography that will guide you to books, trade associations, and other sources of detailed information. Most publications of the SBA are free, others are inexpensive. The monthly seminars touch on functional areas of the small business and often include a session on marketing the new business.

Second, you can get direct assistance at no cost through the Service Corps of Retired Executives (SCORE) and the Active Corps of Executives (ACE). The latter group is composed of persons still active in business. Consultative talent may be available through the nearest office of SBA to help you complete your marketing plans.

The SBA will also help you if you want to do business with the federal government. The SBA has the responsibility for making sure that small businesses participate in certain federal government contracts. Meetings and seminars are held to inform entrepreneurs on how to bid for government business.

Banks

The commercial bank you've been using for your personal banking could be an excellent source of local market information. Contact a loan officer who handles small business accounts. Describe your business idea and marketing plans. Ask the loan officer for advice on the areas in which you need information, and find out what kinds of economic data the bank publishes. The loan officer will have insights into local business conditions and activity and may know about other businesses similar to yours.

There are two other important reasons for visiting with your banker. First, it's important to start early to build good relations with the bank. Although commercial banks won't give unsecured start-up loans, you'll probably need banking services soon after you open your doors for business. Personal contact in the planning phase for your venture will help later on when you may need working capital quickly.

Second, an experienced loan officer will have suggestions on cash flow planning for your business. In day-to-day dealings with clients, the loan officer has intimate knowledge of financial needs of numerous small businesses and can help you avoid the results of poor cash planning.

The Bank of America publishes the *Small Business Reporter*, a series of booklets covering many different kinds of business and treating many subjects that you'll want to know about. Issues of the *Small Business Reporter* come in three categories: business profiles, business operations, and professional management. Business profiles treat fundamental issues in starting small businesses ranging from *Small Job Printing* to *Mobile Home Parks*. Business operations give data on such subjects as *Understanding Financial Statements*, *How to Buy or Sell a Business*, and *Advertising Small Business*. The professional management booklets deal with subjects such as *Establishing an Accounting Practice* and *Establishing a Veterinary Practice*.[1]

In addition to helping you set your sales forecasts, these publications supply much other information that you'll find useful.

Universities

Many major universities have a school or college of business administration that offers small business courses. You may want to enroll in one of these or use the management library facilities on the campus.

Free assistance may be obtained from instructors of small business management courses. Over 300 colleges and universities are members of the Small Business Institute (SBI), which is cosponsored by the SBA. You may want to contact a program coordinator of the SBI in your local university to arrange for a student team to counsel and assist you in planning your business.

The university may also have a bureau of business research that offers services for entrepreneurs in the local area. Often these bureaus prepare market and economic studies, and publish reports of interest for small business operators.

Chambers of Commerce

These organizations represent commercial interests in the local community. The membership is composed of owners and managers from all kinds of businesses. Regular meetings are held and information about the commercial area is usually published. You should join the local chamber of commerce; it's an excellent way to become acquainted with the business community and to learn from other entrepreneurs.

Trade Associations

There are over 5000 trade associations in the United States. Almost every industry has one. The purpose of the association is to help improve the health of the industry it represents. It does this by furnishing its members detailed industry data, market surveys and forecasts, information on technological breakthroughs, representative sales and cost data, and the like. Moreover, the advertisements in trade journals are an excellent source of information about competitors and their products. Attending trade association meetings and visiting with sales representatives can also be a good way for you to assess competition and gain additional business ideas. So you should join the association of your business. If you're planning to open a bookstore, join the

American Booksellers Association; if you're going to open a screw machine shop, join the National Screw Machine Products Association. Your local or university library will have a Directory or Encyclopedia of Associations that lists all the trade associations and the addresses to write to for membership.

Other Similar Businesses
We assume that as a serious entrepreneur you've had direct experience working in a business similar to the business you want to start. We suggest at least two years of such experience. You can check the current situation by consulting a good source of start-up information—successful entrepreneurs. Entrepreneurs enjoy talking about their experiences in starting their own business. Pick businesses you won't be in competition with but which are similar to yours, and choose a day when business may not be heavy—perhaps sometime in midweek. Ask the owners about their marketing approach, their successes and failures, who they bank with, and who they use for an attorney or an accountant. Concentrate on asking questions that published literature may not answer.

PINPOINTING THE MARKETING QUESTIONS YOU MUST ANSWER   SUMMARY

In this chapter we've presented the questions you must answer to analyze and segment your market effectively. We've given techniques you can use to gather information, and we've listed sources of assistance. You'll find additional sources of information not mentioned here as you track down references given in many of the publications you'll study.

Concentrate your market research on those sources that are the most helpful to you in planning your business. Market analysis becomes impossible with too much data. This is known as "planning overkill." We've been selective in our suggestions for collecting information, and you should be also. You'll never be able to eliminate market risk; your goal in seeking market information is to reduce your chance of being wrong and to increase your chance of being right.

Central to this chapter is the notion that all planning activities of the venture must be based on a consumer orientation. You can avoid the entrepreneurial disease we described in Chapter 4 as marketing myopia by following the suggestions made in this chapter and completing the worksheets that follow.

CHAPTER 5/FOOTNOTE

[1]You can obtain a complete index of *Small Business Reporter* publications by writing to: The Bank of America, Department 3120, P.O. Box 37000, San Francisco, CA 94137. A nominal charge will be made for each publication you order.

Your Market and Consumer Behavior

1. Why would customers want to buy your product or service? Ask yourself: What are the advantages or key benefits of my product or service to my customers? What are the disadvantages or negative aspects of my product or service? Be specific. Avoid using generalizations, such as lower price or better quality, without some justification. Be certain to include tangible and intangible benefits the customer would receive from your product or service.

Advantages	Disadvantages

2. After you've completed the preceding assignment, review the steps Ms. Wood-worth followed to determine why consumers might or might not buy her products. Change or adapt her procedures to fit your own business. Develop your action plan, outlined below, to collect data on the advantages and disadvantages of your product or service **as perceived by potential customers.**

Steps or tasks to be completed	Date task is to be initiated	Date task is to be completed
a.		
b.		
c.		
d.		
e.		
f.		
g.		

3. How are you going to segment your market? What demographic, geographic, or other variables are appropriate for segmenting your market? Be sure to include all the factors that will precisely identify your target market.

4. List the sources you'll check to collect information for segmenting your market. Identify the kind of consumer information you expect to obtain from each source. (You may also want to develop an action plan for completing this assignment, similar to item 2 above.)

a. _____

b. _____

c. _____

d. _____

e. _____

f. _____

g. _____

5. Describe the target market you want for your business. What's the approximate size of the *potential* market for your kind of product or service? What are the demographic characteristics of consumers in your target market? Where are they concentrated geographically? Identify other features of your market segment that will help pinpoint the kinds of customers you want—their life styles or buying habits, for example. You probably don't have all the information you need to complete this step. Do the best you can with your own knowledge of the market, and finish this exercise once you've acquired all the necessary data.

_____

_____

_____

_____

_____

_____

_____

_____

_____

_____

_____

6. The next chapter concentrates on developing marketing strategy for your business. Marketing strategy depends on how you define your business in relation to the target market you want. Therefore, before plunging into advertising, pricing, and other marketing substrategies, you should compare your response to the first assignment for Chapter 4 (What Business Are You Really In?), with the results from assignment 5 above. Summarize in the space below the definition of your business and the market segment you'll try to reach through marketing strategy.

**The customer's view of
the business I'm really in**

**The market segment(s)
for my business**

←

→

73

Your local *public or business libraries* are among the richest potential sources of information. Journals and periodicals are an excellent source of data on products, industries, and markets. The title of an article can be a good clue to what it's about. Some useful directories of articles in libraries are:

- *Readers Guide to Periodical Literature*
- *Business Periodicals Index*
- *Applied Science and Technology Index*
- *Wall Street Journal Index*

In addition, most reference libraries keep current and historical material of local civic interest, including newspapers, magazines, and books. Also available are guides to state publications of possible interest.

Marketing Research Procedures is a leaflet (number 9) published by the Small Business Administration. Reference sources for individual types of businesses are given. Available from any SBA field office.

Louis H. Vorzimer, "Using Census Data to Select a Store Site," (Washington, D.C.: Small Business Administration, 1974), *Small Marketers Aid, No. 154.*
This booklet gives detailed examples and step-by-step procedures for using census and census tract data for choosing a store location.

Sales Management and Marketing Magazine can be found in many public libraries and most university libraries. Once each year it publishes its *Survey of Buying Power* issue, which gives figures for every county in the United States and for every city over 10,000 in population. Because the U.S. Census is completely done only once in ten years, this annual magazine report is particularly valuable for years between census dates. The *Survey of Buying Power* report contains information on total population, households, breakdown of retail sales into divisions for different kinds of business firms, and total purchasing dollars represented in each city and county.

Bibliography of Publications of Bureaus of Business and Economic Research, 1957–1975, (Morgantown, West Virginia: Associated University Bureaus of Business and Economic Research). A useful guide to publications primarily concerned with state and local business information.

Chapter 6

Reaching Your Customer

This chapter concludes the discussion of the marketing system for the small business. When you've set marketing objectives and decided on specific strategies for achieving them, the marketing plan for your new business will be complete. It will specify how you expect to reach your target markets. The tools available for reaching these markets are your product or service and your pricing, promotion, and distribution strategies (Figure 6-1). The actual sales you make will depend on the effectiveness of these marketing strategies.

We'll make several suggestions to aid you in completing the marketing plan for your business. The worksheets at the end of this chapter will guide you in this effort.

SETTING YOUR MARKETING OBJECTIVES   2 A (2), 1 B, 5 A

After you have analyzed your market and decided on which market segments to concentrate, you're in a position to develop realistic, but challenging, marketing objectives. An objective identifies an intended result to be accomplished within a specific time, usually one year. Your marketing objectives will answer the question:

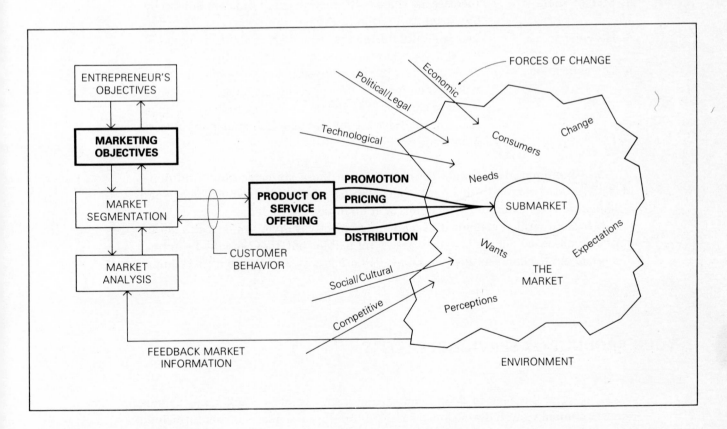

Figure 6-1   The Marketing System of the Small Business

"What results do I expect to achieve in my target markets through my marketing efforts?" Your product or service, promotion, pricing, and distribution strategies must be keyed to achieving one or more marketing objectives. In this sense what you actually do in these areas is programmed by your objectives.

A clearly written set of marketing objectives and well thought out action plans for achieving them serve as the basis for measuring your firm's market performance. Marketing objectives give you a yardstick for assessing your efforts in the marketplace.

The specific objectives you'll set depend on the kind of business you're in and the market opportunities you've identified. But certain categories of objectives appear to apply to most businesses. A few examples follow:

Category of Objectives	Examples
1. Sales	Achieve $8000 in sales from customers located within walking distance from my store within the next six months.
2. Market Penetration	By the end of the current year, complete the mailing of 6000 brochures describing my business to potential consumers who have not shopped in my store.
3. Market Share	Increase my share of the market over local competition by 5 percent during the next year.
4. Growth	Increase sales during the second six months of operation by 10 percent over the preceding six months.
5. Diversification	Add three new products appealing to professional women within nine months after opening my shop.
6. Profit	Achieve after-tax profit by the end of the first year of operation that exceeds my present take-home salary by at least 5 percent.

At a minimum, you should set objectives in these six categories. Additional objectives, for example in the areas of developing a favorable business image and establishing good community relations, will no doubt be needed.

A concise written statement of marketing objectives gives you a road map for your marketing actions. Objectives aren't inflexible, but they should be formal enough to guide you in setting plans and evaluating how well the venture is doing.

YOUR PRODUCT OR SERVICE STRATEGY   1 B, 3 B, 5 A

We've stressed the need to define your business and what you sell from the customer's point of view. If the customer sees your product as a need satisfier furnishing intangible psychological benefits, you should package and display the product accordingly. If technical qualities of the product or service are most important to consumers, this should determine the features to emphasize in performance, in design, and in warranty. Again, try to view what you sell as the customer views it.

The product or service "life cycle" is a helpful guide to use in preparing this part of your marketing plan. Any product or service moves through identifiable and predictable stages from the time it's first conceived and introduced to the market. Four distinct stages in the life cycle of a product or service can be identified as in Figure 6-2: Introduction/Growth, Maturity, Saturation, and Decline.

- **Introduction/Growth Stage.** If a product or service is introduced and catches on, it may enter a period of rapid growth lasting several months or even years. Many firms may enter the industry during this period of expanding demand. Sales volume grows at an increasing rate, and profits for firms in the industry rise sharply. Competition also increases, but the entry of rival firms with their additional promotion efforts may actually enlarge the market.

- **Maturity Stage.** Eventually the level of market acceptance and sales volume reaches a peak. Sales revenue may continue to rise somewhat, but the rate of increase falls off, resulting in a decline in rate of profit. This is a stage of intense competition. Expenses for promotion become heavy, price cutting may occur, and consumers are pressured to be "brand loyal." Firms that can't keep pace drop out of the market or are acquired by others. Large firms begin to dominate the industry.

- **Saturation Stage.** At this stage the consumers who can or will use the product or service are already buying—the market is saturated. Sales volume and profit in the industry begin to fall. Marginal firms have left the market, and the number of competitors stabilizes. The firm's promotion strategies concentrate on taking customers away from others rather than on enlarging the market.

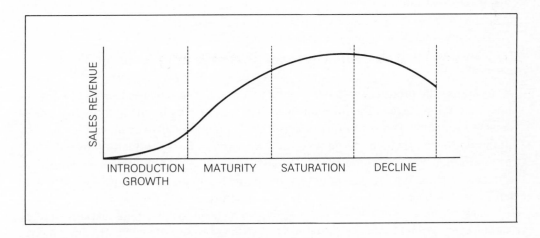

Figure 6-2 Product or Service Life Cycle

79

- Decline Stage. Demand for the product or service falls at an increasing rate at the end of the cycle. Promotion is curtailed and becomes highly selective, and prices are cut to stimulate sales. More and more rivals drop out of the market. New products or services are developed to take the place of those that are now obsolescent.

The total length of the life cycle and the length of each of the stages vary considerably. A new clothing fashion may have a life span of one calendar year with an introductory/growth stage of two months. But the automobile has been in the maturity stage for at least forty years. In any case your firm's market environments—economic, technological, social, and competitive—are constantly changing. When markets change, product or service strategy must change with them. Customers' acceptance of your product or service also changes. Therefore, you'll find it necessary to adjust your marketing strategy to the change.

Extending the Product/Service Life Cycle

It's often possible to extend the product life cycle if actions are taken early in the maturity stage. Such products as Scotch Tape, Jell-O, Arm & Hammer Baking Soda, and nylon have all been given extended commercial lives through marketing efforts designed to find new uses for them.

We all know the spin-offs from Scotch Tape and Jell-O. The new uses for nylon are perhaps not so well known. It was originally used by the military during World War II in the production of parachutes, thread, and rope. The product then revolutionized the women's hosiery industry and has since been used in producing sweaters, tires, carpets, and ball bearings, to name only a few.

Arm & Hammer Baking Soda had been marketed for 125 years when a decision to emphasize a new use revitalized it as a consumer product. Baking soda was promoted as a deodorant for refrigerators. Six months after promotion began, an estimated 70 percent of the nation's refrigerators contained a box of Arm & Hammer Baking Soda. More recently, this baking soda has been promoted as a "natural" deodorant and tooth paste.

The Product/Service Life Cycle as Proactive Management Tool

You can use the product/service life cycle as a tool to evaluate the timeliness of your business. What stage of the life cycle are your competitors in within the area you've selected for selling your product or service? A telephone answering service may be in the saturation stage in one geographical area and in the introductory/growth stage in another. If you conclude that in a particular location your business would be entering during the late introductory or maturity stage, you should be extremely cautious. It's best to be first—not a me-too business.

The product/service life cycle should also be used to anticipate market changes. Knowledge of the natural progression of each stage in the life cycle of your product or service will help you plan your marketing strategy to cope with market changes as they occur. If you know that the saturation stage is approaching, you'll also know that your primary concern should be to extend the cycle by finding new product uses or otherwise modifying your product or service to meet the changing market conditions.

Study of the concept of product/service life cycle reinforces several recommendations we've made in this book, such as the need to be proactive in planning your business and to continually innovate in what you offer consumers. One of the best ways to keep your present customers and attract additional ones in later stages of the life cycle is to offer unique features, to develop and present a new twist to keep customers loyal and satisfied. You'll find this works much better than increasing your outlay for promotion or cutting prices to meet competition. The suggestions we made in Chapter 3 for developing new business ideas aren't limited to the start-up of your venture; they can be used continually after your business is operating. You'll find the product or service market matrix (Chapter 3) particularly useful for this purpose.

YOUR PRICING STRATEGY   2 A (4), **5** A, **6** A, **8** A (6)

Price is a measure of what the customer must exchange in order to obtain goods or services. But price is also an indicator of *value* to the customer. Value, like beauty, is in the eye (or mind) of the beholder. Thus, we return again to the premise that all marketing decisions, in this case pricing, should be based on your customers' perceptions of what you offer and the value they perceive in it. Your prices should reflect what potential customers *believe* to be the value of your product or service.

Price Conveys Image

The prices you charge are part of your business image. Price tags say many things. Price on a tag tells the potential buyer something about the quality of the item: It can indicate extra value for the customer if two figures appear, the higher one marked out; or it can suggest that the very high price is insignificant compared with the status conferred on the buyer. The following case illustrates this point.

Martin Furniture: The Living Room Suite That Wouldn't Sell

Jim and Roger Martin are brothers. They owned one of two furniture stores in a small Midwestern town. A three-piece living room suite had been sitting on their showroom floor for fourteen months but hadn't sold at the marked price of $399.95.

The furniture was upholstered in imitation black leather with small silver stars printed on the material and silver piping around the edges. Jim Martin described the suite as being "in the modern tradition."

The brothers pondered the best way to sell the suite. They finally concluded that rather than put the furniture on sale they'd raise the price substantially because, as Jim put it, "this was a one-of-a-kind design." They priced the three-piece set at $799.99 and placed it just inside the store's entry.

The set sold the following week. Jim described the transaction as a "pay-day sale." "Pay-day customers come in on Saturdays when they have just been paid and have ready cash. They're usually with their families, and they're usually impulse buyers. I don't know what happens, but I don't even have to give them my sales pitch."

It's difficult to determine exactly what role the higher price actually played in making the sale for the Martins, but it's safe to say that with little information and inability to compare quality, consumers often use price as a yardstick of value. In the case of the living room set, perhaps the price conveyed the idea of quality or status or uniqueness to the buyer. Jim Martin told the authors that he was certain that's what had happened.

The ethics of this particular case may be questioned. But the importance of price reflecting what customers believe to be the value of your offering cannot be overstated.

Common Mistakes in Pricing

Two errors in setting prices for their goods or services commonly trap unwary entrepreneurs. The first we call the "I-can-do-it-cheaper" mistake. Rarely can the small business manage to charge less than a larger enterprise. There are several logical reasons why this is so. Production costs per unit will be higher for the small business because of relatively small output. The small enterprise usually can't take advantage of large volume discounts on purchased supplies. In a small service business, overhead expenses may be the same over a wide range of output or sales, resulting in higher costs per unit of sales in the first years of operation.

Chances are that if small business can enter an industry and sell "cheaper," others can do it also. With low barriers to entry this can mean either that competition will be fierce and will focus on price or that the industry is in a late stage of the product life cycle—the saturation or even the decline stage. Neither situation is attractive; and neither holds much promise for the success of the enterpriser.

The other pricing mistake we call "timid undercharging." It often occurs in firms offering services performed personally by the entrepreneur who believes lower prices compensate for lack of experience and furnish a security blanket for gaining market acceptance. Low prices are set during the early months of operation with the idea that they can be raised as more and more customers are attracted.

This policy more often than not proves to be a fatal mistake because it is always easier to lower prices than to raise them. The reason has to do with *image*. During the start-up phase, new businesses usually have to rely heavily on a core group of loyal repeat customers—attracted by the business image—and fringe customers—attracted by word-of-mouth advertising from the core group. The entrepreneur faces the prospect of losing both groups by raising prices. Higher prices change the image of your business in the eyes of your customers. Remember, *price communicates image*. Not only must your customers pay more for what they get when you raise your prices, but also they're likely to be confused about what kind of a business you really are.

If, on the other hand, the entrepreneur continues to undercharge timidly, the message the customer receives is: I can't do this as well as the competitor down the street so I'll charge less. But the image of the entrepreneur and the image of the business are one and the same. It's a second-best image that's difficult, if not impossible, to overcome.

If you really can't do as well as others in the business, our advice is for you to work for someone else until you've mastered the skills required to perform your service expertly. Then charge for it accordingly.

Marketing Approaches to Pricing

The prices you charge obviously must cover all costs of producing the product or providing the service. The financial consequences in pricing are covered in Chapter 8. What we've been discussing here are some of the marketing implications of pricing. Three basic marketing approaches are possible:

- A high-price strategy, often called "skimming-the-cream" pricing. This approach sets prices of the product or service well above costs of production.

- A low-price strategy, sometimes referred to as "market-penetration" pricing. This strategy calls for setting prices just above production costs in the attempt to achieve a high volume of sales rapidly.

- A meet-the-competition strategy, known as "me-too" pricing. This approach is intended to match prices charged by other similar businesses.

The approach you select depends, of course, on the kind of business you want to create. Skimming-the-cream pricing reinforces the uniqueness of your business. The high prices take advantage of any status connotations your product or service may have. Skimming-the-cream pricing is *not* price maximization. At no time do we advocate price maximization. What we do suggest is that your goal should be to set prices that will help you to achieve *maximum sales and profits*. If General Motors wanted to maximize the *price* of a Cadillac, it would produce and sell just one per month or one per year. Instead, GM charges a price well above production costs, consistent with the image of high quality and status the Cadillac conveys to its market.

As we've said before, it's easier to lower prices than to raise them. Many companies regularly use the skimming strategy for new products and gradually reduce price after the product is introduced at a high price. Early adopters, consumers who enjoy being the first to buy the newest, buy the product and tell others about it. Almost all early adopters have high income and are relatively insensitive to price.

As word spreads about the new product, the price is reduced so others can afford to buy it. Products that have been sold through this strategy are numerous:

hand-held electronic calculators, microwave ovens, electric toothbrushes, and digital display watches to name just a few. This pricing strategy enables the company to recover its initial investment costs quickly, to meet competitors' attempts to copy its success, and to reach more segments of the market. Sales and profit are kept high early in the product's life cycle.

Market penetration pricing is usually used for products that become fads; they progress through the life cycle rapidly. Hula-hoops and Superballs are good examples. The products are unique. The objective is to gain quick access to the market, to obtain shelf space in dealers' stores, and to achieve a high level of sales within a short time. Penetration pricing affords the entrepreneur the most profitable way to sell easily copied products that appeal to a large market.

Meet-the-competition pricing is a strategy we do not recommend. If your new business can't charge more for its product or service than its competitors, it's a me-too business. The only conceivable reason to be in it in the first place would be if you were using the product or service as a holding action, giving the customers more value for their money than your competitors, while you were developing a truly unique product or service. We can't emphasize too often or too much that "I can do it cheaper" is not a good reason to start a new business.

YOUR DISTRIBUTION STRATEGY   1 B (2), 5 A (2)

A channel of distribution consists of firms that facilitate the flow of goods from the producer to the ultimate user. It may be viewed as a series of links in a chain, with each link being a business performing specialized functions that add utility to the product or service.

The best distribution strategy for your business depends on which channel affords the greatest utility for your potential customers. Utility defines the degree to which the product or service satisfies the customer.

Your customers can use your product only if it's in their possession at the right time. And to purchase your product it must be in a place convenient to them. Therefore, the channel of distribution you select must offer two kinds of utility:

- Time utility. Your product is available *when* the consumer wants to buy.

- Place utility. Your product is available *where* the consumer wants to buy.

The importance of these forms of utility is obvious. Owning a pound of coffee located in Brazil certainly has drawbacks. And what value to you would tire chains be at the factory during a snowstorm or electric fans in a warehouse during a heat wave?

You may be able to produce the products that consumers are demanding, but no transaction takes place unless you and the buyers can get together. You must match

84

your ability to supply or sell products with the specific time- and place-utility demands of your target markets. The best channel for vacuum cleaners may be direct from manufacturer to consumer through a house-to-house national sales force of 7000. The best channel for frozen pies may be from food processor to agent to merchant wholesaler to supermarket to consumer.

Figure 6-3 illustrates the traditional channels of distribution for consumer goods.

Of the three channels shown in the diagram the third, manufacturer to wholesaler to retailer to consumer, is that most often used by small producers. The small company with a limited line of products usually needs the financial and promotional resources and the market access of large wholesalers to reach the hundreds of retailers who will eventually stock its products. The wholesaler's large sales force is responsible for reaching the market with the manufacturer's output. This channel of distribution carries the lowest distribution costs to the small manufacturer. But it has the disadvantage of the manufacturer losing control of marketing because title to the product passes to the wholesaler.

The first channel shown in Figure 6-3, producer to consumer, gives the producer complete control of marketing and sales. It's also the most costly method of distribution. This means that you may have to make a tradeoff between cost and control in choosing your distribution channel. Such a tradeoff is illustrated in the following case.

The Case of R & H Wall Paneling Company

Jim Ross was a remodeling contractor in the Pacific Northwest. He found that increasingly his jobs involved paneling the walls of basements, family rooms, and dens. Local sources of finished hardwood panels were few. These materials were expensive and availability was unpredictable. It became more and more difficult to keep up with orders for jobs.

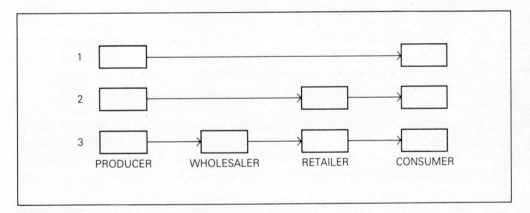

Figure 6-3 Typical Channels of Distribution

85

Ross's partner, Tolly Hansen, was a graduate engineer. Hansen suggested they try making their own engraved panels of enameled tempered hardboard in streamlined patterns. Ross liked the idea, and Hansen built an oven for baking enamel on the raw panels. Ross arranged with a local wholesaler to supply them with 100 sheets of hardboard at a time. Hansen designed and built special tooling for engraving the desired patterns.

Ross and Hansen now thought they could benefit by easing out of the remodeling business and concentrating on manufacturing their prefinished wall panels. They sold their finished wallboard to a wholesaler who in turn sold to retail outlets.

After a few months of following this distribution strategy they found they were just breaking even. Finished wall panels were selling at retail for about 50 cents per square foot. After retail and wholesaler discounts were subtracted from the selling price, Ross and Hansen were collecting just enough to cover their overhead, material, and processing costs. The tradeoff between cost and control of distribution wasn't working to their advantage.

Hansen suggested they try another approach. They would produce, sell, and go back to installing the wall panels themselves; they would employ what is called vertical integration. They'd market "home beautification," remodeling with custom wall panels, directly to consumers. In this way they'd bypass wholesalers and retailers (the third channel of distribution shown in Figure 6-1).

This time the trade off between cost and control of distribution worked in their favor. In spite of increased operating expenses—they had to advertise and maintain a sales force to sell door to door directly to home owners—they were successful. "We had complete control. We sold the concept of custom design, supervised installation, and guaranteed completion dates." The success of the channel of distribution Ross and Hansen chose was in great measure attributable to the superior time and place utility afforded their customers.

R & H Wall Paneling Company expanded rapidly with the use of this distribution strategy. Additional sales people were hired, and new products were developed, such as etched-grain fir plywood paneling. After three years of profitable operations, they started to establish franchises across the country. Ross and Hansen furnished materials to order and trained franchisees to sell and install their products. After ten years of operating R & H Wall Paneling Company with success, both men were able to retire.

Manufacturers increasingly use more than one marketing channel for similar products. In the case of Ross and Hansen, they continued to manufacture and sell directly to customers in their local area and with their franchise operations developed another channel of distribution. They became sole-source suppliers of wall panels for their franchisees.

Another example of more than one distribution channel is the case of the sale of soap products. These products are distributed through traditional grocery wholesalers to food stores to consumer and at the same time through a second channel:

directly from manufacturers to large retail chains and motels. Manufacturers are able to serve different target markets through different distribution channels.

The channel of distribution you choose depends on the kind of business you enter and customer preferences in shopping for products like yours. Tupperware and Avon cosmetics are firms whose marketing moves directly from producer to consumer. Almost all service businesses use this approach. If your business enterprise is a retail store, you'll more than likely be at the end of the distribution line. In this case the distribution channel decision is out of your hands. Your concern would be for the best possible location for your store. But no matter what the nature of your business, you'll have to consider several things in making decisions about distribution:

- *Your Consumer.* Results from your completed assignments about consumers at the end of Chapters 4 and 5 on marketing should give you some insights about the best channel of distribution for your business. In general, the geographic location and the needs of your potential consumer market will influence your choice.

- *Your Product.* The kind of channel, its length, and the functions to be performed within the channel are influenced strongly by the nature of the product you'll move through it: the weight and bulk of the product, its unit value, its technical characteristics, the amount of service it requires, its perishability, and the degree to which it's standardized or custom made.

  Perishable products, such as fruit or fresh produce, typically move through short channels directly to the retailer or consumer. Complex or highly technical products, such as computer equipment, are also sold directly from manufacturer to buyer. A general rule is that the more standardized the product and the lower the unit value, the longer the channel will be. Convenience goods and industrial supplies with low unit prices are usually marketed through longer channels. Installations and more expensive industrial and consumer goods are marketed through shorter, more direct channels.

- *Your Competition.* Which channels your competitors use is an important factor for you to consider. You'll have to decide whether you should use a similar channel or an entirely different one. Similar channels should probably be used for most target markets because of established patterns of customer shopping behavior. Occasionally, however, a unique channel approach is called for.

One entrepreneur we know owes her success to her unique distribution strategy. Her product is a small cake. It comes in six "natural" flavors such as lemon and pumpkin. She bakes the cakes in the morning and carries them from her car in a large basket to sell in beauty salons during the afternoon.

Your distribution strategy should be carefully designed to ensure the greatest utility for intended customers. Your products become accessible within your target markets through the channels of distribution you choose. You should make your decisions about your channels simultaneously with other marketing decisions, particularly those concerned with market segmentation, pricing, and promotion.

Successful marketing of your small business calls for more than developing a good product or service, pricing it correctly, and making it easily available to your customers. An effective program of promotion is also essential for every business that wants more than "walk-in" sales.

Two serious deficiencies are often apparent in promotional activities of small businesses. Many entrepreneurs waste promotional dollars on consumers who aren't potential customers, and promotion is often viewed by entrepreneurs as a one-shot deal—a way to boost sales in slow periods. Promotion should be a deliberately planned and continuing program of communication tailored to the market segment you want to reach. It's probably the most flexible marketing tool you'll have, and you should use it to gain a competitive edge for your business. At the end of this chapter we'll ask you to develop a detailed promotional campaign including schedules to use during your first year of business operation.

Promotion is a special form of communication intended to influence target consumers; it may take any of the following forms: advertising, personal selling, publicity, or sales promotion.

As you read through the discussion of each of these elements, keep in mind that effective promotional strategy communicates continually to the *target* market. It develops awareness of, interest in, and desire for your product or service.

Advertising

Advertising is intended to get your message to a large number of potential customers at the same time. It presents the ideas, goods, or services of an identified sponsor. It is paid for by your business. Advertising includes:

- Direct mail
- Store sign
- Radio and television
- Magazine and newspaper
- Outdoor sign, poster, and skywriting
- Novelties such as calendars, blotters, pencils

Advertising bolsters your personal selling efforts with nonpersonal forms of communication. A McGraw-Hill study called *The Mathematics of Selling* uses an advertisement that illustrates this relationship. The ad shows a salesperson facing an industrial buyer. The buyer's thoughts (shown in a balloon) are:

I don't know who you are.
I don't know your company.
I don't know your company's product.
I don't know what your company stands for.
I don't know your company's customers.

I don't know your company's record.

I don't know your company's reputation.

Now—what was it you wanted to sell me?

Personal selling as the ad suggests can't always handle the whole selling job. Mass selling through advertising can do much of the spadework for you so that your personal follow-up can be concentrated on answers to specific questions and on closing the sale. Your goal in advertising is to increase the likelihood that the customer will buy your product or service.

You'll need to make three basic decisions to achieve your advertising goals. They are:

1. How much should I spend? ⟶ Budget strategy

2. What media should I use? ⟶ Media strategy

3. What should I say, and how should I say it? ⟶ Copy strategy

Budget Strategy

There is no pat answer to how much you should spend on advertising. What you spend will depend on your promotional objectives, your target customers, the characteristics of your product or service, and the type of business you're in. Several methods for deciding on a budget are used successfully by small businesses.

The *percentage-of-sales* method is probably the most frequently used. A percentage of projected sales revenue to be devoted to advertising is predetermined. Suppose you learn from your trade association that firms similar to yours allocate 5 percent of revenue to advertising. You'd estimate the amount of your sales for your first year of operation to determine what your advertising expenditures should be.

The *fixed-dollar-per-unit* method uses an absolute dollar amount in the advertising budget for each unit of product sold or produced. You'd have to estimate how much it would take to sell each unit and then set your advertising budget for the year. A boutique owner who plans to sell 500 dresses might estimate a cost of $1.00 to sell each dress. The advertising budget for the year would be $500.00. The fixed-dollar-per-unit method like the percentage-of-sales method represents "formula thinking"; it ignores the goal that advertising must achieve—to bring sales.

Matching competition can be viewed as a defensive way to develop your advertising budget. Spending as much as your competitors assumes that your advertising strategy should be similar to theirs. It also assumes that your competitors know the "right" amount to spend. And it's pretty nearly impossible to find out how much your competition is actually spending in any case. This is not a method we recommend.

The *affordable method* isn't really a method at all. It simply answers the question: How much am I willing to spend on advertising? Entrepreneurs who use this procedure as a basis for deciding on an advertising budget don't truly understand the function of advertising. Of course, there are practical limits to how much you can spend; the flaw in the how-much-can-I-afford approach is the self-fulfilling prophesy. Advertising leads to sales; the amount you spend on it should be keyed in some way to the amount of sales you want. Suppose an entrepreneur is willing to spend only a small amount on advertising during the first year of operation. At the end of the year, meager sales and disappointing profits—the result of the inadequate advertising program—might lead to even less money being budgeted during the second year. This method of developing an advertising budget could result in the ultimate failure of the business.

As a practical matter **the amount you decide to spend on advertising should be related to planned sales targets and the objectives for your advertising program.** This means you should carefully assess your firm's need for advertising and set specific objectives before you make your budget. The advertising objectives must be based on your sound understanding of the target audience and identification of the results the advertising must produce. At this point you can determine the costs of reaching your objectives. In this way the budget results from what you want to achieve rather than your achievement being limited by what the budget will permit.

Media Strategy

Several forms of communication are available to aid you in meeting your advertising objectives. They offer enough flexibility for you to reach any specific target market by using a particular medium or a combination of media. The suitability of any medium for your advertising strategy depends upon the following four factors:

1. *Your Target Market.* When you begin to advertise, use the media that your customers pay attention to. You'll then have some assurance that your message will be heard, read, or seen by these target customers. Most of the major media use marketing research to develop profiles of the people who buy their publications or live in their broadcasting area. Although they can't tell you exactly who reads each page or sees or hears each show, their data can give you guidelines appropriate to your market segment.

2. *Cost.* One measure that isn't subjective is cost. Two important dimensions of media cost are absolute cost and relative cost. Absolute cost is the actual dollar outlay for running an ad. For example, a message carried by a number of newspapers takes considerably fewer dollars than a message transmitted by television. Relative cost is the relationship between the actual cost and the number of consumers the message reaches. A common measure is the cost per thousand consumers reached. For example, suppose you want to compare the relative cost of a full-page ad in two different magazines. You'd obtain the following information from each:

	Ajax Magazine	Tabloid Magazine
Circulation	30,000	25,000
Percent of readers that appear to be potential customers—persons within a particular age group in a certain kind of occupation, for example.	30%	50%
Potential customers reached with your ad.	9,000	12,500
Cost of ad.	$2,000	$2,500
Cost of ad per potential customer reached.	$\frac{\$2,000}{9,000} = 22.2$¢	$\frac{\$2,500}{12,500} = 20$¢

90

This analysis shows that even though *Ajax* has a larger circulation and the absolute cost of running an ad is less, you'd prefer *Tabloid* because it has a lower cost per *potential customer reached.*

3. *The Right Media.* Some media will be better than others for the message you want to convey about your product or service. For example, for women's cosmetics, radio is limited because it carries only sound, whereas print media can show color pictures. You will also have to consider the message itself—its length, its degree of complexity, its need for repetition, and other factors—to determine which media can best handle what you want to communicate.

4. *Availability of Media.* The local situation may determine the number and kind of media you use. A retailer in a small town wouldn't have as many options as a retailer in a large city. Whether your market is large or small, the medium you choose may not be available at the time and place you desire; the radio station you select may be sold out of advertising time.

Copy Strategy

This is the development of the actual advertising message—the idea or information you want to convey translated into effective words and symbols for your target market. Copy strategy involves formulating what is to be said, and how it's to be said, what form it will take, what its style and design will be. Rather than attempt to master the professional skills of copy design, you'd be wise to rely on specialists—graphic artists and public relations people—for your copy strategy.

How to Use an Advertising Agency

Depending on the advertising needs for your new business, you may want to use an advertising agency. If you do, you should interview two or three agencies to get a line on their services. The case at the end of this section describes how a small agency assisted in developing one of the most successful franchise operations in the world.

Advertising agencies specialize in designing and carrying out tailored advertising programs for their customers. The larger full-service agencies offer these kinds of services:

- Creativity: They can develop unique ideas for promoting your business, product, or service.

- Media selection and use: Agencies analyze and evaluate media to fit your advertising plan, and will schedule and place the ads for you.

- Technical production: They'll apply specialized skills in such areas as preparing illustrations, photoengraving, art work, and setting copy into type.

- Marketing research: The agency's research staff can advise you on the potential market for your product or service and on possible sources of distribution.

- Other functions: Many agencies also furnish such services as developing sales promotion and public relations programs.

You can readily see that the advertising agency can be an organizational extension of your business in performing several marketing services. Small, boutique-type ad agencies are growing in number; some of these specialize in helping small business clients. These agencies have limited services but would be more likely than large agencies to want you as a client.

You'll have to pay for the services of the ad agency. The most common method of compensation is the commission plan. Agencies generally get most of their revenue from selling advertising space and time. You, the customer, pay the list price to the medium in which the ad is placed by the agency. The medium then returns a commission to the agency for placing the ad. Thus, it's the medium—newspaper, magazine, radio, or television—that provides a good share of the agency's income.

In some cases agencies simply charge a flat fee for services to the client; in other cases the "cost-plus-percent" is used. The agency charges the cost of the advertisements placed plus a given percentage of that cost for other services performed. Fees or commissions can be negotiated; you should shop for the best value for the services you need.

Advertising makes your business known to the consumer. The advertising agency can furnish expert talent to make your message effective and get it to your intended customers. The potential value of establishing a working relationship with an agency is dramatically illustrated by a business that is now known to millions.

Baskin-Robbins 31 Ice Cream Stores

Burton Baskin and Irvine Robbins returned to the United States after a stint on a supply ship in the Navy during World War II. They had discovered that of all things they delivered among the South Sea Islands, the troops in the South Pacific enjoyed ice cream the most. They decided to start their own ice cream business after the war to take advantage of the universal acceptance of this favorite confection.

Their first customers, as Irvine Robbins tells the story, were two or three small stores that sold their ice cream to retail customers. Very soon after they had gotten these outlets, a representative of a very large dairy product firm tried to persuade these stores to give up the partners' ice cream and take on their brand. The dairy products firm made attractive promises to the small store owners: new freezer cabinets, counter displays, and widespread newspaper advertising to stimulate the sale of their ice cream. The representative said, "Why do you want to deal with a peanut firm, when you can have our massive support?"

Baskin and Robbins were shaken when they learned of the attempt to take their business away from them. What to do to counteract the attack by the large competitor? The partners saw that if they lost these first outlets for their ice cream they would be out of business.

92

They talked through a strategy to improve their position with their retailers. "Let's put an ad in the *Los Angeles Times*—as big a one as we can afford. That'll show our retailers that we have substance and they can count on our being here permanently to supply their needs."

Checking their bank account, they found that they could manage $500 to buy an ad.

Then came the next question: How do you prepare an ad? Neither knew. So they decided in true entrepreneurial fashion to locate expert help. They found a small, new ad agency formed by two young, competent partners who had spun off a major national firm to form their own, called the Carson-Roberts agency after themselves.

When Baskin and Robbins told these two young men of their predicament, the two decided to take a chance on going along with the young entrepreneurs despite their obviously precarious financial condition. Perhaps they could grow a client relationship that would be sound and profitable for the long haul—if they could help Baskin and Robbins out of their crisis.

After they heard the Baskin-Robbins story, they said to the ice cream makers, "We're inclined to think that putting an ad in the paper is not the best way for you to spend your money. The ad will appear once and that's it. You won't get any mileage out of your investment. Let us think about your problem for a day or two. Then we'll make our recommendation to you."

At the next meeting, the two advertising men said, "Here's what we suggest you do with your $500. Your customers should get the image of fun when they see your company name. We recommend that you develop this image by using a white background with pink and chocolate colored balloons on it everywhere you can. Paint your little ice cream delivery truck white with pink and chocolate balloons on it. Change your stationery to carry the same colored balloons. And paint the inside of your retailers' stores white with pink and chocolate balloons on the walls. That'll carry out the theme you should have—fun to go into these clean stores, select a flavor, and eat a high quality ice cream.

"Oh, yes, one important point—you should have lots of flavors your customers can choose from. That'll make it a game for your customers to enjoy—selecting a flavor."

"O.K.," said Baskin, "that's a great idea—31 flavors."

How did he arrive at that number? There happened to be 31 days in that particular month. As you know, the image of Baskin-Robbins is tied to 31 flavors and pink and chocolate colored balloons on a white background. Variety and fun have evolved a chain of hundreds of Baskin-Robbins stores with a gross business approaching $2 hundred million a year.

The Baskin-Robbins turning point toward success came from that first meeting with the small advertising agency. The relationship has held firm over the years. The outstanding marketing success of Baskin-Robbins 31 Flavors Ice Cream Stores is directly attributable to the advice they got from their advertising agency.

Personal Selling, Publicity, and Sales Promotion

These three forms of promotion, personal selling, publicity, and sales promotion, along with advertising should be part of your overall consumer communication strategy. An advertisement can't make a sale by itself. In any promotion program it is the salesperson who must finally make the sale. Free publicity about your business can give you market exposure that will create consumer interest in your business. And sales promotion can result in temporary stimulation of demand for what you sell.

Personal Selling

Personal communication with customers is vital to the survival of most businesses. It can be used for several purposes: creating awareness of your product, developing preference for your product, arousing interest, negotiating terms of sale, closing a sale, and furnishing reinforcement to the customer after the sale.

It's essential that you recognize the distinction between personal selling and all the other marketing tools: **Face-to-face selling probably furnishes the only opportunity you'll have for two-way communication with customers.** It's an interactive relationship between you and your customers; it involves learning and observing the characteristics and needs of buyers.

The modern approach to selling is not to *sell* customers, but rather to *help them buy.* This is accomplished by presenting both the advantages and disadvantages of your product or service and showing how it will satisfy their needs. The result is satisfied customers and the establishment of long-term buying relationships. Instead of viewing personal selling as just moving products, your direct sales communication with customers should involve personal attention and interest in their buying needs.

Publicity

Another name for publicity is free advertising. When your company or its product comes to the attention of the public simply by being newsworthy, it gets publicity. You pay nothing for the media exposure you receive. Most local daily newspapers will print stories about a new store or business opening in their area. Publicity releases describing your business should be sent to copy editors for possible inclusion in their papers. In addition, new information about your product or information describing your new unique service may gain the interest of editors. Every new business serving local customers should take advantage of any publicity it can get. You might, for instance, have an advertising agency or professional copy writer prepare written materials and photographs to be sent to local media just prior to your grand opening. Then as you add new products or services or perhaps perform special community service, publicity can become a regular component of your promotion strategy.

Sales Promotion

This is a catchall term for promotion tools such as free samples, contests, coupons, discount offerings, and trading stamps. It also covers specialty advertising like giving away calendars, matchbooks, ash trays, and key rings with your firm's name on them.

94

You might use sales promotion for a variety of reasons: a temporary promotion when you open your business, giving away a bonus item with the purchase of your product (called a premium in the trade), or a coupon offering a discount to stimulate sales during low seasonal buying periods to attract new customers or to induce present customers to buy more. However, the coupon really represents a temporary price reduction and may be inconsistent with the image of your business. Furthermore, the price-off sales promotion applies only to products that customers buy frequently. A caution applies to the use of sampling, contests, and trading stamps. In the long run these can involve much more expense than they're worth. Most small businesses should limit sales promotion to specialty advertising and occasional use of premiums.

REACHING YOUR CUSTOMER   SUMMARY

Setting challenging but realistic marketing objectives will guide you in designing effective marketing strategies. Your marketing objectives are crucial to planning since they help to assure that your efforts and expenditures are directed toward reaching a predetermined target.

Marketing strategies spell out how you intend to achieve your objectives and reach your market segments by pricing, promoting, and distributing your product or service. The effectiveness of these strategies will be reflected in sales. They will determine the number of new and repeat customers you attract and the degree of product awareness your business achieves. The acid test for assessing how consumer-oriented you are will be seen in the results of your marketing strategies.

Your product or service strategy should consider the life cycle concept, which identifies four stages marked by a changing set of problems and opportunities. In the introduction/growth stage initial sales expand slowly for a time then rise rapidly as the availability of the product or service becomes known and word-of-mouth advertising spreads. Competition enters as the market success becomes clear. To stay on the offensive, the firm that introduced the new product or service must improve it, add new features or new products, enter new market segments and distribution channels.

The maturity, saturation, and decline stages follow. Sales growth slows down and profits stabilize. Innovation is required to renew market acceptance and sales. Major modification of the product or service is usually needed. Finding new uses for the existing product or service also should be explored.

The product or service life cycle offers a useful framework for identifying the major marketing features of each stage and suggesting marketing strategies to consider in each. It can also be used to evaluate the timeliness of your business in a particular market segment.

Your pricing strategy has two major dimensions. First, the price you set conveys image and suggests the level of quality to the consumer. This is the marketing side of pricing. Second, price has financial implications since the total dollars your business takes in results from price times the number of units (quantity) sold. This chapter concentrated on the marketing dimension.

Entrepreneurs often make the mistake of believing they can produce and price their product or service cheaper than others in the business. Another common error is consciously to undercharge for a product or service with the hope that low price will help them gain entry into the market. These can be serious mistakes that once made are hard to correct.

If at all possible, you should adopt a strategy of "skimming-the-cream" pricing. A high price capitalizes on the uniqueness of your business, conveys a high quality image, and reinforces any status symbol that owning your product or using your service may have. If the price you set seems too high after some experience with it, it's easier to lower price than to raise it. Your strategy may then call for gradually reducing your first high price to attract the more price sensitive consumers, or to meet competitors who enter the market stimulated by your success with your high price strategy.

Distribution strategy varies from direct selling to using one, two, three, or more intermediaries to reach consumers. The best channel of distribution is the one that offers the greatest utility to your potential customers. Distribution here matches your ability to produce and supply products with your customer's needs for time and place utility. The special characteristics of your potential customers, product, and competition have to be carefully evaluated to develop the right distribution decisions.

Your promotional strategy represents your attempt to stimulate sales by conducting persuasive communications with potential buyers. The instruments of promotion are advertising, personal selling, publicity, and sales promotion. Together they may be the most flexible marketing tools you'll have.

Be careful not to waste promotion on consumers who aren't potential customers. Just as important, don't view promotion as gimmickry or as a one-shot deal to boost sales temporarily. Promotion should be a deliberately planned, carefully scheduled, continuing communication program aimed at the market segments you want to reach. And your budget for promotion should be determined by your promotional objectives and the sales results you desire.

Use professionals in designing your promotional campaign. Graphic artists will help in preparing effective, eye-catching symbols or other unique identification for your business, product, or service. An advertising agency can advise you on the best media to use and your copy strategy.

Your marketing strategy will be an ongoing challenge. The tools you use, the skill and creativity with which you coordinate and employ them, and the consumers' response determine whether your business thrives or fades in the market.

Reaching Your Customer

1. Develop concise written statements of your marketing objectives. For each area write at least one objective to be accomplished within one year after opening your doors for business. (Note: You might want to jump ahead to Chapter 15 and read the section on managing by objectives. There you'll find the criteria your written statements of objectives should satisfy.)

   a. Sales: _____

   _____

   _____

   b. Profit: _____

   _____

   _____

   c. Product or Service Strategy: _____

   _____

   _____

   d. Pricing Strategy: _____

   _____

   _____

   e. Distribution Strategy: _____

   _____

   _____

   f. Promotional Strategy: _____

   _____

   _____

2. Evaluate carefully your intended market, competition, available products or services, and apparent trends in each, then answer this question:
   At what stage of the product or service life cycle will your business be entering the market? Then specify the evidence for your conclusion.

   a. The stage at which I'm entering the market is: _____

   _____

   _____

   _____

b. The trends that I've observed as evidence for my conclusion are: _____

_____

_____

_____

_____

_____

3. If you've concluded that your business is entering the market at the beginning or during the introduction/growth stage, develop and describe your marketing plans to deal with the problems and challenges each subsequent stage will bring. Here you should play the "what-if" game. It works like this: Suppose, as we hope, your venture is truly new and unique in your market and your sales grow rapidly. What if all of a sudden a competitor copies your success and opens up a business across the street offering the same products or services? What could you do to stay on the offensive? Remember, the variables *you* control are your product or service, your pricing strategy, your distribution strategy, and your promotion strategy. Describe briefly the kinds of adjustments or modifications you would consider in each area of strategy.

a. Product or Service: _____

_____

_____

b. Pricing Strategy: _____

_____

_____

c. Distribution Strategy: _____

_____

_____

d. Promotional Strategy: _____

_____

4. If you've concluded that your business is entering the market at some later stage in the life cycle, justify clearly why you believe you can succeed. Do so by describing how your marketing strategies will set your business apart from the rest of the pack.

a. Product or Service: _____

_____

_____

b. Pricing Strategy: _____

_____

_____

c. Distribution Strategy: _____

_____

_____

d. Promotional strategy _____

_____

_____

5. a. What will be your basic pricing approach? Will you be skimming the cream, using a market-penetration approach, or a meet-the-competition strategy?

My pricing strategy can best be characterized as _____

_____

b. What price(s) will you charge? What evidence do you have consumers will buy from you at the price you set?

The price I'll set (or range of prices) will be $_____ for my product or service.

I have the following evidence that indicates consumers will buy from me at this

price: _____

_____

_____

_____

_____

_____

6. What is the relationship between the price you will charge and the image of the business you will be trying to create? Is your price compatible; will it enhance the image of the business? Why? (Before you attempt to answer this, review your responses to assignment 6 in Chapter 5.)

The price(s) I'll charge are compatible with the image of my business because: __

_____

_____

_____

7. a. Describe the distribution strategy for your business. Will you go directly to consumers or will you use intermediaries?

_____

_____

_____

_____

b. Justify your distribution strategy in terms of the time and place utility it will offer potential customers.

My distribution strategy will assure that my product is available *when* the consumer wants to buy because: _____

_____

_____

_____

My distribution strategy will assure that my product is available *where* the consumer wants to buy because: _____

_____

_____

_____

8. a. Which method will you use to determine your budget for advertising?

_____

  b. Apply the method you choose to estimate how much you plan to spend for advertising during the first year of operation.

   The method I'll use to determine my advertising budget is: _____

_____

   I estimate my first year advertising budget to be $ _____

9. Listed below are media for advertising. Check the ones you plan to use and beside each one briefly describe its advantages as you see them in reaching potential customers.

	Plan to Use	Advantages
Direct Mail	_____	_____
Store Sign	_____	_____
Radio	_____	_____
Television	_____	_____
Magazines	_____	_____
Newspapers	_____	_____
Billboards	_____	_____
Handbills	_____	_____
Novelties	_____	_____
Others (specify)	_____	_____

10. Prepare a list of specific questions you will ask an expert in advertising for small business to answer (an ad agency, very likely). For instance, if you've checked

100

direct mail and believe it to be most effective in reaching potential customers, you might want to know about cost per potential customer reached, brochure design and production, obtaining good mailing lists, what to expect in sales per 1000 pieces mailed, and many more items.

My questions about the media and their use are:

_____

_____

_____

_____

_____

_____

_____

_____

_____

_____

_____

11. Have you had experience in personal selling?

   Yes _____, No _____.

   a. If yes, describe it briefly, list your strengths and weaknesses in face-to-face selling situations, and describe what you will do to overcome your weaknesses: _____

   _____

   _____

   _____

   _____

   _____

   _____

   b. If no, describe how you will acquire personal selling skills and overcome any perceived weaknesses: _____

   _____

   _____

   _____

   _____

12. When and how will you seek publicity for your business? What media will you contact and what will you say to them that will be interesting enough to print or broadcast? In the space below, write two paragraphs about your business that you'd like to see in your local newspaper. (You might study the business section of a local newspaper and evaluate the articles about new businesses before you attempt this exercise.)

Here's what I'd like to read in the newspaper about my new business: _____

_____

_____

_____

_____

_____

_____

_____

_____

_____

_____

_____

13. What forms of sales promotion fit your kind of business? How do you plan to use them and what results do you expect? _____

_____

_____

_____

_____

_____

_____

14. The best way to coordinate and integrate your promotional strategy is to lay out an action plan for the year ahead that identifies for each month the promotion tasks to be accomplished. This will be your Master Promotion Calendar.

Procedures to follow in completing your Master Promotion Calendar:

a. You will need a large sheet of paper for this—brown or white wrapping paper perhaps. Along the bottom, you should note key dates such as holidays or other heavy buying periods. Under advertising on the left, list the specific media you will use during the year. Then, opposite each form of advertising you plan to use, show target dates for completion. For the other forms of promotion, personal selling, publicity, and sales promotion, you may want to make notes for yourself about the kinds of activities or events that will take place, and their target dates for completion. The general format for your calendar might look like this:

Advertising	Jan	Feb	Mar	Apr	May	Jun	Jul	Aug	Sep	Oct	Nov	Dec
1. Radio												
2. Newspaper												
3. Direct Mail												
4. Other												
Personal Selling												
Publicity												
Sales Promotion												

b. Then make brief notes on what will be done and when it will occur. For example, let's say you're going to conduct a direct mail campaign right after your business starts to announce your opening and to describe what your business offers. This will require designing the brochure and mailing brochures. The direct mail portion of the Master Promotion Calendar might look like this:

1. Direct Mail	Jan	Feb	Mar	Apr	May	Jun	Jul	Aug	Sep	Oct	Nov	Dec
a. Develop and design brochure with graphic artist		■	■									
b. Locate and select firm specializing in direct mailing and buy mailing lists		■										
c. Print brochures and get mailing out				■								

IF YOU WANT TO READ MORE

Louis E. Boone and David L. Kurtz, *Foundations of Marketing*, The Dryden Press, New York, 1977, pp. 163–185. This is a chapter on product strategy from an excellent basic marketing textbook. It presents an overview of the elements to consider in formulating product strategy including the product or service life cycle, how the consumer adoption process works for new products or services, ways to classify products in terms of consumer shopping behavior, and the implications of this for strategy.

Theodore Levitt, "Exploit the Product Life Cycle," *Harvard Business Review*, November–December 1965, pp. 81–94. This article is a classic. It is straightforward and presents specific suggestions for staying on the offensive in each stage of the life cycle. Although published in 1965, the author offers advice for entrepreneurs that applies just as much to today's changing business world.

Benson P. Shapiro, "The Psychology of Pricing," *Harvard Business Review*, July–August 1968, pp. 14–25. This is another classic article. It summarizes studies showing how consumers perceive price in relation product quality and how they make purchase decisions on the basis of price.

Some Guidelines for Advertising Budgeting, The Conference Board, Inc., New York, 1972, pp. 5–13. A discussion of procedures for developing the advertising budget are presented in this booklet. All of the methods discussed in this chapter are covered in more detail.

"The Advertising Agency—What It Is and What It Does for Advertising," *Advertising Age*, November 21, 1973, pp. 34–42. This article presents the services advertising agencies perform in a clear and detailed fashion. Topics covered range from media planning to package design, and the expert advice they can often give on pricing, distribution, and marketing research.

Chapter 7

Marketing the Service Business

The business that deals in products sells tangibles; the service business sells intangibles, which cannot be touched, weighed, or smelled. Marketing services therefore poses more problems and more challenges than marketing products.

Services are often sold as part of the marketing of some physical product. Marketing the service that goes with the product requires special attention. This chapter tells about marketing services and marketing the special services accompanying the sale of a product.

In market analysis, the market segmentation, pricing, promotion, and distribution, as well as the procedures of planning for the marketing of services, are essentially the same as for products. The major differences lie in the distinctive characteristics of services and the resulting close relationship between seller and buyer.

WHY IS THE SERVICE BUSINESS UNIQUE?   1 B, 2 A, 3, 4

A service is an intangible product performing tasks that satisfy consumer needs in chosen market segments. When you market a service, your customer comes away empty handed from the resulting sale. A product can be seen and handled; a service cannot. A product is *produced*; a service is *performed*. As a result, successful marketing of services takes more than conventional marketing methods.

If your business is services, you'll find several features important beyond those required in marketing products. These key features include:

Services Are Intangible

Your customer can't hear, see, smell, taste, or touch your service. This places a heavy burden on your promotion strategy. When physical goods are marketed, the product itself can communicate value to the consumer. Not so with services—**your sales effort must concentrate on the benefits your customer will get from the service rather than on the service itself.**

Because of difficulty in demonstrating, displaying, or illustrating an intangible product, consumers are often unable to evaluate the quality of a service before buying. As a result, the reputation and image of the service business become paramount in buying decisions.

Buyers and Sellers of Services Are Interdependent

This means that the seller performs the service for the buyer, and the buyer frequently plays a major role in the production and marketing of the service.

There is no transfer of ownership in the sale of a service; buyers are usually dependent on the seller *during* the consumption or use of the purchased service. In contrast, after purchasing such items as clothing, food, appliances, or books, the buyer is not dependent on the seller.

As the seller you are often dependent on the buyer in the creation and marketing of your service. This implies that the adequacy of the service depends on the ability of your customers to communicate their specific needs and your skill in perceiving and satisfying these needs. Unlike a product, the quality of a service depends partly on the experience, knowledge, and ability of the consumer to communicate and the opportunities the entrepreneur creates for buyers to tell about their needs.

To summarize, there is a dependency relationship—a personal or professional relationship—between buyer and seller during the creation and consumption of a service. This dependency does not exist to the same extent when products are produced, sold, and consumed. The marketing implication is that **the value of the service to your customer quite often depends on the quality of the personal relationship between the buyer and you.**

The Service and the Seller Are Often Inseparable

In only a few businesses can the service performed be separated from the creator–seller. A broker, an insurance salesperson, a travel agent, for instance, may represent and sell the service actually being offered but performed by another person or institution. In most cases, however, the service cannot be separated from the person of the seller. This follows from the dependency relationship described above and the characteristics of services being performed by activity, which is quite different from the service, or value, offered by a product. Services are created and marketed at the same time. For example, a barber creates a haircut service and dispenses it simultaneously.

Inseparability of seller and service has two important marketing implications. First, it means that in your service business direct personal selling is the only channel of distribution possible. Second, since your customers are buying "you" as much as the service you sell, your capacity for supplying the service limits the scale of operation of your business.

Services Are Perishable

The service business doesn't have inventory problems; it has *capacity* problems. One person can repair just so many appliances in a given time. A beautician can give only a limited number of facials per day. Services cannot be stored and sold according to fluctuations in demand. The usefulness of the service to the consumer is usually short-lived. It cannot be created ahead of time and sold when demand reaches a peak.

From a marketing standpoint the perishability of services means that your strategy will have to address the problem of fluctuating demand. You may find it necessary to discover new uses for idle facilities and ways to stimulate demand during the off-season.

It Is Difficult to Standardize Service Quality

Human beings perform services and, therefore, performance is subject to human frailty. The performance of a service is usually "person intensive"; this characteristic can result in variations in quality of the seller's performance. As instances, customers can experience differences in quality of service performed by an auto mechanic, a psychiatrist, an airline, or an advertising agency. Unless consistent, high-quality performance can be maintained, the entrepreneur in a service business cannot build customer confidence. Positive word-of-mouth advertising is vital to the success of the service business. You must exert every effort, therefore, to keep the performance of your service consistently at a high level.

The marketing of services poses differences from the marketing of physical goods. With few exceptions, services cannot be purchased and resold. Service charges are often expressed in terms of time required, rate, fee, honorarium, or premium rather than as a price in dollars. Moreover, rather than being called customers, service buyers are known as clients, patients, participants, or spectators. Finally, the consumer experiences no pride of ownership in a service. The customer must be satisfied with symbolic value or the functional benefits of an intangible product. In short, the service "product" is different from a product "product," and the reasons for buying a service are different from those for buying a product.

THE MARKETING CONCEPT AND BUYER BEHAVIOR   5

The adoption of the marketing concept in a service business is vital for success. Intangibility, buyer–seller interdependence, perishability, and nonstandardization all add up to mean that customer orientation is even more important for the service firm than for product marketers. Consider that **the buyer almost always has the option of doing it him- or herself.** On the service supplier's side, most sellers think of themselves as creators, producers, professionals, or specialists—not "marketers" of a service. They take pride in performance—their ability to repair an automobile, give advice on landscaping, fly an airplane, or diagnose an illness. We have stressed that you must be an expert in the service you're planning to sell.

There is a special problem facing your small service business: Consumers often believe they can do it themselves, so they have to be convinced they will be better off by letting you do it for them. Although sellers must have a high degree of professional competence and pride, they have to bend and shape their service and performance to the specific needs of the customer.

Inflexibility in serving customer needs can be disastrous, as illustrated by an entrepreneur who operated (we use the past tense because he's no longer in business) a small contracting business. He was a superior plumber, which even his competitors acknowledged. He had worked for his father and had taken over the business when his father retired. His attitude toward customers was shown by comments such as "I don't have customers, I deal with contracts." "I'm so good at this people will always come to me." "I know what's best for them." The result of this attitude was that he was usually late in completing work ("I'm the best, they'll wait for me," he would say). He seldom took the time to explain his work or answer questions. The number of jobs he was asked to bid on dwindled as word got around that he was cold and indifferent toward his customers and took his own sweet time in finishing contracted work. He failed to take advantage of change in the local building codes, which now allowed the use of plastic (polyvinyl chloride or PVC) pipe in residential construction. Potential customers increasingly found they could do many plumbing jobs themselves, because PVC pipe is easy to work with compared to steel or copper pipe. His reaction was: "Let 'em, they'll find out in the long run they would have been better off with a professional like me." He didn't recognize he had marketing problems; he went bankrupt waiting for the long run to arrive. Entrepreneurs of this sort are expert at solving technical problems, but their businesses fail because they refuse to adopt the marketing concept.

Why Consumers Buy Services

As we've indicated in Chapter 5, consumer behavior depends on the actual or anticipated consequences—both positive and negative—of buying. The same principle applies to buying services. Yet there are some notable differences in consumers' motives and predispositions as they evaluate the results of obtaining certain services. These differences stem from the special characteristics of services and the close relationship between buyer and seller. Our approach to these differences is to view them as *opportunities* for successfully marketing the service business.

The consumer's desire for personal attention is often the dominant need satisfied by a service. By appealing to the consumer's need for personal attention, you as the provider of service offer a form of satisfaction the seller of products cannot easily match. This is clearly an advantage for your small service business. You're in a unique position to cultivate the consumer's personal feelings and loyalty toward your service.

The insurance industry is an example of a service business that has lost some of this advantage. Several of the larger companies have introduced mass selling of conveniently packaged insurance policies with lower prices (premiums). This has resulted in a decline in the role of the insurance agent and loss of personal contact with the customer. There are strong indications that consumers dislike the lack of personal attention because sales have not increased as anticipated.

Consumers are more likely to weigh subjective impressions of the service business and its seller when contemplating the purchase of a service. With physical products, the consumer can use appearance and objective performance data to compare similar products. Not so with intangible services. Consumers cannot inspect or sample your service before purchasing. So they turn to their next best source: the comments of friends, coworkers, and neighbors who have experienced your service.

A subtle but extremely valuable *promotional* advantage for service marketers exists because of the key role of personal influence in the selection of services. Upon successful completion of the service—particularly if your customer sees significant value from your personal attention—you can benefit from the referral form of promotion. This offers one of the easiest, least costly, and most effective tools in marketing. You simply ask the satisfied customer to recommend your service to friends who could benefit from it. You may ask your customer personally to contact a prospective customer. After this contact has been made, you follow up with a sales call. In addition to being straightforward, personal, and inexpensive, this way of promoting improves your chances of reaching *potential* customers for your services. In contrast to product marketers, it is the personal involvement of buyer and seller in the service transaction that makes the referral form of promotion a natural and effective tool for you to use.

Sometimes the service business is based upon nothing more than the marketing of a good idea that fulfills an "unrecognized" need. The most important raw material for the service business is usually a novel idea. The world has become more complex, and the hassles and frustrations in contending with day-to-day problems have increased; in defense consumers seek self-expression, personal growth, and involvement in creative endeavors. The result has been a heightened consumer awareness of the tyranny of time. Time-saving services afford the opportunity for consumers to redirect their activities into more satisfying channels.

Remember that consumers have the alternative of doing services for themselves. However, they often perform tasks that a service firm could do better or faster. And the need for the service often goes *unrecognized* by potential buyers until the service becomes available. This is why the reaction of the consumer to a new service business is frequently, "Why didn't I think of that?"

Here is an excellent example of a new service firm that is marketing an idea to satisfy a hitherto unrecognized need. Each household must perform accounting and bookkeeping functions: bills must be paid, bank deposits made, tax records kept up-to-date, and checking accounts balanced. This is usually done by husband or wife and often takes several hours each month. The higher the income of the household, the more complicated the bookkeeping chore. If both wife and husband work, the paperwork becomes even more of a burden. Two women in Southern California recently formed a service firm that deals with this problem. Their idea is simple and effective.

Their firm offers two basic services that relieve the drudgery and frustration of household cash management. They come to the home and, after taking an inventory of all financial transactions of the family, set up an efficient record-keeping system. They classify expenses by type: personal, home improvement, cash, or credit. They schedule payments to minimize interest charges and checking account fees. They prepare ledgers for recording expenses for income tax purposes. In short, they design a complete accounting system for the home similar to that used by small businesses.

The service their firm provides takes care of all the financial transactions of the household for a monthly fee. It works like this: On a predetermined day each month, one partner visits the home. While there, she prepares the necessary checks for signature, records and transactions, balances the checkbook, brings all the ledger accounts up-to-date, and summarizes the family's financial standing. She even prepares envelopes and mails the checks.

Both women had worked as clerks in an accounting firm. Before striking out on their own, they tested their idea by working evenings—moonlighting—with a few selected acquaintances as clients. The response encouraged them to expand. Within three months they had enough referrals from their first clients to devote full time to their new business.

Consumers will want more of a good service than the entrepreneur can supply. This is a "when-it-rains-it-pours" problem unique to the service business. A product manufacturer can satisfy additional demand by adding extra shifts or installing a new production line. But the *capacity* problem for services is not so easily solved because consumers usually buy the *time* of the entrepreneur. (We hope you do run into the capacity problem, for this would be a sure sign that your service fills a real need.)

We have three specific suggestions for anticipating and dealing with the capacity barrier. First, become expert in the management of your own time. There are several excellent how-to books on the subject, some of which are listed at the end of this chapter. Short courses or seminars are offered through university extension programs. Second, we strongly recommend that you carefully schedule service work and take on new clients selectively in order to prevent becoming overcommitted. You should avoid the temptation to accept too many clients during the first few months of operation. You must not rush. You must do a good job with these clients since so much of your future business will depend on favorable word-of-mouth advertising. Third, in early stages of operation you should begin selecting and training a staff of personnel who will be as proficient and reliable as you are in providing the service you offer.

Why Consumers Don't Buy

A service buyer's dissatisfaction with one element of the service may lead to dissatisfaction with the entire service. There is a tendency for customers to remember any negative aspect of a service and to allow this to overshadow the positive satisfaction they've received. For example, an entrepreneur whose accounting practice was growing rapidly suddenly found that his volume of business was tapering off. He finally found the cause when a client complained about the telephone answering device he had installed. He asked other clients about this and they confirmed that, although pleased with his work, they were put off by the mechanical impersonal response and as a result hesitated to call him. Many people are blocked by the need to talk to a tape.

Again we see the crucial importance of regular personal attention. Because consumers don't have something tangible in hand to remind them of the value they received for their money, they will often recall and be guided in their relationship by their most recent personal experience with the seller.

MARKET ANALYSIS AND MARKETING STRATEGY FOR THE SERVICE BUSINESS   3, 4 A, 5, 6

The procedures involved in market analysis and strategy are basically the same whether the firm is selling a product or a service. The service entrepreneur should understand population characteristics as they affect the market for the service. And it is essential that customer buying motives be understood. The guidelines in Chapter 5 for analyzing consumer behavior are just as effective for services as they are for products. The service marketer must also analyze shopping behavior and should answer the *who, when,* and *how* questions by following procedures and consulting the sources of information we've suggested. The following pinpoints some special considerations in analyzing the market for your service and developing your marketing strategy.

Social, Economic, and Competitive Change

The environment for small service firms has changed radically during the recent past, presenting both opportunities and threats for the new service business. As the economy has matured, spending for all kinds of services has soared. Personal spending on services is predicted to surpass total expenditures for durable and nondurable goods within the next few years. Rising discretionary income means that consumers can buy more than basic household and personal necessities. Put another way, increased buying power results in less individual self-sufficiency and more desire for services. Thus, more demand for travel, health, beauty, culture, and education. Services have replaced durable goods as status symbols in many instances. The reaction against materialism has clearly benefited the service sector. It would appear that acquiring experiences rather than acquiring goods fits the current consumer movement toward self-fulfillment. In such areas as education and travel, services more than products enable consumers to reach their personal growth goals.

Other societal trends such as more women in the labor force mean greater markets for services—for example, in childcare, dry cleaning, and transportation. The shorter work week results in more leisure time and the demand for recreation and entertainment. To "do your own thing" usually requires the purchase of services in some form.

As opportunities for service firms have increased, however, competition has become fierce for consumers' discretionary dollars. Inevitably, direct competition between products and services has grown. Recognizing the shift in consumer preferences, manufacturers are adding more conveniences or services to their products. Drip-dry permanent-press clothing competes with the conventional laundry service. Improved household appliances that reduce the need for domestic service help, and custom television programming that competes with other forms of entertainment afford other examples. Perhaps the most significant threat of product competition for services comes from the manufacturers of do-it-yourself products.

Competition also comes from the growing number of other service firms. The barriers to entry into the service field are usually low. As one cynic put it, "With a little knowledge and a great brochure, you have a new service venture." This condition exists because almost anyone can provide some sort of a service. The implication is that competitive service businesses may multiply rapidly. The importance of attracting and retaining a core group of loyal, satisfied customers becomes crucial in this intensely competitive world.

PRICING YOUR SERVICE   **6** A (3) (4), **8** A (6)

The word *price* is seldom attached to services. Instead, other terms such as *fee* or *premium* are used to describe charges for services rendered. Regardless of terminology, the basic approach to pricing applies: Price measures value perceived by customers. To be more precise, since what your customer gets is often intangible or subjective in nature, **your price reflects the quality, degree of specialization, and value of your performance to the buyer.** With the exception of services regulated by government, there is more opportunity for creativity and imagination in pricing services than in other marketing areas. Since the consumer can usually either postpone the purchase of a service or perform the service personally, setting your price is one of the most important decisions you'll make.

In Chapter 6 we stressed the advantages of a high-price versus a low-price strategy. The same arguments apply generally to pricing a service. However, there are some additional factors that can make the high-price approach even more favorable. Instead of lower prices and price reductions having a positive effect on sales, the reverse is often true—especially for the human-intensive service. In most cases, buyers of a specialized service are reluctant to display sensitivity to your price because they perceive a professional–layperson relationship. Furthermore, the price of your service signals to the buyer the quality of your skill and competence. And to complicate matters, **the price you set affects the value your customers perceive.**

To see how this works, consider the difficulty encountered by Ruth Blackstone, an independent child psychologist. She started her own business after serving for six years as a counselor in a local high school. Her marketing approach had two related parts. First, she felt that the effectiveness of her service would be improved if she could observe and deal with behavioral problems in the home—an environment familiar and nonthreatening to the clients and the place where most parent–child interaction takes place. Second, she could charge lower fees than most psychologists because she could operate from her home and avoid office rent and associated overhead expenses. She expected that lower prices would allow middle- and even low-income families to benefit from her inhome service. It turned out that her first assumption was right but that her second was dead wrong.

She set hourly fees at about half the prevailing rate of other independent psychologists. Her first clients were parents and children she had dealt with at the high school. Although she had no problem attracting clients, she found that parents weren't following the recommendations she made. They didn't seem to listen actively or to acknowledge her observations of behavioral problems. "For a long time, I thought the problem was with me," she said. "And I did a lot of soul searching to see if my kind of therapy had something to do with it." Finally, she visited an old friend who had been her major professor during graduate school. She summarized their

114

conversation this way, "He listened patiently to my story, and then he said: 'Your advice to clients is worth just as much as they have to pay to get it.' Then it dawned on me that my clients weren't listening to me because my consultation cost them so little."

It wasn't easy for her to raise her fee since she knew that persons referred to her by former clients would know what she had charged. The solution was to start all over again. Eventually she was able to attract new clients through short courses she taught at the local university and speeches she made on child development at civic and professional meetings.

Ms. Blackstone learned a difficult lesson: The more the buyer is involved in performance and quality of the service, the more crucial the role of price in affecting the perceived value of the service. This is true in almost any professional service; it increases in importance as the degree of specialization increases. Customers are more willing to listen to advice if they have given up something of value to obtain it. To sum up, your clients' perception of your power to solve their problems may be enhanced by charging high prices for your service.

High-price strategy, however, may not be appropriate in all cases. Here are some statements about your service. If you believe them to be true and you answer yes to any of them, then a higher rather than a lower price is probably the way to go.

Yes   No

____ ____ 1. There will be no readily available substitute for my service to consumers. (Or, to get my kind of service, consumers cannot easily shift to less expensive alternatives.)

____ ____ 2. Consumers interested in my service cannot easily make price and quality comparisons. (Or, consumers will not shop around or bargain for a lower price.)

____ ____ 3. Demand for my service will be of a crisis nature. (Or, consumers will not be able to postpone their purchase.)

____ ____ 4. Unlike the purchase of staple food items and necessities like clothing and shelter, my service fulfills higher-ordered human needs. (Or, consumers will not be price-sensitive to my service because it appeals to their need for status, esteem, or intellectual or emotional growth.)

There are other considerations in pricing your service. For example, your pricing decision can be affected by whether your service will be purchased routinely (haircuts), contractually (small construction jobs), or occasionally (travel, recreation, or repairs). A trade or professional association is often the price setter within an industry. Local barber unions frequently set the price of haircuts; dry-cleaning associations set the price of cleaning trousers; professional associations strongly influence the fees of doctors, dentists, accountants, and architects.

Although there are few generalizations possible in pricing a service, we can sum up by reemphasizing the value criterion. Value is an illusive concept. For services, value given by the seller and value received by the buyer can be related to the time required to perform a particular service and the duration that the results of service performed are experienced by the buyer. As you can see, estimating value and attaching a price to it can be a much more complex task for the invisible service than for the tangible product.

In this chapter we have emphasized the differences between promoting products and promoting services. It is easier to sell something that can be handled, tasted, smelled, or demonstrated than it is to sell the benefits of an intangible service. (The principles and procedures are about the same, and the suggestions in Chapter 6 will generally apply for promoting your service. However, you should check to see whether your trade or profession has legal or ethical restrictions on specific promotional methods.) We'll concentrate here on the somewhat different forms of promotion and the alternatives you have in developing your strategy for promoting your service.

Although you may decide to let your service performance speak for itself, communicating with potential customers through advertising, publicity, or personal selling is usually necessary for the new service business. The purpose of promotion for services is the same as for products: to develop awareness of, interest in, and desire for your service. But for services, your strategy should be geared to promoting three key features of your business:

Availability ⟶ Consumers in your target market must know where and when you are available and how to reach you.

Image or Reputation ⟶ Consumers must become acquainted with your capabilities—the quality of performance of your service.

Use Benefits ⟶ Intended customers must understand how the results of your service will benefit them.

Each form of promotion, advertising, publicity, and personal selling can be used to communicate these three features.

Regardless of the forms of promotion you use, you should stress a consistent theme in advertising, personal selling, and publicity messages. For example, if your methods or techniques of service performance are unique they could serve as a unifying theme for promotion. Or if you have key personnel who have established reputations in the service you offer, you could highlight this in promotional messages. You can use a third approach after your new service firm gets going: stressing the benefits already gained by satisfied customers.

Advertising

Your service business will probably attract mostly local customers. Therefore, media that reach just the local market are the ones to use. The yellow pages of the telephone directory, direct mail, and newspapers are examples. Note that with any of these you can display your firm's identifying symbol as well as where, when, and how to find you. Broadcast media are not as effective because of the temporary nature of the message. If your services are to be purchased only on an "as needed" basis by customers, then awareness of your availability is vital. The purpose of the message is to keep your trade name or business location exposed to potential customers so that when your service is needed, they'll remember you.

Special attention should be given to developing an identifying symbol for your service business. Large service firms like the airlines have spent thousands of dollars developing unique corporate identification. A clever symbol is effective in reminding consumers of the availability of your service and makes it easy to remember. Your symbol becomes part of the image your business projects to consumers; it differentiates your service from other businesses offering similar service. The symbol is to some extent a substitute for having a physical product to display. We've found that it is well worth the investment to have a professional graphic artist develop such a symbol for use on your store sign, stationery, and business cards.

Whenever possible show the benefits of your service. Use instore displays showing consumers enjoying or benefitting from your service. An example would be the posters and brochures used by travel agencies. Also, tell of benefits through testimonials of personal satisfaction, often called "the verbal-proof story," or by before-and-after comparisons.

Be sure to relate your message to shopping behavior. For example, if your service will be purchased routinely and repeatedly, stress dependability. Note that banks often feature trust and confidence in their advertising messages. It is even possible for some service businesses to change shopping behavior of consumers by promoting the "preventive" value of their service. Any service business that deals in repairs could well use this approach.

Advertising messages for services are particularly difficult to create because they must appeal to the buyer's imagination. Think of it this way: In a marketing society that emphasizes the acquisition of things, the service advertiser must create a message that appeals to the buying of experiences, the avoidance of inconvenience, or a better future. For these reasons, we suggest consulting a professional advertising agency in preparing your message.

Personal Selling

As in advertising products, it is easier for a salesperson to extoll the virtues of a product than it is for the supplier of a service to promote something the consumer cannot see. The buyer faces greater risk in purchasing services than products. Not only is a service usually completed before its quality can be judged, but also the defective service cannot be returned for refund or substitute. The only recourse unsatisfied customers have in most cases it to try another supplier the next time or do the work themselves.

The personal selling job should concentrate on reducing the prepurchase uncertainty consumers usually experience. To relieve this uncertainty, you might stress (1) your unique methods or techniques in performing your service, (2) the skill and competence of your employees, and (3) significant benefits your firm's customers are already receiving. The task is not easy because to sell your service *you must sell yourself*—without appearing to brag or boast. Therefore, personal selling often requires you to take a more indirect and subtle approach.

117

Your goal is to obtain the maximum amount of *exposure* in your target market. A professionally acceptable practice is to make business contacts through presenting speeches to local clubs, participating in trade or professional associations, making contributions to charitable causes, sponsoring public events, serving in community or civic groups, writing professional articles, or appearing at conferences that suit your business purpose.

After you've established your reputation, the most effective selling tool will be word-of-mouth advertising. How effective this will be, of course, depends on your performance record. But you should always remember that the manner in which the buyer–seller relationship is conducted is a form of personal selling. All client contacts by you or anyone working for you should be viewed as a way to promote new business.

Publicity

A way to obtain free advertising is through publicity releases to local newspapers. These should be written to create a favorable impression of your organization and its employees. This is the principal form of promotion for many service firms since consumers tend to accept the authenticity of news stories more readily than of paid advertisements. You'll find that most service business "news" articles in your local newspaper are originated as publicity releases by the firm itself. The opening of your business, the addition of a new employee, or the offering of a new service would all qualify for favorable and free publicity.

Sales Promotion

Sales promotion techniques have very limited application to the small service business. Tools that may be effective are carefully designed specialty advertising: calendars with your business name displayed on them or premiums giving the customer a bonus item with the purchase of your service. Be sure to choose an approach that projects a professional image of your business if you use specialty advertising.

DISTRIBUTING YOUR SERVICE   1 B, 5 A, 7 A (4), 8 A (4)

The distribution strategy for your service boils down to decisions on business location and service delivery. With very few exceptions, there are no channel alternatives as there are for products since you'll be dealing directly with consumers. However, the concepts of providing time and place utility (discussed in Chapter 6) are important—in most cases more important for services than for tangible goods. Your location and delivery strategy are particularly crucial for success because consumers can perform many services themselves and because demand may be irregular.

Optimum Location for Your Service Firm

The optimum location for your service firm depends upon the type of service to be provided. We'll approach the distribution strategy in two ways: We'll examine consumer buying patterns and implications for the location of your business; then we'll present specific suggestions for site analysis.

Services purchased by consumers can be classified according to three basic kinds of shopping behavior:

Convenience Services

Convenience services are those the consumer knows a great deal about. They are purchased with a minimum of time and effort. Being willing to accept any of several substitutes, the consumer buys the service from the person or firm most accessible. In this case the consumer works to complete the purchase as easily and quickly as possible. Almost any relatively inexpensive service that is purchased frequently would fit here; a dry-cleaning business would be typical. Convenient and visible location is essential for this type of service.

Shopping Services

These services are those for which the consumer wants to compare quality and price before buying. Here the consumer lacks specific knowledge about the service and believes that taking the time to compare costs and benefits will be worthwhile. Location is important but to a lesser degree, since the consumer will expend some effort to seek out alternative service firms.

Specialty Services

These services are those that the consumer has complete knowledge of but insists on buying from only one supplier. The consumer does not compare substitutes; the only problem is in finding the right supplier. Consequently, a low-rent and inconvenient location may be sought out since the consumer is willing to make a special effort to find it.

These classifications are not rigid, since (1) different target markets and even consumers within the same target market may have different buying patterns, and (2) as income, life styles, and demographic characteristics of a target market change over time, service buying behavior may change. As a practical matter, you should view this scheme of classification as covering a range to which the potential customer responds. Consumer behavior in spending time and effort to do business with you depends on the kind of service you sell and how well the consumer knows what you offer.

Analyzing a Location

There is no easy solution to the location problem. The selection you make will probably involve a tradeoff between the high-cost, convenient location and the low-cost, inconvenient location. In making your choice, consider location cost along with promotional cost. In the long run you may incur considerable advertising expense if you don't have a business site easy for your customers to find.

Once you've narrowed down the possible locations for your service business to a few, your task is to conduct a specific site analysis. The factors to consider for the service business are similar to those for the business that sells products.

- *Land and buildings:* For vacant land, the adequacy of site and size. For land with improvements, the suitability of building placement and design, frontage, access, and exposure.

- *Zoning and use restrictions:* Conformity of type of business with local commercial land-use controls.

- *Supporting services:* Availability of fire and police protection, liquid and solid waste disposal, and street lighting. Suitability and quality of streets, alleys, and parking.

- *Cost and carrying charges:* Availability of financing, lease and improvement provisions, taxes, maintenance, and fees.

You'll want to assess these and other features for each site. For physical aspects, such as land and building, you may need to consult an architect or engineer. You'll require the help of an accountant or attorney in evaluating legal and financial aspects of the property you choose.

THE MARKETING OF SERVICES IS DIFFERENT   SUMMARY

Your marketing approach will have to stress the unique features of your intangible services—a harder job than to sell the advantages of tangible products. The special characteristics of intangibility, buyer–seller interdependence, service–seller inseparability, perishability, and difficulty in standardizing service quality have important implications for your pricing, promotional, and distribution strategies.

Intangibility means that your promotion will have to be creatively designed and executed. Buyer–seller interdependence limits your distribution strategy to making choices about business location. And the size of your operation will be limited because customers will be purchasing you and your time instead of a product that could be produced in large quantities. Perishability of your service will result in idle time and the need to stimulate demand during slow periods. Finally, the difficulty in standardizing your quality of performance for customers places a special burden on you to be consistent in satisfying each customer.

Most purchases of a service can easily be postponed, or, in many instances, consumers can perform the service themselves. The consumer cannot evaluate service quality before purchase and therefore relies heavily on the opinions of others who have been your customers. This means you must be technically proficient at performing your service, flexible in meeting specific customer requirements, and skilled in establishing and maintaining good interpersonal relationships. Your com-

120

petence in dealing with people will be as crucial for your success as your professional abilities in the service you actually perform.

The opportunities for the success of the small service business are increasing. They will continue to grow as long as a trend away from consumer self-sufficiency continues. You're on the right track if your service results in added convenience for consumers, enables them to experience personal growth, or improves the quality of their everyday lives.

Marketing the Service Business

Special note: Your completed assignments for Chapter 6 will apply to some of the exercises here, but you may want to review them after studying this chapter.

1. Answer the question(s) following each special characteristic of service.
   a. Intangibility: What will you stress as benefits to your customers?

   _____

   _____

   _____

   _____

   _____

   b. Buyer–Seller Interdependence: What kinds of things can you do to help potential buyers communicate their specific needs so you can adapt your service offering accordingly?

   _____

   _____

   _____

   _____

   _____

   c. Inseparability of Service from Seller: What are your weaknesses and strengths in managing your own time? What will you do to expand the time available for performing your service for customers?

   _____

   _____

   _____

   _____

   _____

   d. Perishability: What actions will you take to boost sales during slow periods?

   _____

   _____

   _____

   _____

   _____

e. Difficulty in Standardizing Service Quality: What standards of excellence will you set in performing your service? How will you assure that your performance is consistently of high quality?

_____

_____

_____

_____

2. After you render your service, what actions will you take to follow up and make sure your customer is truly satisfied and helps to promote business for you?

_____

_____

_____

_____

_____

3. What feature could you incorporate into your service or its promotion that would appeal to potential customers on the basis of saving them time?

_____

_____

_____

_____

4. On what social, economic, or other trends are you basing the need for your service business? Describe them.

_____

_____

_____

_____

5. What price will you charge for your service? How does it compare with prices for similar services? How does your price fit the market image you will try to establish? (You might summarize the results of the pricing quiz in the chapter here.)

_____

_____

_____

_____

6. In the spaces below summarize how you plan to use the various forms of promotion to communicate availability, reputation, and use benefits.

   a. I'll let consumers in my target market know where and when I'm available and how to reach me by: _____

   _____

   _____

   _____

   _____

   b. I'll promote my capabilities and reputation by: _____

   _____

   _____

   _____

   _____

   c. I'll let consumers know how the results of my service will benefit them by: __

   _____

   _____

   _____

   _____

7. If you've made a decision on the location of your service business, describe the factors that you considered and the advantages and disadvantages of your location. Be sure to state whether you've made a tradeoff between the high-cost, convenient location and the low-cost, inconvenient location and your justification for your decision.

   _____

   _____

   _____

   _____

   _____

8. If you haven't decided on an area in which to locate your service business, what specific factors will you consider? Also, point out how the shopping behavior for your kind of service will influence your decision.

   _____

   _____

   _____

   _____

124

IF YOU WANT TO READ MORE

John M. Rathmell, *Marketing in the Service Sector*, Winthrop Publishers, Cambridge, Mass. 1974. This is quite possibly the best book available that deals exclusively with marketing the service business. It contains an in-depth, thorough, and practical treatment of the various facets of marketing services. Numerous case examples are given, too.

Eugene M. Johnson, "The Selling of Services," in Victor P. Buell (ed.), *Handbook of Modern Marketing*, McGraw-Hill, New York, 1970, pp. 12–110 to 12–120. As suggested by the title in which this work appears, this is a how-to coverage of service marketing. It includes suggestions on advertising, sales promotion, publicity, and personal selling.

Sidney P. Feldman and Merline C. Spencer, "The Effect of Personal Influence in the Selection of Consumer Service," in Peter D. Bennett (ed.), *Marketing and Economic Development*, American Marketing Association, Chicago, 1967, pp. 440–452. This material explores purchase behavior as a cause of differences between products and services. Discussion focuses on the nature of purchasing decisions as they relate to proper timing and selection of a source for a service.

Ronald Stiff, "The Changing Role of Professional Service Marketing," in Kenneth L. Bernhardt (ed.), *Marketing: 1776–1976 and Beyond*, Educators' Proceedings, American Marketing Association, Chicago, August 1976, pp. 283–286. This is a concise survey of trends in marketing professional services. It describes the increasing emphasis on promotion, market segmentation, and consumer orientation.

Carl Gersuny and William R. Rosengren, *The Service Society*, Cambridge, Mass., Schenkman, 1973. This is a good book to read if you want to explore societal trends and find out why new markets for services are likely to continue to expand. The author discusses the service revolution and the new dimensions it brings for consumer behavior.

James H. Donnelly, Jr., "Marketing Intermediaries in Channels of Distribution for Services," *Journal of Marketing*, January 1976, pp. 55–57. David L. Kurtz, H. Robert Dodge, and Jay E. Klompmaker, *Professional Selling*, Business Publications, Dallas, 1976; Louis E. Boone and David L. Kurtz, *Foundations of Marketing*, The Dryden Press, Hillsdale, Ill., 1977, pp. 365–386. The first reference is a practical book dealing with many aspects of personal selling. The second is a chapter of a basic marketing book that covers most of the personal selling methods. Both are excellent for entrepreneurs with little direct sales experience.

Ross A. Webber, *Time and Management*, Van Nostrand Reinhold, New York, 1972. This reference covers the typical reasons why managers waste time. It recommends several ways to overcome the factors that cause time to be wasted. The author's point of view is particularly suited to the entrepreneur as it emphasizes the need to lessen the overloading of the present with time-consuming activities and shows how to carve out some time to plan for and make the future less time haunted.

James T. McCay, *The Management of Time*, Prentice-Hall, Englewood Cliffs, N.J., 1959. This book draws on the field of general semantics in a unique way to present a number of practical ways for becoming more effective in the use of time.

Chapter 8

Managing Your Financial Requirements

PLANNING REQUIRED

YOUR PLANNING ASSUMPTIONS AND FINANCIAL PLANS

KEY POINTS IN MANAGING YOUR FINANCES

Recall that competence in financial management is a fundamental strength you must have to run your business successfuly. To become a proactive financial manager **you must do the basic planning yourself.** That's the only way you can get a solid grasp on managing the financing your business will need to survive.

Planning for finances will tell you how much money you'll need and when you'll need it. With these data at your fingertips, you'll prepare for the investments or loans required well ahead of time—and improve your chances for getting the money. Prospective investors, lenders, or bankers will gain confidence in your ability to repay your loans because they'll quickly see that you know what you're talking about.

You'll require three kinds of money: capital for permanent investment in your business; liquid cash, or working capital, for operating your business; and personal money for your family and yourself.

You'll estimate the capital investment you need for fixed assets by totaling the sums for such items as machinery and equipment, cost of freight and installation, storage bins, store fixtures, decoration, office equipment, and sales or use tax. And you'll want to add a reasonable safety factor to the total.

You'll project the liquid cash, or working capital, your business will require to pay for inventory of raw material or stock and for labor and current expenses each month.

And finally, you'll prepare a budget for living expenses for your family. It's a hard fact of life that most new businesses don't return enough in the first year or two to pay the owner a salary. You'd be on solid ground to figure living expenses enough to take care of your family's needs for at least a year and a half ahead. You'll want this money above and beyond that required for the business itself.

PLANNING REQUIRED   1 C

In general you'll find that your funding needs will fall into two categories: long-term and short-term. The long-term funds will be used for capital investment in setting up your business; the short-term funds will be used for taking care of cash deficiencies that occur from time to time in any business, and to cover seasonal bulges, as in businesses that must build a large inventory for the Christmas trade. If your business prospers and grows very rapidly, you'll develop a need for major outside investment in your company. Most businesses don't generate enough profit to furnish the capital to support significant expansion. You'll find a discussion of sources of funding in Chapter 9.

Planning for Long-Term Financing

Each business has unique requirements for capital investment. It isn't possible therefore to give detailed information on what items make up the list of purchases required to open the doors of a business. You'll find it necessary to draw on your own data for this purpose. With technical competence in your business, you'll know the items needed to turn out the product or render the service. You'll draw on your knowledge to compile a list of the equipment and fixtures necessary to open your business. By referring to the planning examples given in Appendix B, you'll pick up some hints about the kinds of items you may have to consider in figuring your capital budget.

Planning for Short-Term Financing

Once you've a capital budget that covers your initial long-term investment in the business, you'll want to prepare your short-term operating plans. These are crucial in controlling your operating affairs day by day, month by month, and year by year. These plans, which are in essence budgets, include projections about sales, expenses, balance sheets, income statements, and break-even analyses. You'll also want to learn how to use financial ratios in your financial planning.

Persist in Your Planning

The characteristics of the planning required for you to know what your financial needs will be just simply will not allow you to do it in one pass. You'll find that your projected results will vary when you change your assumptions. You'll want to develop a feeling that your planning is somewhere near what the actuality is likely to be. To accomplish this, you'll have to make several estimates: optimistic, pessimistic, and what you think reasonable.

Your first plans, even after you've made repeated trials, will still not be what will happen, unless you're very lucky. But that doesn't matter. What does matter is that you've now become a proficient planner; it's in your blood. You now see what a powerful tool it is for controlling your financial affairs—indeed, your whole business. And what you'll do after you open your business is to substitute the real figures for the estimates, month by month. Each month you'll run out your projections and plans for a year and two years ahead, by the month. You'll have a rolling set of plans that will allow you to see very clearly what your financial requirements are likely to be, a long way ahead. Then you'll be able to prepare for those needs in adequate time to be assured of success in meeting them. And the feedback you'll get from the whole planning process will enable you to correct deviations from the course you want and to do more of whatever's producing success.

YOUR PLANNING ASSUMPTIONS AND FINANCIAL PLANS   1 C,
2 A (2), 3 B (1), 6 A (4), 8 A (8), 8 A (1), 2, 4, 5

To start your financial planning for your new business, you'll have to make some assumptions. Some will be easy to make, as you'll have the information at hand. Others will take some crystal ball gazing. But don't despair; in most situations there is a wealth of information to be had. The trick is to know where to look for it. We'll point you in the right direction—give you a number of sources that you can check to find the data upon which to base your planning.

Your Capital Investment

The first planning you'll want to do is to estimate how much money you'll need for permanent investment in your business. As we've said, each business is unique. Therefore, you'll have to list all the items you must have to produce the goods or service you intend to sell. For a sheet metal shop, for instance, you might require shears, sheet metal brakes, welding equipment, work benches, and a variety of other equipment depending upon your particular specialty. You'd also want an assortment of hand tools. You'd need adequate space for shop and office and at least minimum office equipment: desks, file cabinets, typewriters, and miscellaneous items for long-time use. Lumping costs for equipment and permanent tooling together will allow you to prepare a capital budget figure. If you buy a building, the cost of the building and the cost of modification would be a major item in your capital budget.

If you were starting a retail store, perhaps a bookstore, the capital budget for fixed assets would be quite different. It would include such items as display cases, counters, shelves, and office equipment. Your largest single initial investment wouldn't be in capital items like these; it would be in a beginning inventory of books. This would be an operating expense and would take working capital as contrasted with fixed-asset capital.

Once you have the estimated figure for capital equipment, you should add to it a reasonable safety margin. This might be 10 to 15 percent in today's inflationary economy. If you plan to renovate or remodel a building for your purpose, we recommend a higher cushion to protect yourself against rapid rises in the costs of building materials and construction labor.

Your Detailed Planning Assumptions and Plans

With the starting capital set for both fixed assets and operating expenses, you'll now want to establish the basic assumptions for your first try at financial planning. The following are customary items that appear in the assumptions, although your business may need an addition or two because of its special characteristics.

Date of Starting Business
This date sets the schedule for all the rest of your plans. It can also mark the beginning of your fiscal year, which determines when you pay income taxes. You must, however, observe the legal requirements for setting your fiscal year. As a sole proprietor you must use the same tax year in which you report your personal income. In a partnership you must use the same tax year as the principal partners unless you get special authorization. If you have a choice, you may want to choose a fiscal year that gives you the advantage of paying taxes when seasonal sales produce a large amount of cash.

Balance Sheet

The balance sheet is a statement that shows what your company owns, and what it owes. What it owns are termed assets. What it owes, which includes debts of various kinds plus the money invested that represents ownership, are called liabilities, or sometimes "liabilities and equity." (In a sense, the company "owes" the investors the money they put in to form the capital.) The balance sheet shows the financial condition of the company at a specific time. It's like a snapshot picturing the financial condition of the company at that moment.

You'll want to prepare a balance sheet for the opening day of your business. You'll then want to check the health of your operations regularly to see how you're doing; you'll do this through monthly, quarterly, and yearly balance sheets. By comparing current figures against previous ones, you can see whether your business is losing or gaining in net worth.

One way of pinpointing how you're doing is to see how much increase or decrease in each asset and liability there has been in dollars and percentage from the figures in a previous balance sheet. The percent figure will give you another way to see clearly the trend of improvement or worsening of performance. You can use both dollars and percentages as feedback to show you where you're doing well and where you should put more effort to make improvement. The balance sheet also gives you the figures you need to do ratio analysis on your business. A ratio is a comparison of one item with another on the balance sheet. These will give you additional feedback signals on the status of your business. You'll find a detailed explanation of ratio analysis later in this chapter.

Sales Forecast

A critical item in your financial planning is the sales forecast. The ability of your business to generate sales in sufficient volume at the proper price level determines whether your business can survive and grow. Because all other financial variables in your business depend upon sales, you must exert great care to do as good a job as you can of forecasting them.

You may say, "But I've never been in this business before. How can I possibly guess how my sales are going to come in?" The answer is **you must.** You must do the very best guessing you can, because all other plans hinge on sales. And don't despair. Many sources of information are open to you, and most cost nothing or very little. We'll identify some of them here.

You'll find it wise to forecast sales by the month for two years and possibly three years ahead. It's a good idea to try three approaches: optimistic, high estimate; pessimistic, low estimate; and realistic, somewhere in the middle, your best estimate of what may actually happen in sales. You'll recall that we stated early the importance of knowing something about the specific business before starting your own and that if you hadn't had experience you'd better work for a company in that business for a year or two before starting your own. With this background you'd have some feeling for such things as the seasonality of the business and the daily, weekly, monthly, and quarterly pattern of sales. You'd know something about the costs and profitability of the business. And knowing about how many dollars annually you'd like to take out of the business for yourself, you could work backward to see how many dollars in sales you'd need in a year to produce that income. By studying the examples in Appendix B you'll see how you can go about this kind of analysis and planning for your business.

In Chapter 4 we gave some sources of information for segmenting and understanding your market. You'll find these sources also useful in gathering data for financial planning. Therefore, we'll list them briefly here and add to them some other sources in which you can find basic financial information:

- Data from your own experience in the business.

- Daily newspapers. Although not a prime source of financial information, you may get leads that will help you gain such data.

- Weekly newspapers. The same holds for weekly papers, but here your chances for getting to entrepreneurs who can help you are probably a bit better than with the dailies.

- The Small Business Administration (SBA). You should check with the closest office of the SBA to see what pertinent publications are to be had and what other help they can give you in gathering the financial information you're after.

- Banks. Your banker can very likely put you in touch with successful entrepreneurs in businesses similar to yours; you can talk with them about financial and other matters.

- The Bank of America's *Small Business Reporter,* which is an excellent publication that gives financial information on specific businesses. You should check their list for titles to see if there are *Reporters* you can use.[1]

- Chambers of Commerce or Business Development Departments in your community. It would be good practice for you to see what help these organizations can give you.

- Universities. The professors of management or finance in graduate schools of business can sometimes be helpful in your quest for information. They often seek live projects for their students. The best way to get help here is to make sure you know exactly what you want to ask, identify the professor, phone and make an appointment. You may be able to get a team of two or three bright students to compile the information you need and to help you with your financial planning.

- Trade Associations. The association in your industry can furnish all kinds of important financial data that you'll find basic to your needs. Don't overlook this very important source.[2] You'll be able to get figures for companies of different size on such matters as sales, expenses, capital requirements, profit percentages, and many other basic inputs you'll need for your financial planning.

- Other Similar Businesses. As we've said, successful owners who have built their business from scratch can give you a wealth of information of all kinds. Take advantage of their hard-earned store of financial wisdom. Draw on it as well as on their marketing and other knowledge.

- Financial Data from Dun and Bradstreet Reports.[3] This organization publishes several kinds of reports that give useful information. One report that you may find helpful is *Key Business Ratios*. This gives figures in each of several business ratios, ranging from current assets to current debts, to funded debts to net working capital. Three figures are given in each case: the median, and the upper, and the lower quartiles. The ratios represent the experience of many companies in a given business and cover what may be considered good, average, and not-so-good performance. The companies surveyed tend to be rather large "small" companies, usually over $100,000 in net worth. Nevertheless, the ratios will give you some feeling for good management practice. The businesses reported upon include retailing, wholesaling, manufacturing, and construction.

- If you're planning to enter a retail business you'll find The National Cash Register Company publication, *Expenses in Retail Business*, particularly useful.[4] This booklet gives operating percentages that will help you set the level of sales for your forecasting. It contains much other valuable information about expenses in retail business. The booklet can serve as a guide not only for sales forecasting but also for many other aspects of financial planning. Retail businesses covered range from Appliance Dealers to Women's Apparel and Specialty Stores.

- Don't overlook libraries! A recent report published by a Louisiana university says that only three percent of a large number of small businesspersons interviewed ever set foot in a library. Yet the public library and business school libraries are great reservoirs of information. Many libraries, particularly in metropolitan areas, have research librarians who would be pleased to help you dig out specific data. In the library you can find all kinds of reference books on business and the financial reports of many small publicly held corporations. These can furnish you with operating ratios, data about sales, and much other important information.

The foregoing are some, but by no means all, of the sources of basic information available to you. Most of them are free; some can be had for a small fee. By pursuing these sources and the references given in most of them, you can track down what you'll need to know to do your sales forecasting and other kinds of financial planning. And you can do this yourself. Indeed, that's the best way, for then you'll become an expert in your own business.

Cash Flow Analysis

Cash moves in and out of your business as your customers pay their bills and as you pay for goods, services, and labor. You'll be vitally concerned with what is called cash flow. Cash flow is the difference between what you take in and what you spend. It's usually figured by the month. If your business pays out more than it takes in, you'll find yourself short of cash.

If, however, you know several weeks, or months, ahead that you're going to need money to avert a cash crisis, you can take the steps to have the money on hand when you need it. As you know, if you suddenly find on a Friday afternoon that you'll need ten thousand dollars next week to keep your business going—pay your labor and cover some critical bills—your chances of raising the money on time are pretty slim. If you knew that you'd need ten thousand dollars of working money two or three months ahead of time, ordinarily you'd be able to arrange for a loan without too much trouble. The tool you'll use to anticipate your cash needs is cash flow analysis. This is one of the most important management techniques you can learn.

Cash flow analysis not only tells you about shortages of funds that are likely to develop, but it also tells you when you are likely to have surpluses of cash. Knowing this, you can plan for ways to invest the surplus in improving your business.

Your cash flow analysis is a proactive management plan that forecasts the amount of dollars you'll have on hand at the end of each month. You'll develop your cash flow by projecting your income each month and subtracting from it what you must spend to keep your business going. The first cash flow chart you make will necessarily be based upon many figures that will be estimates. Some, like your rent, you'll know exactly. Others, like sales for each month ahead, will be estimates or forecasts. You'll do the best you can in making these forecasts, relying on the sources of information we've outlined previously and those you'll add yourself. Next to the estimated figures for each month you'll leave a blank column for the actual numbers. After you start your business, you'll replace the estimated numbers with actual numbers from the month's records. And you'll rework your projections for cash flow (and the other financial projections we cover in this chapter) for a full two years ahead by the month and the third year ahead by the quarter. In this way you'll gain a sharp insight into the financial requirements of your business. You'll know if you'll require cash and how much, month by month. You'll be able to anticipate your needs for loans well ahead of time, and you'll be in a favorable position to get the money to meet your needs.

Because the cash flow analysis is simply a statement of income from which expenditures are subtracted for each month, its basic form can be set up as shown in Figure 8-1.

Detailed examples of cash flow analysis are given in Appendix B, including a discussion of the assumptions upon which the key figures were based. Refer to the assumptions if you've any doubt about where the figures came from. You'll then be able to follow a similar pattern in making your own projections.

Income Statement

You'll want to know month by month how much you're making or how much you've gone in the hole. To do this, you'll prepare an income statement each month. This statement is made by subtracting the cost of goods sold and the operating, selling, and administrative expenses for the month from the gross sales made during the month. This procedure follows the general statement that revenue less expense equals net income. Examples of monthly income statements appear in Appendix B.

A useful management tool for guiding your planning can be made by comparing income statements for current against previous years, month by month. You can do this best by placing your data in parallel columns as shown in Figure 8-2.

The increases or decreases in percentages of the various items will give you clues about trends in sales, costs, and expenses. You'll then be able to adjust your

CASH FLOW ANALYSIS FOR THREE MONTHS ENDING MARCH 31						
	January		February		March	
	Forecast	Actual	Forecast	Actual	Forecast	Actual
Forecasted receipts						
Cash sales						
Credit sales						
(1) Total cash in						
Forecasted cash payments						
Cost of goods sold						
Purchases of goods needed						
Salaries, proprietor						
Salaries, other						
Payroll and other taxes						
Rent						
Utilities						
Telephone						
Supplies						
Advertising						
Bank borrowing						
Interest						
Repayment of loan						
•						
•						
•						
•						
Miscellaneous						
(2) Total paid out						
(3) Net cash increase (or decrease): Difference between (1) and (2)						
Beginning cash on hand Add (or subtract) Item 3 = Cash on hand at end of month						

Figure 8-1 Typical Form of Cash Flow Analysis

INCOME STATEMENT					
			Increase or (Decrease) $; %	Percent of Total	
	Jan. 1978	Jan. 1977		1978	1977
Sales	15 600	13 700	1900; 13.9	100.0	100.0
Less cost of sales	8 736	8 080	656; 8.1	56.0	59.0
Gross margin	6 864	5 620	1244; 22.1	44.0	41.0
Less operating expenses:					
Cash payments*	2 262	2 130	132; 6.2	14.5	15.5
Administrative	1 200	1 000	200; 20.0	7.7	7.3
Interest	270	—	—	1.7	—
Depreciation	75	75	0	.5	.6
•					
•					
•					
•					
•					
•					
•					
Miscellaneous	90	110		.6	.8
Total expenses	3 897	3 315	582; 17.6	25.0	24.2
Before-tax profit	2 967	2 305	662; 28.7	19.0	16.8

*(For labor, materials, supplies, and services)

Figure 8-2 Typical Form of Income Statement

planning to improve the efficiency of your operations; you'll know exactly where to concentrate your efforts.

Yearly Income Statement

The yearly income statement collects the gross income for the year and subtracts from it the cost of sales, the total of expenditures in the various categories, and the taxes that will have to be paid on the year's business. The resulting after-tax profit (or loss) is combined with the proprietor's capital at the start of the year to show increase (or decrease) in the value of ownership at the end of the year.

When you prepare a yearly income statement, you'll have a greatly condensed financial summary of the complex of activities and events that have taken place in your business, just as you've been able to do with month-by-month income statements. By comparing percentages of the different items, you can see trends that will allow you to take proactive management steps for improvement.

Break-even Analysis

You should know what sales volume you'll need in a given period of time to break even. This is the point at which there's no profit and no loss. A straightforward way to find out is through the construction of a break-even chart. This chart will show you graphically how many dollars in sales you must have during the period to break even.

Although there are many variations of break-even analysis, we've chosen as an example a simple version coming from the records of a small electromechanical manufacturing firm. The company grossed about $1 million annually and employed fifty people. The business and employment had been steady during the year and could be expected to stay at this level for the four-week period we want to look at. The break-even chart was constructed for the four-week period ending June 11. What we want to do is to construct a chart that will show the total cost of sales versus gross sales for this period. We consider sales as **shipments out the door for which we bill our customers**—not orders.

We take our data from the comparative statement shown in Figure 8-3. These are figures we have for the twenty-three weeks of the year to date and for the current period of four weeks in which we're interested. Gross costs include five categories: administrative expense, which covers salaries for management and office personnel, plus miscellaneous expense connected with running the office; direct labor cost in making the product; manufacturing expense, which includes engineering salaries and supplies and services; cost of materials; and marketing expense, which covers salespersons' salaries, advertising, promotion, and sales administration. We assume that administrative, direct labor, and manufacturing costs are essentially constant during the four-week period. Also, because the business and employment have been steady during the year, we can average costs of direct labor for the year to date. The weekly value found in this way would give us a figure suitable for our immediate proactive management purposes.

(You should note, however, that direct labor and manufacturing expense are variable expenses. They increase and decrease as sales volume goes up and down. But what we're after is not precise accounting data at this point. We want to know reasonably closely what our break-even volume is for management purposes, and the assumptions we've made for this specific four-week period will give an answer accurate enough for telling us what to look for in improving our business performance.)

We start the chart by drawing a horizontal line (x) and a vertical line (y); along these we place numbers corresponding to dollars, using the same scale for each. Cost of sales is shown on the vertical scale, dollars in sales on the horizontal scale. Next we draw the break-even line at 45 degrees to the horizontal, from the zero point. You'll note that a horizontal line and a vertical line projected from any given point on the breakeven line will intersect the x and y lines at the same number of dollars.

We now extract cost data from the comparative statement and plot it on the chart:

$$\text{Administrative expense} = \frac{68,469}{23} \times 4 = \$11,900 \text{ (per four-week period)}$$

This number is the administrative expense for an average four-week period in the elapsed twenty-three weeks of the fiscal year to date.

138

COMPARATIVE STATEMENT FOR PERIOD ENDING JUNE 11

PERIOD			YEAR TO DATE	
AMOUNT	%	ACCOUNTS	%	AMOUNT
73,500	100.0	Sales	100.0	530,796
42,560	57.9	Cost of Sales	56.9	302,008
30,940	42.1	Gross Margin	43.1	228,788
17,934	24.4	Marketing Expense	23.3	123,669
11,980	16.3	Administrative Expense	12.9	68,469
1,026	1.4	Gross Profit (Loss)	6.9	36,650
502	.7	Est. Income Taxes	1.6	8,461
524	.7	Net Profit	5.3	28,189
		Cost of Sales		
17,787	24.2	Material Used	22.5	119,423
17,419	23.7	Direct Labor	24.3	128,977
7,354	10.0	Manufacturing Expense	10.1	53,608
42,560	57.9	Total	56.9	302,008
		Inventory Analysis		
160,710		Opening Inventory		182,604
31,327	42.5	Material Purchased	30.6	162,416
33,957	46.2	Labor & Mfg. Expense	34.4	182,585
(213,084)		Closing Inventory		(213,084)
42,560	57.9	Cost of Sales	56.9	302,008
		Manufacturing Expense		
2,940	4.0	Engineering Salaries	3.5	18,577
4,414	6.0	Supplies and Services	6.6	35,031
7,354	10.0	Total	10.1	53,608
		Marketing Expense		
17,947	24.4	Salaries and Services Total	23.3	123,669
		Administrative Expense		
11,980	16.3	Salaries and Misc. Total	12.9	68,469
4 W/E June 11				23 weeks

From A. Kuriloff, *Reality in Management* (New York: McGraw-Hill, 1966), p. 55.

Figure 8-3   Comparative Statement

Next we draw a horizontal line at this number on the chart, the administration line.

Direct labor + manufacturing expense:

$$\text{Direct labor} = \frac{128{,}977}{23} \times 4 = \$22{,}400$$

$$\text{Manufacturing expense} = \frac{53{,}608}{23} \times 4 = 9{,}300$$

$$\text{Total} = \$31{,}700 \quad \text{(per four-week period)}$$

We plot this line a distance marked B (equal to \$31,700) above the administration line. You will see that the distance $A + B$ represents a dollar value that's constant. The volume of sales doesn't affect these costs.

However, the costs of material and marketing are assumed to increase directly with the volume.[5] The comparative statement shows that these costs are 22.5 percent and 23.3 percent, respectively, of gross sales, average for the year to date. These lines are plotted on the chart as shown, starting at a distance $A + B$ above zero.

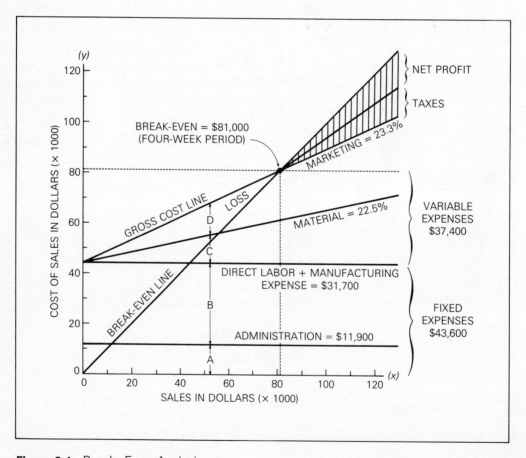

Figure 8-4 Break–Even Analysis

140

We've now placed on the chart all the elements we need for our purpose. We can see the total cost of any dollar volume of the gross sales during the period. By dropping a vertical line through any gross sales dollar value, the total cost of the volume of sales can be found. It is, on any vertical line, the sum of the distances A, B, C, and D, and its value may be found by projecting the point of the intersection of the vertical line with the gross-cost line (marketing line) horizontally to intercept the cost-of-sales scale.

Now we can find our break-even point by observing the dollar value of the intersection of the break-even line with the gross-cost line. On our chart it's $81,000. In practical terms, this means the company must ship $81,000 worth of goods in this four-week period before it can make any money at all. The gross profit possible to make is shown by the crosshatched area.

You'll see from the foregoing that the break-even chart shows the fixed and variable costs of doing business. The total expenses are plotted against sales at all volumes of sales. Your break-even chart will give you valuable information in planning in many areas: in budgeting, in pricing, in controlling expenses, and in setting sales policies, among other things.

Another example of break-even chart is given in Appendix B; it's been prepared for a retail bookstore and should prove informative as a model in any retail business.

Using Ratio Analysis

Another type of analysis that will help you guide the financial affairs of your company is *ratio analysis*. A ratio is simply a comparison of one item with another, from the balance sheet or operating income statement. By checking your current ratios against previous ratios on a regular basis, you can see how you're doing; these data permit you to improve the quality of your management decisions—and therefore the performance of your company. You'll also want to check the ratios from your operations against those customary in your kind of business. This will tell you if you're doing better or worse than the average firm in the business you're in. You'll find information on the ratios typical to your business in the publications we've listed earlier, such as those of Dun and Bradstreet, of the National Cash Register Company, and of the various trade associations.

Current Ratio
An important financial ratio is the current ratio. It's given by:

$$\frac{\text{Current Assets}}{\text{Current Liabilities}}$$

This will tell you how healthy your financial condition is. For example, if current assets = $12,600 and current liabilities = $5,950, the current ratio would be 12,600/5,950 = 2.12. In figuring this ratio, you should omit any prepaid expenses from current assets. Current assets are those you could turn into cash if the need arose; therefore, it's good practice to omit prepaid expenses from this calculation.

The figures you use to calculate the current ratio also tell you how much working capital you have available. In this example, the difference between $12,600 and $5,950 is $6,650, which is the **working capital.** This shows the ability of the business to pay for current operations after taking care of its current bills.

The customarily acceptable current ratio for most businesses is at least 2:1. This means that your business should keep current assets at twice the figure of current liabilities. The 2:1 ratio shows a reasonable safety margin. If your business had some slow moving merchandise in stock, these would be considered assets. But you'd have trouble getting rid of them at a good price in case you wanted to raise money quickly. You can see from this the importance of having a safety cushion in this ratio.

Some businesses may do with a ratio smaller than 2:1; such might be the case in a conservative business dealing in nonperishable goods in a stable market. A higher ratio than 2 should be maintained when the current debt must be paid off quickly or on demand. You should find out what is customary in your business and try to keep your current ratio at least at that level.

Acid Test Ratio

A refinement of the current ratio is the **acid test ratio.** It's similar to the current ratio but shows the comparison between the quick assets and the current liabilities. Quick assets are limited to those that can be readily turned into cash; these include such items as cash, collectible receivables, and securities that can be sold immediately.

You find the acid test ratio by dividing your quick assets by your current liabilities. Suppose your company has quick assets of $8,400 and current liabilities of $7,600, then your acid test ratio would be:

$$\frac{\text{Quick Assets}}{\text{Current Liabilities}} = \frac{\$8,400}{\$7,600} = 1.13$$

A business is customarily considered in good shape when this ratio is at least 1. This means that the company of the example could raise enough money on short notice to pay off its existing liabilities. The 1.13 ratio is a sign of financial health.

Proprietorship Ratio

The relationship of the owner's investment in the company and the total assets being used in the business is the **proprietorship ratio.** It's simply the owner's investment divided by total assets.

Suppose the balance sheet of your company at the end of a fiscal year shows total assets to be $25,490 and the proprietor's capital on the liabilities side shows $15,590. Your proprietorship ratio would then be:

$$\text{Proprietorship ratio} = \frac{\text{Your Investment}}{\text{Total Assets}} = \frac{\$15,590}{\$25,490}$$

$$= 0.61 \text{ or } 61\%$$

This figure would show you that you're well above the 50 percent level considered to be a conservative minimum in any business.

142

Ratio of Net Profit to Net Sales

One of the more significant ratios is the **ratio of net profit to net sales.** It shows the number of cents profit for every dollar of sales. The most informative way for the small businessperson to view net profit is to see this figure as the one remaining after taxes, and net sales as sales for which money has been collected and is due for product or service delivered. There are other ways of setting these figures for other purposes. But looking at them as we've said is a clear, hard-headed managerial way which gives the percentage that is the real measure of the efficiency of a business.

Let's say for illustrative purposes that your company has had profit of $129,300 after taxes for the fiscal year and that your net sales have been $1,645,000; your ratio of net profit to net sales would be:

$$\frac{\$129,300}{\$1,645,000} = .0786 \text{ or } 7.9\%$$

You should study the variation in this percentage on a regular basis. By comparing statements for past periods, you'll be able to put your finger on items that have caused deviations from the performance you'd like. Searching examination of the items in the comparative operating statements such as that shown in Figure 8-3 can give you the clues you need to reduce costs and increase efficiency. Or you may find it imperative to raise prices. However, you should increase prices cautiously, recognizing that raising prices too much can seriously cut your sales. You may find that what you need to do is to increase your volume of sales. Reference to your break-even analysis will help you decide how much money to put into increased advertising, promotion, and sales efforts to move your operation higher into the profit area.

Explore the Use of Ratio Analysis

A number of other ratios that you may want to use for specific purposes are those derived primarily from figures on the balance sheet and from items on the income statement. Because these are intended for rather special purposes we prefer not to include them in this text. Instead, we give you several pertinent references at the end of this chapter in which you'll find excellent information on how to prepare and use many different kinds of ratios.

KEY POINTS IN MANAGING YOUR FINANCES

SUMMARY

You'll need three kinds of money to start your business: capital asset investment, working capital, and personal money. Therefore, you should plan for both long- and short-term financing. Capital assets take long-term money; working capital and personal financing may be thought of as short-term. In all cases you should do the planning yourself. This will give you the knowledge and skill you'll need to guide the financial affairs of your company.

Before you start your business, your planning will necessarily be based on assumptions. In this chapter and in the chapters on marketing, we've given a number of sources of information you can draw upon to start with. As you do business, you'll be able to replace the figures you've assumed with actual figures. We recommend that you redo your financial planning every month, projecting from the actual figures into the future. You'll gain both speed and accuracy of prediction as you do this planning each month.

We suggest that you prepare the following plans each month: A balance sheet to see what the financial picture looks like; a sales forecast twenty-four months ahead by the month and perhaps a forecast for the third year by the quarter; a cash flow analysis in the same time frame as the sales forecast; an income statement, projected at least twelve months ahead; and a break-even analysis from time to time, to see how much you need to sell by the month just to break-even.

You should learn to use ratio analysis as a check on different aspects of your financial condition. Of the many variations of ratio analysis we suggest the following as of key significance for your management purposes:

- Current ratio, which is your current assets divided by your current liabilities. Most businesses are considered to be financially healthy when this ratio is 2 or a bit above.

- Acid test ratio, which is a refinement of the current ratio. You find the acid ratio by dividing your quick assets by your current liabilities. Quick assets are those you can turn into cash immediately: collectible receivables, securities, and cash itself. Your acid ratio should be at least 1, which would show that you could pay your existing debts quickly in case of need.

- Proprietorship ratio, which is your total investment divided by the total assets of your company. This number should be at least 50 percent to show a healthy ownership position.

- Net profit to net sales. This ratio is obtained by dividing your after-tax profits by the net sales for your fiscal year.

To practice the best kind of proactive management, you should compare your figures in these various plans on a regular basis, month by month and year by year. This practice will alert you to potential difficulty so you can take corrective steps quickly. It will also show what you're doing well—and what you should be doing more of, and better.

CHAPTER 8/FOOTNOTES

[1]The *Small Business Reporter* is available from: Small Business Reporter, Bank of America NT & SA. Dept. 3120, P.O. Box 37,000, San Francisco, Calif. 94120.
[2]You can find out about the trade association in your business in *National Trade & Professional Associations of the United States and Canada*, Columbia Books, Inc.,

Publishers, Room 601, 734 15th St., N.W., Washington, D.C. 20005. This directory is published in an up-dated version every January.

Another source of information about trade associations is the *Encyclopedia of Associations*, a three-volume set, published by the Gale Research Company, Detroit, Michigan. Vol. 1, National Organizations of the United States; Vol. 2, Geographic and Executive Index; Vol. 3, New Associations and Projects. Vol. 2, arranged geographically, includes association names, addresses, phone numbers, and executives' names.

[3]A list of Dun & Bradstreet publications may be obtained from the Business Economics Department, Dun & Bradstreet, Inc., 99 Church Street, New York, N.Y. 10017.

[4]This publication may be obtained from the Marketing Services Department, The National Cash Register Company, Dayton, Ohio 45409.

[5]Note that in the small business just starting the cost of marketing may not increase with sales volume. The cost of the marketing effort may be considered a steady cost such as administrative costs and would be shown as a horizontal line on the break-even chart.

Managing Your Financial Requirements

This worksheet is a bit different from the others in that you'll want to take advantage of standard accounting sheets with vertical columns to prepare your financial plans. These are available at any stationery store. We'd recommend that you buy a dozen five-column sheets and a dozen thirteen-column sheets to work on. You'll find these standard forms a great convenience in tabulating your figures.

1. Prepare a budget for your living expenses for eighteen months ahead. Stationery stores usually carry printed forms that you'll find easy to use for this purpose. This is a good point to involve your spouse and family. You'll want their support and commitment to your venture. By preparing the family budget as a team, you'll improve the chances for a healthy climate of cooperation in the affairs of the new business.

2. Prepare a list of equipment, machinery, fixtures, or other equipment you'll need for your business. Find and assign costs to the items and add these figures to find your required fixed asset capital investment. Be sure to add a reasonable safety factor to the total. Don't forget to consider the possibilities of leasing or renting equipment to conserve cash.

3. Prepare your short-term operating plans. Here you'll want to follow the text of this chapter. You'll also want to check your planning by referring to the examples in Appendix B. Beginning with setting the date for starting your business, include the following plans:

   - Balance sheet for the day you start your business.

   - Sales forecast for two years ahead, by the month. You may find it good practice to try forecasting the third year by the quarter.

   - Cash flow analysis for two years ahead by the month, possibly the third year by quarters.

   - Income statement for two years ahead by the month, possibly the third year by quarters.

   - Break-even analysis for the first year. (You'll very likely want to find your break-even point by the month, four-week period, or week once your business is rolling.)

   - You may want to compare your estimated figures against those considered appropriate for your business through ratio analysis. Check these ratios by quarters, for example:
     Current ratio
     Acid test ratio
     Proprietorship ratio
     Ratio of net profit to net sales.

As a concluding reminder, be sure to repeat your planning on the basis of three approaches: optimistic, pessimistic, and at a moderate middle level. Later, as you use real figures from your business to replace your estimated figures, your planning will show reality. You'll be able to practice proactive management effectively.

IF YOU WANT TO READ MORE

Dan Steinhoff, *Small Business Management Fundamentals*, McGraw-Hill, New York, 1974. This is a fundamental text that tells about financial planning and forecasting for the small business. It's an excellent basic book for the beginner. The text focuses to a considerable extent on the small retail firm.

Hal B. Pickle and Royce L. Abrahamson, *Small Business Management*, John Wiley, Santa Barbara, Calif., 1976. This text presents a simple explanation of financial record keeping and cash control. It's aimed at the beginner in small business.

J. K. Lasser, *How to Run a Small Business*, 4th ed., McGraw-Hill, New York, 1974. A simply written handbook on small business management, the text gives examples of the use of financial data for controlling business operations. In addition, the book contains many practical suggestions about managing a small business.

S. B. Costales, *Financial Statements of Small Business*, Racine Printing of Connecticut, Danielson, Conn., 1970. The author develops a simple primary set of examples of financial statements for the small business. He takes the reader through an uncomplicated study of interpreting and analyzing the financial conditions of a small commercial enterprise. There are several actual examples of financial success in small business.

Spencer A. Tucker, *The Break-Even System*, Prentice-Hall, Englewood Cliffs, N.J., 1963. This reference tells about break-even analysis in detail. You'll discover here the many variations of break-even analysis and how to use them for all kinds of proactive management purposes. The text has numerous illustrative examples, which make it easy to see how break-even analyses apply in practice.

How to Read a Financial Report, 4th ed., Merrill Lynch Pierce Fenner & Smith, Inc., New York, 1973. This pamphlet, available through any office of this well-known investment brokerage firm, takes readers by the hand and leads them through the basic financial statements of balance sheet, ratio analysis, income statement, and accumulated retained earnings statement. Explanations are clear and are tied to figures given in a set of typical financial statements for a small manufacturing business.

Richard Sanzo, *Ratio Analysis for Small Business*. Small Business Administration, Washington, D.C., 1970. This booklet offers a straightforward, simple explanation of business ratios and how they work. It also contains examples, information on evaluating and interpreting ratios, and sources of data on ratios for various industries.

Chapter 9

Raising Money for Your Business

Small businesses often fail from lack of adequate capital. You should have a sound estimate of how much money you'll need and where it will come from early in the game. By completing the exercises at the end of Chapter 8, which deals with financial requirements, you'll have a good idea of *what* funds and amounts you will need for fixed assets and working capital and *when* you'll need these monies. This chapter will help you determine *where* these funds will come from.

Your ability to raise the required funds is an extremely important factor in determining the type and size of business you can enter. Keep in mind that there is no one best method of financing and that financing methods vary over time as a result of legal, legislative, and economic changes. More importantly, the way you finance your business will depend upon the stage of development of your enterprise.

There are three typical stages of business development, each requiring different financing approaches. We've organized this chapter around these different stages. We'll discuss start-up financing, but it's also important for you to understand how business financing requirements usually change during the growth of the business. This will help you do the right things early so that financing your business later will be easier.

The generalizations we'll make about financing the business during each stage of development will not apply in every case. For example, there are a few instances in which an entrepreneur with an exceptional business idea and a carefully prepared business plan has marched into a commercial bank and obtained a sizeable start-up loan on the basis of his or her signature. These cases are rare. They usually occur when the entrepreneur has contracts in hand and has a proven financial and business track record. But even when this has happened, in every instance *the entrepreneur has had to contribute a sizeable proportion of the needed seed money.* We know of no exceptions.

And don't forget that you'll need money for personal expenses. Few new businesses produce enough revenue in the first year to eighteen months to pay the owner a salary. As a rule of thumb, you should have enough money set aside to support yourself and your family for about eighteen months. Funds for personal support should be above and beyond those needed for the business.

THE START-UP STAGE 1 C (1) (3), **8** A (2) (3), **8** (8) (e), **9** A (1) (4) (a) (b)

The first stage we'll call the *start-up stage*—the period when the entrepreneur needs seed money for rent, supplies, inventory, equipment, wages, advertising, licenses and fees, and other expenses associated with starting the business.

You, and your business partners if you have them, will be the major source of cash during the start-up stage. Besides putting up savings you've accumulated, other personal resources might include borrowings backed by secured collateral, such as stocks or bonds, loans against the cash value of existing life insurance policies, or borrowing against the equity you've built up in your home. Most small service firms, boutiques, manufacturers, and other types of businesses, start in this way: Funds come from personal resources and personal borrowings of the entrepreneur.

Knowledgeable investors will not put money into a new business unless they have concrete evidence that the entrepreneur has personally made a sizeable *financial* commitment in the business. They know from experience that if the venture turns sour it will be easier for you to back out if you don't have your own money at stake. Thus, to obtain sufficient financing, you will have to invest a substantial portion of your *personal* net worth in your venture.

Investors, whether financial institutions, venture capital firms, or individuals, invest in people as well as in companies, products, or ideas. Your money talks when you demonstrate your personal commitment to the venture by putting up your own resources. And investors will not usually listen to you unless you do.

Numerous studies have shown that when the entrepreneur's cash contributions are insufficient to finance initial business operations, outside funding usually comes from wealthy individuals. As a general rule, try to put in at least 50 percent of needed seed money yourself. There are two reasons for this: (1) Individual investors probably won't be interested unless you've contributed about this proportion, and (2) contributions by individuals will frequently take the form of equity or ownership interest in your business. As you put up more than 50 percent of the total capital, the greater becomes your independence in controlling the business—and the more substantial your share of the profit.

Seed money from friends or relatives is common in start-up operations even though borrowing from friends or relatives is generally frowned upon by experienced business people. It's dangerous to mix social or family relationships with business. Friends and relatives can, and often do, interfere with business policy and operational matters.

It will probably be best if you can arrange a loan with favorable repayment terms instead of giving up ownership interest in your business in exchange for seed money. The agreement should be clearly understood, with specific written arrangements for retiring the loan, provisions for early repayment, and procedures if loans become delinquent.

When wealthy individuals supply seed money for new ventures, it's usually in the form of *equity capital.* It's not easy to locate wealthy investors, but there are persons called *finders* who specialize in matching entrepreneurs searching for seed money with private individuals interested in new investment opportunities. Commercial loan bank officers, stockbrokers, lawyers, and others involved in financial matters can sometimes refer you to a good finder. A finder may be able to steer you to individuals specifically interested in your type of business.

If you must seek outside sources for seed money be careful not to accept more than you need. It may be comfortable to have a capital cushion, but the cost will be either dilution of your ownership and control position or early burdening of your cash flow with excessive loan repayment charges. The financial performance of your business becomes more impressive to future investors if it has been achieved with a small rather than a large amount of seed money. And this will make it easier for you to obtain the additional funding you'll need as your business grows.

The second, or growth, stage is the period when you will need additional financing for business expansion—the hiring of full-time sales personnel, building new production facilities, purchasing new equipment, or investing in new product development. By this time the business will have developed its product or service, successfully marketed what the business offers, and generated respectable sales revenue.

Several alternatives now exist for acquiring growth-enabling funds. Your suppliers may be persuaded to finance inventory and equipment; commercial banks, the Small Business Administration, venture capital groups, and others become interested at this stage of development.

Suppliers

Your firm's suppliers can give financial assistance. Most important are suppliers of inventory. Wholesalers who want a retailer's business will often offer attractive terms for paying invoices, and manufacturers will do the same for a desirable wholesaler. For example, if you can buy a $100,000 inventory that will sell within one month for $50,000 as the down payment, with the balance due in 30 days, your wholesaler will have supplied you with $50,000 worth of capital.

Another form of trade credit is the discount offered when inventory is sold to a retailer. For example, a discount often used is the 2/10, net 30. This means that the retailer gets a two percent discount off the total due if payment is made within ten days; if not, the full amount of the invoice is due in thirty days.

Trade credit is a way you can either postpone payment until your inventory itself is returning cash or realize savings on your accounts payable by taking discounts by paying for inventory immediately. Planning for use of trade credit is essential. Its effective use is the principal reason large businesses buy products for less money than small firms. Do not depend too much on trade credit from one supplier. If you run into difficulty in paying on time, you may find your source of supply cut off when you most need it to fill your customers' orders.

You can often finance capital equipment and plant facilities like shelves, display cases, counters, and delivery trucks through your suppliers. It's usually easier to obtain financing on these items than it is to get a loan for ordinary working capital because the equipment itself secures the loan. Suppliers will often give favorable terms to sell their equipment, even to new companies. A modest down payment of 10 to 20 percent with the balance spread over two to three years is not unusual.

Commercial Banks

Banks supply debt financing; they don't want an ownership (or equity) interest in your venture. They will lend money for working capital or for purchasing fixed assets when they have clear evidence that your firm's cash flow can meet principal and interest payments. They'll want to know how and when their money will be repaid, and they'll usually want some form of collateral to secure their loan.

As we've stressed earlier, you should select a bank and establish good relations long before your need for financing growth arises. The sooner you do so, the sooner you'll learn what types of loans and how much credit will be available to you.

Select your bank on the basis of your business and financial needs. Compare services offered and get to know key officers you'll be dealing with. At some early point in the growth of your business, assess their willingness to lend you money. Show them your business plan and keep them informed of financial developments. Invite them to see your business in operation during the start-up phase. After you've selected a bank, do all your business banking and personal banking there; don't split your accounts among banks. By following these suggestions you'll improve your chances of getting money when you need it.

Here are some of the types of financing a bank supplies:

- Short-term commercial loans: These are the most common kinds of loans to small businesses. The loans are for short periods, 30 to 180 days; they are usually made to cover seasonal or other temporary needs for personnel or inventory. Repayment is usually made in one lump sum, which includes interest.

- Longer-term loans: With longer repayment terms of up to five years, these loans have a regular repayment schedule, usually monthly, including interest to date plus payment against principle. These loans are for such purposes as buying fixed assets, equipment, or other items for business expansion.

- Accounts receivable financing: Banks will often lend money on your accounts receivable if they are pledged as collateral. You must pay the bank if the accounts pledged are not paid on time. You would still own the receivables and would yourself go after your customer for collection. This type of financing is frequently used by small retail and service businesses for purchasing additional operating inventory or operating supplies.

- Other types of financing: Commercial banks will lend money for building construction or improvement and for buying land. The loan is usually long-term and is always secured by the asset for which the loan was made.

Bank credit cards offer another form of financing. By accepting them for payment from customers, the business affords credit to customers without having to assume any credit risk or financing the sale. But it costs the entrepreneur 3 to 6 percent of the sale price to use this service.

Banks provide other valuable services that will help you to expand your business. They can perform credit checks for sizing up potential large customers. The bank can help you develop a financially sound product leasing plan to offer customers if you market capital equipment. Larger banks have international departments that can assist in product exporting or importing. Banks increasingly offer their commercial customers payroll accounting and data processing services at competitive rates. Finally, your loan officer may prove to be a valuable business adviser in helping you locate sources of additional business, in dealing with overdue accounts, and in setting up your accounting system. Cultivate good relations with your bank and your banker; you'll need their services.

The Small Business Administration (SBA)

The information and management assistance offered by the SBA has been described previously. The SBA is also a source of financing. It is prohibited by law from granting financial assistance unless the entrepreneur is unable to obtain funds from the private sector on reasonable terms. It does not compete with the banking industry; instead the SBA works with private capital suppliers to assure availability of funds to potentially profitable small businesses.

These are the major SBA loan programs:

1. Direct loans: Loans can be made directly to qualified small businesses if adequate collateral can be pledged. The loan limit is currently $100,000, but funds available for direct loans are small compared to demand.

2. Guaranteed loans: These are loans made by a commercial bank but guaranteed up to 90 percent by the SBA. The bank lends all of the funds and incurs at least 10 percent of the loan risk. In effect, the SBA acts as cosigner for a sizeable portion of the loan, enabling the entrepreneur to get a loan that otherwise could not be obtained. This is the most frequently used loan program of the SBA.

3. Participation loans with banks: In this case, the SBA actually supplies the major portion of money lent—up to 75 percent—and the bank puts up the rest. Loan payments and servicing are handled by the bank.

4. Special loan programs: These include Displaced Business Loans for small businesses that have suffered economic loss due to federally financed construction such as urban renewal or highway projects. Economic Opportunity Loans are also available for entrepreneurs who are physically handicapped or are members of a minority group. In addition, there are several disaster-related loan programs. A little-known form of assistance is the Lease Guarantee Program. The SBA will guarantee the rental payment for the small firm to the land owner or building owner, allowing the entrepreneur to compete with larger firms for commercial space.

It is outside the scope of this book to describe fully all the SBA's assistance programs. New legislation constantly creates new loan programs and changes existing programs. Your best approach will be to visit your local field office of the SBA, study the literature, and discuss the programs with their financial and management assistance officers.

Small Business Investment Companies (SBICs)

These privately owned companies are licensed and regulated by the SBA and were created to supply equity capital, long-term loan funds, and management assistance to small business. They exist in most states and are ready to help firms with attractive potential. The excellent financial record of SBICs reflects the success of the small firms they have helped. The SBA or your bank can assist you in contacting an SBIC.

Business Development Corporations (BDCs)

These organizations exist in every state and supply financing similar to SBICs. They are privately owned and their capital base is made up of funds from private sources. Private businesses and individuals form these corporations to promote local commercial growth by attracting new and different types of business. They will often grant long-term business loans to small firms that have been turned down by banks, and on occasion they will buy stock in a promising new venture.

Venture Capital Firms

These are firms specializing in supplying equity capital for businesses with high growth potential. The venture capital firm looks for unique, exciting, fast-growing companies in an expanding field.

Venture capitalists become interested in the small business when it has demonstrated (1) *market acceptance* for its products by sizeable sales generated over a period of time, (2) its *potential* for rapid growth, and (3) *competence* in managing other people's money. This source of capital will want large returns for supplying equity financing. It would not be unusual for venture capital firms to expect ten to twenty times their initial investment within five years. Although venture capitalists would have an ownership interest, they do not want management control of the business unless things go wrong. Instead, they look for a well-balanced and experienced management team with technical, marketing, and financial competence.

Don't waste your time (and credibility) by seeking financing from a venture capital firm before you've met the requirements we've just described. Several sources of information about them are given at the end of this chapter. Learn about them and what they can do for you before you approach a venture capital firm for an infusion of capital.

Summary: Debt vs. Equity Financing

We have outlined several sources of funds for financing the growth stage of your business. Some, such as banks, supply loans to small businesses. These debts must be repaid out of current earnings. Others, such as venture capital firms, offer only equity financing. Funds of this kind represent ownership interest in the business for which a handsome financial return is expected.

Some equity financing during the growth stage is usually required. There are several reasons for this. First, growth requires cash—cash to pay for increased facilities, new personnel, research, and promotion efforts. Meeting fixed repayment schedules for loans can place an undesirable strain on your cash flow at a time when you'll want to conserve cash for expansion. Second, loans are extremely difficult to obtain for such intangible purposes as new product development and market research. Loans are usually made to help a firm acquire tangible assets like equipment or inventory. Third, you'll multiply the risk of business failure by not having the protection of long-term equity and the resulting financial strength required to borrow money on favorable terms when you need it.

Permanent equity financing is something to plan for. It involves strategic decisions and technical knowledge of the capital market. This is another area where professionals, such as your accountant or attorney, can help.

THE MATURITY STAGE

During this stage the enterprise tends to outgrow its ability to finance further expansion with cash generated from its own internal operations and the external sources described previously. At this point the business will want to move into new markets, construct new plants or distribution outlets, and purchase more equipment. Sizeable sums of money for marketing may be needed to meet increased competition. Large sums of equity money are usually sought from such sources as public sale of stock or merger. We will examine these sources only briefly since financing at maturity is a highly complex and technical subject beyond the purpose of this book.

Public sale of stock is a viable alternative for raising capital when the business has a well-established track record. The public equity offering sometimes has the dual purpose of raising additional funds for the company and enabling original investors to realize a financial gain by selling a portion of their shares. The expenses involved in "going public" are significant. There are legal and auditing expenses as well as the cost of good placement services—the reputable investment banking firm that agrees to underwrite or sell the stock offering. Often these costs can amount to 20 percent or more of the total proceeds of the stock sale. The company will have to devote a lot of its efforts to maintain good relations with its stockholders and the Securities and Exchange Commission. There will be strict disclosure and reporting requirements. And if the company doesn't perform well with its equity capital, additional public financing will be out of the question.

On the other hand, sale of public stock can net the company more debt-free funds than, say, venture capital firms can supply. Going public will often produce a higher stock price than selling stock to a single buyer.

Finally, although managerial efforts may be diverted to reporting requirements and public investor relations, working with private investors, banks, and venture capital firms also takes time.

Expanding markets, new technology, and need to diversify often mean that large infusions of cash will be needed beyond the company's own resources and credit available from financial institutions. A public offering of stock permits the owners to retain control of their company while reaping the benefits of an increasingly valuable equity position if growth continues. But it should be noted that buyers of stock in a public offering look primarily at the potential for capital gain rather than dividends. This means that for the stock offering to be attractive, the company's growth record must far exceed the industry average.

In addition, going public alters the character of the company and changes the way the entrepreneur is accustomed to operate. Profit margins, market share, and other information may have to be disclosed, which could affect the firm's competitive position. Stockholders, analysts, auditors, and brokers will also want access to information and will feel they have a right to question a variety of decisions and actions management has made. The effect is that the closely held company accustomed to a low-profile and free-wheeling operation now becomes accountable to many outsiders.

Another way to raise funds for continued expansion of the business is through merger with a larger company. Although this may not be the answer for financing, small businesses often do not consider this alternative until they've found no other way. At the maturity stage merger should be viewed as one tool available to meet the company's goals—a means to conquer new markets or develop existing ones fully, expand production, or increase productivity.

A merger is a transaction in which the seller is the small business and the buyer is the larger acquiring business. From the seller's viewpoint, there can be personal and business reasons for considering a merger. The seller's original investment will be more valuable and marketable if the acquired company is healthy and growing. And the buyer will have to give up enough cash, perhaps combined with stock in the larger company, to compensate the owners of the small business for their success. The benefits to the acquired business is that by merging it achieves a better position to grow. There may be advantages in marketing, production, and management by combining the talent, assets, and financial strengths of the companies.

COST, FLEXIBILITY, AND CONTROL   SUMMARY

There are several sources of funds for the small business with a good record. But in the start-up phase, your personal funds and borrowings will almost always be the major form of capital. There is ordinarily no substitute for putting your financial assets on the line in starting your own business.

Trade credit is an excellent way to finance inventory; if you use discounts wisely, it can be very economical. New equipment may be financed on an installment basis or by leasing from the supplier.

Establishing and maintaining good relationships with your bank will assure ready access to short-term funds and even term loans up to five years. These will usually have to be secured by existing business assets. Your need for bank loans should be anticipated well in advance. You should assess bank services and select the bank to deal with before opening your doors for business.

Continued growth of your business will require you to consider long-term financing. Loans from the SBA, SBICs, and SBDCs are available. Equity financing may become necessary with growth to prevent burdening the cash flow of the business with fixed repayment expenses. SBICs, BDCs, and venture capital firms can supply this form of funding, but they'll want a well-balanced management team guiding a rapidly growing business and selling unique products or services.

The cost of obtaining capital must be weighed against the benefits. Loans must be repaid—interest and principal—out of business earnings. But they will not affect your ownership interest in the business, unless things go wrong. Nor will they impair your flexibility in making decisions that affect your business operations.

One of the most difficult strategic decisions you'll have to make concerns long-term financing. This usually boils down to whether or not you want your company to grow. If you do, you'll probably have to sacrifice some of your ownership and control in the business. And your entrepreneurial flexibility may be diminished. You'll have to reexamine the reasons you went into business for yourself in the first place. It may be possible to stay small and remain profitable. If your firm grows too large to suit you, it may be better to sell out and start another business. This will very likely be your course if your dominant need is for achievement through entrepreneurship. As you'll see in the next chapters, surviving business growth will require you to develop skills beyond those it takes to be an entrepreneur.

Raising Money for Your Business

1. (a) Of the total start-up capital your business needs, what percentage will you be contributing? ____%

   (b) What personal assets will you use to come up with the amount needed? List them and indicate how much each will supply:

	Item	Amount
a.	_____	$ _____
b.	_____	_____
c.	_____	_____
d.	_____	_____
e.	_____	_____
f.	_____	_____

2. Are there other investors who will supply seed money for your venture? List them below along with how much you expect them to contribute and the terms (debt or equity position) on which you are willing to let them come into the business.

	Investor	Amount Expected	Terms
a.	_____	_____	_____
b.	_____	_____	_____
c.	_____	_____	_____
d.	_____	_____	_____
e.	_____	_____	_____

3. What are the sources you'll seek for capital to finance business expansion? What will you use the money for? Rank sources in order of importance as you see them for your kind of business, and describe the purpose of money they'll supply.

	Sources	Purpose of Funds
a.	_____	_____
b.	_____	_____
c.	_____	_____

160

d. _____   _____

e. _____   _____

f. _____   _____

4. How much have you set aside for maintaining yourself and family for the next year and a half it usually takes to get the business rolling—in addition to the funds you need to start the business? $ _____.

IF YOU WANT TO READ MORE

"Financing Small Business," *Small Business Reporter*, Bank of America. This is another pamphlet in the Small Business Reporter series published by the Bank of America. It describes sources of capital and credit for the small business and the risk and cost associated with each. Especially useful is its discussion of developing good relations with your bank and bank services.

"Borrowing Money from Your Bank," Small Business Administration Publication 1.10/2:2, Annual No. 2, No. 33, and "What Kind of Money Do You Need?" Small Business Administration Publication 1.10/2:11, Annual No. 11, No. 150. These two SBA publications tell you how to determine the kind of money you'll need and about conventional sources that supply it. Bank borrowing is discussed: What banks want in the way of collateral and for what purposes banks will lend money to you.

Stanley M. Rubel, *Guide to Venture Capital Sources*, 4th ed., Capital Publishing Corp., 10 S. La Salle St., Chicago, 1977. Sanley M. Rubel, *Guide to Selling a Business*, Capital Publishing Corp., Chicago, 1977. Leonard E. Smollen, Mark Rolloson, and Stanley M. Rubel, *Sourcebook for Borrowing Capital*, Capital Publishing Corp., Chicago, 1977. These three references are placed together because they are complementary and come from a publishing house that specializes in financial texts designed for the businessperson.

These publications are financial encyclopedias for the entrepreneur. The initial chapters in the first book, *Guide to Venture Capital Sources*, not only present some basic information on raising venture capital but also discuss the pros and cons of going public. There's a directory section that lists all venture capital firms, their officers, who to contact, and descriptive information on the areas of investment and investment limits they prefer.

The first sections of *Guide to Selling a Business* discuss the characteristics to look for in the buyer company, working out the terms of the merger, and how intermediaries can help sell the company. A directory lists corporate acquirers and merger intermediaries, who to contact, the industry, geographic, and size preferences for potential acquirees. Acquisition policies and recent activity are also discussed.

The final volume, *Sourcebook for Borrowing Capital*, discusses private financing sources such as commercial banks and insurance companies; government financing sources such as federal, state, and local programs; and guidelines for obtaining loans. There are lists of commercial finance and leasing companies, SBICs, and community development corporations. It also suggests people to contact, geographical and industry preferences, and types of financing the company engages in.

A particularly valuable section presents various types of deals on which money has been lent. This will permit the potential borrower to preview the lender's approach and thus minimize the time to obtain financing.

Venture Capital, Technimetrics, Inc., 919 Third Ave., New York, N.Y. 10022. This book lists over 400 venture capital firms with brief descriptions of who to contact, preferred areas of investment, approximate range of financings, special help proffered to the recipient of financing, and some examples of recent investments.

Sam Adams, "What a Venture Capitalist Looks For," *MBA* June/July 1973, vol. 7, no. 6, pp. 6–9. As the title suggests, this article gives specific suggestions for entrepreneurs who are looking for venture capital.

Chapter 10

Deciding on Some Key Legal Matters

Three basic forms of business structure are available to you in setting up your business. These are the sole proprietorship, the partnership, and the corporation. Each has advantages and disadvantages. You'll want to check carefully before you decide which to choose, because of two fundamental variables: cost of setting up and the tax consequences attached to each form.

You'd be wise to seek professional help in making your decision. Two professionals who can help are a lawyer and an accountant; both should be familiar with small business. They can help you decide which form will give you the best breaks on your taxes and which will protect your assets in case of financial claims against your business. They can also help you estimate the fees for setting up your business in the form you choose.

SOLE PROPRIETORSHIP   1 A

The sole proprietorship is the easiest way to start a business. As the sole proprietor you own all the assets of the company. The legal requirements are minimum: You may need only to buy a license for doing business in your community. If you operate under a fictitious name—that is, a name other than your own—you'll have to register that name with the appropriate authority. It's necessary that you publish your fictitious business name in an authorized newspaper and show that you're the person legally behind it. You can then open a bank account in the fictitious name. Without this formality, you might be unable to sue or collect debts due you because your business wouldn't exist under the law.

Advantages of Sole Proprietorship

To start your business as a sole owner, you have merely to offer your product or service to the public and to make your first sale. You're in business when you've made that sale.

The sole proprietorship is the simplest and easiest to start. It's also the least expensive, requiring the least legal documentation of all forms of business ownership.

Another advantage that attaches to the sole proprietorship is the ease of making decisions. As the owner you can decide what to do as quickly as you make up your mind. You don't have to consult with anyone, but you'd be wise to ask for expert help in matters that are outside your own competence. In any event, one of the great advantages you have as the sole owner is the speed at which you can operate. You can see and seize an opportunity for making money quickly. And you can get under way before a larger partnership or corporation can decide to move.

The sole proprietorship uses an elementary form of organization, which may be diagrammed as shown in Figure 10-1.

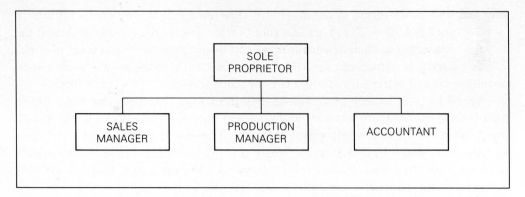

Figure 10-1 Typical Organization Chart for a Small Proprietorship

With the key people reporting directly to you and taking their orders directly from you, the sole proprietorship gives you the advantage of the shortest and most direct lines of communication. You'd be able to keep up with what's going on, to see how well your people are performing, and to manage proactively with minimum time lost.

Disadvantages of Sole Proprietorship

A major disadvantage of the sole proprietorship is that it offers no shelter from claims or creditors. If you are sued as the sole owner of the business, all your personal assets are subject to lien for the satisfaction of creditors' claims. That means that what you own could be taken from you to pay off the claims of a successful law suit against your business.

You may protect yourself against many kinds of claims by having adequate insurance. If you have proper insurance coverage, you'd be protected—for example, if a customer slips and is injured in your store or if a customer suffers injury in using your product. Here again you'd do well to get expert advice to ensure that you take the right steps.

Another disadvantage of being the sole owner is that you're alone. As the chief executive you must wear many hats. Your position demands tremendous amounts of time and energy. And you have no one to share the load.

PARTNERSHIP   **1** A, **7** A (1) (2) (3), **9** A (3)

A partnership may be thought of as an association of two or more persons who carry on a business as coowners with the intent of making a profit. A partnership may be established by oral or written agreement. It's assumed to exist when there's a clearly

166

perceived intention to be partners, when there's coownership and community of interest in the business, and when there's sharing of profit and loss.

You may enter into a partnership simply by talking it over with an acquaintance or a friend and agreeing to go into business together. However, this way of doing it has some dangers as the partnership is such a close relationship that it's almost like a marriage. A new business, like a new marriage, almost always goes through difficult periods. Because the partners are human beings, subject to differences of opinion and emotional responses to trying situations, it's most important that the partnership agreement be spelled out in detail before the business starts. This suggests that you carefully consider two aspects of your intended partnership: (1) Choose your partner or partners with great care. Make sure you can get along well together under difficult circumstances, and that you can work through differences and come to satisfactory agreement. (2) And get *expert legal help* in setting up the partnership. That means you should put in writing in a binding form the responsibilities of the partners and the ways in which foreseeable problems are to be solved or decisions made when these problems arise.

Your objective here should be that of proactive management. You should anticipate possible contingencies with your partner or partners. Then you should agree on how they are to be handled to produce results that all consider fair. These procedures should then be put in a legally binding document prepared with the guidance of your attorney. In this way all partners will have foreknowledge of their rights and obligations. You and your partner or partners will be able to put your energies into making the business prosper without draining energy in avoidable disputes.

Rights and Obligations of Partners

The relationship of partners in the conduct of business has been spelled out in the Uniform Partnership Act. This model partnership law was developed by the National Commissioners on Uniform State Laws. Many states have adopted the Uniform Partnership Act in its entirety; others have enacted variations of it. You should follow the legislation in force in your state if you enter into a partnership. In any event, the Uniform Partnership Act gives useful guidelines for a partnership, in outlining both rights and obligations of partners.

Rights
Under the Uniform Partnership Act, each partner has the right to:

- Share in the management and conduct of the business

- Share in the profits of the firm

- Receive repayment of contributions

- Receive indemnification for, or return of, payments made on behalf of the partnership

- Receive interest on additional advances made to the business

- Have access to the books and records of the partnership

- Have formal accounting of partnership affairs

Obligations

Under the Act each partner has the obligation to:

- Contribute toward losses sustained by the partnership

- Work for the partnership without pay in the customary sense, but rather for a share of the profits

- Submit to majority vote, or arbitration, when differences arise about the conduct of affairs of the business

- Give other partners any information known personally about partnership affairs

- Account to the partnership for all profits coming from any partnership transaction, or from the use of partnership property

As you can see from this list, the partnership relationship must rest on good faith and honest dealing. The Uniform Partnership Act was drawn up on the basic principle that each partner has a *fiduciary* obligation to other partners—that is, the relationship is founded in trust and confidence.

The importance of trust and confidence in a partnership cannot be overstated. For example, any partner may bind the partnership to a deal without the knowledge of the other partners. This means that your partner could commit your partnership business to a costly action without your agreement, and the commitment would be legally binding. Your whole fortune, all your personal assets, could be put at risk without your knowledge or consent. For this reason, the interpersonal relations among partners must be founded on complete honesty and trust. There can be no secrets in a partnership if it's to be successful.

New Partners

Persons entering into an existing partnership are generally held responsible for obligations of the partnership existing at the time of their entry. However, for the protection of new partners, a special provision of this rule states that incoming partners' responsibility for preexisting debts shall be limited to only the partnership property. In other words, new partners' personal assets may not be attached to satisfy preexisting debts of the old partnership. Some states still have legislation governed by common law. Here the incoming partner is not liable for debts of the firm current at the time of entry, unless there's an agreement to assume this liability.

If you consider taking in a partner after your business is established, you should carefully think through and agree on the responsibilities the new person will take on when joining the firm. Here again, you'd do well to have a written agreement prepared by an attorney.

Tax Implications for Partnerships

If you don't yet recognize the complexities of federal and state tax laws, you will, soon after you start your business. We can't begin to deal with the intricacies of taxation for partnerships in this text. However, you should know some key points about taxation of partnerships. We'll cover them here.

The federal income tax laws give a unique status to partnerships. They aren't taxable as partnerships; partners are individually liable for their share of taxes resulting from the partnership's business.

Although partnerships don't file an income tax return, they're required to file an information return (Form 1065), signed by one of the partners. This form reports gross income, deductions, and the names and percentages of the firm's business shared by its members. Partners are individually liable for their proportionate share of taxes resulting from the business.

What this means for you as a partner in your business is that you must determine your own individual income tax, taking into account your share of the partnership income, gain, loss, deduction, or credit.

Gain and loss must be apportioned among partners in accordance with their profit-and-loss ratios, unless the partnership agreement specifies some other arrangement. In some partnerships, certain members will contribute capital and others only services. The usual agreement states that losses are to be borne only by those contributing capital. Partners who contribute only services usually bear losses limited to the extent of their accumulated earnings.

Tax consequences will usually follow the partnership agreement. The initial partnership agreement can, of course, be changed by mutual consent.

Termination and Dissolution

Termination of a partnership is defined somewhat differently for tax purposes than for closing out the relationship and the business. The Internal Revenue Code of 1954 states that a partnership is considered terminated: (1) when partnership business activities cease, or (2) when there's a sale or exchange of an interest of 50 percent or more in capital and profits of the partnership within a twelve month period.

Termination in either case is significant for tax purposes for three reasons:

- Termination closes the taxable year of the partnership; if the partner and partnership are on different taxable years, the partners may experience a bunching of partnership income that could materially increase their income taxes.

- Termination may stop the use of a favorable fiscal year for the partnership business. If the business is succeeded by another partnership, the successor partnership will be regarded as a new partnership and will need consent from the Commissioner of Internal Revenue for the adoption of a fiscal year different from that of the principal partners.

- Termination of a partnership results in the properties of the partnership being deemed to be distributed to the partners.

Termination is defined somewhat differently for purposes other than taxation. Under the Uniform Partnership Act, termination is the final act of winding up the business; another term, *dissolution*, is defined as the change in the partnership relationship caused by any one partner ceasing to be associated with the business. Dissolution is not considered a termination of the partnership. Nor is it considered a termination of the rights and powers of the several partners. Many of these rights and powers continue during the closing-out process that follows dissolution. Termination occurs after the intent to cease operations of the partnership is expressed (dissolution) and all the affairs of the partnership are concluded.

Dissolution may be caused by any of the following:

- Expiration of a specified period of time (term certain) or the finishing of an undertaking spelled out in the partnership agreement

- Expressed wish of any partner when no definite term or particular undertaking is specified

- Expressed wish of all partners, either before or after the expiration of a term certain or specified undertaking

- Expulsion of a partner under the provisions of the partnership agreement

- Withdrawal, retirement, or death of a partner (except when a partnership agreement provides for continuation under any of these circumstances)

- Sale or transfer of substantially all of the assets of the partnership

- Bankruptcy of any partner or of the partnership

You can see that the partnership is a close personal relationship. When a change of partners occurs for any reason, the partnership dissolves in the eyes of the law, unless otherwise provided by agreement.

Dissolution of a partnership doesn't free the partners from the debts to creditors or from their obligation to act equitably toward one another. These duties remain until all are taken care of and the partnership is terminated. In other words, the partnership and the partners, including the estate of a partner who may have died, must fulfill all obligations of the past until these preexisting matters are taken care of. Winding up affairs for termination includes the performance of existing contracts, collection of debts or claims due the firm, and payments of debts owed by the firm.

At the time of dissolution, the partners lose their power to act for the partnership in all matters except those involved in liquidation of the partnership. They can't legally take on future obligations; potential creditors in this situation would be subject to being defrauded.

The partnership agreement should provide for the amount and method of payment of a partner's interest upon disability, withdrawal, retirement, or death. If this isn't done in the legal partnership document, bitter controversy may occur among partners when the partnership is dissolved.

Limited Partnership

The limited partnership is usually used in real estate developments and some kinds of international business. It's a particular form of partnership that gives investors special tax advantages and shielding from liability.

A limited partnership is set up in the same way as a general partnership. However, in some states a special notice must be filed in the county or district where the limited partnership has its principal office.

A limited partnership is a creature of statute. Unless the legally required recording and publishing of notice are carefully followed in all details, the partnership will be considered a general partnership in the eyes of the law.

The limited partnership includes one or more general partners and one or more limited partners. The general partners manage the affairs of the partnership; the limited partners are investors only. They have the advantage of limited liability. If the business fails, the most they can lose is their original investment, any additional capital contribution, and their portion of the assets of the firm. General partners, who manage the firm, have unlimited liability as in any ordinary partnership.

Limited partners legally may have no say in the management of affairs of the firm. Those partners who violate this proscription automatically dissolve the limited status of their partnership. They then become general partners and have the same unlimited liability for the debts of the firm as the originally designated general partners.

If the assets of a limited partnership are sold or transferred, the limited partners, as major investors, usually have control of the transaction.

The duration of the limited partnership is stated in the original agreement and certificate filed with the appropriate public authority. Procedures for transfer of limited or general partners' interests should be agreed upon at the time of formation of the limited partnership.

Tax Implications

The limited partnership, as with the general partnership, is not itself a taxable entity—the partners are the taxpayers. Financial information must be reported, but taxes are levied on the individual partners. The special tax treatment of limited partnerships is the primary reason for the adoption of this form of organization. Without risking unlimited exposure, the limited partners can receive the benefits of noncash losses. This can be particularly beneficial in real estate ventures of some size. Here depreciation allowed by law can produce a substantial "expense" item without producing a similar cash drain. The "expense" is deductible from income by individual partners. The limited partner, usually an investor in a high income bracket, gets the tax advantages of an individual but is exposed to none of the consequences of personal liability if the project fails.

CORPORATION   **1** A, **7** A (1) (2) (3), **9** A

The corporation is an "artificial being" sanctioned by law in each of the fifty states. The powers granted the corporation are those spelled out by legislation in each state. Differences in the legal requirements among the states are numerous; therefore, the discussion that follows concentrates on characteristics of corporations in general.

A typical organization chart for a modest-sized corporation is shown in Figure 10-2.

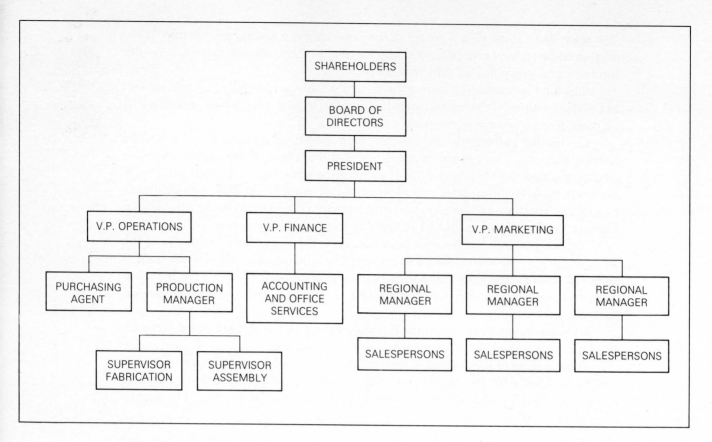

Figure 10-2 Typical Organization Chart for a Small Corporation

Limited Liability

The corporate form of organization has several advantages, but high among them is that of limited liability. The liability of shareholders, who own the company, is limited to the amount of their investment in stock of the company. This means that if you set up your business as a corporation, your investment is reflected in the shares you own. Your personal liability is now limited simply to the amount of the money you used to buy the stock—provided you run the company in a way that fulfills the legal requirements for corporations in your state.

The same is true for those who may invest in your business by buying shares. Sole proprietors expose their entire net worth for the satisfaction of creditors if the business gets into difficulty. Partners have similar exposure; in addition, their responsibility is collective, and this may result in strained relations among partners in time of financial stress. Investors in the shares of a corporation, however, avoid this total exposure. Their liability to corporate creditors is limited to the purchase price of their shares.

As the owner and principal shareholder of a small business, you may find the corporate form of less importance as a shield against exposure of your personal net worth in some circumstances than in others. You may have invested everything you own in the business on setting it up. You may therefore have little of consequence to

172

own in the business on setting it up. You may therefore have little of consequence to protect. Also, you may find that major lenders and suppliers to your company want your personal guarantee and those of your principal shareholders in doing business with you. They believe that the added exposure will increase your desire to make your venture successful and that through your increased commitment they'll be more likely to be paid. The personal guarantee gives them additional security, in other words. Smaller, less sophisticated creditors don't normally need, nor would you want to grant, this additional protection.

You may find it good policy to insure your corporation against loss of various kinds. However, many businesses face major risks that aren't insurable—for example, performance requirements under the terms and conditions of specific contracts. Here you'd find the limited liability of shareholders in the corporation particularly attractive.

Need to Comply with Legal Requirements

Sometimes in going to the law to collect a debt from a small corporation, creditors will try to show that the small corporation has been behaving like a sole proprietorship—and therefore the principal shouldn't enjoy the protection of personal assets normally given shareholders. This attempt can result in what is often called "piercing the corporate shield."

As the owner-shareholder of a small corporation, you must protect yourself against this kind of attack by meticulously meeting the requirements of corporate law. You mustn't influence, govern, or dominate the affairs of the company *too* greatly. This doesn't mean you shouldn't manage proactively. You should. But you must make sure that your personal affairs and corporate affairs are kept separate. You shouldn't commingle corporate funds and personal funds. You shouldn't pay your personal expenses with corporate funds. Here are some other points that you should be careful of: Keep your personal affairs and corporate affairs as separate entities in all transactions and in bookkeeping; be sure to qualify the stock under the state security laws when you want to issue shares; make certain you have adequate capitalization to be seen as financially responsible; conform with the corporation laws in holding shareholders' and directors' meetings.

The factors that you should be aware of in making sure that your company behaves like a good corporate citizen vary from state to state. Your attorney can give you appropriate guidance here.

Tax Implications for Small Corporations

On January 1, 1979 a new Federal Income tax schedule for corporations was put into effect. Starting on that date, corporate income is taxed according to the following schedule:

Taxable income	Percent
$ 0 to 25,000	17
25 to 50,000	20
50 to 75,000	30
75 to 100,000	40
Over 100,000	46

The closely held small corporation has certain flexibility in developing its capital structure that is not available to the large corporation, which must go to the public for financing. For example, you may be able to have your few shareholders contribute some part of the corporation's capital in return for promissory notes rather than for stock. This becomes a bona fide debt of your company on which you must pay interest. The interest so paid is deductible by your corporation, and the repayment of the principal doesn't result in taxable income to the lending shareholders.

When your company pays dividends to its shareholders, this payment is not deductible by the corporation. The shareholder must include dividends in reporting income for tax purposes.

Tax planning, as we've said before, can be exceedingly important in the overall planning for your corporation. You should give careful consideration to debt financing by your associate shareholders. In your closely held corporation you should weigh the tax benefits available to you and nontax disadvantages that you can foresee. You should take into account such items as the disadvantages of fixed maturity, fixed interest-bearing obligations, your corporation's potential need for credit from third persons, and the effect on credit of debt owed to shareholders.

If you decide to use debt financing you must face the questions of "how much?" and "what kind?" The wrong answers to these questions can lose the tax benefits you expect. And, what can be worse, if for several years your company has engaged in financing practices that are later shown to be improper, your tax benefits may be replaced by liabilities for back taxes plus interest. This discussion should suggest to you the desirability of consulting professional counsel—a qualified accountant or tax lawyer—before deciding in these matters.

Transferability of Ownership Interest

The corporate form carries with it another advantage. It's easy to transfer ownership. You can add to the owners by simply allowing outsiders to buy stock in your corporation. Or if a shareholder wants to sell out, the procedure is straightforward; the shareholder's stock is sold to someone else and ownership of that portion of the company represented by the shares automatically transfers. In any circumstance, you must observe the legal formalities required in the sale of shares.

If you, or those of you who formed the corporation, want to hold the ownership to a small select group, you may readily restrict the transferability of stock. You may make provision for such restriction in the charter or articles of incorporation, in the bylaws, or in a separate agreement among the shareholders. An agreement among the original shareholders is usually the simplest way of keeping the shares among those you prefer. This agreement would provide for a first refusal or option to purchase from shareholders wishing to sell their shares.

Board of Directors

The top management of a corporation rests in a board of directors by law. Too often the small businessperson overlooks the possibility of getting sound advice and counsel from a board composed of experienced and knowledgeable members. A small, closely held corporation will very often have on its board the principal shareholder, spouse, or other relative, and perhaps one other person, a close friend. These may be the people most easily available to you as principal shareholder. You should, however, spend whatever energy it takes to assemble a "working" board rather than the "titular" board you may have with relatives and friends.

Your working board should have individuals who can give your company strength where it's needed. You'll recall the three basic strengths a small company can't do without (or any size company for that matter): production—ability to get out the product or service in good style; marketing—competence in identifying the right market segment and developing effective techniques for reaching it at the right price in the right quantity; and financial management expertise—ability to make appropriate financial plans for the business and to control the flow and use of money to the company's best advantage. You may use these requirements as a guide in choosing people for your board of directors. If your strength is in production, you will want to make sure that you have one person on your board with a solid marketing background and one with wide experience in financial management and control. Your working board will then be a source of counsel and strength in helping you make the proper decisions needed to run your company efficiently and profitably.

A word of caution: In the past many people took on directorships in corporations for the prestige of the title or for the sake of helping a friend. Titular boards were common. This has changed today. Court decisions have recently imposed severe personal penalties on directors whose companies suffered large losses attributable to their negligence in performing their duties. In typical cases, directors have relied on financial data supplied by company management without their own independent analysis, or they have failed to use independent business judgment in assessing management recommendations. Because of this, many experienced business executives are now wary of becoming directors. You must be able to show competent people that you're willing to listen to and take sound advice if you want them to become directors of your corporation.

Inside versus Outside Boards
Boards of directors may be classified in another way as "inside" or "outside" boards. If the majority of your directors are chosen from within the company, your board is called an inside board; if the majority come from outside the company, your board is considered an outside board. You can readily see the advantages of an outside board for giving you advice based upon an objective point of view. Contrary to the case with inside board members, outside board members aren't dependent upon you for their jobs. They can use their best judgment in independent fashion to chart a course of action for your company. They're not swayed by the specter of losing their positions if they should disagree with you, the chief executive officer.

Although it's sometimes hard to accept advice from outsiders, you'd be in a much better position to form sound judgments by listening carefully to what a competent director might say. But no matter whether you choose to have an inside or an outside board, you should select only competent people to serve as your directors.

175

Tax Treatment of Corporations

Corporations are treated like individuals for federal income tax purposes. This is different from partnerships, which are tax-reporting but not tax-paying entities. As long as the corporation observes legal requirements and behaves like a corporation should, its identity will be honored. This means that the corporation has been set up for a legitimate purpose, that there is no fraud or sham, as for example, the intent to avoid taxes.

A taxpayer has the right, of course, to reduce taxes or to avoid them by legitimate means. One technique for reducing taxes under special circumstances is the adoption of what is known as a Subchapter S corporation.

Special rules and regulations of the Internal Revenue Code of 1954, commonly known as Subchapter S, permit the setting aside of the corporate entity at the request of the shareholders. The effect of setting aside the corporate entity is, for tax purposes only, to have the shareholders treated as individual taxpayers. In other words, the income or loss of the corporation passes through to the individual shareholders as if they were partners.

Subchapter S status can be obtained only by small business corporations. These corporations are defined as having only one class of stock and no more than 15 shareholders. Shareholders must be natural persons, estates, or trusts.

If you and your shareholders have appreciable outside income, and you forecast losses for your company for a couple of years ahead, you could decide that Subchapter S would allow you to reduce your income taxes for that period. If so, you'd follow the required procedure to achieve Subchapter S for your company.

You may elect Subchapter S for the next fiscal year any time within the current fiscal year or within the first 75 days of the new fiscal year. However, a new corporation desiring to start under Subchapter S must elect to do so within 75 days of filing papers of incorporation. If you miss this time period you'll have to wait until the end of the current fiscal year to qualify for Subchapter S status for the following year.

You must have the consent of all the shareholders to get the Subchapter S status. Once achieved, the status continues until you voluntarily terminate it. Termination may also come about by transfer of stock to a new shareholder who doesn't consent to the election or by the corporation ceasing to qualify as a small business corporation. The penalty for terminating is that you can't renew Subchapter S status for the year of termination plus four years.

EXPENSES OF DIFFERENT FORMS OF BUSINESS ORGANIZATION   **1** C (3), **9** A (1)

Cost may be an important consideration in adopting the corporate form. You'll find relative costs for forming the sole proprietorship, the general partnership, the limited partnership, and the corporation in Table 10-1.

The sole proprietorship is the least expensive to start. The partnership involves

Table 10-1   Comparison of Expenses for Organizational Set-Up (State of California)
(Estimated for 1980)

Expense Item	Proprietorship	General Partnership	Limited Partnership	Corporation
Licenses and permits	Varies with local government imposing fees	Varies with local government imposing fees	Varies with local government imposing fees	Varies with local government imposing fees
Fictitious business name statement	$10.00 for each fictitious name	$10.00 for each fictitious name	$10.00 for each fictitious name	$10.00 for each fictitious name
Attorney's fees	Varies with amount of work done; attorney's fees ordinarily will be less than for other business formats	Varies depending primarily on complexity of partnership agreement	Varies depending on complexity of partnership agreement and certificate and qualification of securities, if required	(See below)
Certificate of limited partnership recording fee			$3.00 plus $1.00 for each page after first page	
Qualification of limited partnership interests under California Corporate Securities Law, if required			Same as corporation	
Articles of incorporation filing fee				$65.00
Recording fee				$2.00
Secretary of State				$3.00 per copy if furnished
Certification				$2.00 plus $.30 per page, if Secretary of State prepares copies
Recording fee, county clerk, county of principal place of business				$3.00 plus $1.00 per page after first page
Prepayment of minimum franchise (income) tax				$200.00
Attorney's fees for preparation of articles of incorporation, first minutes of first meetings, and other initial documents				Varies, depending on complexity of corporate structure and work required for tax, securities, and other regulatory problems ($400 to $1000 for standard, new incorporations)
Qualification of securities, if not exempt				Fees of department of corporations vary depending on type of qualification and value of securities to be issued
Purchase of minute book, seal, and form stock certificates				Ordinarily under $160

relationships with another or others. To protect the parties in the relationship, an agreement should be drawn by a lawyer. This means that fees for this service will have to be paid.

Incorporating will take the most money in the beginning. In the long run it may prove to be the best arrangement for many of the reasons indicated before. The primary costs of incorporation are:

- Those payable at the time the charter or articles of incorporation are filed with the state agency. A state franchise tax or a minimum state income tax may be included.

- Attorneys' fees.

- Miscellaneous charges and costs including stock certificates, corporate seal, and minute book.

These costs are amortizable over a period of usually not less than five years.

Licenses and Permits

You'll have to comply with several requirements for licenses and permits when you incorporate.

You must get a federal identification number for use on federal tax returns, statements, and other documents. This number may be obtained through the Internal Revenue Service or the Social Security Administration.

You'll have to comply with state and local requirements for business licenses. If your company plans to sell tangible goods, you must check for sales and use taxes, both state and local. You should obtain the necessary permits before you open for business.

Other Taxes

Your company will have to withhold income tax and Social Security tax (FICA) from the taxable wages paid your employees. It must also pay a Social Security tax equal to that withheld from your employees' wages and must deposit the withheld taxes in an authorized commercial bank depository or a federal reserve bank, with an accompanying form, Federal Tax Deposit Form 501. The deposits are to be made semimonthly, monthly, or quarterly, depending upon the amount of the tax. Your company must also file an Employer's Quarterly Federal Tax Return (IRS Form 941).

Officers or other persons charged with the responsibility of withholding employee taxes must fulfill this responsibility meticulously. If they fail to do so, they may be personally liable for a 100 percent penalty for failure to collect those taxes.

As a corporate employer, you may be subject to the Federal Unemployment Tax. If so, you'll be required to deposit taxes together with the Federal Tax Deposit Form 508. This procedure is similar to that of handling withholding tax. You'll be required also to file an Unemployment Tax Return (IRS Form 940) and pay any balance due on or before January 31 of each year.

178

You must find out what you need to do to comply with workmen's compensation laws, which are different in each state. Generally, as an employer, your company must be insured against workmen's compensation liability by an authorized insurer or be self-insured with the consent of the appropriate government agency.

You'll want expert guidance in fulfilling these various federal and state legal responsibilities. You'll want to count on your attorney and your accountant in these matters, both to make sure that all bases are covered and to save your time for the important management duties your business will demand.

Other Forms of Organization

Other forms of organization are available to you besides the three basic ones we've dealt with. They include joint ventures, real estate investment trusts, condominiums, and not-for-profit corporations. These are special adaptations of the three primary structures we've discussed.

A joint venture is really a partnership but for a special limited purpose. A condominium is a form of property ownership but not a form of business. These variations are intended for special purposes. You should seek legal advice before adopting any of them.

PROTECTION OF IDEAS AND CONCEPTS   **1** A (1), **2** A (1), **3** B (4), **4**

If you have originated a new or useful concept for a product or process you should take precautionary steps to protect it from being pirated. Ideas of various kinds, depending upon their intent, may be protected by patents, trademarks, service marks, or copyrights.

Patents

Patents may be obtained on any: "new, useful, and unobvious process (primarily industrial or technical); machine; manufacture or composition of matter (generally chemical compounds, formulas and the like); or any new, useful, and unobvious improvement thereof." Patents may also be obtained on any distinct and new variety of plant, other than tuber propagated, that is asexually reproduced; and on any new and unobvious original and ornamental design for an article of manufacture.

You should note that ideas in themselves aren't patentable. Neither are methods of doing business, an inoperable device, or an improvement in a device that's obvious or the result of the "application of mere technical skill."

The Commissioner of Patents, U.S. Department of Commerce, issues patents. A patent gives the inventor the exclusive right to make, use, or sell the patent for a period of seventeen years in the United States, its territories and possessions. Design patents for ornamental devices are granted for three and a half, seven, or fourteen years, as the applicant elects.

Disclosure Document Program

When you conceive of an idea that you think patentable, you should take advantage of a service called the Disclosure Document Program offered by the U.S. Patent Office. To use this service, you or your attorney or agent prepares and submits a document with the aim of establishing priority of your invention. The Patent Office keeps this document in its files for two years. It is then destroyed unless it's referred to in a separate letter in a related patent application you have filed within the two-year period.

You shouldn't think of the two-year period as a period of grace; you can't wait until the end of the period to file application for patent. If you do, you risk losing the benefits of the procedure. You must show diligence in completing the invention or in filing application for patent after sending in the Disclosure Document.

The Disclosure Document isn't a patent application. It doesn't lessen the value of the conventional witnessed and notarized records as evidence of the conception of an invention. When you submit a Disclosure Document, you're establishing a more credible form of evidence that you've originated the concept than you would by sending yourself or someone else a disclosure letter by registered mail.

Your disclosure document should be clear, with enough explanation so someone with a reasonable knowledge in the field could make and use your invention. As in other matters having to do with legal protection, you should choose an expert to negotiate the complex procedures of securing a patent.

Trademarks and Service Marks

A trademark is a distinguishing name or symbol identifying a product used in commerce subject to regulation by Congress. The "design of a flying red horse" is one example of the description of a trademark. A trademark can be protected by registration against use by others for a period of twenty years. It may be renewed for an additional twenty years. Registration is done by the Commissioner of Patents, U.S. Patent Office. In addition to the federal government, most states offer trademark registration and service mark registration.

A service mark is similar to a trademark in that it's a distinguishing name or symbol identifying a service rather than a product.

You'll find the following descriptions of trademarks and service marks helpful in clearing up the differences between them. These are as given by the State of California Division of Business and Industry Development.

Trademark

A trademark is a work; a name, a symbol; a device; or a combination of these elements. ("Device" means generally a "design" or an "artistic figure.")

A trademark is used to identify an applicant's merchandise and to enable customers to recognize applicant's products and to distinguish them from the products of others.

A trademark should not be described ordinarily as a label. The word "label" is

180

not included in the definition of a trademark. The trademark most usually consists of part of the matter printed on a label.

Not everything printed on a label or on a container is part of the trademark. Statements of ingredients, the name and address of a business, cautions, instructions for use: these are not part of the trademark. A trademark is the customer's recognition factor. It is intended to be something that will catch the customer's attention and enable him to buy again a product he previously bought and liked.

Service Mark

The description must be brief but accurate. Most service marks are very simple. For example, the words "The Fog Cutters" is a service mark identifying restaurant services.

A service mark is a word or words, or a design or designs, or combinations of a word or words and design or designs. A service mark is used to advertise services. The function of a service mark is to distinguish one person's services from the services of others. Prospective customers are made familiar with the service mark by the advertising thereof. If the services are excellent, the customer in theory will deal with the person using the service mark when he again needs the particular service.

The following are examples of services: banking services; real estate broker's services; motel services; entertainment services by a musical group.

You should take advantage of the commercial benefits of a distinctive trademark or service mark for your business. These marks help your customers to identify and remember your product or service. And if they've once liked what you've offered, they're going to ask for more when they have need. Your special symbol will help to stimulate repeat business.

Copyrights

You may get protection of your *literary* or *artistic* work through a copyright. Copyrights are processed through the Copyright Office attached to the Library of Congress, Washington, D.C. In a fashion similar to patents, trademarks, and service marks, copyrights provide a legal monopoly to the holder. Copyrights are effective for the life of the author plus fifty years.

As a small business owner, you may wish to copyright material you use in promoting your business: catalogs, catalog sheets, brochures, and instructions on how to assemble or use your product. To get copyright protection, you must first make a claim by imprinting a copyright notice in front of the item you're planning to publish. You can follow this standard form: © Copyright, followed by the year of publication and the name of the individual or company originating the piece. After publication, you must make application for copyright to the Copyright Office, Library of Congress.

Marketable But Unpatentable Ideas

Once in a while you may hit upon an idea for a product or service that's not patentable but that might be good for some firm other than your own. You may want to get paid for your idea, but you may be reluctant to disclose it for fear of its being pirated. There's a way you can get the protection you would want in a situation like this. However, you can readily see that to work out a successful deal with a company capable of capitalizing on your idea presents substantial difficulties. You'd probably be approaching a company much larger than your own, with many more resources. You'll find most such companies chary of inventors or "idea persons." Nevertheless, you may be able to find the rare company that's willing to listen to you. And it may be possible to come to a mutually satisfactory arrangement based upon a binding contractual agreement.

You should know that ideas become public property under the law as soon as they're divulged. You shouldn't disclose your idea in its entirety, therefore, before you've reached agreement with the firm you're dealing with, and the agreement has been put into a binding contract signed by them and by you.

The Small Business Administration suggests use of a letter, which when signed by both parties, becomes a contract. It should be prepared in duplicate so each party may have a copy. A typical letter is shown in Figure 10-3.

This contract binds the firm to hold in confidence any features not already known to it. It may not use your idea without paying you as stipulated in the contract. By the same token, the company is protected from any unwarranted claims you may choose to make.

Advantage of Counsel

To protect your creative idea, whether through patent, trademark, service mark, copyright, or in the disclosure of a unique idea to an outside firm, you should depend upon professional counsel. You'll find that's what it takes to ensure proper attention to the details of these legal procedures. And you'll surely recognize the wisdom of using such help in the beginning. It's far less expensive—and far less stressful—to avoid legal entanglements by proper procedure up front than to resolve a legal problem later by law suit.

FINDING AN ATTORNEY AND AN ACCOUNTANT

We've said that it's good practice, indeed it's essential, that you have the help of two kinds of professionals when you go into business: an attorney and an accountant. We're often asked, "How do you locate a competent attorney and a competent accountant?" The procedure most often used seems to be similar to that in finding a doctor or a dentist, that is, reference from others.

Friends, relatives, or neighbors may have been satisfied with a lawyer or accountant and will give you their names. You should also check with your banker. In any event don't limit your choice. Get the names of two or three in each category. And a very good way to locate competent professionals is to talk with the owners of

John Doe Co.
123 Fourth Street
Anytown, U.S.A.

Gentlemen:

I have developed a new idea for the packaging of your product which I believe would greatly increase your sales and profits. The new method of packaging would not raise production costs.

If you are interested in details of the idea, I shall be glad to forward you complete information if you will kindly sign the enclosed agreement form. Promptly upon receipt of the signed form, I shall forward to you all information I have regarding the idea.

Sincerely,

Robert Roe

AGREEMENT TO REVIEW IDEA

We, the undersigned, agree to receive in confidence full details about an idea for product packaging to be submitted for our consideration by Robert Roe.

It is further understood that we assume no responsibility whatever with respect to features which can be demonstrated to be already known to us. We also agree not to divulge any details of the idea submitted without permission of Robert Roe or to make use of any feature or information of which the said Robert Roe is the originator, without payment of compensation to be fixed by negotiation with the said Robert Roe or his lawful representative.

It is specifically understood that, in receiving the idea of Robert Roe, the idea is being received and will be reviewed in confidence and that, within a period of 30 days, we will report to said Robert Roe the results of our findings and will advise whether or not we are interested in negotiating for the purchase of the right to use said idea.

Company _____

Street and Number _____

City _____ Zone _____ State _____

Official to receive disclosures (please type)

_____ Title _____

Date _____ Signature _____

Accepted: _____

Robert Roe, Inventor

Figure 10-3 Suggested Contract for Submission and Review of Ideas

small businesses comparable to yours, but not directly competitive. Ask who handles their legal and accounting problems and find out if they've been satsified with the services they got. Check with professors who teach entrepreneurship and small business management in colleges or universities in your community. They usually have contacts with attorneys and accountants who specialize in small business clients. Compile a list of prospects among these attorneys and accountants.

Make an appointment with each. Say that you're interested in an exploratory meeting as you're starting a new business and want to locate competent professional help. Ask if there will be a charge for a preliminary meeting. Most professionals won't charge for a preliminary meeting or, if they do, will charge only a minimal fee. Be prepared to tell the attorney or accountant what your plans are for your business. Be prepared to ask the questions you consider important. Ask what clients are typically served by the individual's firm. Make sure that the firm doesn't handle direct competitors. And don't be afraid to talk openly about fees.

By following this procedure you'll be able to decide on an attorney and an accountant who would suit your business—and you personally. You should feel comfortable with the person because you'll work together for a long time. Your attorney and your accountant will be intimately involved in your affairs. The closer the association the more likely you are to get beneficial results from their efforts, and the happier the relationship will be.

Once you decide on an attorney or an accountant, that person can very likely help you find the other.

DECIDING SOME KEY LEGAL ISSUES   SUMMARY

In this chapter we've discussed three basic legal structures you can choose from in setting up your business: sole proprietorship, partnership, and corporation. Each has advantages and disadvantages.

The sole proprietorship is the easiest to start and has the lowest first costs. You can open your doors for business with the least amount of red tape and the least cost. However, as a sole proprietor, all your personal worth is exposed to the demands of creditors. You can protect yourself from some risks through insurance. In other cases your entire worth would be open to attachment in case of a major law suit.

The partnership, which involves you in an intimate relationship with one or more people, permits combining different strengths in building competent management for your company. You should take great care to prepare an agreement among the partners that would spell out actions to be taken in case of disagreement, dissolution, or termination of the partnership. Because any partner can commit the others to a business activity without their knowledge, it's of the utmost importance that you make sure you and your partners can get along well under all conditions before you work up the partnership agreement.

The partnership doesn't provide protection for the personal assets of the partners. The situation here is similar to that of the sole proprietorship. A special

184

form of partnership does provide this protection for those partners who wish to invest money but not time in the venture; this is the limited partnership, which is used mainly for financing and managing large real estate projects.

The third major form of business structure open to you is the corporation. The corporation may be considered an artificial person sanctioned by law. If you elect the corporate form, you gain two great advantages: You and your investors are protected against exposure of your personal assets in case of suit as long as your corporation observes legal requirements; and your company has the capability of enduring beyond the active participation of its original owners.

The corporation is the most expensive form of structure to launch and requires more legal steps. Its advantages may sway you to adopt it, if not in your start-up condition, perhaps at a later point in the growth of your company.

A special form of corporate structure, known as Subchapter S, permits the shareholders in a small corporation to assume the losses or profits of the company as individuals, thus bypassing the tax consequences to the corporation itself. Under some circumstances, as when the corporation is just starting and is losing money and the individual shareholders have substantial outside income, the shareholders may offset some income by assuming the losses of the corporation in proportion to their shares in the company. This, of course, could be advantageous to you if the circumstances fit.

In this chapter we've outlined some procedures you may take to secure patents, copyrights, trademarks, and service marks. We've suggested a way of selling an original concept to another company and protecting your interests while doing it. But we've also said that you'll find it a difficult process as most companies are not inclined to listen to outsiders.

Finally, we've suggested ways of choosing an attorney and an accountant. And we've stressed the advantages of having competent counsel in legal and financial matters.

Deciding on Some Key Legal Matters

This worksheet covers some major points you'll want to consider in deciding on the legal form of business structure to adopt. Because each business is unique, it's not possible for us to suggest all the items you should think through when you begin to deal with the legal procedures. A good way to check your thinking about these matters is to review the other worksheets in the book when you work on the agreements you want and the legal requirements you'll have to meet. Studying carefully these aspects of going into business is time well spent. It's much less expensive—and much less anxiety producing—to take care of possible legal contingencies ahead of time, rather than to have to resolve them by law suit.

1. On the basis of the advantages and disadvantages of the three legal forms of business structure given in this chapter, decide on the form that appears best for your business.

    I have chosen the following form for my business: sole proprietorship _____; partnership _____; corporation _____; other _____.

    Here are my reasons for preferring this form:

    _____

    _____

    _____

    _____

    _____

    _____

    _____

    _____

    _____

    _____

2. If a sole proprietorship, I'm going to use my own name _____. If I'm going to use a fictitious name, I've recorded it with the proper agency in my community _____. If a partnership, I've chosen my partner or partners with special attention to the following:

    I've known _____ _____ for _____ years. I have a firm knowledge that we can get along well together, even in times when things go wrong _____. The following typical experience shows that we can talk things out and come to a happy solution when we hit a difficult situation:

    _____

    _____

_____

_____

_____

_____

_____

_____

_____

3. We've agreed to refer to a third-party arbitrator if we can't resolve an argument ourselves. The person or arbitrator we'll go to is _____

4. My main strength in the business is: technical _____; financial management _____; marketing _____. In addition, I believe I can add the following competencies to the management of the business:

_____

_____

_____

_____

_____

5. My partner or partners will add the following strengths to management:_____

_____

_____

_____

_____

_____

_____

6. We've talked through the basis for a written agreement of partnership and have covered the following points:

- Percentage of contribution of capital and therefore of ownership and sharing of profit and loss

- Buy–sell agreement if a partner wants to get out

- Succession of ownership if one of us dies

- The fiscal year we should use

- Assigned duties and responsibilities

- Set up a formal accounting arrangement for partnership affairs

- The name of the company is to be: _____

- Have agreed on an attorney to help us prepare the partnership agreement. The attorney's name is: _____.

■ Have decided on an accountant to help us with financial matters: The accountant's name is: _____.

7. If I'm going to the corporate form, there are to be a limited number of shareholders, and they are:

_____   _____

_____   _____

_____   _____

_____   _____

8. We've decided on the following attorney to incorporate and advise us: _____.

9. We've chosen this name for our company: _____

_____.

10. We've decided on the organization chart for starting our company. It looks like this:

11. Attached are resumés of the people on the chart.

12. We've chosen the following, and they've agreed to act as directors of our company:

_____   _____

_____   _____

They have these special strengths in giving us advice and counsel: _____

_____

_____

_____

13. Special Notes. Note here any special items you've thought about, for example, the possibility of adopting the Subchapter S form of corporation; the use of an inside or outside board of directors; patent applications; trademarks; service marks; copyrights; insurance coverage; or anything else that has legal implications for the business and the shareholders.

_____

_____

_____

_____

_____

_____

_____

_____

The legal procedures in establishing the form of a business can become quite intricate as you have probably noted from some portions of this chapter. It's beyond the scope of this book to get into elaborate detail on legal matters—indeed, it's a waste of time for the prospective businessperson to try to become a legal expert. The following references are therefore intended to give you additional general information and other points of view on the legal forms of business enterprise.

Dan Steinhoff, *Small Business Management Fundamentals*, McGraw-Hill, New York, 1974. You'll find a clear and easy-to-understand presentation of the three basic forms of organization: the sole proprietorship, the partnership, and the corporation. There is an excellent section on the federal tax implications attached to these forms of organization.

J. K. Lasser, *How to Run a Small Business*, 4th ed., McGraw-Hill, New York, 1974. In Chapter Six, "Choosing a Form for Your Business," there's a description of the advantages and disadvantages of the three basic forms of ownership. The chapter is short and takes the form of a somewhat expanded outline. You'll find it useful as a quick refresher on some of the more important points about each of the three forms of business structure.

H. N. Broom and Justin G. Longenecker, *Small Business Management*, 3rd ed., South-Western Publishing Co., Cincinnati, 1971. This is a well-recognized college text. Chapter 8, "Legal Considerations in Starting a Business" presents a well-organized summary of key points from selecting an attorney to taxes and government regulations. You'll find its concise approach welcome in checking basic concepts about legal matters in forming a business.

Patrick R. Liles, *New Business Ventures and the Entrepreneur*, Richard D. Irwin, Inc. Homewood, Ill., 1974. A note called, "The Legal Forms of Business Enterprise," pp. 75–101, contains a summary treatment of the several forms of business organizations. Their relative advantages and disadvantages and the complexity of setting them up are treated in a well-organized way.

Chapter 11

Buying a Going Business*

TO BUY OR NOT TO BUY

FINDING THE BUSINESS TO BUY

SCREENING THE OFFERINGS IN DEPTH

PICKING A LOSER

PERSONAL FACTORS IN THE TRANSACTION

EVALUATING AND PRICING THE BUSINESS

CLOSING THE DEAL

---

*Code numbers referring to the Outline for Developing Your Basic Business Plan
(Appendix A) are not used in this chapter. The worksheets in this chapter will guide
you through the planning required to assess the desirability of buying an on-going
business. When you have finished the Worksheets check the items in Appendix A,
point by point, to make sure you haven't omitted any important considerations.

"**S**ome of my friends said I'd paid ten thousand dollars too much for my auto wrecking business in White Plains," said Dave Romney, newly retired and enjoying life in the Florida sun. "The owner was a middle-aged bachelor who'd been spending more and more time sailing on the Hudson in the three years before I bought. He'd let the business run down; one of his employees managed it in his absence—and it was just barely eking out a living for him.

"But I saw opportunity there. I felt I could turn the business around fast. After all, I'd had years of experience in auto wrecking and used parts sales. I could see two major ways to increase profits. One was to concentrate on late model cars by building good relations with insurance companies—offer prime prices for wrecked cars they covered. The other was to get the word around that parts for late cars were available at my place. I called on the local repair people and put ads in the town papers.

"Well, I was right. The business made good money. Not long ago I sold it—and here I am, my wife and I, quite comfortable as retired senior citizens."

What Dave Romney had done was to build a run down business to prosperity through the skills he had achieved in his past experience. If you have the background and can see ways to improve the earning power of the business, you may be able to do what Dave Romney did. In most cases, however, you'd avoid the dying business.

Either way requires detailed study to dig out the facts you need to make up your mind to buy or not to buy. To evaluate the potential of the going business, your investigation should follow essentially the same pattern you'd use if you were starting a new business. Study of the pertinent chapters and the appendixes in this text will allow you to arrive at key ideas, methods, and techniques to:

- Raise important questions you may not otherwise have hit upon

- See how to analyze significant factors in the operations of the business

- Make the necessary projections in marketing and financial planning to estimate future earnings of the business.

You'll find that the potential earning power of the business will very likely be the pivotal factor in your decision to buy—and in your decision about the price you'd be willing to pay.

TO BUY OR NOT TO BUY?

Your investigation of going businesses will reveal both advantages and disadvantages in buying. Before you decide to buy you should make sure that the advantages clearly outweigh the disadvantages because *one major disadvantage can easily overbalance any number of advantages.*

Advantages in Buying

Significant advantages in buying a going business can be as follows:

- Reduced risk. Buying a business that is already successful is less risky than starting one from scratch. The firm has a proven market segment with an established clientele. Management has established sound relations with bankers, suppliers, and customers. If location is important, the business shows by its record that the location is satisfactory. A usable inventory will very likely be on hand. And acquiring some experienced and expert employees with the purchase of the business is not uncommon. All these advantages tend to reduce the risks encountered in starting a new business.

- Faster profits. The successful business will return a profit much faster than the new business. As the buyer, you would not have to struggle through the problems of building a business from the start. You'll recall that most new businesses don't bring in enough money during the first year or so to pay the owner a reasonable salary, if any at all. The going concern can pay you a salary right from the start if you make the transition to ownership smoothly.

- Easier planning. Financial and market planning are much easier for the going concern than for the new business venture. Historical records afford a much firmer basis for projecting financial and marketing data than the information gathered in planning for a new venture. Knowing the strengths and weaknesses of the existing company, you'd be able to build on the strengths and overcome the weaknesses. Using the market/product-service matrix described in Chapter 3, for example, you could plan improved or new products or services for further penetration of existing markets, or expansion into new ones. And reference to Chapter 6 will help you to identify the point of the existing product or service in its life cycle, so you can judge when to launch the new product or service.

- One financial transaction. The new business venture usually takes more than one financial transaction before it becomes capitalized, well-launched, and stabilized. Buying the going concern, however, can ordinarily be accomplished in one transaction. Once through this you can focus on marketing and delivering the product or service; your energies are concentrated and you can manage more effectively to achieve the profit you're after.

Nevertheless, where you find advantages more than likely you'll find disadvantages also.

194

Disadvantages in Buying

Major disadvantages that may occur in buying a going business can be:

- Inheriting ill will. As the buyer, you may inherit ill will. The product or service may have been allowed to deteriorate, alienating customers. Or the attitude of sales personnel toward customers may have destroyed a good image. In taking over ownership, ill will can get you off on the wrong foot.

- Inheriting incompetents. It is possible to acquire incompetent personnel with the purchase of the going business. Indeed, one reason for owners wanting to sell may be their inability to acquire or hold competent help. This can be a serious flaw in the business. You should check it carefully.

- Bad precedents. Some bad precedents in policies, procedures, or customs may be inherited with the business. These could be in external relationships, such as selling to poor credit risks or long delays in paying company bills. Also, bad conditions could exist in internal operations, such as not having a consistent and well understood salary review program for employees, or having unsafe working conditions.

- Antiquated facilities. The buildings and equipment may need modernization. Nothing is so frustrating as trying to fit a manufacturing line into chopped up floor space or turning out accurate screw machine parts in quantity on an old-fashioned, slow machine. Make sure that the facilities are up-to-date and adequate for your purpose.

- Obsolescent inventory. The inventory of merchandise, raw stock, or supplies may be obsolescent. The usability of inventory is often extremely difficult to determine, yet you should conscientiously make the effort. The seller may be carrying inventory on the books at original value when in fact it may be essentially worthless. If you are not aware of this, you might pay good money for worthless stock.

- Uncooperative landlord. In buying a business in leased premises, you may inherit an uncooperative landlord. On occasion, this can not only be exasperating, but also frustrating. If you wind up with a landlord who won't make major repairs to plumbing in the plant or repair a leaky roof, you may have to spend precious time in argument, or in legal procedures, which take both time and money to get a satisfactory solution.

- Overpaying. A major disadvantage in buying can come from overpaying for the business. If you should overpay significantly, you'll find that your profits will be limited. It will take a long time to recover from this hidden loss. You'll need to plan proactively to increase the profitability of the business.

You can see from this list of possible disadvantages in buying a business that you must be careful not to take on any more problems than you have to. What is needed is your careful, systematic study and analysis of the proposed purchase. This doesn't mean that uncovering one or two disadvantages should prevent you from buying the business; if you see your way clear to overcoming a couple of minor disadvantages with effort you can comfortably manage, then you might use them as bargaining points to arrive at a reduced price for the business.

STEPS IN BUYING A BUSINESS

You'll go through several phases in assessing and buying a business. The list given here suggests a logical set of steps to follow. These are not necessarily in sequence. You may have to back up a bit on occasion to pick up some details that occur to you as a result of your findings as you go. But this list will give you an overall guide to help you on your way.

Look at Yourself

If this is your first venture into business, examine your own entrepreneurial characteristics. Reread Chapter 2 and check your answers to the questions raised in Worksheet 1. Assuming that you're satisfied with your entrepreneurial qualities, you should then answer the next question, about the business.

Look at Your Business Experience

What business do you know and like? Recall that we've recommended that you should be technically competent to produce the product or the service of the business you enter. Such competence keeps you clear of the pitfall of trying to learn the business while managing it. It goes without saying that you should really like the business. You'll spend so much time at it that it would be disastrous not to enjoy what you're doing.

FINDING THE BUSINESS TO BUY

When you search for a business to buy you'll find that it takes much time and energy. You must be prepared to be patient and to spend some money in the effort. You'll use several sources of information in your search: newspaper and trade journal ads, business brokers, bankers, lawyers, accountants, and people in the business.

Advertisements

Newspapers carry business opportunities advertising. Ads in this category tend to be sketchy, telling little of importance about the business. Here are a couple of examples drawn from a leading metropolitan paper:

LANDSCAPING Co., set up for $1 million operation per year. Under capitalized. Good business opport. Owner, 919/624-4911.

PAINT SALES (exper. a must) to invest in small but profitable paint mfg. co. Owner to retire. P.O. Box 701 Elk Grove, N.Y. 40905.

As you can see, ads like these don't offer much information. All they do is give you some general idea of what the business is. They say, "Here's a door labeled landscaping or paint sales. Open it and find out, if you're clever enough, what this business really is and what opportunity it offers."

In one case you're to phone the owner; presumably you could arrange an appointment to explore details. In the other case the owner is hiding behind a box number. On inquiry, you may find yourself dealing with a business broker, not the owner. If it turns out to be the owner, you may ask why he or she should choose to hide behind a box number.

Box numbers are used for a variety of reasons. They can conceal the broker behind the number (prospective buyers usually think they can get a better deal directly from the owner). Public advertising of a business for sale can have bad effects on the business. Key employees may decide to leave. Creditors may get edgy, particularly if the firm's credit is shaky. Customers may search for new suppliers if they are uneasy about a firm that is for sale.

Many approaches are used to advertise businesses for sale and to reply to ads. In some cases all parties are frank and open. In others, they are secretive. Both approaches have worked in practice. However, in the overall picture, everyone saves time (and therefore money) by laying the cards on the table. Owners pinpoint the requirements for prospective buyers when they are specific about the business: what kind of business, cash requirements, price, and other important points. Searchers can shorten the search by being frank about what they're looking for, and how much they can pay.

Although frankness may put you on a few sucker lists when you search for a business to buy, it can give you clear advantage not only with owners, but also with brokers. Brokers will see that you mean business and are not merely shopping. Knowing what you want, they'll try to find what you're looking for. Their income comes from a percentage on the sales they make—and they don't want to waste time and effort in making a living. One of their most annoying tasks is to rid themselves of prospects who are just shopping—who have no intention of buying.

Business Brokers

Your search for a business to buy will inevitably lead you to the business broker. Business brokers work like real estate brokers. They are paid by percentage commission on the sales they arrange. Commissions, regulated by the state, can amount to ten percent of the sale price.

Business brokerages tend to be small, often one-person operations. In smaller towns and rural areas business listings will often be part of the typical combined real estate and insurance office. In metropolitan areas, brokerage firms may be larger and will often specialize in one kind of business, such as electronics manufacturing or bars and restaurants. Brokers who specialize develop a keen feeling for pricing the businesses they deal in. For example, one broker who deals in liquor stores, bars, and restaurants, states that these properties are valued at five times their net profit, regardless of the worth of the fixtures, equipment, and furniture. This is one way to judge the worth of the business; for the entrepreneurially minded seeker a better way—setting the price on the future earning power of the business—will be discussed later.

The business brokerage is a service business. It requires little capital to enter. This accounts to a considerable extent for one-person brokerages. Some of these may be seedy operations working from a rented desk in a run-down office building. On the other hand, you'll find well-managed operations that can be of real service to you. You'll want to use several brokers in your search because their small size usually limits their selection of businesses available to them.

Getting Leads through Other Sources

Don't overlook your ability to get leads through your personal connections. Your banker can be helpful in identifying businesses that can be bought. Through their own experience bankers can direct you to reputable brokerage firms. Your attorney and accountant come across prospective opportunities in their work with their clients. They know when a business client wants to retire and sell or when a business must be sold to settle an estate. Another source of information about a particular business is someone who is familiar with the industry you want to enter. You can usually find such a person by asking among your friends. Suppliers to the business also may prove to be good sources of information. They know what's going on in the industry and can often tip you off to a firm that might be for sale.

Pointers in Personal Observation and Search

When you have set out in earnest to search for a firm to buy, you'll find it helpful to focus your activities by deciding what business or businesses you will consider, what limitations you'll put on where you want to locate, and what major reasons owners have for selling.

You'll discover that only by the rarest kind of good luck will you be able to locate the business you want in the area where you want to live. This suggests the need for flexibility in your thinking. You'll probably have to compromise to get the best of the available choices. And it may take a long time to find an acceptable compromise. Trying to find the right kind of business in the right place and understanding why people want to sell underlines the need for flexibility and patience. Meeting your needs and those of the seller will take care and study. The effort will be time consuming. But the payoff can be productive—and profitable.

Preliminary Search

Preliminary search is the next step. The ideal search would locate potential purchases in a business you know and like—and in places where you'd be willing to live.

Stages of Screening

If things look good at this point, you'd go though the following three stages of screening before you'd consider closing the deal.

First Stage: Rough Screen
Following the preliminary search, you'd use a rough screen to narrow the number of possibilities. Your aim would be to eliminate all but one or two likely businesses for more careful study.

Second Stage: Medium Screen
In this step you'd assess the strengths and weaknesses of these concerns. You should concentrate primarily on the three basic requirements we've dealt with in this text. How do the businesses you are considering shape up in technical, marketing, and financial management qualifications?

Third Stage: Fine Screen
Once you've satisfied yourself on the performance of a company in the foregoing respects, you would conduct a fine screening. At this time, you'd make a carefully detailed analysis of the financial and management history of the company. And you'd prepare your own projections of *what you could expect the business to do for you after you buy it.* You should take into account the seller's biases, and your personal desires. Your ultimate goal would be to arrive at an acceptable price for the business.

Closing the Deal

In the final step, you'd close the deal. At this time you should get the help of your attorney and your accountant to take care of the many details of legal and tax issues. They will protect your interests in buying the business.

SCREENING THE OFFERINGS IN DEPTH

The foregoing three levels of screening should be done whether you are looking for a retail, manufacturing, service, or other kind of firm. And as you might expect, you'll go into greater and greater detail as you conduct these levels of investigation.

Preliminary Screening

In your first stage investigation, you'll visit and inspect the premises and operation and interview the seller. In interviewing, the trick is to get the owner to talk—and to listen *actively* to what you hear. In a productive interview the interviewee is encouraged to do 90 percent of the talking. Listen for discrepancies and distortions; let the owner talk, but when you want to check a point, guide the conversation by a well chosen question. The owner will try to make a positive (and usually glowing) sales pitch. This need not bother you because you'll search for hard data that will allow you to form your own opinion in the checking you'll do later. Your task will be to remember the main points and try to verify them.

Observe the Premises

Are things neat and tidy? If a retail store, is the interior attractive; would you like to walk into the store as a prospective customer? If a manufacturing operation, is the shop well laid out? Does the flow of the manufacturing process follow the recommendations made in Chapter 11? How efficiently is the inventory or raw stock managed? If a service organization, how are client contacts made, and how are jobs scheduled? Do procedures ensure adequate attention to the needs of customers? You should raise and answer questions like these in your preliminary survey of the business.

Before you leave, make a first check of financial data. Ask to see a current balance sheet: What assets does the business own and what does it owe? Look at income statements for the last two or three years, and the current one too. Does the income show a seasonal pattern? Or is it steady by the month? Check several years of income tax statements, the last five years if the company has been in business that long. And by all means, get copies of these items to take along with you for further study.

Second Stage Screening

Your purpose in the second stage screening will be to eliminate unpromising prospects. Several considerations will help you to narrow your choices.

The Facilities

Are they adequate to serve the needs of the business, at least to start with? If so, you can plan to add equipment, tools, or other facilities as you see the necessity or desirability.

Estimated Financial Strength

Another check you should make is to compare financial ratios of the company against those of others in the same business. See the section, Using Ratio Analysis, in Chapter 8 for suggestions on how to use ratio analysis. Ratios that differ widely from those customary should raise red flags pointing to the need for careful investigation of underlying causes; comparative financial data afford the chance to verify the internal financial strength of the firm you're considering.

Character of the Investment

If you're assessing a small corporation, it's important that you know who owns the stock. Your investment would be essentially nonmarketable should a small group of shareholders own more than half the stock.

Capital Requirements

You'll want to estimate the capital you'll require to keep yourself out of trouble in taking on the business. You should judge the potential of the business for growth—and your assessment of the capital you'll need should include an allotment to support such growth.

Qualifications of Personnel

Do you believe the personnel you may be acquiring with the business have the potential to grow with the business if you buy it? Are they reliable? Would you feel comfortable for the long haul in working with them? Can you trust them without question? If so, you'll acquire an asset of great worth. If not, you should face the issue of staffing your new business with help you can rely on.

The Marketing Program

Look carefully at the program the company has been following. Check the market segment the business has been serving. Does it seem right for the business? Can you see ways to expand the market? Check back on the product-service/market matrix in Chapter 3 and the product or service life cycle on pages 78–81 to see the possibilities in the existing market and in developing new markets. Read through the discussions on marketing, Chapters 4 through 7, to pick up important points to check. This review will prepare you to examine the marketing questions you'll want to study thoroughly, not only in this second stage of your investigation, but also in the third stage.

Some Special Questions

These final questions should be answered to the best of your ability at this second stage of investigation: (1) What exactly would you be buying? Would it be physical assets such as plant and machinery; a fully equipped retail store; patents that have real value; good will in an existing clientele of repeat customers; an exclusive franchise in an established chain of fast food outlets; or other assets? (2) If you can trust the accuracy of the financial records you've gotten, would the business be a profitable investment at the asking price? If not, what is your best estimate of a proper price? (3) Finally, in view of your answers to these questions, would you be better off by starting a new venture than by buying the existing business?

If you decide that you'd be better off buying the going business, then you'd be ready to do the final screening.

Final Screening

Although you may approach the final screening of the business from many points of view, we suggest that an effective start can be made by analyzing the market that the business serves. We recommend that you follow the procedures given in Chapters 4, 5, 6, and 7, which cover market feasibility analysis in sequence and in detail. When you review the subjects presented in these chapters you'll prepare yourself to answer the questions they raise. You'll find numerous hints and suggestions about points you'll want to check to satisfy yourself in deciding about present marketing effectiveness and the potential for making significant improvements in the marketing effort.

If you're examining the possibilities of buying a service business, read Chapter 7, "Marketing the Service Business," for pointers. Pay particular attention to the unique aspects of the service business—its intangibility, the need to maintain a consistently high level of peformance, the special requirements in advertising and promotion, and the importance of setting the right price for the service. In Chapter 7 you'll find guidelines that will help you assess the effectiveness of the existing business in meeting these needs. And you'll very likely see ways to make improvements should you buy the business.

Looking at Intangible Assets

The intangible assets of the company, particularly in the service business, may be the most important part of the package you'd be buying. Some typical questions you'll want to answer are these:

- What kind of image does the existing business project—favorable or unfavorable? What kind of reputation does the company have with its suppliers, customers, and banker?

- Are there negative things about the product or service you'd have to overcome?

- Is the business dependent upon special skills or personal relations the present owner shows with customers? If so, could you acquire them upon buying the business?

If any of these factors are adverse, you should think hard about what you would have to do to overcome them. Changing the image or reputation of a company may be quite possible if you can apply the elements of proactive management we've stressed throughout this book. If the task looks overwhelming after due study, you'd probably be better off starting a new business.

Evaluating Physical Assets

Any business you are contemplating buying will have some kind of equipment and inventory that you'll want to evaluate. Appraise what's offered cautiously. Whether a small manufacturing plant, a retail store, or a service facility, examine the equipment to find out if it's in good shape, modern, and really suitable for the function intended.

■ Can you see ways to improve productivity or profitability by adding modern equipment or changing procedure or process?

■ How much would the machinery or equipment bring as used merchandise?

Check the status of inventory. Is it valued at the prices at which it was bought? Or at current prices?

Be sure that you consider the effects of inflation on asset evaluation and replacement costs. You may want to set what you'd be willing to pay for assets in the light of present prices. (When you do your financial planning you *must* take inflation into account.)

Appraisal of this kind will give you a realistic value of the physical assets and put you in a sound position to negotiate for the business.

AVOIDING LEGAL PROBLEMS

Be sure to check legal issues that can be critical in buying a business. The following questions will suggest legal points to be investigated in your assessment of the business you're thinking of buying:

■ Does the business have any encumberances against it or the property such as mortgages, judgments, liens, zoning restrictions, environmental requirements, or condemnation proceedings?

■ What is the status of patents, trademarks, service marks, copyrights, and logos owned by the company?

■ Does the company have clear title to land and buildings? What are the terms and conditions of existing leases on buildings, machinery and equipment, trucks or automobiles?

■ Are there any restrictions on free access to alleys, driveways, streets, or parking?

■ How can you deal with ongoing contracts to buy or sell goods?

■ Will you experience any problems in getting city, state, or federal licenses to do business? This can be an especially critical issue in food, drug, and liquor businesses.

■ Can you ensure that all outstanding debts, accounts payable, notes payable, or other outstanding obligations are shown on the books?

These are typical subjects for investigation. You'll become aware of other significant items you'll want to look into when you study the worksheets at the ends of the chapters in this book. Your lawyer and your accountant can give you the expert help you'll need to check the legal issues involved in buying the ongoing business you're considering. Be sure to draw on their help.

PICKING A LOSER

For some persons it makes good sense to pick a loser. If you can find a company in which you can clearly identify opportunities the present management can't see, and you are certain of your ground, you may find it profitable to buy. Once more we must point out the importance of technical competence. You must know the business well enough to see how to move it toward the achievement you want.

Your study of possibilities for turning the business around can start with the concepts of the market-product/service matrix of Chapter 3. This will help you see how the existing market may be expanded or how you may gain new market segments.

In considering the possibilities, you would be wise to think as if you were starting a new company. Go through the stages of market analysis and financial projections we've given in this book. When you have arrived at what is essentially a prospectus for a new business, on the basis of data gathered from the existing business, you'll have a sound background upon which to form your *buy* or *reject* decision.

PERSONAL FACTORS IN THE TRANSACTION

When looking for a business to buy, you, the buyer, and the seller too, bring personal factors to the transaction. When you have some understanding of these factors and their implications, you're in a better position to negotiate and have the deal meet your expectations.

Personal Factors the Seller Injects

The seller will probably have open and, more than likely, hidden reasons for selling. Your problem is to do the best you can to become aware of both. Some of the apparent reasons for the owner wanting to sell can be:

- The owner may want to retire because of ill health or old age, and therefore to convert the business into cash.

- The owner hasn't the desire to learn to be a professional manager, as the growth of the company demands, and prefers to cash out and start another business.

- The owner has been unable for financial or for personal reasons to arrange for adequate management succession.

- The company has grown so fast it needs an infusion of capital, which the owner can't find.

204

The owner will often have hidden reasons for selling. Some point to declining profitability or fading of the market. Among these hidden reasons are the following:

- The company is experiencing a diminishing market and the owner doesn't know how to cope with it.

- The technology of the business is changing rapidly and the owner is unable to adapt to its complexity, which may require the acquisition of new skills or a massive capital investment.

- The owner fears that the product or service is obsolescent and can't be improved or replaced.

- Fear about the financial future of the business and supporting the family may trigger the owner's desire to sell. The owner may be poor in cash but rich in the resources of the company and sees converting the assets to cash as the way out.

Personal Factors the Buyer Injects

Just as the seller has personal reasons for wanting to sell, so you, the buyer, will have your own special factors that will influence the deal. You'll want to compare the prospective return on your investment against other forms of investment. Does the return compare favorably with those available from stocks, bonds, rental property, or Treasury bills? Would you be able to draw a reasonable salary for actively managing the company, perhaps including some perquisites, or fringe benefits, such as a company car, season tickets to sports events or theater, boat, or the like? If the foregoing seem to be favorable, you might be willing to pay a little more for the company than you would under other circumstances.

Or perhaps your own special desires would lead you to offer a somewhat higher price than you would otherwise. You may understand the business and like it. You may want to live in the area where the business is located. You may have any of a number of other personal requirements that would cause you to offer a substantial price for the business. Only you can judge the impact of such personal factors on the price you're willing to pay.

EVALUATING AND PRICING THE BUSINESS

You may set the price for buying a business in three different ways, depending on your point of view or the circumstances in which the business exists. The business can have any of these three values: its *liquidation value*, its *market price*, or its value as an *investment* capable of producing profit.

Liquidation Value

The liquidation value (sometimes called the doomsday value) is the lowest. It is computed from a pessimistic estimate of what the tangible assets would bring at a forced sale. These assets include accounts receivable reduced to a reasonably safe value, machinery and equipment figured at second-hand prices, and inventory estimated at distressed prices for quick sale. The total would represent the value in case of bankruptcy.

Market Price

The market price for a going business reflects the rule-of-thumb estimate of the business broker. Although this estimate can be helpful, it is important to know that exceptions to the rule abound. Some hardheaded business brokers' ways of judging the price for typical small businesses, as quoted by Thomas P. Murphy, follow.[1]

Franchised Business
Where a contract is signed for protected territory, set the price at the amount of one year's net profit plus the inventory at cost.

Bakery and Pastry Business
A six-day operation with $1,000 weekly gross sales is worth $10,000; $1,500 weekly gross is worth $15,000 to $17,000; and a bakery or pastry shop with $2,000 weekly gross is worth $25,000 to $30,000.

Manufacturing Concern with Product Involved
Pay the appraised value of machinery plus the actual cost of raw materials, packing materials, and finished goods; also add to the price from one-half to one year's net profit.

Restaurant
Pay replacement value of equipment plus food inventory at cost, plus one-half annual net profit.

Service Business
Example: Dry-cleaning pick-up store (not plant or unit). Pay $3,500 for every $100 per week of net income up to $250. Pay $5,000 for every $100 weekly net over $250.

Soft Goods and Ladies' Ready-to-Wear
Pay 25 to 50 percent of cost of fixtures plus inventory at 50 to 100 percent depending on salability, styles, and brand names. Very little good will is usually paid in this classification.

These rules of thumb are just that—rough estimates. Nevertheless, they can be helpful in estimating a fair price for the business you want to buy. Note that these approaches don't allow for good will. The underlying assumption is that the business for sale is in a bad way financially. Although this approach may give you some idea of the price for a business, it will not meet your personal needs for buying for profit.

Another approach to estimating the range of fair market price for a business is given in the following guide (Table 11-1). In this guide, net income is considered earnings before interest expense and income taxes, but includes the salary, if any, of the seller.

When buying shares in a corporation, the quantities given in columns 3, 4, and 5 are usually included in the net book values as shown in corporation statements. Therefore, only the information given in column 2 should be used. The multiplier would be applied to the adjusted net income. For example, assume the book value for a large manufacturing firm is $100,000. Column 2 shows the multiplier as one-and-a-half to three times net. If the net income is $50,000, using the lower multiplier of one-and-a-half gives a value of one-and-a-half times $50,000, or $75,000. Adding $75,000 to the book value of $100,000 results in a sales price of $175,000. If the multiplier at the high end had been used, the sales price would be three times $50,000 plus $100,000, or $250,000. The range of sales price in this case would be from $175,000 to $250,000.

The information in all the columns, 2 through 5, would be used in buying the assets of a small company.

You should be aware that these data give a rule-of-thumb way of estimating selling price ranges. The actual price will be set by your negotiation with the seller, as we have recommended throughout this chapter.

Buying for Profit

You will note that the liquidation and rule-of-thumb methods rely on appraisal of the physical assets. We recommend a third way, which seems to fit the entrepreneur much better. That is to set the price on the basis of the business's power to make profit. You should figure profit after deducting a reasonable salary for your efforts in running the business. The profits of the business should be at least equal to or better than what you could earn by investing an amount equal to the purchase price in securities, mortgages, or other worthy investments.

The next two steps outline the procedure for arriving at a price for the business: This price is based on the future earning power of the business.

- ■ Step One. Assess the company's power to earn.

- ■ Step Two. Capitalize these earnings at a rate in keeping with the risks involved in the business. (Capitalization means the sum total of the owner's investment and the borrowed capital invested in the business. Sometimes it is defined as the owner's equity plus the long term debt of the business.)

To estimate the future earnings of the business you should analyze its earnings from income statements for at least the past five years. Make adjustments for non-recurring items that you would not expect to encounter in the future.

Table 11-1 A Guide to the Evaluation of Small Business (Under 2 Million in Gross Sales)

1 Type of Business	2 Guide to Price Multiplier	3 Inventory	4 Fixtures and Equipment	5 Hard Assets: Cash, Accts. Rec., Real Estate, etc.	Check the Following, and *Use Common Sense*
Full service car wash	1 yrs. gross income	add	include	add	Labor & utility bills may verify income
Coin operated business	1/2 to 1 yrs. gr. inc.	add	include	add	Utility bills & supplies verify income
Liquor stores	3 to 5 × 1 mo. gr. + license	add	include	add	Check sales tax receipts
Beer bars	3 × 1 mo. gross	add	include	add	Verify cases & barrels bought
Cocktail lounge	3 to 4 × 1 mo. gr. + license	add	include	add	Verify cases of liquor, beer & wine bought
Fast foods	1 yrs. net income	add	include	add	Personally count people at different times and register receipts
Full service restaurants	1 to 1 1/2 yrs. net + license	add	include	add	Verify food & liquor bought
Small retail	1 yrs. net	add	include	add	Check sales tax receipts. Have professional company take inventory
Large retail or chain	1 to 2 times net	add	add	add	Check sales tax receipts. Have professional company take inventory
Small manufacturing	1 to 1 1/2 × net	add	include	add	Check if line is too limited
Large manufacturing, over 1 million gross	1 1/2 to 3 × net	add	include	add	Is line too large? Check for outdated inventory
Small distributor	1 to 2 × net	add	include	add	Same as small mfg.
Large distributor, over 1 million	1 1/2 to 3 × net	add	add	add	Same as large mfg.

Business	Formula				Notes / Questions
Service business	1 to 2 × net	include	include	add	Check contracts if any
Phone answering service	3 to 4 × net	include	include	add	Is there a rapid turnover of employees?
Insurance	1 1/2 to 3 × net	include	include	add	Is bonus included in gross? Is company rated?
C.P.A., M.D.s, etc., professionals	1 1/2 to 2 × net	add	add	add	How long will seller stay with you?
Auto & appliance repair	1 yrs. net	add	add	add	Are customers happy and how many repeats?
Bookkeeping service	1/2 yr. gross	include	include	add	Will seller stay on for 1 year?
Beauty & barber shops	25% to 50% of 1 yrs. gross	add	add	add	Check turnover of help
Employment agency	1/2 of 1 yrs. gross	include	include	add	Any contracts with large co's and repeats?
Florist shop	1/4 to 1/2 yr. gross	add	add	add	How many repeats & how many commercial accts.?
Newspaper	1 yrs. gross	add	add	add	50% of lineage should be paid advertising
Publishing company	1 1/2 to 2 × yrs. net	add	add	add	Industrial better than retail book type
Pet shop	1/2 yrs. net	add	add	add	Pet supplies are important for profit
Print shop	1/2 to 1 yrs. net	add	add	add	Check equipment if modern & are clients industrial?
Real estate office	1/2 of 1 yrs. gross commission	include	include	add	How long have salespeople been there?
Travel agency	1/2 of 1 yrs. gross commission	include, if any	include	add	How long have salespeople been there?

This guide, © 1978, reproduced by permission of Lester L. Lynch, President, American Acquisitions, Inc., Encino, California.

These could include such expenses as the purchase of a patent or the purchase of a special machine tool. Deduct unusually large bad debts, inventory writeoffs for obsolete mechandise or supplies, and excessive salaries. Estimate the reduction in earnings from the impact of raising low salaries that would have to be increased to hire good help. Take note of the accounting procedure used; it can have a direct effect on reported earnings. For example, one company may charge off the whole cost of tools, jigs, dies, or fixtures in the year bought; another may amortize these costs over several years, thereby increasing earnings.

As the buyer, you should adjust for nonrecurring items and varying accounting practices to judge what future earnings might be *under your management*. The return on your investment (ROI) must come from future earnings.

You can start, as we've indicated, on the basis of adjusted historical earnings. But you should project for five years ahead, figuring as the business *would be run under your management*. You can follow the recommendations we've given in this book for the needed proactive management planning in the critical financial variables. These should include at least the following:

- Identification and analysis of the market segment or segments suitable for the business

- The assumptions upon which you base your financial estimates

- Balance sheets

- Cash flow projections

- Income statements

- Profit and loss statements

From these statements you can capitalize the business's earning power. The higher the risk of generating projected earnings, the lower should be the capitalization rate. In a business considered to be high risk, the return customarily expected ranges from 15 to 20 percent; in a business of moderate risk, 5 to 10 percent. Here's an example of how this might work, comparing two companies, each earning $50,000 per year on a current basis:

Company A	*Company B*
Small specialty paint manufacturer	Small pest control company
Established ten years	Established three years
Steady growth for last seven years	Growing slowly, but not firmly established
Highly favorable prospects for future	Highly competitive industry
Might be capitalized at twenty times earnings, or $1,000,000	Buyer would need a high ROI, perhaps 20%; might be capitalized at five times earnings, or $250,000

In this example, the lower risk paint manufacturer would be worth four times more than the higher risk pest control company would seem to be. The results of analyses such as these reflect what might be called internal variables of the business. Before beginning negotiations to buy it you would be wise to weigh external factors in modifying the rate of capitalization.

External Factors in Setting the Capitalization Rate

After you've found the capitalization rate as described in the foregoing section, you should check the impact of external forces on the business. You may find factors here that would cause you to modify your first estimate of capitalization rate. In Chapter 4 we outlined several environmental forces that could cause sudden change in a business: economic, political or legal, technological, social or cultural, and competitive. What effect could any of these forces have on the business you're thinking of buying? Refer to Appendix A, Outline for Developing Your Basic Business Plan, particularly item 3, Background of Proposed Business, for clues to details in the possible effects on the business of changes in the above forces. It might be disastrous, for example, to buy a business specializing in the manufacture of a proprietary herbicide if the Food and Drug Administration has plans to prohibit that product from being marketed. Similarly, it would be a grave error to buy a retail nursery without knowing that it was in the path of a proposed freeway. Changes in any of these external forces can have serious effects on the proposed business.

Selling Price Formulas

We have indicated previously some rules of thumb for setting the price for several kinds of retail businesses. In most businesses there are no such guidelines: What is needed, as we have said, is a way of arriving at a proper price on the basis of the present earning power and the potential for profit in the future *under your management.* The Bank of America suggests a useful formula, which is given in Figure 11-1, Suggested Price Formula.

One stumbling block that often poses a problem in using a formula such as this is *goodwill.* Goodwill, the value of intangibles, is defined by the U.S. Treasury Department as "the value attached to a business over and above the value of the physical property." The assumption behind the concept of good will is that the firm has developed a clientele who are repeat customers, and who therefore are a valuable, although intangible, asset.

As the buyer, you should deal with the question of goodwill with reasonable skepticism. The past effort of the owner in building effective customer relations will undoubtedly be seen in a high figure for goodwill. However, the future earning power of the business should be the key variable in your estimating the worth, if any, of the goodwill. Figure 11-1 gives two examples of how to treat the evaluation of goodwill, one showing it at substantial worth, the other at none.

Figure 11-1 Suggested Price Formula. (Reproduced by permission of the *Small Business Reporter*, Bank of America.)

Step 1. Determine the adjusted tangible net worth of the business. (The total value of all current and long-term assets less liabilities.)

Step 2. Estimate how much the buyer could earn annually with an amount equal to the value of the tangible net worth invested elsewhere.

This is just an arbitrary figure, used for illustration. A reasonable figure depends on the stability and relative risks of the business and the investment picture generally. The rate should be similar to that which could be earned elsewhere with the same approximate risk.

Step 3. Add to this a salary normal for an owner-operator of the business. This combined figure provides a reasonable estimate of the income the buyer can earn elsewhere with the investment and effort involved in working in the business.

Step 4. Determine the average annual net earnings of the business (net profit before subtracting owner's salary) over the past few years.

This is before income taxes, to make it comparable with earnings from other sources or by individuals in different tax brackets. (The tax implications of alternate investments should be carefully considered.)

The trend of earnings is a key factor. Have they been rising steadily, falling steadily, remaining constant, or fluctuating widely? The earnings figure should be adjusted to reflect these trends.

Step 5. Subtract the total of earning power (2) and reasonable salary (3) from this average net earnings figure (4). This gives the extra earning power of the business.

Step 6. Use this extra, or excess, earning figure to estimate the value of the intangibles. This is done by multiplying the extra earnings by what is termed the "years of profit" figure.

This "years of profit" multiplier pivots on these points. How unique are the intangibles offered by the firm? How long would it take to set up a similar business and bring it to this stage of development? What expenses and risks would be involved? What is the price of goodwill in similar firms? Will the seller be signing a noncompetitive agreement?

If the business is well-established, a factor of five or more might be used, especially if the firm has a valuable name, patent or location. A multiplier of three might be reasonable for a moderately seasoned firm. A younger, but profitable, firm might merely have a one-year profit figure.

Step 7. Final price = Adjusted Tangible Net Worth + Value of Intangibles. (Extra earnings x "years of profit.")

	Business A	Business B
1. Adjusted value of tangible net worth (Assets less liabilities)	$50,000	$50,000
2. Earning power—at 10%*— of an amount equal to the adjusted tangible net worth if invested in a comparable-risk business, security, etc.	5,000	5,000
3. Reasonable salary for owner-operator in the business	12,000	12,000
4. Net earnings of the business over recent years— this means net profit before subtracting owner's salary	20,000	15,500
5. Extra earning power of the business (line 4 minus lines 2 and 3)	3,000	−1,500
6. Value of intangibles— using three-year profit figure for moderately well-established firm (3 times line 5)	9,000	None
7. Final Price — (lines 1 and 6)	$59,000	$50,000 (or less)

In example A, the seller gets a substantial value for intangibles (goodwill) because the business is moderately well-established and earning more than the buyer could earn elsewhere with similar risks and effort. Within three years the buyer should have recovered the amount paid for goodwill in this example.

In example B, the seller gets no value for goodwill because the business, even though it may have existed for a considerable time, is not earning as much as the buyer could through outside investment and effort. In fact, the buyer may feel that even an investment of $50,000 — the current appraised value of net assets — is too much because it cannot earn sufficient return.

CLOSING THE DEAL

Assuming that you've done the analysis, considered your personal requirements and the other key points made in this chapter, you're ready to close the deal. Don't work alone in this final step. Legal requirements and tax implications tend to be much too complicated for the nonexpert; you'll want expert counsel in these matters.

You should consider the impact of taxes on the method of payment. Some ways are available for reducing the tax load—effecting savings—in choosing the method of payment. For example, by making a smaller down payment and incurring interest on the balance, the interest may be deducted in figuring income taxes. Or the purchase price can be reduced and the previous owner taken on as a salaried employee or consultant. Here, too, the expense would be deductible. With a noncompeting agreement with the seller for a definite period of time, a value may be set on the agreement and payment for it may be deducted over the life of the agreement.

As we've said, consult your attorney and accountant in closing the deal. Follow your entrepreneurial inclinations—get the best counsel you can to ensure that your interests are well served in this final phase of buying the business.

MAJOR POINTS IN BUYING A GOING BUSINESS   SUMMARY

Buying a going business has both advantages and disadvantages. The trick is to ensure that the advantages can make for a profitable outcome.

We've pointed out several avenues for finding the business to buy. Among these are ads in newspapers and trade journals; services of business brokers; contacts with bankers, lawyers, and accountants; talks with owners and managers in similar businesses, and those who supply the business with goods and services.

You'll protect your interests by going through several steps in studying a business to buy. After you're sure of your own qualifications to run the business you're attracted to, you'll screen the deal in more and more detail as you gather information and numbers. When you're reasonably sure that physical, financial, and marketing data look sound, you'll check to clear away any existing legal problems.

Some entrepreneurs can do well by picking a loser—if they have the necessary experience in the particular business and can see how to make it a winner. If this description fits you, you may find it advantageous to buy a rundown business and turn it around through your special skill.

Remember that both you and the owner bring personal factors to the deal. Your task is to uncover the owner's hidden reasons for selling. You must then see how to overcome any problems posed by these reasons. If you're sure you can solve them and you feel good about the prospects of the business, you'll choose to close the deal.

When you've selected a business to buy, you'll need to evaluate and price it. We've suggested that a business can be valued in three ways: 1) at its liquidation value, 2) at its market price, or 3) at its value as an investment. We recommend the third way, buying for earning power. We've outlined several ways of estimating the price for the business, including recognized selling price formulas. Unless the deal is unique in its prospect for profit, the entrepreneur would be well-advised to buy a going business on the basis of its potential to earn a profit appropriate to the investment.

In closing the deal, you should work with a well-qualified lawyer and accountant to be sure of a sound purchase agreement.

CHAPTER 11/FOOTNOTE

[1]Thomas P. Murphy, *A Business of Your Own,* McGraw-Hill Book Co., New York, 1956, pp. 184–185. In these pages the rules-of-thumb for market pricing some small businesses are quoted from the experience of a well-qualified New York business broker. Although this book was published in the mid-fifties, the quantities and ratios quoted are still useful; inflation has raised the dollar quantities but has not changed the relationships.

Buying a Going Business

You'll find that the text of this chapter carries the questions you should answer in each of the sections listed below. We've allowed space under each heading for your answers to the questions given under that heading within the chapter.

TO BUY OR NOT TO BUY

I've studied the first sections of this chapter and have decided that buying a going business is right for me.

■ I've searched and identified a business I might want to buy.

Name of company _____

Individual proprietorship ____ Partnership ____ Corporation ____.

Principals _____

_____

Address _____

Phone _____

ADVANTAGES IN BUYING

■ Here are the advantages I see in buying:

_____

_____

_____

_____

_____

DISADVANTAGES IN BUYING

■ Here are the disadvantages I see in buying:

_____

_____

_____

_____

_____

PRELIMINARY SCREENING

■ In this first stage of investigation, I've visited the premises, interviewed the seller, and observed the operation of the business. Here's some background data on the business:

_____

_____

_____

_____

_____

SECOND STAGE SCREENING

■ What needs to be done to the facilities to fit them for the business as I project it under my ownership:

_____

_____

_____

_____

_____

■ I've made a preliminary check of the financial condition of the company. I have copies of the following: current balance sheet __; income statements for the past __ years; income tax statements for the past __ years. Notes on financial information:

_____

_____

_____

■ I've checked the financial ratios in the operation of the company (as given in Chapter 8) and here are my notes on these ratios:

_____

_____

_____

■ If this is a corporation, here are the principal stockholders and the percent of the shares they own:

_____   _____

_____   _____

■ The amount of capital I will need to buy the business, make improvements, and support growth:

_____

_____

■ How I'll judge the quality of the personnel I'd acquire with the company:

_____

_____

_____

■ I believe the market segment the company has been serving is appropriate for the business: Yes ___; No ___. If no, here's what I'd do to improve the marketing program:

_____

_____

_____

_____

_____

■ A special question. What exactly would I be buying: physical plant; retail store with inventory; patents; franchise; good will; or . . .?

_____

_____

_____

_____

_____

FINAL SCREENING

■ At this point we recommend that you perform a market feasibility analysis as given in Chapters 4, 5, 6, and 7. Note your conclusions and the ways you've found to improve marketing effectiveness if you buy the company. Include your findings about the intangible assets and the physical assets of the company. Use the space below for your notes.

_____

_____

_____

_____

_____

217

AVOIDING LEGAL PROBLEMS

■ Note here your responses to the questions raised in this section of this chapter. Include the answers to other questions that may have occurred to you as you've worked through those given in the text.

_____

_____

_____

_____

_____

_____

_____

PICKING A LOSER

■ If you've found a loser that you believe you can turn around, state here the specific plans you've developed to make the business profitable.

_____

_____

_____

_____

_____

_____

_____

_____

_____

PERSONAL FACTORS IN THE TRANSACTION

■ I recognize that the owner will give me some open reasons for wanting to sell—and will have some hidden reasons. And I'll have my reasons for wanting to buy. It will help me to weigh these reasons side by side to balance them.

Reasons for Selling	*Reasons for Buying*
_____	_____
_____	_____
_____	_____
_____	_____
_____	_____
_____	_____
_____	_____
_____	_____
_____	_____

EVALUATING AND PRICING THE BUSINESS

■ I've estimated these values as guides in negotiating the price for the business:

Liquidation Value _____

Market Price _____

Buying for Profit _____

In setting these prices, be guided by the recommendations made under the section on Evaluating and Pricing the Business in this chapter.

CLOSING THE DEAL

■ In closing the deal, I've considered the tax implications in deciding on the best way to pay off the seller. I've arranged to consult with my attorney and accountant in taking this final step to buy the business.
Notes:

_____

_____

_____

_____

_____

IF YOU WANT TO READ MORE

Kenneth J. Albert, *How to Pick the Right Small Business Opportunity*, McGraw-Hill Book Co., New York, 1977. This book, simply and directly written, will be found particularly useful in helping you decide on the business that fits your personal strengths. Chapter 12, "Selecting an Ongoing Business" offers comprehensive check lists of items to investigate and gives practical suggestions for pricing the business.

Hal B. Pickle and Royce L. Abrahamson, *Small Business Management*, John Wiley & Sons, Inc., New York, 1977. In Chapter 7 the authors present a condensed discussion of the advantages and disadvantages of buying a going business and the factors that should be considered in evaluating the prospective purchase. The text emphasizes the desirability of buying for the future profit of the firm. The price should be keyed to the expected profit and the estimated degree of risk attached to the business.

Nicholas C. Siropolis, *Small Business Management*, Houghton Mifflin Co., Boston, 1977. Chapter 4 of this book, "Search for a New Venture," contains an excellent discussion of the financial aspects of buying an existing business.

Patrick R. Liles, *New Business Ventures and the Entrepreneur*, Richard D. Irwin, Inc., Homewood, Ill., 1974. In a special *Note*, "Evaluating a Going Company," pp. 186–201, this book examines the valuation of a going company at a relatively sophisticated level. Different aspects of asset valuations and earnings valuations are analyzed in depth. If you want to learn some of the more technical aspects of evaluating the worth of a going company, you'll find these pages rewarding.

Chapter 12

Buying a Franchised Business*

ADVANTAGES AND DISADVANTAGES OF THE FRANCHISED BUSINESS

HISTORICAL BACKGROUND OF FRANCHISING

TYPES OF FRANCHISING ORGANIZATIONS

NATURE OF THE FRANCHISE RELATIONSHIP

EVALUATING THE FRANCHISE RELATIONSHIP

EVALUATING THE FRANCHISE AGREEMENT

TRENDS IN FRANCHISING

---

*Code numbers referring to the Outline for Developing Your Basic Business Plan
(Appendix A) are not used in this chapter. The Worksheets in this chapter will
guide you through the planning required to assess the desirability of a franchised
business. When you have finished the Worksheets check the items in Appendix A,
point by point, to make sure you haven't omitted any important considerations.

You may find that owning a franchised business may be more attractive than starting a business from scratch. A franchise is a prepackaged and widely known business that benefits from the national image and promotion of the franchisor. Tested operating methods and proven products lower risk of doing business and mean that the franchise operation may yield you profit sooner than a business you start yourself.

If you go the franchise route, you'll very likely find trade-offs in your quest for independence. You'll be required to follow standard procedures and operating methods and you'll have little to say about product and marketing strategy. On balance, you'll have to make up your mind about chosing a franchise on the basis of its advantages and disadvantages.

ADVANTAGES AND DISADVANTAGES OF THE FRANCHISED BUSINESS

This chapter examines the advantages and disadvantages of owning and operating a franchised business instead of starting a business from scratch (discussed in Chapters 1 through 10), or buying an established enterprise (covered in Chapter 11). If you have the technical know-how, owning and operating a franchised business—becoming a franchisee—is an alternative you may want to explore. For those who've already decided that a franchised venture is the way to go, each of the previous chapters should be helpful, especially Chapters 4 through 7 and Chapter 11.

Applied research in franchising spells out clearly the characteristics of successful franchisees:[1]

- They conduct their own independent market research and analysis in evaluating the franchised business they enter.

- Before purchasing the franchise, they use independent financial and legal counseling to assess the potential worth of the business and to prevent contractual conflicts with the franchisor.

- They develop thorough business and marketing plans, not relying completely on the franchisor, to chart the future of their business.

- They have prior work experience in the business the franchisor offers.

These findings should come as no surprise because, as we've stressed, the basic requirements for starting any kind of business are the same.

In this chapter, we'll concentrate on the special characteristics of franchising, the relationship between franchisee and franchisor, and on how to evaluate a prospective franchise venture. Several excellent sources of information on franchising are available; you'll find them listed at the end of the chapter.

HISTORICAL BACKGROUND OF FRANCHISING

Franchising, one of several systems of distribution by which a producer may bring products or services to the consumer, performs a major and growing distribution function in the United States. Today franchised enterprises number about half a million and account for about one-third of all retail sales.

The term *franchise* comes from the old French word "franchir," which originally meant "to free from servitude." The term gradually came to mean a right granted to an individual by a sovereign. Nowadays franchise means the granting of a positive right to use or do something commercially. Most often the right involves use of a recognized name or method of operation belonging to someone else.

Franchising in one form or another has existed since the Middle Ages as a method of establishing outlets for selling a manufacturer's products. In modern times, shortly after the Civil War, the Singer Sewing Machine Company seems to have been the first to introduce an extensive franchising system. The system gradually declined and franchising did not become an important part of the country's distribution system until the automobile and soft drink industries adopted it early in this century. Growth in franchising was spurred during the 1930's when oil companies adopted it as a major system of distribution.

The present boom in franchising came in the early 1950's. Growth areas included food retailing (Super Value stores and IGA), drug retailing (Rexall and Walgreen), hardware and auto parts retailing (Ace Hardware and Western Auto), and variety goods retailing (Ben Franklin variety stores). These distribution arrangements were primarily wholesaler-retailer franchise systems.

The franchise form that's shown the most spectacular growth during the past twenty years has been the service-firm-retailer-sponsored system. Several well known examples include McDonald's, Hertz, Howard Johnson's, Kentucky Fried Chicken, Mister Donut, Holiday Inns, Pizza Hut, and Weight Watchers. In this system the franchisor offers a recognized trade name and a system of doing business, which are granted to the franchisee. The franchisee or dealer typically receives a variety of marketing, management, financial, and technical services in exchange for a specified fee. The growth economy of the 1960s and early 70s created an environment in which franchising flourished. The number of organizations relying on this kind of franchised distribution increased more than 300 percent.

Then during the 1974–75 recession many franchises, sponsored by well-known names but run by inexperienced newcomers, disappeared almost as quickly as they entered the market. Do you remember Dizzy Dean's Beef and Burger? Minnie Pearls? or Broadway Joe's? Undoubtedly influenced by bankruptcies that were occurring in some operations, franchising attracted fewer and fewer entrepreneurs during the economic downturn of 1974–75. Well managed franchised businesses survived profitably even during this recession.

The heyday of expansion of franchising has passed but excellent opportunities still exist for entrepreneurs in franchised businesses. We'll explore these opportunities later in this chapter. For now we'll give you a rundown on the types of franchises available and the criteria to assess the characteristics and quality of the franchise relationship.

224

TYPES OF FRANCHISING ORGANIZATIONS

Franchises range from marketing products such as fast food, ice cream, and candy to marketing services such as motels, dry cleaning establishments, and coin operated laundries. We'll identify four basic types of franchises, each of which have distinguishing economic and legal characteristics.

1. *Manufacturer-Retailer Franchise System:* In most cases the manufacturer franchises an entire retail outlet to stock and market its product line. Examples include manufacturers of automobiles and trucks, farm equipment, petroleum products, shoes, and paint.

   In this system the major role of the franchisee is to establish an outlet in a defined market where the consumer may readily obtain the manufacturer's product. The franchisee has very little discretion about what products are to be marketed.

2. *Manufacturer-Wholesaler Franchise System:* Beverage companies, soft drink and beer primarily, dominate this form of franchising. In soft drink franchising the manufacturer supplies the syrup or concentrate to the franchised wholesaler who adds ingredients, packages the product, and distributes to local retailers. In this system the franchisee performs some of the production activities and distributes the product to the retail level. As in the manufacturer-retailer franchise system, the franchisee has little control over the products to be distributed or their characteristics.

3. *Wholesaler-Retailer Franchise Systems:* In this system the wholesaler sponsors retail franchises; the franchisor recruits independent retailers to become contract franchisees. Western Auto Supply, Firestone, Goodyear, Butler Brothers, and Super Value Stores, Inc. are good examples.

4. *Trade Name Franchises:* This is the system that has enjoyed the most rapid growth in the past two decades. In this arrangement the franchisor possesses a known trade name and proven methods for profitable operation of retail outlets. Well known examples can be found in motel chains (Holiday Inn, Best Western, Sheraton Inn), restaurant chains (Howard Johnson's, McDonald's, Kentucky Fried Chicken, Burger King, Baskin-Robbins), and auto rental firms (Hertz, Avis, National, Budget Rent-A-Car).

   The franchisee may manufacture or modify the product (depending on product or service) but, as in other types of franchises, must follow strict operating and marketing procedures.

In the first three franchise systems the franchisor is the producer and the franchisee the distributor. In the fourth, the franchisee can be either a producer or a service supplier. All types involve trademarked or nationally branded products. Franchisors usually emphasize the quality control imposed on products made or services offered by their franchisees.

Growth in all four systems of franchising, especially in trade name franchising, has been influenced by trends toward national branding and increased mobility of consumers. Consumers seek the reputation of a national brand that results from mass advertising. As recreation and business travel have increased, so too have consumers' preferences for consistent standards of service and known costs of accomodation. In cases like these, franchising offers unique opportunities where local ownership and operation are advantageous.

National reputation, image, and promotion are of overriding importance and influence economic and contractual obligations between franchisor and franchisee. These vary widely among the four types and within each type. The particular franchise relationship specifies the amount of entry capital required and degree of control held by the franchisor over the franchisee.

NATURE OF THE FRANCHISE RELATIONSHIP

The heart of the franchise relationship is a contractual agreement governing the freedom of the franchisee to do or use something that is the property or right of the franchisor. This binding agreement establishes your relationship and controls your distribution of products or services. You, the entrepreneur/investor, pay an agreed-upon sum for the right to sell a certain product or service, use a certain brand name, trademark, technique of operation, or technical process owned by the franchisor.

But a franchise relationship involves more than granting a license to use certain trademarks or business techniques in return for a specified consideration. Two additional features are present: first, the success of the franchise venture calls for a *continuing relationship* between the franchisor and you; and second, you agree to maintain certain standards of operation specified by the franchisor.

Most forms of the franchise relationship involve the sharing of decision-making and management control, the transfer of specific management or technical expertise, and, in many cases, the advantage of unique products or services developed by the franchisor.

The International Franchise Association defines franchising in these terms:

> A franchise is a continuing relationship between the franchisor and the franchisee in which the sum total of the franchisor's knowledge, image, success, manufacturing and marketing techniques are supplied to the franchisee for a consideration.

In short, when you purchase a franchise you buy a prepackaged business. But you operate the venture under contract and in cooperation with the franchising company. Thus, careful evaluation of the particular franchise relationship will be crucial to your success.

226

EVALUATING THE FRANCHISE RELATIONSHIP

In this section we'll explore the franchise relationship and address these questions:

- What is the franchisor's role in the relationship? What makes franchising so attractive that franchisors choose this method of distribution over other methods?

- What is the franchisee's role in the relationship? How does being a franchisee differ from being a wholly independent entrepreneur?

The Franchisor

Knowing the motives of the franchisor—"what's in it for them"—will help you to objectively evaluate your prospects as a member of their distribution system.

Capital Acquisition

In recent years the most important reason for firms to adopt franchised distribution has been to acquire or conserve capital.[2] Several well known fast food companies use the initial fees paid by their franchisees as a major source of working capital. This is obviously an attractive funding technique since in many cases fees are collected long before the actual opening of an outlet. In effect, the franchisor receives hundreds of thousands of dollars in interest-free loans from franchisees.

Reduce Marketing Costs

Franchising can reduce marketing costs. If the company owned its stores, it would have to pay all the costs of doing business in many different locations—costs such as labor, overhead, insurance, personnel administration, employee training—expenses that continue regardless of sales volume.

Entrepreneurship

Successful franchisors believe that the local entrepreneur-manager is a crucial factor in the peformance of the franchise system. For many franchisors, the best type of franchisee is someone who can conform to an established way of doing business without being driven to try to improve it. Often franchisors seek a "sergeant type," a person who can operate well at a rank between an officer who gives orders and a private who follows them. Franchisors have found that franchisees are more likely to work hard in marketing and in controlling operating costs than are salaried employees in company owned outlets. The large financial stake the franchisee has in the business induces intense commitment.

Our experience shows that success of almost any franchise system and its franchisees is linked directly to how effectively the franchisor has created and maintained favorable conditions for entrepreneurship among the franchise owner-managers.

The Franchisee

Personal factors will have much to do with how you judge the franchise relationship and your "fit" as a franchisee. You should carefully review Chapters 1 and 2, where we presented the characteristics of successful entrepreneurs. Franchisees in well-run systems tend to view themselves as entrepreneurs and important local businesspersons. The question you must answer is: Under the franchise relationship I'm studying, will the franchisor consider me an entrepreneur, or will I be treated as an employee of the parent company?

Many people know that they want to go into business for themselves, but are hesitant to take the drastic step in starting a wholly independent business venture. As we've said, it is a risky endeavor and the failure rate is high. Lack of seasoned business experience quite appropriately makes would-be entrepreneurs uneasy about going it alone. Although many people know that operating a small business is what they want to do, they lack a specific idea, product, service, or business location.

Franchising has very special appeals for such individuals, and perhaps for you. Buying a franchise means that you would not be venturing into completely uncharted waters. Buying a franchise appropriate to your capabilities could gain you the following advantages:

- The business and its methods would have been thoroughly tested.

- You would begin with a known product or service that has already achieved customer approval and acceptance.

- There would be a proven track record of financial and marketing success that can be transferred to the specific franchise you'll purchase.

- Expert help would be available to you in launching and operating the business—in such areas as site selection, store layout, merchandising, inventory control, and accounting.

- For many franchised operations, and perhaps yours also, significant benefits would be found in group purchasing and national brand advertising.

Many franchisees welcome group identity and participation in a franchise system. Observers have noted that many franchisees really don't want to be totally independent, but rather seek to be part of a large successful organization and yet maintain their individual identity. The right franchise would offer you the opportunity to enter a field of business that might be prohibitively expensive to enter on your own.

Important trade-offs occur in choosing a franchised business. Even with the best franchise operations the franchisor tends to hold the advantage, especially in operating practices and in purchasing materials and supplies.

If you want to escape taking orders by operating a franchised business you may be frustrated by your lack of autonomy. You'll have to prepare and submit detailed reports. You may have to set inventory levels and mix inventory items by rules, regardless of local customer preferences. You may have no say in your store location.

228

You may be limited to prescribed sources from which you buy supplies. And, although you may disagree with the franchisor's advertising program, you will probably not have any say in it.

The franchise you should look for would combine the proven expertise and marketing sophistication of the franchisor with your need to exercise your entrepreneurial drive and your ability to manage the required capital investment. In evaluating a specific franchising operation, you should determine whether the combination results in mutual value and benefits. To do so, you'll need some guidelines on what to expect in acquiring and operating the franchise. You'll also want to know what the franchisor's obligations are.

EVALUATING THE FRANCHISE AGREEMENT

The franchise agreement, or contract, spells out the responsibilities of the franchisor and the franchisee. The agreement should clearly set forth what the franchisor will supply in initiating your franchise and the on-going forms of services you'll receive. The agreement will also describe, often in detail, just how your business is to be run. Legal conflicts arise because commitments and responsibilities are not made sufficiently clear. All promises and agreements, oral and written, should be thoroughly checked by your attorney and spelled out in the franchise contract.

We'll examine here some of the common elements of franchise agreements.

Start-up Costs and Continuing Charges

The franchisor will usually require a franchise fee. This fee can run anywhere from hundreds to hundreds of thousands of dollars. The purpose of the fee is to obtain working capital for the franchisor, and to cover the expense of site location (sometimes charged as a separate fee), training, and other services necessary to create a prosperous franchise outlet. Also the fee is supposed to assure the franchisee's personal involvement in running the business. Franchisors are increasingly skeptical of nonmanaging investors. Franchise fees have risen rapidly in the past decade; many have tripled or quadrupled. Several successful fast food chains that charged $25,000 a few years ago now charge their franchisees $100,000 or more.

Some retail and service station chains do not charge any initial fee. The franchisee pays rent for use of the franchisor's facilities and the franchisor realizes most profits by selling products to the franchisee. In some instances, such as muffler shops and the like, the franchisee acts as a volume purchaser and profits by this advantage. In others, soft drink manufacturers for instance, franchisors derive most of their revenue from sale of syrup to franchised bottlers who convert the syrup into a marketable product. In still others, such as "instant" printing franchises, the franchisor sells the franchisee all the equipment for operating the business, plus supplies used and products offered.

In a franchised service business, such as accounting, travel and employment agencies, an initial fee may be the only financial charge made. Seldom are there monthly or percentage of sales charges. This is because the franchise fee covers the use of the franchisor's name, operating methods, and business forms, but there is no continuing relationship. In instances where continuing services are supplied, such as national promotion, the franchisee usually pays the franchisor a set percentage of sales.

In addition to initial fees, rent, and charges for supplies and products, royalty fees may be charged. In the typical case the franchisor charges an initial fee, plus a set royalty fee that is usually levied regardless of the profits earned by the franchise.

The amount you invest to obtain the franchise and any continuing charges you pay the franchisor should depend on the value you receive. The central question is: *What can the franchisor do for me that I can't do for myself?*

The Business Location and Facility

The success of most franchised ventures depends heavily on the location of the business. In the past, franchisors would recruit the franchisee and then acquire the location for the outlet. This practice has now been reversed. The franchisor identifies and purchases the site for the outlet and then recruits the franchisee. Three major factors have caused this reversal of procedure. First, the growth of franchising has caused the number of desirable locations to decline sharply. Second, the price of land tends to escalate when it's known that a national franchisor is interested in a particular site. And, third, local zoning restrictions contribute to the increasingly limited supply of attractive locations.

Franchisors often deal through intermediaries in purchasing business property. But more important, franchisors are becoming more thorough in researching and selecting potential sites for their outlets. Often several thousand dollars may be spent on the marketing research and feasibility studies necessary to evaluate a specific store location. You should analyze these studies. We'll give you some guidelines for conducting your own low-cost assessment of market potential.

In most cases the franchisor will define territorial boundaries for the franchised outlet, taking into account the size of the market or population. Franchisors increasingly stipulate in the franchise agreements that, if population grows, the franchisee's territorial boundaries may be adjusted or that additional outlets may be located in the original territory.

Franchisors typically follow one of two location strategies. They may, for example, deliberately choose to locate their retail outlets close to directly competitive units. These franchisors usually cater to a largely undifferentiated mass market. This practice is no doubt influenced by local zoning restrictions, but it follows from the belief that increased customer traffic that results from a cluster of competitive outlets will more than offset the impact of competition.

Other franchisors choose not to compete directly with franchise businesses like McDonald's and Burger King. Tastee Freeze, for example, usually locates in smaller towns with populations of 20,000 or less. Several of the larger franchisors aim at metropolitan areas with a population of 30,000 or more but still small enough to be without direct competition from huge franchise operations.

In many cases the concentration of several competitors in a small geographical area has saturated the market. And in some instances franchisors in rural areas have experienced declining population. Each franchise location is unique. You should evaluate the location offered by the franchisor in terms of its *future* market potential.

Training in the Business

Most reputable franchisors offer the franchisee thorough training in operating the business. Often they require such training as a condition of obtaining the franchise. You'll want to check out how much background the franchisor expects you to have in the type of business you'll be running. Many actually prefer that the franchisee have no experience, nothing to "unlearn," and therefore can more easily be trained in the franchisor's way of doing business.

Franchisee training should not only cover policies, procedures, and methods, but also should emphasize the entrepreneurial and management skills needed. The problems in initiating and running a franchise business are no different from those encountered in any other kind of small business. Training should also prepare franchise managers for long working hours, stress, and frustration during the first several months of operation.

The best training programs are about equally divided between classroom instruction and field experience gained through working in a franchise outlet. Programs are usually four to six weeks in length, often conducted in the franchisor's special training facilities. Your franchise fee usually covers training costs and any on-the-job or follow-up training conducted by the franchisor.

One of the more common complaints of franchisees is that despite training that features the technical, managerial, *and* emotional aspects of initiating a small business they still do not feel adequately prepared. We strongly recommend that before investing you check out the franchisor's training program thoroughly, especially if you lack specific business experience. Before you start your own franchise business be sure that the training offered by the franchisor includes field experience and is supplemented later on by training designed to update and expand your skills.

Franchise Operations

The franchise agreement often sets rigid standards and spells out specific operating procedures the franchisee must follow. These controls on the business assure consistent practices among franchised outlets and serve to enhance trademark awareness, community identity, and consumer image. This means that the franchisor's operating requirements can affect every aspect of your business, including store layout and design, equipment and furnishings to be used, products produced and their quality, and promotional efforts.

The amount of control the franchisor exerts directly affects the amount of discretion and entrepreneurial freedom you'll have. You should check out the mechanisms used to govern business operations. Five ways in which franchisors can control the franchise are:

1. *The franchise agreement.* Typically the franchise contract will describe in painstaking detail standards, rules, and procedures to be followed. The agreement will also set the duration of the contract and the conditions under which the contract can be terminated. As the franchisee you would be legally bound by the contract.

2. *Franchisor policy.* Most franchisors spell out additional rules and guidelines in their official operating manual. These operating manuals cover required day-to-day business practices such as hours of operation, employee hiring and firing, employee qualifications, record-keeping systems, and product storage, preparation, and handling.

3. *Franchisor approval.* In some cases, franchisors require franchisees to obtain approval for certain business decisions. For example, the franchisor's approval might be required before the franchisee could expand the business, or add new products or services.

4. *Franchisor recommendations.* Franchisors sometimes simply recommend ways to perform certain business tasks or kinds of business activities rather than impose prescribed procedures.

5. *Franchisee reports.* Reports on unit sales, revenue, costs, and profit will be required monthly or quarterly. The franchisor's representative will probably discuss the reports with the franchisee.

The franchisor may use one or some combination of these governing methods. You should understand the particular way these control mechanisms are applied. It will be important to pinpoint those areas of business operations over which:

- You have no control and in which strict compliance to standards is required

- You have some control, but your decisions must be guided by franchisor recommendation, or your actions must have prior approval of the franchisor

- You have total control and can make local decisions without consulting the franchisor.

Duration, Termination, and Transfers

Other aspects of the franchisor-franchisee relationship you should explore concern the *duration* of the contract, the details of *termination* of the contract (whether franchisor or you, the franchisee, wants to cancel), and the *conditions* under which the franchise may be sold or transferred.

Duration
The trend has been towards longer and longer franchise contract periods. Contracts that now run 10 to 20 years or more are common. In most cases the length of the franchise contract depends upon the duration of the lease on the property where the outlet is located. The franchise agreement and the property lease agreement are often contained in one document because most franchises have no value without having a specific business site.

Termination
The franchisor properly reserves the right to cancel, or refuse to renew, the contract of a franchisee who does not cooperate, mismanages, or fails in the business. But conditions for terminating the franchise contract should be examined closely. Franchisees are often at a disadvantage in influencing the franchisor's right to cancel or refuse to renew the contract. Franchisors have threatened franchisees with cancellation to force them into accepting corporate decisions or unreasonable obligations. We urge extreme caution if the franchisor requires high minimum purchase of inventory levels, or unreasonably high sales quotas. Your planning and decision making should be based on careful analysis and strategy, not on fear of unreasonable demands from the franchisor.

Transfers
The franchise agreement will stipulate the conditions under which the franchise may be sold or transferred. Generally the franchisee does not have the right to sell the business or bequeath it to heirs without formal approval of the franchisor.

The franchisor usually reserves the right to recover or buy back a franchised outlet upon termination of the franchise contract. If the franchisee has not reserved the right to renew the contract, the franchisor can deal with others in negotiating the new contract.

The "guaranteed buy back" offer of franchisors—to buy back a franchise business that doesn't make a go of it—was the bait that lured hundreds of franchisees. However, buy back usually didn't mean the franchisor would share in the franchisee's financial losses. Buy back clauses should be examined carefully.

Some major franchisors tend to repurchase franchise outlets and operate them themselves or to sell some or all outlets to larger companies. The point is that since the franchise agreement will favor the franchisor in some way, the franchisor can pressure the franchisee to sell out. When the franchisee sells a successful business back to the franchisor, there's the problem of setting a value on the business. Our recommendation is that your contract contain a provision for independent arbitration to evaluate the business fairly in the event of termination. The value should include tangible assets such as equipment and fixtures and intangible assets such as goodwill.

Special Problems to Watch For in the Franchise Agreement— a Summary

The franchise agreement establishes the responsibilities of each of the mutually dependent parties. Conflicts arise if the agreeement does not precisely spell out the rights and obligations of the franchisee and franchisor. One study identifies more than sixty well-known franchisors who have been involved in significant franchise litigation.[3] You should be aware of the more frequent sources of disagreement in evaluating a potential franchise agreement.[4]

Table 12-1 shows the ten most common legal problems reported by franchisees.

Sharing advertising costs is the most common legal problem according to the table. Franchisees who are required by contract to contribute money for national advertising indicated that in some cases they had not received their "fair share" of advertising locally. The complaint is that the franchisor, who controls the scheduling and placement of advertising, had not devoted enough attention to the franchisee's market. Thus, franchisees sue to reduce their assessment for advertising or to increase the amount of advertising in their locality.

The second most common problem involves provisions for inspection or evaluation by the franchisor. Here the complaint is that franchisors are not consistent in enforcing strict adherence to standards among all members of the franchise chain. Failure of the franchisor to insist that all franchisees meet standards damages the image and reputation of those who do.

The third most prevalent source of disagreement is really the reverse of the problem just described. Disputes arise about the interpretation of minimum performance standards. As might be expected, this tends to occur among low-performing franchisees who complain that they must comply with inflexible or arbitrary minimum performance standards.

Table 12-1 Ten Most Common Legal Problems of Franchisees

Problem	Rank
Frequent Problems	
Sharing advertising costs	1
Inspection/evaluation by franchisor	2
Minimum performance requirements	3
Occasional Problems	
Royalty payments	4
Fees for support services	5
Territorial limits	6
Rare Problems	
Penalties for violation of contract	7
Restrictions on products or prices	8
Employee conduct/training requirements	9
Limits on competitive business	10

Source: James L. Porter and William Renforth, "Franchise Agreements: Spotting the Important Legal Issues," *Journal of Small Business Management*, Vol. 16, No. 4, October 1978, p. 28.

Pay careful attention to whether the franchise agreement sufficiently covers the problem areas listed in Table 12-1. Give special consideration to the first three since they occur most frequently and can be critical to successful franchise operations.

Litigation is costly and can be avoided by adequate planning. Having prior business experience, consulting your own independent legal counsel, and conducting your own market research are the best ways to avoid serious disputes.

Key Factors in Marketing

Be sure the investment you make will significantly help you market your outlet. The franchisor's products or services must be thoroughly tested and meet an important consumer need. There should be evidence of new product development and continual innovation. The franchisor should have a recognized trade name and a national reputation. Advertising should be geared to promote franchise outlets and to expand the market for the franchisee's products. Creative sales promotion that appeals to the potential market for your outlet should supplement advertising.

Doing Your Own Market Research

Conducting your own market research is the most important element in choosing the right franchise business. Franchisors wanting to expand distribution rapidly feature the franchise opportunity in the best possible light. They may have elaborate location studies or consumer surveys to support their claims and fancy ways of presenting the benefits of winning one of their outlets. Doing your own market research lessens the likelihood of your being misled.

Profitable marketing for the franchise business is no different from that for other types of businesses. The marketing concepts, strategies, and tools covered in Chapters 4 through 7 are important to successful operation of the small franchise business. What *is* different is that some of the marketing responsibility—primarily nationwide marketing—is assumed by the franchisor.

Before investing, you should thoroughly check out the marketing expertise of the franchisor, particularly in the areas of product innovation, site location, national trademark and trade name image, advertising, and creativity in sales promotion. These are the marketing responsibilities and benefits you buy with your investment in a particular franchise. It's up to you to determine how well these responsibilities are performed *before* you sink your money into the venture.

Product Innovation

Does the franchisor introduce new products and ways to improve on existing products? Are the products or services offered truly unique? Have the franchisor's products been tested thoroughly under market conditions? What are the franchisor's plans (not promises) for new product development and introduction?

You can answer these questions through your own observations of the franchise chain, by interviewing existing franchise owners and customers, and by critically reviewing reports or product studies conducted by the franchisor. If you're not satisfied with the answers, it may mean that the franchisor is attempting to "sell you a franchise" rather than a business that caters to a consumer need and sells proven and continually improving products.

The marketing concept, you'll remember, places the consumer first. Products or services offered by the franchise business must fulfill a consumer need. Huge outlays of money for advertising, site locations, and capital cannot compensate for shoddy products or inadequate services.

Site Location

The success of most franchise businesses depends on a good location convenient to the customer. Knowing the amount and type of consumer traffic close to the outlet is essential because, the products are purchased by consumers not only on the basis of quality and need, but also on the basis of convenience.

Franchisors follow several location strategies. They sometimes locate in areas where there is a cluster of outlets selling similar, but differentiated, products; sometimes they choose not to compete directly and locate "free standing" outlets in individual market areas; some locate in shopping malls, or adjacent to other retail outlets in shopping centers.

The approach the franchisor uses to locate outlets depends on the market segmentation strategy being used. The franchisor should be able to give you hard data in well documented, professional market research studies that describe the market segment to be reached and confirm the appropriateness of the site location to that market segment.

If the outlet you're thinking of buying is new, you should review the franchisor's market studies critically. Check the franchisor's data on consumer traffic, for example, by counting the number of cars and people passing the store during a typical week—Mondays, Thursdays, and Saturdays during time periods when you'd expect business to be good usually will give good data. And check the experience of other franchisees to see how traffic count translates into customers for the outlet. Compare these data with the franchisor's.

You should also check with the local government traffic department that controls street use around the potential site. Will there be changes in traffic patterns? Will parking ordinances be changed? Will streets be widened, or major traffic arteries improved? In many cases you can get accurate traffic surveys from local city or county governments or police departments.

You should interview small business owners in the vicinity of the proposed site for your business. Ask their opinions about the future of the commercial area and its potential, the appropriateness of the site for your outlet, and any related problems they foresee.

Study residential construction patterns and visit with real estate brokers to find out if and how population and property values are changing. Is the area growing or declining? Local government officials who issue business permits are knowledgeable about the kinds of new businesses being attracted to the area. Editors of local newspapers and the local Chamber of Commerce may be helpful.

Image and Advertising

The marketing of products and services sold by franchise outlets requires effective mass advertising. Fast food products, motels, tax services, auto mufflers, paint, hearing aids, and auto rental services need a large investment in advertising to create trade name or brand awareness on a national scale. Carefully designed advertising messages that saturate the consumer market and are repeated frequently are critical in order to differentiate the franchisor's products or services from competitors'.

Most franchisors conduct national advertising campaigns to draw customers to their outlets. Initial fees and often other charges paid by franchisees help to support the mass advertising effort. For a new outlet, national advertising will usually be supplemented by targeted local sales stimulation.

Two important aspects of the franchisor-franchisee advertising relationship need to be checked out. First, find out what your financial commitments are in the franchisor's advertising program. Does the contract specifically state how the franchisor and franchisee will share in advertising expenditures? How much of your initial investment goes for this purpose? What contributions will you have to make over time for the franchisor's national promotion campaign?

Second, look into the nature of the advertising program itself. Ask the franchisor for the year-ahead advertising plan. Figures should be available to show how much advertising your market will receive compared with the franchisor's other markets. From your own experience, does it appear that the mix of mass media to be used in advertising—radio, TV, billboards, magazines, newspapers—will be the right one to reach the potential market for your outlet? Will the advertising message appeal to the market for your outlet?

The franchisor should be able to show you media studies that document the effectiveness of the advertising campaign. Copy tests, for example, will demonstrate the believability and attention-getting impact of advertising messages. An analysis of the reach of the advertising program should be available to show how many consumers heard or saw the franchisor's messages. The analysis should also indicate demographic and consumer buying characteristics. The franchisor should also be able to show you how advertising will be scheduled in your local market—the media to be used, when ads will run, and how much will be spent.

Sales Promotion

As competition in franchising has increased, so too has franchisors' reliance on sales promotion as an important tool to entice consumers to their outlets, and to build customer loyalty. These promotion efforts may include special point-of-purchase display materials, in-store demonstrations, coupon redemption deals, and premiums. It is usually the franchisor's responsibility to design and execute creative sales promotion programs. Advertising is frequently used to inform consumers of the sales promotion. And concrete plans for sales promotion must be set well in advance, at least six months to a year, so that advertising and franchisee participation are properly coordinated.

Ask the franchisor for sales effectiveness studies of past sales promotion programs. Review the plan and approach to be used in the coming year. Will you have to pay for a share of the cost? Will particular sales stimulation tools be appropriate for your market? Will they be enough, or will you have to supplement such promotion with your own local campaign?

TRENDS IN FRANCHISING

Although the franchising industry is stabilizing, it shows signs of continued vitality. The era of fast, at times chaotic, growth during the 50s and 60s resulted in a healthy shake-out in the early 70s. This was caused by a combination of overexpansion, incompetent management, and poor business conditions. During the second half of the 70s increased legislation and surveillance by government at all levels corrected earlier abuses. Today there are far more assurances that companies offering franchise ventures are reputable and professional. The earlier rapid growth has slowed, but total annual sales volume of franchised outlets has increased an average of about 10 percent each year through the 70s.

Before citing some obstacles to future growth, we'll examine notable trends in franchising, including increased legislation, more power for the franchisee, and expansion in franchising services.

Government Control

More than a dozen states have enacted legislation requiring franchising companies to register and to disclose fully their financial condition. Several other states have such legislation to govern franchisor-franchisee relations.

In one of the worst abuses in the past, franchisors withheld information from prospective franchisees on how well the outlets in the chain were doing. Instead, some franchisors would present the financial data on only a few of their more profitable outlets.

Now, in addition to public disclosure, franchisors must meet tougher restrictions in the kinds of claims they can make in recruiting their franchisees and about the means by which they can terminate franchise agreements.

Franchisee Control

The rights of the franchisee have much better legal protection now than in the past; recent court decisions have tended to favor the franchisee. For example, court decisions have revoked the once-common practice by some franchisors of forcing franchisees to buy supplies and merchandise from them alone.

In several instances, franchisees have organized into associations to negotiate more effectively with franchisors. In addition to the growing collective power of franchisees, the more profitable franchisees have substantial influence on the franchisor. There are numerous cases of franchisees, who have become successful, leaving the franchisor's chain and starting their own competitive franchise operation.

Company-owned Outlets

Increased government regulation and franchisee control have heightened the interest of franchisors in buying back their franchised businesses. Moreover, to several major franchisors, the profitability of franchised outlets has made it good economic sense to begin developing company-owned outlets. Franchisees' earning profit ratios of as much as four-to-one more than the franchisor has produced the incentive to acquire outlets. Pizza Hut, Ponderosa Systems, and McDonald's have been active in acquiring their own outlets.

As we noted earlier, examine the termination conditions in your franchise agreement carefully. Guard against indirect methods that might be used by the franchisor to pursuade you to sell out. Know your legal rights before you sign.

Growth in Franchising Services

The service sector of the U.S. economy is larger than the manufacturing sector and is growing rapidly. Demand is strong and rising for consumer and industrial services. The number of franchised businesses has soared in the fields of recreation, entertainment, travel, and business services.

The financial requirements for starting the franchised service business tends to be much less than in the product business, since most are not capital-intensive. Further, as we've stressed in Chapter 7, the rendering of services takes more personal involvement and interaction with consumers. Thus, small franchised businesses, owned locally and serving a limited geographical area, tend to be an ideal vehicle for expanding distribution.

Key Trends in Franchising

The factors we've examined here have produced a more stable industry with tighter controls and better protection for franchisees. As the more mature phase continues, there are clear signals that responsible franchisors will pursue a more orderly, soundly based, growth pattern.

Opportunities in service-oriented franchises look promising. And as capital becomes increasingly scarce, other types of businesses, not now using the franchise method of distribution, will be attracted to franchising. Finally, franchisors may improve the attractiveness of obtaining and operating their franchised outlets because of the short supply of good franchisees.

Obstacles for Future Growth

We've already noted the problem of obtaining good site locations. In addition, franchisors increasingly face capital shortages in expanding operations because of rising land and construction costs. Even when good locations are available, local regulations are growing more stringent in controlling building design, size of signs, building setbacks, and parking space requirements.

Increased competition and the difficulty of finding good franchisees are also problems facing franchisors. Some key markets may be nearing a saturation point. Also, franchisors who received many applications a few years ago report that recruiting an effective franchise team is now more difficult. This has resulted in more public appeals and advertising by franchisors to locate franchisees.

A franchise contract is a legal agreement between a supplier (franchisor) and a retailer or wholesale distributor (franchisee) under which the supplier grants the right to handle its products or services to the retailer or wholesale distributor in a mutually agreed upon way. The franchising relationship means that you operate your own business under certain defined conditions and in connection with a chain of similar businesses. As a franchisee you are given the right to represent and market the product or service of the franchisor in a specific geographical area. The franchisee also receives training and other assistance to operate the business successfully.

In some cases, either with or without an initial fee, franchisors receive continuing revenue from franchisees' payments for royalty, leasing the outlet, and supplies furnished by the franchisor.

A major benefit of franchising is the cooperative buying power, which results in reduced cost of supplies, equipment, sales promotion material, and advertising.

In return for your investment, the franchisor should offer tested products, a national, pre-sold market, proven selling methods, less business risk, and a shorter time before your business shows a profit. Other services normally include operating manuals, management training, site selection, facility design and construction, lease negotiation, and, in some cases, financing the franchising venture. Once the business is launched, continuing services often include sales promotion, merchandising, national advertising, and retraining.

The franchise contract spells out the responsibilities of the partners involved. Legal problems occur most often because of confusion in interpreting clauses within the contract. You should get competent legal counsel to review the contract in detail before you sign.

You should check the reputation of the franchisor with bankers, the Better Business Bureau, and other franchisees. Extend your investigation to the product or service to be offered, the potential market in which your outlet will be located, and the advertising and sales promotion efforts of the franchisor. Make sure you are familiar with the community's building and zoning regulations, growth pattern, highway and street plans, real estate trends and outlook, and changes in population and income. The time and effort you spend in planning for your franchise venture will reduce your risk and make your investment more secure.

CHAPTER 12/FOOTNOTES

[1]A recent study reinforcing these findings may be found in James L. Porter and William Renforth, "Franchise Agreements: Spotting the Important Legal Issues," *Journal of Small Business Management*, Vol. 16, No. 4, October 1978, pp. 27–31. Summaries of several previous studies on franchising can be found in Charles L. Vaughn, *Franchising*, D. C. Heath and Company, Lexington, Mass., 1974, especially pp. 37–42.

[2]Interestingly, obtaining working capital by collecting franchise fees constitutes a self-liquidating debt obligation. The fee has to be repaid only if the franchisor does

not meet all contract requirements. In the early 1970s several franchisors were reporting franchise fees as current earnings. This artificially inflated their earnings per share value. Practices of this nature existed in several franchising companies. Investor support declined sharply when it was found that rapid accumulation of franchise fees was being used to boost performance figures. Records of profitability through good management would show legitimate figures.

In addition to its interest-free feature, capital financing through franchising avoids restrictions on use of funds and procedural delays in setting up a stock corporation. Within very broad limits the franchisor can spend funds collected— even on business activities not directly connected with the requirements of new franchisees.

Franchising offers a clever acquisition-of-funds technique since the interest-free loans (initial joining fees) do not have to be repaid so long as the franchisor honors the contract with the franchisee. It has been estimated that $450 million would have been required for Kentucky Fried Chicken Corp. to establish its first 2,700 stores. This large sum of money was available only from franchisee-supplied capital.

Other forms of financing are much less attractive to the franchisor. Obtaining funds through sale of stock often takes a long time and imposes significant under-writing costs that reduce the total capital acquired by the sale. Equity financing techniques, such as sale of common stock, result in diluting ownership. Debt financing through borrowing weakens cash flow because of the interest and repayment obligations.

[3]Harold Brown, *Franchising—Realities and Remedies*, Law Journal Press, New York, 1973, p. 6.

[4]The more frequent problems causing franchisee-franchisor litigation are summarized here, as reported in James L. Porter and William Renforth, "Franchise Agreements: Spotting the Important Legal Issues," *Journal of Small Business Management*, Vol. 16, No. 4, October 1978, pp. 27–31.

FRANCHISING

Special note: Your completed assignments for Chapters 4 through 6 will apply to some of the exercises here. If you are considering a service franchise, Chapter 7 will also apply. You may want to review them all after studying this chapter.

1. List the advantages and disadvantages to *you* for choosing the franchise route to owning and running a business compared to starting your own business from scratch. The central question to address is: What can the franchisor do for me that I cannot do for myself?

Advantages	Disadvantages

2. Develop an action plan for carrying out your own independent marketing research to evaluate the franchise opportunity you are considering.

   a. Product or service innovation: _____

   _____

   _____

   _____

   b. Site location: _____

   _____

   _____

   _____

c. Image and advertising: _____

_____

_____

_____

d. Sales promotion: _____

_____

_____

_____

e. Overall market trends and_____

prospects: _____

_____

_____

_____

3. Before you've made any financial commitments: How will you verify and evaluate the services the franchisor will supply you once you've made your investment? Make notes for actions you'll take to assess each category below.

a. The business location and facility: _____

_____

_____

_____

b. Training in the business: _____

_____

_____

_____

c. Franchise operations: _____

_____

_____

_____

4. In evaluating a particular franchise agreement, specify below the areas of business operations over which:

a. You'll have no control: _____

_____

_____

_____

243

b. You'll have some control: _____

_____

_____

_____

c. You'll have total control: _____

_____

_____

_____

5. List below the specific features of the franchise contract you'll want evaluated by your legal counsel.

a. _____

b. _____

c. _____

d. _____

e. _____

f. _____

IF YOU WANT TO READ MORE

BOOKS

Charles L. Vaughn, *Franchising*, Lexington Books, Lexington, Mass., 1974. Gives a complete overview and history of franchising. Describes the nature, scope, and advantages in a nontechnical way. Good case histories are given covering legal and marketing problems.

Robert M. Dias and Stanley I. Gurnick, *Franchising: The Investor's Complete Handbook*, Hastings House, New York, 1969. Although somewhat dated—the book was published just prior to the shake-out in the industry in the early 70s—it is still one of the best nuts-and-bolts treatments of franchising from the viewpoint of the prospective franchisee.

Urban B. Ozanne and Shelby D. Hunt, *The Economic Effect of Franchising*, Small Business Administration, Washington, D.C., 1971. This book reports some of the serious pitfalls in franchising, from the franchisee's viewpoint, that occurred during the early 70s. The effects of some of the abuses franchisors inflicted on franchisees are instructive, and ways to avoid them are given.

Harry Kursh, *The Franchise Boom—How You Profit in It*, Prentice-Hall, Inc., Englewood-Cliffs, N.J., 1968. An encyclopedia of franchise information, this volume gives tips on how and where to find franchise opportunities, how to investigate before investing, and how to finance the franchised venture.

MONOGRAPHS

E. Patrick McGuire, *Franchised Distribution*, The Conference Board, Inc., New York, 1971. This is a detailed report on research findings in the franchise industry. Areas covered include franchisor operations, franchisee recruitment, contracts, site selection, and training.

Franchising, a report published by the *Small Business Reporter*, Bank of America, San Francisco, 1975. Practical and succinct, this report covers the contractual and financial aspects of franchising.

DIRECTORIES

Franchise Opportunities Handbook, U.S. Department of Commerce, U.S. Printing Office, Washington, D.C., 1972.

Directory of Franchising Organizations, Pilot Books, New York. Published annually.

NEWSLETTERS

Continental Franchise Review, National Research Publishing, Inc., Denver, Colo. Published 26 times per year.

Chapter 13

Controlling Your Manufacturing Operations

f you plan to go into manufacturing, you'll be dealing with issues that are quite different from those in other kinds of business. These issues will be more complex in many cases, and there will likely be more of them. As a beginning manufacturer, you must plan in such a way as to make every dollar you put into the business pay off. To do this, you'll have to set sound policies in managing production and operations.

Policies are guides to action; sound policies beget sound action. You'll want sound policies for gaining control of assets and operations. These will include policies for buying, leasing, or building a plant; buying or leasing equipment; making or buying parts, components, or subassemblies; designing your product line; managing inventory; and controlling production and costs of all kinds.

Like most entrepreneurs starting a venture, you probably have limited funds. Your very first policy should therefore say that you'll husband your money in every way that makes sense. Rather than put a large amount of money into a huge purchase of raw stock at a bargain price, you'd buy less at a higher price in order to preserve your cash. Rather than invest a large sum in a high-speed screw machine, you'd arrange to buy it on terms—again to conserve your available cash. These are a small sample of the kinds of decisions you'll be faced with early in the game.

You'll want to adjust your policies as your company grows and prospers. Then you can take advantage of bargains and the desirable features of new and expensive equipment. You'll be able to capitalize on your company's strengths and build to overcome its weaknesses. You'll adjust your policies, expanding their scope to achieve broader objectives, as your business gains in resources.

DESIGNING YOUR SMALL PLANT   7 A (4), 8 A (4)

Whether you plan to build, buy, or lease a plant, you should follow three guidelines in making your decisions. These have to do with plant location, community features, and plant layout. If you lease or buy, you may not be able to meet the guidelines in full. Whichever way you go, you'll find some of the items suggested here to be mandatory and others to be desirable. You'll want to meet those that are musts in full; you should try to meet the others to the greatest possible extent.

Location

When you choose the location for your plant, look for ease of access to your market and to the raw materials you'll need. If your product uses large quantities of lumber, these materials will come from the mill or distributor by rail or truck. You'll want easy access by railroad siding or road. Your plant should have a loading dock at the right height to unload and load boxcar or truck readily. If your product is light and easy to handle, you may need only the simplest facility. Electrical measuring instruments, for example, can be boxed in small cartons and carried to airport or post office by pickup.

Watch Zoning Restrictions

Choose your plant site with careful attention to zoning restrictions. Zoning ordinances in today's world require attention to the ecological impact of your operations. Many communities don't want plants that spew out noxious fumes or emit smoke, noise, dust, or waste products. Special areas are usually set aside for heavy industry. Whatever your current requirements, you should choose your site with both present and future requirements in mind. If you think that the characteristics of your business will change in time, you should locate your plant in an area where zoning restrictions won't prevent you from making the change. Planning for the future may save you disruption of your business when you want to change.

Make Sure of Your Labor Supply

The kind of labor you'll need in your manufacturing operation will depend on the kind of work to be done. You should make very sure that you can draw on a labor market adequate to meet your needs. Local agencies can usually give you information about labor in your community. Your product may not require highly skilled people. If so, your problem is lessened. You may need only semiskilled people whom you can train without too much effort.

This was the case with the Howard Products Company, which made small components used by the electrical manufacturing industry. This company, owned by a sole proprietor, Jack Howard, hired an assembly force composed mainly of women to do the assembly of tiny parts. His plant was located in an isolated backwater area near a large metropolitan city. Public transportation wasn't available, and it was difficult for many of his people to get to work. Even those who had cars found the drive to work tedious. Howard was faced with a high turnover in the labor force. Despite this problem, his company had prospered in the seven years of its existence, and he wanted to move to a more attractive location.

After several months of searching, Howard found a beautiful small town nestled in the hills not far from the sea. The town offered several advantages for his small plant: A new industrial park on the outskirts gave him the chance to buy ten acres at a reasonable price. His operations didn't emit fumes, noise, or dust and therefore conformed with local ordinances. The town was a haven for older people who were semiretired and would welcome part-time employment. And a nearby college with a school of business afforded the opportunity to hire and train supervisors and potential managers.

Howard had a competent architect design his plant. He developed a four-day workweek that permitted his workforce a great deal of flexibility in setting their personal working schedules. As he hired the older personnel in the new plant, he put them through a carefully worked-out training program staffed by experienced people he had moved from his old plant.

Howard followed the guidelines we give here in building his new plant. It has turned out to be a model of a good place for people to work. It's clean, attractive, and efficient. His company has developed a stable and productive work force.

250

Make Sure About Utilities: Power, Gas, and Water Supplies

When you select your plant site, make sure that the supplies of power, gas, and water are adequate for your intended operation. Work out your needs for these requirements ahead of time. If you plan to use a significant amount of electricity, be certain that it's available in the right quantity, voltage, and phase. Be sure that your supply of electric power can meet the growth you expect. Be certain also about gas and water supplies. If you need large quantities of water in your process, be sure that you can get approval to dump the outflow into the sewer system.

Watch Those Taxes

Find out what your tax burden will be in the location you select. Some communities offer special tax relief for new plants moving in—at least for a given period. If this is your situation, be certain that the tax benefit doesn't override the more important items we've listed above. You'll find that local taxes will run about 2 to 5 percent of the estimated true value of your real estate and property. This would be a rather small portion of your total investment; nevertheless, be careful to check the tax assessment policy and rates in the community you choose.

Design Features

Use expert architectural help in designing your plant or in remodeling an existing plant. Through this kind of help, you can arrive at a design that permits expansion for future growth *and* meets your current needs at minimum cost. You'll be able to select from the many modern construction methods one that gives this kind of flexibility. Methods available include modular construction, shell structures, geodesic domes, independent steel frame, or independent long-span concrete frame construction.

You'd do well to be influenced by the needs for good citizenship in planning your new plant. Measures should be incorporated for the abatement of possible public nuisances such as noise, smoke, fumes, or other pollutants. Very often the capital investment for abatement may be more than recovered through an improvement in efficiency or the reclamation of waste products. For example, if you use a heat-treating furnace in your operations, you'll find that a furnace that burns clean uses its fuel efficiently; the amount of fuel used will be less and will cost less than if your furnace emits smoke.

Build a Good Looking Plant

Be certain that the design of your buildings and grounds meets aesthetic requirements. Your buildings should be kept in good repair and the grounds around them carefully landscaped and well tended. You'll make your plant a pleasant workplace for your personnel by taking care of the appearance of your buildings and grounds. Pleasant, well-kept, tidy surroundings will help to keep the morale and productivity of your work force high. Your investment in appearance will help you establish good relations with your community as well.

Your physical plant is the tool you use to combine the input of people, material, and money to make the product you sell. It should be so designed to give a smooth and therefore efficient flow of process. Anything that interferes with the smooth flow of process costs money, and that lowers the profitability of your whole manufacturing operation. Use the greatest care in designing the plant layout to make the flow of the manufacturing process as smooth as you can make it. However you do it, be certain that working conditions are safe and comfortable.

Make Your Layout Work for You

You can arrive at a straightforward efficient flow of your production process by observing certain precautions in designing the layout of your plant. These include provisions for storing, handling, and moving material and work in process.

The layout can be visualized through a scale drawing showing the arrangement of the facilities and equipment within the plant. It may also take the form of a scale model displaying the physical arrangement in miniature. In either case, the objective is to arrive at a layout that allows material and work in process to be moved easily over the shortest possible distances while permitting the manufacturing process to be carried out smoothly, step by step.

You should seek ways to move material with minimum handling over the shortest route. Moving material and work in process costs money; therefore, anything you can do to eliminate a stage in handling or to shorten the distance that material must be moved will save you money. You can try different arrangements by changing the layout until you arrive at the most efficient location of facilities and equipment.

Building in Flexibility of Design

You can be sure that you'll want or need to change your product design or add new products to your line as your business grows. You should therefore incorporate in your basic plant design features making it easy to adjust your plant to new production requirements. The features you can build in for ready adaptability include: clear floor space without posts or columns; high enough roof and sturdy enough supporting structure to accommodate overhead handling equipment such as traveling hoists for moving material, or for installing tall equipment or machinery; under-floor ducts or overhead conduits for carrying high voltage electric lines; movable mounts for ease in relocation of production equipment; and floors strong enough to take highly concentrated loads. You'll find that some of these features will add some expense to construction costs. But forethought in these matters will allow you to save much more money later when you need these facilities.

Make Your Plant Maintenance Easy

Great care should be taken in choosing your building materials. Some are easier to maintain than others. By careful selection of materials, you can lower the long-range costs of maintenance. No building materials are free from maintenance, but some are

252

more suitable for a given purpose than others. Natural concrete walls may not need paint, but they may need to be steamcleaned on occasion to get rid of soot and dirt. Tile or stainless steel panels are easier to keep clean in washrooms than other materials. Whatever you select, you should consider the cost over the long term when you choose building materials. Savings over time may be worth a somewhat higher first cost.

Select Adequate Machine Capacity

When you select a machine to do a job, you'll find it wise to choose one with somewhat more capacity than you think you need. A machine that can handle larger jobs or more work can easily take care of the first job for which you bought it. But it can do more and will be on hand when you want to make the move to more demanding jobs. The larger capacity machine will require less maintenance than the smaller, and it will be there when you want it. The extra capacity will cost a little more, but it will pay off the extra cost many times over in the long run. It will especially pay off if you're careful to make provision for regular maintenance of it and of all of your production machinery and equipment.

WORKING YOUR PLANT MORE THAN ONE SHIFT?　　7

It seems clear that you can turn out more work in your small plant if you work your facilities more than one shift per day. Under some conditions you may find this profitable. However, you should weigh the disadvantages as well as the advantages before adding shifts to your operations. If you adopt a three-shift operation, you'd be using your equipment *intensively*; in a single shift operation you'd be using your equipment *extensively*.

You'd probably reduce your overhead costs per unit of production by going to a three-shift operation. This would hold for certain items of expense such as taxes, building depreciation, interest on investment, and obsolescence of machinery. You might also be able to take advantage of lower rates for electricity during night operation.

Unfortunately, other costs usually offset these gains. Cost of labor is higher for second and third shifts. Saturday and Sunday work commands even higher labor rates than off-normal shift rates. Labor on other than first shift tends to be somewhat less productive, thus increasing unit labor costs.

Maintenance of machinery and equipment is easier on one-shift, five-day operation. Repairs and adjustments may be done without interfering with production.

The experience of many small plant executives shows that, all in all, it's generally more desirable to have a larger plant that can produce what's normally needed in a standard workday and workweek.

Many plants use part of their facilities intensively and part extensively. If you have one or two very expensive special-purpose machines, you may find it profitable to work them more than one shift per day. You'd then work the rest of the plant during normal hours.

Changing Trends in Working Hours

You may find advantage in going to a four-day workweek in all or part of your manufacturing operations. The four-day workweek was first adopted by small manufacturing firms in the late 1960s. Since then all kinds of organizations have gone this route: retail trade, hospitals, banks, trucking firms, wholesalers, and a variety of service firms. But small manufacturing concerns still seem to be at the forefront of this movement.

If you were to adopt the four-day workweek, you'd want to study the requirements of your business for labor and production very carefully before you introduced the new schedule. Some companies place the total work force on four days, including men and women employees. Others exclude employees who must serve customers, such as clerks and salespersons. Each firm must plan the move to the four-day workweek on the basis of its special needs.

You'd also want to adjust wage rates so neither your firm nor your employees experience inequities. Some firms reduce the standard forty hours to thirty-five, thirty-seven, or some similar figure. Hourly rates are reduced a bit to minimize the effect of higher overtime rates. In this way the worker's take-home pay is the same as it was before the change.

Surprisingly, companies that have adopted the four-day workweek have experienced few disadvantages. It takes a while for people to adjust to the new schedule, and customers must be educated to the new business hours. But once running smoothly on the four-day schedule, very few problems seem to arise. The advantages that come with the four-day workweek are primarily person-related. Most people like to have a three-day weekend. The plant on the short workweek can often attract a superior work force of qualified personnel for this reason. Managers find the long weekend a positive feature in that it allows them sufficient time to regenerate their energy for the next week. And you, as the owner of the business, may find the quiet time the long weekend permits extremely beneficial in doing your thinking ahead and planning for the future of your business.

Learning from Learning Curves

When we approach a strange new task, we tend to be slow and relatively inefficient. As we experiment with ways to perform the task, we correct our errors and inadequate ways of doing things and we become more efficient. We use less time to do the job and we do it better. This is particularly true in production.

You'll find that as your personnel acquire skill through experience in a new production task productivity will go up and costs will come down. The curves of Figure 13-1 show the typical relationship between productivity and costs of production as learning takes place.

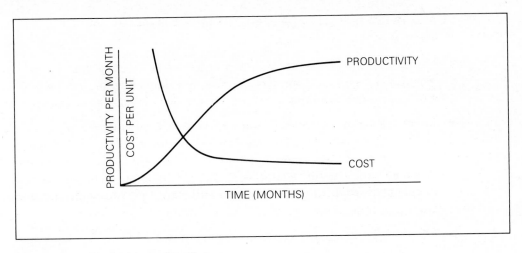

Figure 13-1 Typical Learning Curve

The reduction in time and cost stems from a variety of factors. You can find ways to speed up the learning and cost reduction process by studying the implications of these factors: better planning by management as they learn the elements of the production task; increased skill by workers; improved tooling, jigs, and fixtures; specially developed production equipment; and reduced scrap. You'll be able to predict quite accurately the unit cost when you rerun a product. One guide you can use comes from the aircraft and electronics industries: Every time your production quantity doubles you can expect that your direct labor cost will decrease from 60 to 80 percent of its former level.

You'll predict your costs with increasing accuracy as you collect data. It's an important procedure to keep careful records of cost and production. If you develop your own learning curves as you go, you'll soon have a sound basis for predicting the costs of new runs and of runs of new products.

Manage Seasonal Change

The business of some manufacturing plants is highly seasonal. Sporting goods like skis and tennis rackets have up and down manufacturing requirements during the year. Toy manufacturing and apparel manufacturing have their ups and downs. If your business has seasonal characteristics, you'll face the critical problem of managing your cyclical manufacturing demands. In all likelihood you won't want to hire and fire personnel at the demands of the season. You couldn't build an effective work force for the long haul if you did. Seasonal demands can be handled in ways that have been found helpful by manufacturing firms faced with cyclical production. Here are some suggestions for handling peak loads:

- Do some building to inventory. The extent to which you can follow this course will depend upon the strength of your financial position, of course. You won't want to tie up too much cash in stockpiling inventory. However, you can often finance building inventory through a relatively short-term bank loan.

- Use special marketing efforts to stimulate sales in off-season periods. You might mount an export sales effort, develop a new market for your existing product, or offer special discounts for off-season orders.

- Increase the number of shop hours during peak manufacturing periods and decrease them in off periods. You'll have to be skillful in doing this to make sure that your personnel go along with you in this procedure. You may be able to hire a supplementary group of retired or semiretired people to work during peak-load periods; these people often prefer to work part time; therefore, their desires would fit your needs.

- Keep a small steady workforce and farm out work during heavy production periods. Bring the work back into your plant when you come to slack periods.

You can use any of these approaches singly or in combination to take care of the ups and downs of your production requirements. Whatever course you take should be taken on the basis of sound proactive planning.

MANAGING RESEARCH AND DEVELOPMENT   4 A (2) (3), 7 A (5)

If you're dependent on research and development (R and D) in your business, you'll very likely have to work on a limited budget, as is the case with most small new firms. This means that you'll seek ways through your own ingenuity and that of your personnel to solve your R and D problems.

You can turn to the services of many small firms that specialize in a variety of technical fields to bolster your own efforts. Some companies offer services such as electroplating, precision grinding, chemical milling, dynamic balancing of rotating parts, and tool and die fabrication.

Knowing that you can add outside special services to your own, you should concentrate on building an R and D facility suited to your special requirements. If, for example, you're entering the electromechanical manufacturing field with the intent to supply other manufacturers with small precision components, you'll want a model shop equipped with three or four basic precision machine tools, perhaps a lathe, grinder, drill press, and milling machine. You might require a small sheet metal shear and welding equipment also. You'd want some simple tools to handle the electrical fabrication and testing: soldering tools, small printed circuit equipment, and electric measuring instruments: an oscilloscope, voltmeters, and ohmmeters.

The model shop shouldn't be used for production. You should view it as a highly specialized tool designed to support your efforts at creating newer and more attractive products or improvements in products you're making.

256

The model shop should be seen as an arm of the marketing function. It's the tool you'll use to bring innovative ideas to actuality—a highly important aspect of your practice of proactive management. If you should fall into the trap of using your model shop for production, tempting as this may be on occasion, you'll have set a precedent that can do nothing but harm to the future of your business. The focus of your attention would be drawn away from the main purpose of the model shop, which is to develop the products upon which the very future of your firm depends. The model shop develops the products, or the improved features, you'll badly want to take up the slack caused by obsolescence or competitive forces. Model-shop myopia can be as disastrous inside your firm as marketing myopia is outside your firm. **Don't trade the future for the sake of a bit more profit today.**

It follows that your model shop operation should be keyed to the marketing function. When a new idea for product or feature comes up within your plant, you should test it for commercial worth from the outside in, which means that you should use the marketing techniques given in previous chapters to find out how well the idea may be received in your segment of the market.

When you consider an idea for a new product, you should make certain that it fits your capabilities. You might well take on the development of a new type of digital electric switch. But you'd be in a bad way if you attempted to develop a turbo-prop aircraft engine. The characteristics and scope of the development job should fit the resources you have available or can readily manage.

The R and D function takes just as careful management as the financial affairs of your firm. Your project leader, or you yourself, if you assume the job, works with people, money, materials, and time to achieve the objective of the development program. You can set your plans on the basis of three criteria: a product that meets the specifications that have come from your marketing study, completed on time in accordance with the schedule you've laid down in your planning, and within the financial budget your planning calls for. You may choose any of several simple techniques for controlling the development project: Gantt charting, Program Evaluation and Review Technique (PERT), Critical Path Method (CPM), or the equivalent.

An example of a Gantt chart actually used by a small company of fifty people is shown in Figure 13-2. This kind of charting should fit most development tasks you may want to do in your small company. If you take on a more complex program, you'll probably find PERT or CPM suited to your planning purpose. You'll find information on these approaches to planning in the references at the end of this chapter.

Development Program for an Electronic Measuring Instrument

The first thing the project manager of this development program did was to list the important tasks in the total program. The end point of each task is considered a *state point.*

Development Program and State Points

1. Start of development project, receipt of marketing specifications

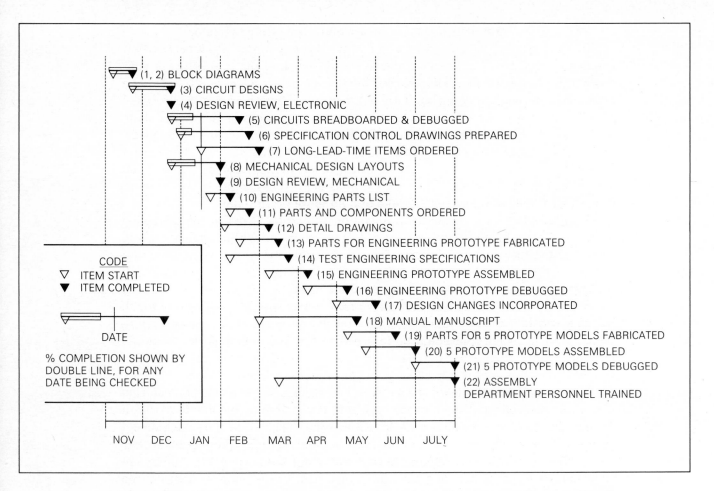

Figure 13-2 Sample Progress and Control Chart for a Development Program (Gantt Chart)

2. Conceptual development complete; basic block diagrams established; inputs and outputs, with tolerances, established

3. Circuit design for each block complete

4. Design review, electronic

5. Circuits breadboarded and debugged

6. Specification-control drawings prepared

7. Long-lead-time items ordered

8. Mechanical design layout finished

9. Design review, mechanical

10. Engineering parts list compiled

11. Components and parts for five prototype models ordered

12. Detail drawings completed

258

13. Machined parts for engineering prototype fabricated

14. Test engineering specifications prepared

15. Engineering prototype assembled

16. Engineering prototype debugged

17. Design changes incorporated

18. Service manual prepared

19. Machined parts for five prototype models fabricated

20. Five prototype models assembled

21. Five prototype models debugged

22. Instrument assembly personnel trained

Whatever technique you use to plan and control the progress of the development job, you should make sure that it's planned carefully and thoroughly. That's the only way to exert the kind of managerial control that will ensure a project well done, on time, and within the funds you've allocated.

Designing for Production

Parts and components may be fabricated and assembled in a manufactured product in many ways. Some ways take expensive production equipment but require little hand labor. Some take much labor but need little production equipment. What's important to the small manufacturer is to choose a design that will allow the item to be made at a cost compatible with the resources available—and sufficiently low so that the product can be sold at a profit. The original design, down to its smallest details, controls these possibilities.

Don't overlook the importance of tailoring the design of your product to your resources in equipment and skilled labor. Study the tradeoffs in costs of large capital investment in production machinery versus the ongoing costs of labor to do the same job. As a simple example, you can join two sheets of metal in many different ways. You might choose spot welding as against riveting or seam bending as against sheet metal screws. Or you might adopt fastening with a special adhesive. You'd want to make careful estimates of relative costs once you've decided that the fastening method is suitable for the purpose intended. And you'd want to estimate for different production quantities. From these analyses you could single out the best way to do the job, taking into account the funds you could make available for fixed asset capital investment in production equipment as against the cash flow requirements you'd take on in performing the task manually.

You'd be very careful also to keep in mind the end use of the product in laying out the basic design. Performance to the specifications identified by your marketing study will help to ensure the acceptance of your product by your intended customer. Your product must do what you claim it can do. And you *must* be able to manufacture it economically with your resources.

The small manufacturing entrepreneur very quickly discovers the critical importance of the purchasing function. Purchasing isn't merely a matter of buying. It proves to be a linking element between the major functions of the company that make the product and the distribution channel that serves the customer's needs. Purchasing contributes to and is involved in every aspect of company operations: production, sales, engineering, distribution, marketing, and other functions, in greater or lesser degree.

Anything that's done at any place in your company affects several other functions. In the R and D process, for example, engineering will depend upon purchasing to find suppliers for hard-to-get components. In distribution, purchasing will be asked to locate a dependable source for cartons with inserts designed to protect your product during shipping. And, of course, keeping production supplied with the right parts at the right time at the right price is a major purchasing requirement.

Purchasing personnel can do their job best when they know the sales you expect within the foreseeable future. This suggests that purchasing personnel should be involved in the production planning schedule on a continuing basis. A good way to do this is to have regular planning meetings involving people from sales, production, engineering, and any other part of the firm you think necessary. Knowing the status of current sales and what sales can be expected, purchasing can schedule with due regard to lead times, quantities, costs, and availability of the necessary components, parts, and services.

You should insist that purchasing personnel keep abreast of what's going on with your vendors. They should know immediately of any change in price, delivery, quality, or availability of goods and services. You can often take advantage of a profitable opportunity by building close relationships with your vendors. Your purchasing people can ask for, and get delivery of, items you need in a tight market. Friendly relationships with your vendors may allow you to stretch your credit in a time of stress. Be careful not to overdo this practice, but once in a while you may find it a good way to overcome a tight cash flow position.

You'd be well advised to have purchasing work closely with receiving inspection. Indeed, you may find it a good idea to attach receiving inspection to purchasing. Purchasing can then keep on top of the quality of the items they buy. If there's any problem, purchasing can let the vendor know and get it solved immediately. This approach gives purchasing the power to enforce the delivery of parts and components that meet the specifications to which they were bought.

Watch Your Costs of Ordering and Inventory

You should watch your costs of ordering and inventory. The major costs, which you should identify and control, include placing orders, receiving and inspecting material, and handling and stocking inventory. Study each step and make certain that there's no wasted motion in the process. In ordering and record keeping adopt the simplest kind of paperwork. A purchasing form with three or four copies should take care of your needs in ordering, receiving and inspection, payment, and record keeping.

Keep careful control of inventory to avoid tying up more money than you need to. Costs you should watch are those for investing in, handling, stocking, and insuring inventory. You'll be concerned with a variety of purchased items, the methods of assembly of your products, the shelf life of perishable materials such as paints or chemicals, and perhaps the seasonal characteristic of your sales. When you view the problem this way, you can see the importance of teamwork among marketing, sales, engineering, and production in planning for production. The part purchasing must play is to keep sufficient materials of the kind required on hand without building up too much inventory.

Manage Your Inventory
You can take straightforward steps to manage your inventory. Just as in managing your financial affairs, the first planning that enters into control of inventory is to schedule sales. A good way to do this is to key your planning to three categories of orders: those in hand, those likely to come in during the next standard period—say one month, and those that may possibly come in in the following two months. You can set a reasonable schedule for production for perhaps three months ahead with this information. The purchasing effort can then be weighted to buy at full scale for the certain orders and to use some care in buying for future requirements.

You'll want to control your inventory to ensure that materials, components, work in process, and finished goods don't become obsolete on the shelves. The profitability of your business depends to a great extent on the immediate usefulness and worth of your inventory. The surest way to guard your inventory against decay is to exercise ongoing control of the status of the items that make it up.

Control Your Small Parts and Components
The *two-bin* method is a practical device you can use to make sure you don't run out of small parts and components used regularly in production. Storage bins for these items are divided by a loose panel of plywood between a reserve stock on the bottom of the bin and a supply stock on top. Quantities in each section of the bin are set by your manufacturing requirements. When the top stock is used up, the part or component is reordered. Sufficient quantity is kept in the bottom section of the bin to give enough lead time for delivery so no stockout occurs. Reserve stocks of very small items like washers, screws, or rivets may be placed in bags or boxes rather than stored beneath a partition.

Control Mixed Inventory by the ABC Method
The ABC method gives you a practical way to control inventory if your company requires a variety of items ranging from inexpensive to costly and from small and easily handled to large and heavy. In this method, parts, components, and supplies to be purchased are classified in three groups: A, B, and C.

You assign items to the A category if they fit the following description:

- High cost

- Expensive to handle, if the part is delicate or bulky

- Likelihood of spoilage or rapid obsolescence

- Long lead time, which can disrupt production schedule or increase the chance of stock outage

- Irregular use of part, so that it must be watched carefully to make sure it's on hand when needed

B and C parts take less attention than A parts. You can control them with an automatic system like that of the two-bin method. You may give responsibility for keeping stock up to production requirements to a clerk for B and C parts. You should give responsibility for A parts to a supervisor.

You identify B parts on the basis of such variables as cost per unit, lead time, annual usage, size, weight, and rate of spoilage or obsolescence. You can use the following list as a guide for identifying B parts:

- Moderate cost per unit

- Intermediate lead time—three to four weeks as against ten to twelve weeks for A parts

- Moderate quantities compared with C units

- Moderate size and weight (can be lifted readily by one person)

- Not likely to spoil or become obsolete within a reasonable period—three to four months

- Seasonal usage

C parts are generally small, inexpensive, and used continually. You'd classify items such as washers, small fasteners, rivets, nuts, and bolts as C items.

The classification of parts in A, B, and C groups takes judgment. With experience and some practice the procedure becomes relatively simple and routine and can prove well worth the time by keeping your company free from delivery delays caused by stock outages.

Graphing Inventory

You'll find that one helpful device in controlling inventory is to keep an up-to-date graph of the total inventory. The surest way to get a reliable picture of the status of inventory is to make a physical count and evaluation on a regular basis, say every fourth week. We suggest four weeks rather than a monthly count. The four-week period gives you an equal caliper of time in your measurement. Your profit will ordinarily depend on the last day or two of shipments in the period. By using a four-week time span, you'll avoid the irregularity (except for one period in the year) of unequal numbers of days in the months.

Your graph of the value of inventory will show a fairly regular ebb and flow; it will go up and down during the year. You'll be able to see irregularities at a glance. You can then take steps to correct unwanted variances by applying corrective measures to the causes. A comparative financial statement like that described in Chapter 8 will be helpful in this effort.

One way you can add a measure of control over the amount of money tied up in inventory of materials is to work with your purchasing personnel to set maximum and minimum figures for the total of money represented by inventory at any time. You can do this by estimating the needs for inventory to meet the existing and near future production requirements. You should include a small cushion on the high side. You can then increase these values gradually as your business grows. You'll help your purchasing people understand how their efforts contribute to the orderly management of cash flow and to the profitability of the firm by involving them in this planning process. This effort will gain their commitment to practicing good husbandry in their purchasing activities.

MANAGING YOUR PRODUCTION VARIABLES   7 A (6), 8 A (1) (2) (3), 8 A (8) (e)

The objective of successful management of production is to produce a sound product as efficiently as possible. This implies careful control of costs at every point in the manufacturing process, from scheduling for production to minimizing waste.

It's the customer who sets production goals. Every aspect of the manufacturing operation is governed by the need to fill the orders of the customer. Therefore, planning for production starts with the sales forecast.

A good way for you to schedule production is to classify your orders in groups, as we've suggested previously: those actually in hand, and those that you expect within the next one-, two-, and three-month periods. Set percentages according to the best estimates you and your salespersons can make about the possibilities of orders being realized: 90 percent for those that seem quite sure and 50 percent for those that seem fairly likely to materialize. You may then work out schedules for production for the next quarter by comparing expected deliveries and sales orders with shipping dates. You'll want to use your experience and judgment to smooth the figures for sales. As you work with your salespersons, you'll find out who's optimistic and who's pessimistic in estimating future sales. You'll then be able to adjust the information accordingly. Through this suggested procedure, production and purchasing will have guidelines for their operations.

Plan to do your production scheduling on a rolling schedule. Involve those people who have key responsibilities in the firm in planning and scheduling sessions on a regular basis. Representatives from marketing and sales, production, purchasing, and engineering might form a typical planning team. A proven way to schedule these planning meetings is to start with weekly meetings. As the team gains experience and skill the time between meetings can be stretched. You'll probably find that a four-week period will serve the company very well after a year or so of experience with the procedure.

The advantages of the team approach to planning for production is that it gets everybody involved. You and your key people communicate with each other. The chances are improved for clear understanding of what's required to do a first-rate job of meeting your customers' delivery needs. You gain efficiency in your plant and improved morale among your people.

Schedule Your Production

Production volume and the rate of production govern the tempo of the manufacturing operation. Both are influenced by variables such as required delivery dates; availability of raw materials, parts, components, and services; lead times for procurement; and seasonal ups and downs in the business. Production scheduling is therefore affected not only by the customers' delivery requirements but also by the cooperativeness of your suppliers in delivering materials and services as needed. Lead times are critical in meeting production schedules.

As the chief executive officer your problem is to make sure that you have first-rate working relationships with your suppliers and that you have a trim inventory. You can take two actions to keep a balance between the outflow of materials and services built into the products going to your customers and the inflow of raw materials and services from your suppliers: Develop, and have your people develop, warm relationships with your suppliers, and adopt the rolling planning procedure we've described. When you build a favored relationship, friendly but not too close, with specific suppliers you incline them to deliver materials as you need them. This can be very important in times of shortage or if you must have special quality in the materials. Proactive planning and scheduling will support sound husbandry in managing the flow of materials in your manufacturing process.

Control Your Product Cost

As the owner of a small manufacturing business, you'll seek a high level of productivity together with efficiency. In most small manufacturing companies labor costs are a large part of the cost of making the product. Anything you can do to increase productivity will help your company make profit.

But you won't be able to tell if your operations are gaining in productivity unless you keep regular records. You'll get the feedback you need to see how well your management effort is doing from these records. With these data you'll be able to plan and apply corrective steps for overcoming problems and you'll be able to increase effort that's paying off.

You should know the cost of every part and component that goes into your product. To do this you must have up-to-date information. You'll want to examine the time that each operation takes, for you'll find that time threads through all operations in your manufacturing process. Whatever you can do to shorten the time required for an operation will pay off in increased profit. You can judge the advantage of a capital investment in a more efficient production machine by comparing the new against the old in a time and cost framework.

And, of course, in a similar way, anything that reduces the scrap in an operation contributes to profitability.

Manufacturing costs can be divided roughly into *fixed* and *variable* categories. You can think of fixed costs as being spread uniformly through the year. These include expenses such as rent, insurance, indirect labor, telephone, advertising, and miscellaneous small supplies. These tend not to vary significantly throughout the year. However, variable costs change with the volume of production. By and large, these include the cost of direct labor and material. To these you'd want to add the costs of electricity, gas, or water if used in the manufacturing process.

You'll want to control your variable costs carefully, as they contribute in large measure to the cost of the manufacturing operation.

Control Your Scrap and Waste

Three variables influence the amount of scrap and waste in your manufacturing process: (1) complexity of your product, (2) suitability and condition of your production equipment, and (3) the skill and experience of your workforce. You should study these variables closely to see how you might make improvements in each.

Complexity of Your Product

As the product gets more complex it becomes more difficult to produce and the amount of scrap is likely to increase. To hold the concentricity of a precision ground gear to .0002 of an inch is an exceedingly demanding task. It's many times more difficult than to hold the tolerance to .005 of an inch, which is a close tolerance in itself. The skill in craftsmanship to produce the tighter tolerance would necessarily be much higher to assure getting the fine job done right. We would expect to see more scrap in the fine job than in the relatively rough one.

Rougher work takes less skill, of course, and we would see less waste of material. For example, to make scrap books with plywood covers and leather string bindings doesn't take highly skilled workmanship. Tolerances here would be about plus or minus one-eighth of an inch in sawing the covers from a sheet of plywood. Scrap could be limited by getting the maximum numbers of covers from a standard-size sheet of plywood.

To minimize scrap in your product, you should design in such a way as to use the material to best advantage and to keep tolerances as wide as possible without impairing the performance or appearance of the final product.

Suitability and Condition of Your Production Equipment

You should be certain that any production equipment you use has sufficient capacity to handle the job and that it's maintained at peak efficiency. It makes sense for you to buy equipment that's somewhat oversized for the first task you intend to use it on. The cost will be a bit higher, but the extra capacity is more than likely to pay off the day you want to tackle a task that's just a little bigger than the ones you've been doing. A sheet metal shear able to cut an eight foot panel can't handle a nine-foot size, but a ten-foot shear can do it with ease. The extra cost of the larger piece of equipment is certain to pay off as your company grows and you find it desirable to take on bigger jobs.

We need hardly call your attention to the importance of proper maintenance of your production equipment and tools. Machines should be kept clean and well lubricated. Parts that wear should be replaced before the wear impairs the performance of the equipment. Cutting tools should be kept sharp at all times and lathes and milling machines supplied with the right cutting fluid for the task in hand. Proper maintenance will improve the profitability of your production effort.

Skill and Experience of Your Workers

You can cut scrap and waste in production by hiring workers with the skill and experience to do the job properly. The more complex the job, the higher the level of skill required. You can improve your chances for hiring the kind of craftspeople you need for the work by screening applicants for jobs in accordance with sound hiring practice. You'll find some suggestions on how to go about this task in Chapter 14.

It may be that your production process involves proprietary procedures or special equipment you've developed yourself. You may find it necessary in this case to train people to do the work.

Performance at all levels in your company follows from skill and mastery of the job that's to be done. But people don't gain skill without training. As a proactive manager, you have the opportunity to see that your people get the training and practice to help them acquire skill and mastery. You can see to it that training takes place in production, which is a good place to start. Training at this level could start you on a systematic program of training your personnel throughout your firm as it grows.

Skill and mastery of the task not only cut scrap and waste but also afford the trained person the chance to grow with the company. Many a top manager learns the business from the ground up—starting on the workbench and, by acquiring skill and mastery through training, moving up as the company grows.

Salvage Your Waste Materials

Scrap and waste materials can often be salvaged or sold for recycling. For example, if your screw machine operation is large enough to make it worthwhile, you can centrifuge cutting fluid and reuse it. Or if you fabricate steel pipe for overhead fire-control sprinkler systems, you can make pipe nipples from left over short ends and you can find other concerns that can use the short lengths left from your fabrication process. Whatever your business you'll usually be able to find profitable ways to make use of scrap materials that otherwise might be dumped beyond retrieval.

Put Value Engineering to Work

You'll undoubtedly find, as do most entrepreneurs entering a manufacturing business, that your need to get your product into production and on the market prevents you from making an elaborate search for the most economical design. Your effort will be aimed at making a satisfactory product at a reasonable cost. But once you're rolling, you should search for less costly ways to get equivalent value. Better still, you can often seek and find better performance at lower cost. You can do this through value engineering, sometimes called value analysis.

Value engineering may be described as a creative study of every material, part, or process used in a product with the objective of achieving comparable, or better, performance at less cost. You can use value engineering to study your material selection, fabrication methods, and manufacturing processes. In applying value engineering you must take two broad steps:

- Discover through creative thinking promising ways for cutting the designed-in, production, or purchase cost of each item, part, component, or assembly of your product.

- Decide through study and evaluation of alternatives on the changes you want to make in the design, production process, or selection of material, to maintain or improve performance at a reduction in cost.

You'll need comprehensive sources of information to do a good job of value engineering. Your engineering and purchasing personnel should work together to find materials, processes, and components that will do an equal or better job at less cost. They'll search through data sheets, catalogs, test records, and cost records to specify cases in which improvement may be made. You'll apply design and production experience, drawing on the background of your people in manufacturing, fabrication, shop practice, and materials handling. You and your people should look at every step of the production process, every bit of material, and every design feature to see how costs may be lowered while performance is maintained or improved.

Above all, you'll find that value engineering can best be done in a climate that supports innovation and creativity. The idea is to freewheel in looking for ideas and concepts without criticising them in the beginning. You'll avoid squashing your people by scoffing at what might seem like an outlandish suggestion. Only after you've gathered a number of ideas on one subject should they be subjected to careful checking and analysis. Then your effort becomes critical but constructive. It's important that you support a climate in your firm that makes it easy for your people to speak out with new ideas. This will be helpful not only in value engineering, but also in many other areas—from marketing to inventory control.

As an instance of how value engineering made practical and reduced the cost of an operation in processing decorative wall panels, a small company found it difficult to control the application of enamel in straight grooves cut the length of four foot by eight foot panels. An expensive semiautomatic device that was supposed to roll paint into the grooves at a uniform rate proved erratic. Paint overflowed the grooves in some places and didn't fill them in others. Hand labor had to be used to clean up overflows and to fill in misses—an exasperating and time-consuming procedure. Workers were asked for ideas and suggestions, as were all key personnel. One workman finally hit upon a simple, inexpensive solution. He found that the grooves could be painted neatly by allowing the enamel to flow from a ten-cent oil can while the can was drawn by hand along a groove. Although this is a simple example of solving a small problem, many instances in any manufacturing operation afford opportunities for improvement and cost reduction. The following section lists some questions you can use to guide your procedure in value engineering.

Test for Values

We suggest that you check the answers to the following questions to judge whether it's worthwhile to do a value engineering job:

- Does it really add value?

- Is the benefit worth the cost?

- Do we need all the features in the present design?

- Can we find something better for the purpose?

- Can we make a usable part by a method that costs less?

- Can we find a standard part to replace one we make specially?

- Is our tooling right for the quantities we make?

- Can we find another dependable supplier who can furnish the part for less?

- Are our competitors buying it for less?

- Are our costs for labor, material, and overhead in line with those in our industry?

You can decide by asking and answering these questions, and others of a similar nature that will occur to you, whether it's worthwhile to tackle a value analysis for any given purpose.

What About Quality Control?

The product you send to market must do what it's supposed to do. If it doesn't perform to specifications, you'd put your business in jeopardy. To ensure quality and performance in your product, you must start with a sound concept, a sound design, and a thorough testing program.

Most firms use quality control procedures to make sure that the product being manufactured is well made and meets specifications. Quality control usually requires careful inspection of components, parts, subassemblies, and final assemblies to make certain that they meet the details of design and performance specifications. In a sense, this approach is like a policing action—it's after the fact.

The small manufacturer can seldom afford the necessary staff for quality control. You may find this situation a blessing in disguise. For you can avoid the necessity for inspection, with the exception of final performance testing, by practicing proactive management in a special way. You can see to it that your people are properly trained to do a good job every step of the way. You'll agree that it makes sense to do a high-class job at each step. When your people have skill and master each task in the manufacturing process, then they'll build quality into your product at every step. The need for you to have a quality control function would vanish (or certainly be reduced to a minimum).

As your company grows, you may want to add a *quality assurance* function. Personnel in quality assurance would act primarily as coaches and trainers. You'd give them the authority to check the performance of products taken at random from final stores. If they found defects in craft or performance, they would help the person who did the job improve in skill by coaching and teaching, using the defective item as a takeoff point.

Take Advantage of Group Assembly Methods

We know from much study of assembly line methods that people on the line tend to get bored and depressed. The result is often poor morale and slovenly workmanship. Boredom can take strange directions: More than one high-priced auto has come off the line with a pop bottle or a banana skin entombed in its tailfin. As a small manufacturer, you have the opportunity to take advantage of what may be called a group-participative method of putting things together. Where you think you can use this group method of assembly you'd do well to try it. In so doing you may underwrite improvement in productivity and in morale.

The trick is to let the members of your firm experience job enrichment. Give them the chance to learn more and to acquire more skills by letting them do a whole job. Let them assemble a whole piece of equipment or at least a complete subassembly so they can see the fruits of their labor. People working in small groups can communicate, be friendly, and fulfill some of their needs as human beings. That this way of doing things pays off becomes more and more certain as evidence from industry grows. Some companies are now building even automobiles this way.

Some products or parts, of course, may not lend themselves to production through group methods. You can be guided by giving routine operations that can be best performed by automation to machines—and by giving relatively complex problems that are better handled by human beings to your workforce.

KEY ISSUES IN MANUFACTURING   SUMMARY

We pointed out the need for your small manufacturing business to be managed by sound policies. Because policies guide the actions you'll take in every aspect of your operation, you'll find it of overriding importance to set your basic policies carefully and clearly before you take action. The first policy you should set states that you'll husband your funds with care, making every dollar pay off.

Whether you buy, build, or lease a plant for your purpose, you'll want to take into account the features of the location: zoning restrictions; availability of labor; electric power, gas, and water supplies; and local taxes. If you build a plant, use materials that are easy to maintain. Make sure the design is flexible to provide for growth and that it's aesthetically pleasing.

The overall plant layout should support the smoothest and most efficient flow of material and process possible. The layout should permit the shortest possible paths for moving material and the most direct routing through the steps in the manufacturing process.

We discussed the possibilities of working your plant effectively by operating more than one shift. The evidence from many plants that have used this approach suggests that you'd do better to install enough capacity to handle your normal workloads on a one-shift basis. The exception here would be the desirability of working very expensive special equipment on a two- or three-shift schedule.

We also suggested that you may want to consider the four-day work week as a way of encouraging the hiring of a stable workforce, and of allowing your managers to have more time to relax and rest before tackling the management chores of the week ahead. If you adopt the four-day work week, be sure to study the procedures you'll need to change and ways for acquainting your customers with your new schedule.

As you take on new production tasks you'll find that your workforce will acquire the new skills needed on a learning curve. The cost of production will come down gradually as learning takes hold. One rule of thumb you'll find applicable to production says that every time you double your production quantity your direct labor cost will decrease to 60 to 80 percent of its former amount.

If your business is seasonal you can take care of peak loads by: building to inventory; stimulating sales through special campaigns in the off season; increasing working hours during peak periods and decreasing them during slack periods; or keeping a small steady workforce and farming out work during peak periods. You can use any or all of the tactics singly or in combination.

You'll want to build up your own model shop if you're doing research and development. Your shop should be capable of handling your unique needs. Many of the more conventional requirements such as electroplating, dynamic balancing, and casting can be done for you by outside sources. You should *never* permit your model shop to be used for production; you should think of it as a highly specialized tool to be used only for innovative model building purposes. And whatever you do in developing a new product be sure it fits your resources. The scope and kind of project should fit your equipment, know-how, and pocketbook. The development project should be carefully planned and managed. Techniques such as PERT, CPM, and Gantt charting are appropriate tools for controlling the progress of the development project. Be careful to design your new product so it can be manufactured readily and economically. And above all it must perform as you claim it will.

Your purchasing function links together many other functions in your company. Its relationship with production is crucial—but so is its contribution to several other functions: engineering, marketing, sales, receiving inspection, and the control of inventory. Require your purchasing people to build good relationships with reliable suppliers. You'll then be able to count on getting materials in a tight market and receiving special consideration when you need credit.

We've recommended some techniques you can use to manage your inventory. These are the two-bin method for controlling inventory of small parts and the ABC method of controlling a wide variety of items from inexpensive to costly and from small to large. Keeping a graph of the value of inventory allows you to see deviations from normal and to take steps to make corrections when such variances occur.

We've also recommended a way to go about planning for production by classifying orders into those in hand: those you're 90 percent sure to get in a short time, and those that seem 50 percent certain. From these figures you can work out a schedule for production for some time ahead. You can arrive at a reasonable estimate of your production and purchasing requirements by adjusting the figures on a continuing basis. Planning for production should be done by teamwork among purchasing, marketing, sales, and engineering people, as a typical team.

You'll want to control the cost of your product very carefully. To do this you'll need regularly kept records of parts and labor costs. Labor is ordinarily a large part of the cost of manufacture; whatever you can do to improve productivity will reduce your labor costs. Scrap and waste, for example, are a function of the complexity of your product, the suitability and condition of your production equipment, and the skill and experience of your work force. Any steps you can take to increase efficiency or utility of material will help to make your production more profitable. You may find ways to make gains in these matters through the application of value engineering.

Finally, we've suggested that the quality of your product can be best supported by training your work force. When people know what to do and have the skill to do it well, your product will have built-in superior quality. The need for an old fashioned policing type of quality control can be replaced by quality assurance. This policing role becomes instead a teaching and coaching function, helping your people to acquire skill and mastery over the work. This effort can often be supported by the use of teamwork in building or assembling the product. Here you'd take advantage of the ability and the desire of people to do complicated, challenging tasks. You'd open the doors to gaining effectiveness in work through the human use of human beings.

Controlling Your Manufacturing Operations

This worksheet presents a checklist for helping you make sure you've taken care of the major items involved in controlling your manufacturing operations. Some of these items may not apply to your particular business. What may be important in other operations may not be in yours. Each business is different. You may find therefore that you can skip some of the items listed here. However, be certain to do a careful job of gathering the information you'll need to complete those you do find important in your business.

FEATURES OF YOUR MANUFACTURING PLANT

This section of the worksheet lists the features you should check in locating, building, or leasing your plant. Place checkmarks at the points appropriate to your answers.

Location

The raw materials for my product are:

- Heavy, bulky, or otherwise hard to handle _____.

- Moderately heavy (up to 50 pounds) and can be handled by one person _____.

- Light and small, little problem to handle _____.

- I will need a railroad siding _____; access by truck _____; normal street or highway access _____. If I plan to ship by air, the nearest airport is at _____, _____ miles from my proposed plant site.

Zoning Restriction

- I've checked the local ordinances for zoning restrictions _____; I've found there are no restrictions against foreseeable changes in the kind of business I'm planning _____.

Labor Supply

- I've checked the local labor market and find there are enough skilled people available for my purpose _____. Enough unskilled people are also available to serve the needs of my business _____.

Utilities

- My operations require electric power of this kind: _____ phase, _____ volts, _____ kilowatts maximum load. I've been assured of adequate service to meet these requirements _____.

- My requirements for gas are: _____ thousand cubic feet per month. This is available to my proposed plant _____.

- The manufacturing process in my business takes _____ gallons of water per hour. This quantity of water is available _____. I can dump the outflow into the sewer system _____. If not, I can recycle the water _____, or drill a return well to pump it back into the ground _____.

Taxes

- I've checked the local tax assessment that my plant may have to carry _____. I'm certain I can live with these taxes _____.

FEATURES OF ARCHITECTURAL DESIGN

- I've selected a competent architect to help me plan the new plant (or remodel an existing plant). We've agreed on floor plan, method of construction, maintenance, appearance, parking, and the general landscaping around the plant _____.

Plant Layout

- An analysis of the production process has given me a plant layout that I'm satisfied with: I'm reasonably sure that I've taken proper care of storing, handling, and moving material in efficient and economical ways _____.

Flexibility of Design

- I've studied the needs I may have for flexibility in the plant: clear floor areas without columns, high and strong roof structure to carry heavy movable loads, conduits for electric power lines, movable mounts for production machinery, and floor construction adequate to support heavy concentrated loads _____.

Easy Maintenance

- My architect and I have chosen materials that look well and are easy to keep clean _____.

Adequate Machine Capacity

- I've chosen production machines with somewhat more power and capacity than my first production needs require, understanding that this is a conservative and wise approach to ensure my ability to meet more demanding production requirements in the future _____.

WORKING MORE THAN ONE SHIFT

■ The results of my study of my production needs show that I would gain some financial advantage by operating my plant more than one shift _____. If so, I've decided on the following shift schedule: _____

_____.

■ If it appears desirable to work certain production machines more than one shift, here's what I plan to do:

_____

_____

_____

USING THE LEARNING CURVE

■ I've studied the learning curve given in this chapter and I'll apply the concept to my cost of production _____.

■ I'll keep records of my production costs and will use the learning curve data to adjust my costs on successive runs of the same product _____.

■ I'll also use these figures to help me estimate costs for the production of new products _____.

MANAGING SEASONAL CHANGE

■ My business is subject to wide seasonal variation in sales _____. If so, I'm adopting the following ways of handling peak demands, as suggested in this chapter: _____

_____

_____

_____

MANAGING RESEARCH AND DEVELOPMENT

■ My approach to building my R and D facility is as follows: _____

_____

_____
_____
_____
_____
_____

■ I understand the need for carefully controlling development costs
_____. I plan to use Gantt charting (or equivalent) to help control these
costs _____.

Designing for Production

■ The design of my product has been carefully worked out to make sure that
I can build it with the facilities I'll have, with the skills of the people who'll
work for me, and within the funds I can assign to the job. I'll try to test the
product sufficiently to know that it will do for the customer what I claim it
will _____.

MAKING PURCHASING EFFECTIVE

■ I understand the importance of building teamwork among my purchasing,
marketing, sales, engineering, and production people _____.

■ I'll see to it that they all work together in projecting production requirements to meet sales for the near and farther out future _____.

■ My purchasing people will understand the desirability of building friendly
relations with selected suppliers, so our needs will be taken care of at all
times _____.

■ I'll see to it that purchasing works closely with receiving inspection to
ensure our getting the quality we need in our purchased supplies _____.

Costs of Ordering and Inventory

■ I'll study the costs in placing orders with suppliers, receiving and inspecting
material, and handling and stocking inventory _____.

■ I'll eliminate waste motion and excess cost in these steps _____.

■ I'll also study my costs for investing in inventory, for handling, stocking,
and insuring the materials that make up my inventory _____.

Controlling Mixed Inventory

■ The two-bin method of controlling small components makes good sense
for some of my inventory; we'll use it _____.

■ I've studied the ABC method of inventory control for mixed inventory and
find it fits our requirements; therefore, we'll adopt it _____.

Graphing Inventory

■ I understand the benefit in keeping a running graph of the value of total inventory: raw materials, work in process, and finished stores _____.

■ I'll keep this graph up to date on a regular four-week or monthly basis _____.

MANAGING PRODUCTION VARIABLES

■ We'll use teamwork to plan and schedule our production _____.

■ The planning team will be composed of representatives from sales, purchasing, production, engineering, and _____.

■ We'll meet on a weekly, biweekly, monthly, or _____ schedule.

■ We'll follow the idea suggested in this chapter for assigning probabilities to expected sales on the following basis: _____

_____

_____

_____

_____

Controlling Product Cost

■ I understand the need for knowing the cost of parts, components, and labor in producing my product and I'll keep accurate records of these costs _____.

■ I'll compile the fixed and variable costs in my business _____.

■ I'll concentrate on getting these costs as low as I reasonably can, with the knowledge that the variable costs are the ones most likely to require the most careful attention _____.

Controlling Scrap and Waste

■ I'll take steps to widen the tolerances in my product as much as possible without impairing its performance _____.

■ The design is such that we'll make the most efficient use of raw materials, taking into account standard sizes of these materials _____.

■ The production machinery we plan to use is of adequate size and performance capacity to handle the assigned operations efficiently _____.

■ I'll make sure production machines are kept clean and well lubricated, and that cutting tools are kept sharp _____.

- My work force will have the skill necessary to do the quality of work required in our production process _____.
- I'll hire people who have the kinds of skill necessary to do the work _____.

Salvaging Waste Materials

- I've studied ways to recover some money from waste materials and scrap produced in our manufacturing process _____.

- Here's what I'm going to do: _____

_____

_____

_____

_____

Using Value Engineering

- I've studied the section in this chapter on value engineering _____.
- I'm going to put these concepts to work in the following ways: _____

_____

_____

_____

_____

Quality Control

- I've thought about the difference between quality control and quality assurance as described in this chapter _____.

- I've decided we can avoid the need for quality control by training our people to do a first rate job in each step of the process of production _____.

- Quality assurance as a training and coaching function makes good sense for my production operation _____; I'm going to adopt the idea as soon as practicable _____.

- I do want a quality inspection function and am going to arrange for it _____.

Group Assembly Methods

- My product lends itself well to group assembly methods _____; I'm going to put this approach into practice _____.

OTHER ITEMS

Your business may need items not included in the foregoing. Here's some space to make notes about them:

_____

_____

_____

_____

_____

_____

_____

_____

_____

_____

_____

IF YOU WANT TO READ MORE

It's impossible to do more than suggest a few representative examples of the many books in the field of operations and production management. These cover every aspect you can think of, and more, about manufacturing. Every book in the following list has references in it. You can find out in detail about any subject by looking it up in specific references.

Franklin G. Moore, *Production Management*, 6th ed., Richard D. Irwin, Inc., Homewood, Ill., 1973. This book, highly regarded as a text in the field, is full of useful information about many aspects of the management of production. You'll find, for example, a thorough treatment of the problems of locating a manufacturing plant.

Elwood S. Buffa, *Modern Production Management*, 4th ed., Wiley, New York, 1973. The level of this text is quite sophisticated compared with others we've listed. For those who want to investigate some of the more technically advanced ways of dealing with operations in manufacturing, the material presented will be found informative.

Riva Poor, ed., *4 Days, 40 Hours*, Bursk and Poor Publishing, Cambridge, Mass., 1970. This paperback is composed of articles written by different authors on the many aspects of the four-day, forty-hour workweek. It's extremely valuable as a reference telling of the advantages and the disadvantages of the short workweek and the precautions that should be taken and planning that should be done before adopting the short workweek.

Walter Rautenstrauch and Raymond Villers, *The Economics of Industrial Management*, 2nd ed., Funk & Wagnalls, New York, 1957. A classic in its field, this text treats the economic implications of decisions in industrial management. It's an advanced text primarily suitable for entrepreneurs who've managed the business through the first awkward stages of growth. Dr. Rautenstrauch was the inventor of the break-even chart; ways of using the chart for many different management purposes are given throughout the book.

Robert S. Morrison, *Handbook for Manufacturing Engineers*, 2nd ed., Western Reserve Press, Cleveland, Ohio, 1974. The author of this book has had many years of business experience in manufacturing. At the time of writing this book he was the chief executive officer of a moderate-sized company. The text is directly and plainly written, covering many subjects of interest to the small manufacturer. Section IV, titled "Manufacturing," gives 100 pages of useful information about many facets of the manufacturing operation, from packaging and shipping to quality control and inspection.

Delmar W. Karger and Robert Murdick, *Managing Engineering and Research*, 2nd ed., The Industrial Press, New York, 1969. The entrepreneur needing to know about the management of research and development will find this text an excellent reference. Although some chapters are addressed to big business, those treating new product development and organizing for development hit at fundamentals useful in the small manufacturing concern.

Small Business Administration Publications. The SBA publishes many leaflets on all kinds of subjects of interest to small business owners. Many among them treat the manufacturing business. Some are free and others cost a small amount. Check with your nearest SBA office to get up-to-date lists of titles.

Alvar O. Elbing, Herman Gadon, and John R.M. Gordon, "Flexible Working Hours; It's About Time," *Harvard Business Review*, January/February 1974. The authors describe the benefits of flexible working hours and some of the problems of changing over from the standard workweek. Among the more significant benefits are less absenteeism and happier employees.

Chapter 14

Managing Your Personnel Function

When you first thought of starting your own business, you had a gleam in your eye, a vision of the future—your company as a substantial enterprise resulting from your driving entrepreneurial spirit. By the time you've read this far, you'll have learned that you can't reach this goal alone. You'll need to surround yourself with capable people to make your vision come true.

With growth comes complexity. You reach a position in the growth of your company where you just can't wear enough hats or switch them fast enough to cover the increasing variety of tasks your business will demand. You'll have to parcel out authority to others to accomplish most of these tasks. How well they get done will depend on the competence of the people you've hired.

DEVELOPING A SOUND PERSONNEL POLICY   7 A (1) (2) (3)

As in all the other areas of management, you'll want to work from sound policy in hiring and managing personnel. Entrepreneurs in most small new businesses don't realize that they set a precedent when they hire their first employees. Owners of small new firms suffer from two deficiencies in personnel matters: lack of sufficient funds to hire the very best people and lack of appreciation that they'll be setting a style that's likely to stay with them forever after. The beginning firm is too likely to hire the first warm bodies that happen to walk through the door when it needs help. The entrepreneur who usually does the hiring isn't ordinarily trained to do the screening necessary to assure getting competent people who can do what's needed now and who have the potential to grow with the firm.

Indiscriminate hiring in the beginning generally causes a difficult situation at a later date. The company one day finds itself burdened with more than a few incompetents; it's grown beyond the capacities of a considerable portion of its employees. The chief executive–owner then faces the disheartening problem of selecting those to eliminate from the organization. By this time friendships have developed. It's hard to terminate people who've been with the company from its beginning. We'll make some suggestions later in this chapter for doing this with the least unpleasantness. Once the disagreeable task's been done, it's necessary to replace those who've been fired with competent people who can take on positions of responsibility. The time lost in allowing incompetent people to fill positions can never be regained. How much better to have hired people with the right qualifications in the first place!

Don't fall into the trap of hiring indiscriminately. Learn the importance of setting high standards in employing people from the very beginning. Think through and set policies for both hiring and managing personnel to ensure staffing your firm with people who can do today's job and can learn to do tomorrow's job as the firm grows.

Guidelines for Hiring Policy

You can be guided in establishing a sound hiring policy by observing these criteria:

1. Make sure the candidate can do the job that needs doing now.

2. Make sure the candidate you hire will work well with others, because of the importance of teamwork in your business.

3. Gauge the potential of the candidate for growth, for becoming more competent with time, because growth of your employees is important to the growth of your company.

4. Make sure you feel comfortable with the people you hire. You'll work closely together to make the company grow both technically and financially. It's important that you get along well together.

If we look closely at these statements, we see that they cover two broad subjects: technical competence in the work and interpersonal competence in relationships with others. Any business must have technical competence to survive; it must do a good job of turning out the product or service. And a high level of interpersonal competence supports the firm's technical competence because it improves the ability of the members to identify the important problems of operations that need to be solved *and* to solve them through teamwork of the most effective kind. Not only that, but by practicing teamwork effectively, members also learn to contribute their special knowledge in solving these important problems. The practice of interpersonal competence helps to improve the team's problem-solving ability.

Once you've thought about these foregoing guidelines and have determined your hiring policy, you're ready to adopt practices that will help you hire people who are right for your organization.

RECRUITING THE RIGHT PEOPLE

If you're a sole proprietor, you'll do the first hiring yourself. You can use a straightforward, well-tested procedure to make sure that you're doing a good job of getting the right kind of person for the job and for your firm. The same procedure should be adopted by anyone you delegate to do the hiring. In using a uniform approach to hiring you'll be setting standards for sound practice in acquiring personnel; sound practice will help you build an effective workforce now and for the future.

Hiring is a three-step process: (1) defining the duties and responsibilities of the position to be filled and the skills, knowledge, and experience required to meet them, (2) finding and attracting those people who have the qualifications for the position, and (3) screening the candidates to identify the most promising and then hiring them.

Finding Qualified Applicants

Assuming that you've defined the requirements of the position you want to fill, the duties and responsibilities and the background needed to do the work, your next step is to find qualified candidates. You won't have the advantages of the large company with its specialized recruiting staff, package of fringe benefits, and high salaries. You'll have to concentrate on offering the advantages of the small company. This suggests that you'll have to use every resource at your command to find candidates who measure up to the standards given in the hiring policies you've set.

Among the many resources you can draw on to find the right people are the following:

- Newspaper advertisements. You should outline in your ad the specific duties and responsibilities of the position and the requirements the candidate must bring to it. State clearly the advantages your small company has over the behemoths: the great opportunity for innovative work, the chance to move up fast with the growth of the company, the pleasure of working closely with other competent people in a friendly environment where everyone knows everybody else, the uniqueness of your product or service, and any other features you think attractive to prospective personnel.

- Business friends and acquaintances. You'll meet your counterparts at various functions, at a dinner or at a business meeting. Tell them about the position you have open and about the kind of person you're looking for to fill it. Many times your business acquaintances will be able to suggest a person who may qualify.

- Suppliers and customers. Let your suppliers and major customers know about the open position. They too can often suggest likely prospects to fill it.

- Technical publications. Place a carefully worded ad in the technical publication in your field. This approach may take longer than a newspaper ad because of the publication schedule of the journal. However, it can be effective because the readership will include persons acquainted with the field; some will undoubtedly have the competence you're looking for.

- Trade associations. The United States boasts over 5000 trade associations. Check with the secretary of the association that represents your business to see if the association has an employment service. If so, you may find that service helpful in your search for qualified candidates.

- Employment agencies. You'll find a great variety of employment agencies available to help you in your search. These range from free governmental agencies to consulting firms that specialize in finding high level management personnel for a fee. If you choose one of the latter be careful to check their record for integrity and success. The management search firm can often do a first-rate job of finding well-qualified, high-level managers. Employing a firm of this kind poses several problems for the new entrepreneur, not the least of which are cost and time. Good search firms charge high fees, perhaps several thousand dollars. And their searching period could run several weeks or months. You probably won't be able to absorb the cost of the management search firm when your company is new. But you may find this approach quite useful when your company grows to a size that can afford it.

- Universities and technical schools. Universities and technical institutes have employment services for their graduates and alumni. You can often find qualified candidates among their young graduates or their mature and more experienced alumni.

- Friends and relations. Discreet inquiry among your friends and relations may identify a candidate or two. This route can sometimes lead to difficulty. If you hire a person you've found through friends or relations and that person doesn't work out, you run the risk of losing a friendly relationship. You'd be well advised to reserve this approach for the last.

- Personal file. It's good practice to keep a personal file of likely prospects for positions with your firm as you meet them in the course of business or at social affairs. Keep a notebook with you to jot down names, addresses, phone numbers of likely prospects whom you meet. Make notes about their background and your impressions of them. When you have to fill a position you can occasionally locate a potential employee in your notebook.

- Self-help clubs. Use organizations such as Forty Plus to find unemployed mature executives who may fit nicely into your organization. More than one small company has recognized the worth of seasoned executives who've had wide experience in precisely the work of the position that's open. Many executives who've been displaced for one reason or another beyond their control are just reaching their prime after forty. They seek work eagerly and are often willing to accept positions at salaries considerably lower than they had when previously employed. You may find a powerful manager at a price your company can afford by checking with the self-help clubs in your community.

Assuming you've located two or three prospects who seem to fill your requirements for a position, your next step would be to select and hire the most promising.

The Interviewing Procedure

When you tackle the inverviewing job, be careful to avoid a pitfall common in most interviews. It's been found from careful study that most interviewers form an opinion about the candidate in the first three minutes. They then spend the rest of the interview hour seeking proof to justify that opinion. Avoid this common pitfall; when you tackle the interviewing job try to be as objective as you can. Withhold judgment until the interview is over and you've had time to sift through what you've learned about the candidate. The people you interview will often be flustered at the start of the conversation. If you jump to a conclusion about them at that point you can be seriously wrong. Wait and see; candidates will generally settle down after a few minutes and give you a much truer picture of themselves.

A screening procedure that has proven itself in the practice of many companies goes through three steps. If you're the only manager in your company, you would do all three steps yourself. You might even decide to combine them into two or even one. If your company has a personnel manager, that person should handle the first interview, which serves as a preliminary screening. The second interview should be done by the supervisor for whom the candidate would work. You'd do the third step yourself to ensure that the candidate fits the guidelines you've established in your hiring policy. Whichever way is suitable for your business setup, you shouldn't omit any of the important points given in the three steps we recommend here:

1. *Preliminary screening.* This first step aims at gaining some background information about the candidate. A good way to start is to have the person fill out a simple application form listing many of the usual bits of data needed for the record. A typical form is given in Figure 14-1. The form can then be used as a guide in the interview.

In the preliminary screening you'll seek the answers to some basic questions: What has the candidate's experience been? What has he or she done in previous jobs? What special skills have been acquired during this experience? What are the candidate's motives, drives, interests, and aspirations? From answers to questions such as these you can begin to form a judgment about the person's potential, both for doing the job you want to fill and for growth in the future.

2. *Second Interview.* The purpose of the second screening is to check on the technical competence of the candidate. The aim here is to find out if the candidate brings to the job the necessary qualifications to perform well. Does the individual have the needed skills to manage a small office, design and machine a stamping die, work up a campaign for a sales promotion, or do whatever the specific job needs done?

Your supervisor or you should try here to ensure that the person being considered has the experience and skill needed to fill the technical requirements of the job. By making a telephone call to the candidate's previous immediate boss you can verify the judgment made about the person's ability. People tend to talk more freely on the phone than they would in a letter. They'll say things that they might not want to put in writing. You'll be able to check what the candidate has told you in both interviews and can judge how truthful the candidate is likely to be.

3. *Third Interview.* In the third interview you'll try to check the information you've gathered, and you'll solidify your impressions about the candidate. You'll reach answers to questions about the candidate's interpersonal competence: Would this individual fit my organization? Would he or she work well with others? Could I expect straight replies to tough questions? Does this person impress me as having potential for growth? With answers to these and similar questions that will occur to you, you'll make up your mind to reject or to hire.

You understand, of course, that even though you've taken great care in putting the candidate through a rigorous three-step screening procedure, you can't be cer-

PERSONAL

   Name: Social Security Number:

   Address: Phone Number:

   Date of Birth*:

*The Employment Act of 1967 prohibits discrimination on the basis of age with respect to individuals who are at least 40 but less than 70 years of age. (Follow requirements of law that prevent discrimination on the bases of sex, race, and religion also.)

EDUCATIONAL

   High School and Location: Dates: from _____ to _____

   College or University: Degrees Obtained:

   Other educational training, including trade, business, or military:

REFERENCES

   Name three persons, preferably former supervisors or teachers familiar with your qualifications, whom we have your permission to contact:

   Name   Address and Phone No.   Position

   1.

   2.

   3.

PERSONAL COMMENTS

   Use this space for comments about your special abilities, special work you have done, or special work you would like to do.

WORK EXPERIENCE

   List all periods of employment since school; start with the most recent employment:

                                                                From: To:

   Company:
   Address:

   Company:
   Address:

   Company:
   Address:

   (If more space is required for work experience, please attach additional sheet.)

_____

I authorize _____ Company to obtain information about my employment and educational records from former employers, school officials, and persons named above as references, and I release all concerned from any liability in connection with the release of such information.

                                                  _____

                                                  Applicant's Signature   Date

Figure 14-1   Typical Application Form

TELEPHONE REFERENCE

(Applicant) _____ is being considered for a position as an _____ and has

given us permission to contact you (Ref., Title) _____ for a confidential reference.

We would appreciate your evaluation on the basis of the following questions:

What was his or her technical assignment? (Company, relationship, time supervised, etc.)

How was his or her performance?

Does he or she get along well with people?

Do you have any reservations about recommending him or her for hire in our proposed work assignment?

Would you rehire him or her if the opportunity arose?

Additional Comments: (Potential, goals, interests, etc.)

_____   _____
Interviewer   Date

Figure 14-2   Telephone Reference

tain that the person *will* work out on the job. Your screening efforts will improve the odds for success, but it's the actuality of performance on the job that will determine whether the candidate should be kept on. You'd be well advised therefore to make it clear that the new employee starts on a trial basis. If he or she doesn't work out well in a given period, say one to six months depending on the job, then that person will be terminated. A clean severance under those circumstances is the best answer for both parties.

Don't overlook the point we've stressed before: With the first person you hire you set a standard for your firm. The careful screening procedure we've outlined here will help you develop the kind of organization you can count on for successful and profitable growth. You fulfill this requirement by building a staff of technically and interpersonally competent people.

APPRAISING PERFORMANCE

With the hiring of your first employee you've taken on the task of appraising the performance of those who work for you. This is, of course, the responsibility of the immediate manager. Therefore, as your organization grows you'll be appraising the performance of people at higher levels and increasing scope of responsibility. In this practice, as in many others, you'll set the pattern and the style for your firm. You should be aware of the pitfalls of the traditional performance appraisal so you can avoid them and so that you can take advantage of more modern thinking that has come from extensive research.

The old approach to performance appraisal has been to tell employees first what they've done well and then to tell them what they've done wrong. The idea was to take the sting out of the criticism by starting with a word of praise. The underlying concept seems to be that people can be changed by telling them to change. We've learned that this way of going about it is psychologically unsound. People don't learn much by being told.

We human beings learn better by involving ourselves in the task or process of what has to be done. We make our mistakes and correct them—*particularly with adequate coaching.* In this way we gain skill.

Criticism, no matter how supposedly constructive, no matter how kindly intended, tends to make persons being criticized experience it as a frontal attack. They become defensive to protect their egos. When this happens, interviews with the boss miss their constructive intent.

We suggest then that as a manager your appraisal of performance should be carried on in a more modern way. Instead of being a critic you should be a coach. This implies that you'll be working with those who report to you in an ongoing fashion. Your role will be one of coach and counselor rather than of judge and critic. You'll automatically appraise in working with your personnel, but you need not make a formal event of the process.

Your appraisal should hinge on the question: Could this person do the work if his or her life depended on it? This is a *can-do* question. If the answer is *yes* but the person's performance is not up to snuff, then you should look to yourself as not doing a satisfactory coaching job. So you should see that the individual gets the training or help needed to ensure improved performance, whether you do it yourself or get someone qualified to do it. If your answer to the question is *no*, then your problem is different. The employee should be moved to another kind of work that he or she can do. If this fails you may have to discharge that person.

TERMINATING PERSONNEL

Letting employees go is, at best, a distasteful procedure; it can be less so if you observe some important managerial considerations. Before you let someone go, you should think about: proper timing, giving the unsatisfactory performer adequate warning, deciding on severance pay, conducting the terminal interview, and filling the open job.

The way you handle these factors will depend upon whether you want to let the employee go or whether the employee wants to quit.

Firing Employees

Before you decide to let employees go, it's only fair that they be told that their performance is not up to snuff. Then you should make the necessary training available so they have the chance to improve. Specify a date by which you expect their performance to improve to the level you want. If the improvement hasn't come about by the cut-off date, you should let the person go. Give your employee notice. One or two weeks is customary in most cases. Once you've made up your mind to let the employee go, you should immediately start to find a replacement.

Employees Firing You

If a person wants to leave your employ, on the other hand, it's good practice to arrange for an immediate severance. A statement of intent to quit shows that the employee's heart is no longer in the work. The sooner that person is gone, the less chance for rumor and perhaps disaffection to be spread among others in the organization. Your best course is to give reasonable severance pay and send that individual packing.

Firing Key Employees

You may run into a situation occasionally that demands some careful thinking before you decide to fire a key employee. Your decision may require answers to questions like these: Does this employee have special knowledge that should be transferred to someone else before being severed from the company? Is there an important negotiation with a customer going on that takes a special input from this employee? Is there someone else who could take over after this person leaves? What would it cost your company to have this employee leave right now as against putting an untrained individual in the spot? Should you try to keep this person because despite some negative factors it seems clearly to the benefit of the company? These are the kinds of questions you should ask and answer when deciding whether or not to fire a key employee. If you finally decide to let the person go, you can gain much valuable information by conducting a terminal interview with the employee.

Set aside a private place and an hour or so of uninterrupted time to carry out this interview. By careful probing you can get some important and useful feedback on how employees see your ways of managing your company. As a result, you may be able to correct deficiencies that will help to improve productivity and morale in your operations. These improvements, in turn, will enable you to develop a stable and effective workforce.

During the terminal interview, the employee will likely want to know why this severance procedure. If you've been through the warning and trial period we've discussed previously, there will be little need for elaborate explanations. Speak openly and straightforwardly about the reasons for the termination. Don't permit the meeting to degenerate into a debate. If you've taken the time and trouble to tell the individual about performance deficiencies in previous meetings, there should be no need for debate. Be decisive. A clean severance is the healthiest way both for the individual and for your company.

Firing Long-Term Employees

After your company has been in business for a few years, you may have to face a somewhat different problem of termination; you may have to deal with discharging a long-term employee who has been unable to work because of a prolonged illness. You will have to face issues of conscience and equity. You may wish to treat the employee generously, but your company, like many small companies, may not have the financial resources to enable you to be as generous as you'd like. You'll have to decide how far you can go. You can guide your decision by answering these questions: How long has the employee been with the company? How long is the illness likely to keep the employee away from work? How adequate is our medical insurance coverage? Does it provide funds for convalescent care, for maintenance of family as well as for medical bills? Can my company afford to make up the difference between what the insurance pays and what is needed to sustain the family? Would a loan be a feasible solution for the employee's financial problems? What's a reasonable length of time for the company to help?

You may decide that the company can afford to help for several months. But you'll more likely be forced to compromise between doing what your moral judgment suggests and what your best business judgment indicates. If you make your decision conscientiously with the help of the foregoing guidelines, at least you'll do the best thing possible under the circumstances.

TO UNIONIZE OR NOT TO UNIONIZE: THAT IS THE QUESTION!

Most entrepreneurs believe that through hard work, carefully calculated risk taking, good management, and fair play toward their employees they can run their small company without benefit of or interference from a union. The very thought of a union operating within your company may be unsettling to you.

When your company has achieved a modest level of success, when it employs between 20 and 200 people, it may be open to unionization. And federal law says that you'll have to sit down with a union representative and bargain in good faith.

When you reach this point in the growth of your company, you should put aside any preconceived notions you may have about unionization; you should instead devote your energies to managing the negotiations in a proactive fashion—for the best interests of your company.

Dealing with Unionization

If you wish to avoid unionization, you must understand the forces that drive employees to seek a union and through proper management prevent these forces from developing. Employees usually want unions for some quite clear reasons: to get better pay, to overcome inability to correct treatment seen as unjust, to ensure job security, to gain means for recognition, or to be protected from unpredictable behavior of the boss. If we look at these major forces for unionization you can see what you, as a small business owner, can do to minimize their impact.

To overcome adverse effects resulting from low pay, make sure you know what the prevailing wage rates are in your community for the kinds of work done by your work force. Check with your Chamber of Commerce for sources of this information. Local personnel managers associations usually gather and publish up-to-date wage rates for different kinds of labor in your area. Your state or city may have a department that does the same. With information from these sources, you can adjust your pay rates from time to time to keep them current or slightly above average. This action would remove pay as a reason for unionization.

The problem of job security is a delicate one. You must treat it carefully, with special consideration for the feelings of your personnel. Reduction in your work force should be done on the basis of a carefully thought out policy that is made clear to your employees. Should you observe priority in letting people go—last in, first out? Should you minimize the effect on your operations by letting go first those whose skills are least important to your operations? Whichever course you choose, you should make it clear to your employees before you let anyone go. And you should use a systematic approach in reducing your work force when it becomes necessary. You may want to review the section in Chapter 13 that treats the different ways to handle widely varying workloads to keep a stable work force. Sound managerial practice that affords reasonable job security for your work force will do much to allay efforts to unionize in the attempt to overcome perceptions of insecurity.

In the other matters of treating employees justly, giving recognition and behaving in a consistent manner, you must look at your own behavior as a boss. Most entrepreneurs tend to be rugged individuals, sure of themselves and straightforward in their dealings. They are often critical of the shortcomings of others and quite directive or even abrasive in their dealings with people who work for them. Their perceptions of how things are being done may not be anywhere like those of their personnel of whom they're critical. Employees called down in a forthright manner will more than likely resent the criticism, even though it may be warranted. They may see their safety in the job threatened by, to them, the boss's uncalled for and often unexpected behavior. Their response may be to look toward a union as a shield against a threatening management. They believe the union will force more dignified, courteous treatment and give them a way to redress what they see as a wrong.

Patterns of behavior that might cause your employees to seek unionization can be corrected. To do this you must be alert to your relationships with people. Building good interpersonal relationships starts with the boss. You're the one who sets the standards of behavior in your firm—the model whom your people respond to and imitate. Practice firmness coupled with respect and kindness. People respect honesty, and they also respect the boss who treats them with dignity, as responsible human beings.

If, despite your best efforts to avoid unionization, your firm should face an organizing effort, proactive management will be of inestimable value in dealing with it.

Your immediate task should be to seek competent help. This means hiring a labor lawyer to help you plan to meet the union challenge. The lawyer will also represent the interests of your company in negotiating with the union. Don't stint on fees for such counsel. The expenses for capable professional help will prove to be but a tiny part of the savings such help can secure for your company. Together with your counsel you should answer questions such as these:

- Are the wages I pay competitive in the community? What wages can I afford?

- What are the benefits my company pays? What are the maximum benefits my company can afford to pay?

- What is the best estimate of how much my company will have to concede in wages plus benefits as compared with what my competitors are paying?

- What managerial powers must I and my executive group retain at any cost? These include hiring and firing policies, overtime scheduling, administration of benefits, and similar matters.

- What are the terms of my competitors' union contracts?

If you plan proactively with counsel on the basis of the answers to these and similar questions that will suggest themselves during your deliberations, you'll be prepared to come out of negotiation with a contract that your company can live with, that costs the least, and that preserves your management rights.

The contract resulting from the negotiation should be seen as fair by the union, by your work force, and by you; it should spell out a win-win solution for all.

KEY POINTS IN MANAGING PERSONNEL   SUMMARY

When you hire your first person in your new business, you automatically set the style for the future. Before hiring that first employee, you should work out a sound policy for handling personnel matters. You'll recall that policies are guides to action. With carefully thought-out guides, you'll prepare yourself to take on people who can do the work that needs doing now and have the capability of growing, of meeting more demanding tasks as your firm grows. You'll be aware of the desirability of choosing those who not only can do the work, but also appear able to work well with others. You should feel comfortable with your new employees.

We've suggested sources for finding qualified personnel. By referring to these sources, you'll expand your field of choice. You should then be able to identify more than one candidate for an open position. And by following the three-step interviewing procedure we've outlined, you can improve your chances for hiring well-qualified people for your company.

We've also pointed out the negative effect of the old-fashioned way of appraising the performance of those who work for you. Criticism, no matter how well intended, usually doesn't produce the results you may intend. It's difficult to change people by telling them to change. A much better approach requires that you act as a coach. By working with your people, by showing them what and how you want things done and by guiding their actions in the process, you can help them improve their competence. You also can judge their performance without going through a formal appraisal procedure that's more likely than not to become abrasive, to develop self-defensiveness on their part. If you find that the person can't do the job, you may want to move that individual to another kind of work. Should that prove unsatisfactory, you may find it necessary to terminate that employee.

You can often learn some important things about how the employees perceive your style of management by conducting terminal interviews with personnel leaving the company. You can use the feedback from such interviews to adjust your management practices to improve the climate in your organization.

After your company is well established you may run into the problem of what to do for a long-term faithful employee who has served the company well but who is suffering a long, disabling illness. You'll have to decide how generous you can afford to be in proffering financial support to that employee. You'll try to do what's reasonable, deciding between what your conscience says and the financial implications of your decision for your company.

You may some day face the problem of unionization. This may happen after you've achieved recognizable success—perhaps when your company has reached an employment level of 100 or so. You probably won't like the idea that your people want a union. But federal law says you must bargain in good faith with the union.

Employees seek unionization for well-known reasons: to increase their wages, to gain protection from what they perceive as unjust treatment, to improve their job security, to achieve ways for being recognized, or to be protected from unpredictable management behavior.

In this chapter we've given some suggestions for avoiding unionization by practicing proactive management in dealing with each of these issues. If, despite your best efforts, you must meet the challenge of unionization, be sure to hire expert counsel to head your negotiation. Find an experienced labor lawyer to work with you in planning your approach to the negotiation. Prepare to deal with the issues of pay, benefits, and management prerogatives you must retain under any circumstances. In this way you can achieve an agreement that your company can live with, that costs your company the least, and that preserves your management rights. The labor contract that results from negotiation should be seen as fair by your work force, the union, and you—a win-win solution that will ensure a healthy relationship among all parties.

Managing Your Personnel Function

This worksheet is designed as a checklist to help you work out policies for managing your personnel function. Because policies afford guides to action, you will prepare yourself to handle personnel issues effectively without the difficulty of having to decide what to do on the spur of the moment. Preparation in personnel management is as important as in financial planning, marketing, or any other phase of proactive management.

1. I understand the importance of hiring people who are both technically competent and show evidence of interpersonal competence. I'll observe the following guidelines:

   a. I will make sure that those I hire can do the work that is required in the position. To support my effort to hire a technically qualified person for a position, I will write out the duties of the position, its responsibilities, and the experience needed to do the work well. This will prepare me to interview candidates competently in the first screening interview.

   b. I'll refrain from forming a too-early judgment about the candidate. I'll use an employment form to guide my preliminary screening interview, being sure that it conforms with legal requirements in not probing into prohibited personal areas.

   c. In addition to finding out about previous experience and special skills, I will try to gauge the applicant's motives, drives, interests, and aspirations. Answers to these kinds of questions will give me some insight into the likelihood of candidates performing the tasks required, their technical ability, and potential growth.

   d. In the next step I'll phone the candidate's immediate superior in the previous job to check on his or her experience. This will give me some feeling for the applicant's capability and will allow me to check on the truthfulness of what I've been told.

   e. I'll use the third step to come to a final assessment of the applicant's interpersonal competence. I want to be as sure as I can that the individual will fit well in my company, work well as a team member, and be able to grow with my company.

   f. I recognize that even the most careful screening may not guarantee that the person will work out on the job. I will therefore make sure that a new employee understands that the first period of employment is a trial period. This period shall be stated, one, two, or six months, whatever appropriate for the kind of work to be done. If the employee doesn't work out, we will part friends.

2. I will try to avoid an authoritarian approach in appraising performance of those who work for me. My attitude will be that of coach rather than critic. By working as closely as I can with my employees I'll gain knowledge of their strengths and weaknesses. This will allow me to help them build on their strengths; I will see ways to help them overcome weaknesses.

Following this managerial style will support my efforts to build a permanent, effective organization.

3. My practice in terminating unsatisfactory performers will be to warn them about their inadequacy. I will set a time for and specify the improvement I want. I will also make training available to them so that they can overcome their deficiency. If that doesn't work, I'll move them to another job that I think they can do. If that effort fails I will let them go.

4. If employees state that they want to quit, I'll arrange for immediate severance. There's no use keeping on people who have lost their desire to stay with the company.

5. If it becomes necessary for me to discharge key people, I'll make sure that the company is not hurt for special reasons: expert knowledge that should be transferred to others who'll remain on the job, close relationship with important customers that others should take over, or other important considerations that I'll examine before I authorize severance.

6. I'll have a terminal interview with anyone who leaves the company. This will give me feedback that may help me see and correct problems in the way my company is managed.

7. If it becomes necessary to discharge a long-term faithful employee because of prolonged illness, I'll be as generous as company finances will allow me to be in granting aid to that person and family.

8. I would certainly prefer not to have a union in my company. I understand the reasons people want a union. These are to get better pay, to overcome their inability to correct treatment they see as unjust, to achieve job security, to have a way of being recognized, and to be protected from management they see as behaving unpredictably. I'll take the following steps to avoid unionization:
   a. I'll make sure that our pay rates are equal to or slightly above those prevailing in similar jobs in the community.
   b. To improve feelings of job security, I will work out policies and procedures for dealing with reduction in work force if it becomes necessary. I will let my employees know the policies and the procedures as a matter of routine practice.
   c. I understand that my behavior must be consistent; as the boss I must respond in the same way under the same circumstances, so my people won't be confused and worry about what's likely to happen when they encounter me on the job. I will work conscientiously to establish trust with my people, because I know that good interpersonal relations make for good teamwork and company effectiveness.

9. If I cannot avoid the effort to unionize my firm, I'll hire the most competent labor lawyer I can find to help me meet the challenge. My objectives in the negotiation will be to reach a contract that my company can live with, at the least cost, and without losing any of our management rights. I accept the idea that the practice of proactive management requires the union contract to be fair to all parties—to the company, to the union, and to my work force.

IF YOU WANT TO READ MORE

We've selected the following publications as sources that you can probe as deeply as you feel the need in the several subjects covered in this chapter. You'll find additional references in each of these books.

George A. Steiner and John B. Miner, *Management Policy and Strategy*, Macmillan, New York, 1977. In Chapters 2 and 3, the authors treat the development of business strategy and policy from the point of view of the chief executive officer. You can gain from this text an important set of ideas that will help you develop your policies for managing personnel *and* for managing the other functions of your business.

Richard A. Fear, *The Evaluation Interview*, 2nd ed., McGraw-Hill, New York, 1973. This is a highly regarded how-to-do-it book that tells in step-by-step fashion how to become a good interviewer and how to interpret the facts gathered in the interview. You'll find the procedures given very much on target in helping you gain skill in the interviewing and selection process.

Douglas McGregor, *The Human Side of Enterprise*, McGraw-Hill, 1960. This is a great classic that has influenced the practice of management toward more human treatment of personnel. Chapters 6 and 7 discuss the problems of the old-fashioned or traditional performance appraisal and give suggestions of how to conduct performance appraisals and administer salaries and promotions in a psychologically sound manner. The whole book is well worth reading. It will give you insight into the modern way of viewing the people who work for you, and it will help you build a business philosophy well suited to the practice of proactive management.

William Wayne, *How to Succeed in Business When the Chips Are Down*, McGraw-Hill, New York, 1972. You'll find in this pungently written book some interesting and practical suggestions for finding, hiring, and firing personnel. Refer to Part 4 of the text for some hardheaded experience-based advice on administering your personnel function. Chapter 9 will give you some sound advice on how to keep unions out of your company.

Gordon B. Baty, *Entrepreneurship: Playing to Win*, Reston Publishing, Reston, Va., 1974. In Chapter 17 the author outlines key points in acquiring and divesting people. Points covered include compensation packages, recruiting, interviewing, and reducing the work force. The chapter gives a brief summary of various aspects of personnel administration; you'll find it a handy reference.

Chapter 15

Surviving: Managing for Productivity and Growth

If you've stayed with us this far, you've completed the worksheet assignments. You've initiated the basic plan for and have very likely started your business. This chapter deals with the problems, pitfalls, challenges and opportunities that will face you almost immediately after you've opened your doors.

At no point in this book have we suggested that staying in your business will be easy once you've started it. We've tried conscientiously not to give you a pep talk on the glories of entrepreneurship. We've spelled out principles and techniques for improving your odds for survival in your small business. We now turn your attention toward solving particular problems of survival and growth of your firm.

You'll face predictable, and unavoidable, stages of development after you begin your business operations. Each of these stages will present a crisis of one kind or another unless you anticipate and plan for them during the first year or two. It will be necessary for you to put aside some of your entrepreneurial qualities to perform successfully as a manager of a going business. This will require a good deal of study and hard work.

We'll point out some of the common pitfalls to avoid during the growth stages of your business. We'll suggest ways to identify the strengths and to detect the weaknesses in your business. You'll then be able to build on the strengths and overcome the weaknesses. And we'll discuss ways for you to gain the special management skills you'll need to carry out your business plans during the first years you're in business. As you acquire these skills you'll be taking steps toward becoming a professional manager.

WHAT IS EXPECTED OF A GOOD MANAGER?

When we teach venture initiation to potential entrepreneurs, we use the following exercise to illustrate the importance of knowing and living up to the behavior people expect of a good manager. We ask participants in our workshops to think about the best managers they've ever worked for and to develop a list of ten specific attributes or characteristics the ideal manager demonstrates. (Put this book aside for a moment and do this yourself before reading further. Note: the term *good leader* is too general!) A composite of such lists follows:

PROFILE OF THE IDEAL MANAGER

Attributes expected

(most frequently mentioned)	*Typical participant comments*
■ Empathic	"sensitive to needs of others"
■ Trusting, fair, honest	"open and honest in dealing with others"
■ Encourages innovation	"wants people to come forward with their ideas"

- **Good listener** "reacts to what I say; listens to me actively and sincerely"

- **Delegates authority** "lets others have control and freedom over some things"

- **Self-confident** "acts positively and decisively with the available facts"

- **Loyal and supportive** "backs up employees on controversial things"

- **Creative and technically competent** "knows the business inside and out and has good ideas"

- **Good planner and organizer** "looks ahead and can pull together what's needed to get there"

- **Gives feedback on performance** "tells people how they're doing and is a good teacher"

In examining the list closely, you'll find there are three categories of expectations mentioned by potential entrepreneurs. First, they expect *technical competence* in the ideal manager. This needs no further elaboration since we've stressed it throughout the book.

Second, attributes such as "good planner and organizer" can be interpreted as meaning they expect *system competence*—skills in fitting all the pieces of the business together, with the planning and organizing ability to direct them toward a desired future. Although technical competence deals with intimate knowledge of physical products, job skills, manufacturing processes, and the like, system competence has to do with ideas and concepts. The business plan you'll develop is the hard evidence of your system competence.

Third, *interpersonal competence* is a category that includes most of the role traits desired by our respondents. Being empathic, trusting, loyal and supportive, and the rest, have to do with people; these are the attributes that usually head the lists. The results of this exercise are consistent although the terms and descriptions used vary somewhat from group to group. There is no reason to believe the results would be substantially different if the list makers were your employees. Individuals you'll employ will expect you to have and to show these same managerial qualities. They'll value above all your competence in dealing with people. As the manager–leader, the degree to which you show such competence will greatly affect the amount and quality of "followership" you achieve with them.

Your business will require the collaborative effort of individuals with different backgrounds. Cooperative effort will become ever more essential as your business expands. Your behavior should induce an environment of openness and trust. You won't needle, demean, or block others. Instead you'll encourage your people to deal forthrightly with their ideas and feelings in their relationships with you. The employee group will very likely respond in kind, reflecting your style. You show high interpersonal competence when you interact with people openly and fairly.

If you have this kind of interpersonal competence, it will also be seen in the way you isolate the important problems facing your organization. It will be seen in the supportive way you deal with employees in solving these problems, and in the universal acceptance of solutions by the group once individual differences have been resolved. Demonstrated interpersonal competence will be a major factor in facilitating the growth of your business for it welds human resources in building a successful business venture.

Entrepreneurial Qualities as Potential Liabilities in Managing

Some of the very qualities it takes to start a new business can cause problems in the operation once it's underway. The behavior patterns of the entrepreneur often include independence, stubbornness (sometimes to the point of bullheadedness), impatience, argumentativeness, and anxiety. These can be intensified by the uncertainties and extraordinary pressures of the early days of the business and can show themselves in alternating periods of elation and depression.

The entrepreneur wants desperately to achieve—for the business to succeed. The drive to be achieving and to create a unique enterprise is fueled along the way by the entrepreneur's boundless energy. This quality helps propel the venture forward. But the volatile entrepreneur needs to be cautioned against allowing personal and behavioral assets from becoming liabilities. There are two ways to deal effectively with this problem.

First, recognize that if carried to the extreme some behavioral tendencies will detract from your ability to run your venture well. This doesn't mean that suddenly you have to become a new person. It does mean that you'll need a thorough understanding of yourself and the willingness to adapt your behavior to the hectic, confused, and emotionally charged environment of your fledgling business.

Entrepreneurs who don't adjust properly typically exhibit negative behavior in these ways:

1. *Reinventing the wheel.* You may automatically reject techniques successfully practiced in other businesses. Convinced that *you* have a gift of perception and sound intuitive judgment, you may tend to insist on reinventing the wheel and perhaps to use practices that have failed elsewhere.

2. *Overreacting to business problems.* The high-risk environment of the new business and the compulsion to make the business successful often result in entrepreneurs overreacting to problems. A shipment of goods that doesn't arrive on time, faulty production equipment, a misplaced order, phone calls that aren't returned in a "reasonable" time, the newly hired receptionist who doesn't show up for work, all seem to happen at once. Thus, harried and impatient, you may react impetuously. You may damage future relationships with suppliers, customers, or employees by blowing up. Or your frenetic activity to solve an immediate problem may not keep the problem from popping up again.

   You must cultivate an even temperament to deal with each problem on its own merits. The tardy supplier won't know the receptionist didn't show up. The equipment supplier won't know that you can't locate an important order. You must approach each problem-solving situation with an eye to resolving it so it stays solved.

Tendencies to overreact and reinvent the wheel result in continual surges of unresolved problems and misdirected activities that center around your special interests and desires.

3. *Dealing ineffectively with hired help.* This most serious problem for the newly operating business only partly results from the two weaknesses described above. As your new venture struggles to its feet, all the personnel problems that plague older companies surface quickly. The principal reason we devoted a full chapter to managing personnel (Chapter 14) is this: *Your solutions to personnel problems or your inability to arrive at solutions rapidly become part of your management style.* They become habitual and ingrained and difficult to change later on.

Entrepreneurial qualities conflict to some extent with the objective capability needed to select, hire, train, mediate conflict, and harmonize the purposes of diverse human beings. You're starting your business because of your need to achieve through marketing a new product or service. You didn't get into business for the purpose of working with others. As a result, you're product- and market-oriented, and rightly so. Equipped with entrepreneurial characteristics and with everything at risk in your new venture, you're ill-prepared to deal with people problems. While making your transition from entrepreneur to manager, this will be a difficult but most important area in which you should gain competence.

Much of the discussion that follows relates both to personnel management in a broad sense and to the varied management skills so crucial to surviving the first year or two of operation.

THE MANY HATS A MANAGER MUST WEAR

Entrepreneurs are doers; they are independent and action-oriented and rely on their own ingenuity and energy to plan and accomplish desired results. To get the business going, the entrepreneur must use his or her own financial, intellectual, and emotional resources. Once underway the picture changes subtly but substantially. Now you'll need to develop and maintain effective, ongoing relationships with employees, customers, lenders, investors, and suppliers. You could rely primarily on yourself before you opened your doors for business. But once underway you'll have to depend on others to help you get the results you want. This will require you to make transition from being a loner-doer to being a professional manager.

Of the many highly successful entrepreneurs we've known, those who've built eight- and nine-figure businesses, the special quality that sets the very successful apart from the less successful has been their ability to make this transition—usually during the first years of operating their business. As we've pointed out, most businesses don't survive the first two years. The principal reason emerges as the entrepreneur's inability to *manage*. Again, this doesn't imply that you'll have to change your basic character. It just means that you must acquire and use new skills in addition to the positive entrepreneurial skills that drove you to create the business.

Ten Basic Roles of Management

As a manager you'll have to fill ten basic roles. It would be absurd to suggest that you must be expert in all these roles; nevertheless, you should have background and general knowledge in these areas and expertise in a number of them. Here, then, are the ten major roles in which you should develop skill, together with a brief summary of the competence pertinent to each role:

1. The manager as *communicator*. Understanding of, and competence in, developing effective communications in your organization; including understanding of business performance data and keeping your employees informed about these.

2. The manager as *integrator*. Ability to coordinate activities of individuals and groups; competence in dealing with outside community groups.

3. The manager as *planner* and *decision maker*. Knowledge of planning techniques; knowledge of techniques for identifying and assessing alternatives in decision making; knowledge about budgeting and control; understanding of the management of financial resources.

4. The manager as *organizational designer*. Knowledge of methods for determining organizational needs to meet market changes and ability to design organization structure to accommodate these needs.

5. The manager as *innovator*. Understanding of creative ways for using organizational resources, human and physical; competence in implementing organizational change; understanding of the impact of market forces on the organization; competence in the continual revitalization of the organization.

6. The manager as *problem solver*. Competence in the techniques of problem analysis and solution; ability to diagnose conflict and resolve it.

7. The manager as *coach* and *counselor*. Ability to encourage and assist in the personal growth of individuals. Ability to help subordinates overcome blocks interfering with their performance.

8. The manager as *teacher* and *learner*. Understanding of the proper use of human resources; understanding of the development of leadership qualities; knowledge of alternate ways of functioning in the management role.

9. The manager as *advocate*. Knowledge of the processes through which negotiation, acceptance, and action take place in decision making; understanding the nature of interdependence in the organization; competence in diagnosing and improving intergroup relations.

10. The manager as a *model of style*. Understanding of how management style influences organizational effectiveness; knowledge of the concepts of motivation in work.

These roles suggest areas in which the acquisition of knowledge and skill will prove desirable for your personal growth as your company grows. They are presented as a guide to the kinds of competencies you'll need to make the transition from entrepreneur to professional manager.

YOUR BASIC CONCERN AS A MANAGER: PRODUCTIVITY

The foregoing discussion focused on the roles you'll need to assume once your venture is launched. Performance of these management roles has this unifying purpose: **achievement and maintenance over time of the highest level of productivity possible for your enterprise.**

Definition of Productivity and Relationship to Profit

Productivity is the relationship between inputs and outputs. The term productivity encompasses both the resources (inputs) used in producing and marketing your product or supplying your service and the market results you achieve with them (outputs). Productivity refers to the amount and cost of labor, supplies, equipment, fuel, and capital required to produce and distribute your product or service in order to develop consumer acceptance and achieve sales.

The ultimate aim of any business is profit. Profit is the measure of financial performance that reflects the difference between inputs and outputs. In this sense productivity and profit are parallel terms. Profit is expressed as a dollar figure on the income statement at the end of the year. But the concept of productivity is broader: It focuses on a manager's conscious actions taken during the year to stroke the proper relationship between inputs and outputs needed to reach a desired *level* of profit.

Efficiency vs. Effectiveness

The proper balance between inputs and outputs is not easy to manage. Inputs represent time and expenditures you make to obtain revenue from consumers. On the input side your management concern is with *efficiency*: "Are we *doing things right;* are we keeping expenditures low?" And on the output side the concern is with *effectiveness:* "Are we *doing the right things?* Are we achieving maximum exposure in (or impact on) the market?"

Efficiency and effectiveness conflict with one another to some extent. If efficiency were carried to the extreme, the most efficient operation would have zero costs. Your concern for efficiency will be seen in day-to-day business operations, such as making sure material waste is kept to a minimum, keeping operating costs as low as possible, taking advantage of discounts on supply orders, and controlling personnel costs. Effectiveness, on the other hand, deals with the future and change. Here, your concern will focus on issues such as whether the business is positioning itself properly in the market, whether promotion is reaching potential customers, whether new products are needed, and in general, whether the market segments you want are responding to your marketing program.

In managing, efficiency matters deal with the here and now and require attention to details and cost control. Effectiveness looks to the future and requires innovation and creativity. Efficiency means that you must be proficient at being a *system regulator;* effectiveness requires you to be a *change agent* for your business. Figure 15-1 summarizes this discussion.

When you are in the process of regulating your business system, you may overemphasize efficiency at the expense of effectiveness. For example, if you overstress efficiency with your employees, they may be fearful of experimenting with new ways of performing tasks or may become reluctant to suggest new ideas for improving customer satisfaction. On the other hand, stressing effectiveness too much may

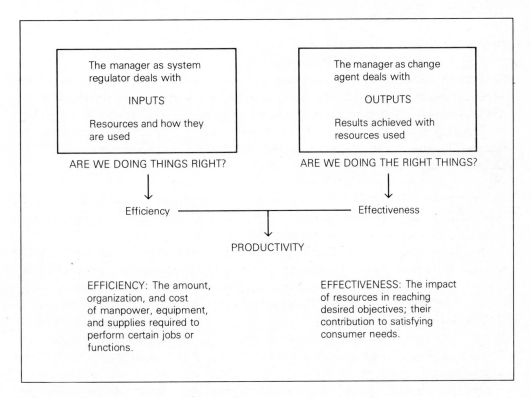

Figure 15-1 The Concept of Productivity

lead to chaos—too much experimentation on the job to get the work out, lack of consistency in work methods, and overspending on marketing to get customers.

Your organization will reflect your management style; good managers blend change agentry with system regulation. As we've said, striking the proper balance between efficiency and effectiveness is difficult. But recognition of the nature of productivity will help you to achieve the necessary balance as you deal with the issues of efficiency and effectiveness that arise as soon as you begin operations.

A MANAGEMENT SYSTEM FOR IMPROVING PRODUCTIVITY

Productivity improvement comes from:

1. Keeping resources used constant while improving results achieved

2. Keeping results constant while reducing resources used

3. Increasing resources used but improving results at an even higher rate.

But how is productivity to be achieved? Surviving the first year or two depends on your ability to adapt to change. This early period will be filled with uncertainty as you attempt to get a toehold in the market. You'll be stretched to the limit. You'll be squeezing every ounce of production out of equipment and people who work for you; you'll be spending every waking minute in building consumer awareness and patronage; you'll be dealing with brush fires that flare up—in cash flow and marketing, for example.

You'll be working harder during the first year than you've ever worked in your life. What you'll need is a system of managing that allows you to work *smarter*. The management system you employ must therefore have the necessary flexibility to adjust quickly to change and bring order out of chaos.

The system of *management by objectives* (MBO) is a tested and proven way to increase the productivity of your enterprise during the first critical period of operation—and ever after.

Management by Objectives

The concept of management by objectives was first stated by Peter Drucker in 1954.[1] He said that after he had observed how good managers achieve and maintain high productivity in successful companies he found that they followed a similar pattern. Instead of being directive bosses, they tended to act as teachers, coaches, and counselors with their subordinates. They helped their people set goals for work in keeping with their own goals. They let people have a great deal to say about their jobs and how they did them. Drucker called the basic strategy *management by objectives and self-control*.

In 1960 Douglas McGregor expanded on Drucker's approach.[2] He called the management strategy *management by integration and self-control*. He suggested

308

that to increase productivity and build teamwork and commitment throughout the company, all members should be working toward the same end. As your company grows and you add managers, you'll be able to introduce them into the MBO system from the day they go to work. The way to do this is to have all members of the company set their own objectives in collaboration with their boss. Starting with you, all personnel would set their key objectives in keeping with yours.

When the process is properly done, your company operates from an integrated network of plans. All who work for you have had a great deal to say about their contribution to the mainstream effort of the company. And all see how their effort fits with those of others in achieving the overall productivity objectives of the company.

People tend to support the plans they have themselves developed. They are committed psychologically to making them work. After all, you don't throw your own baby out the window; you nurture it and see that it grows healthy and survives.

Putting Management by Objectives to Work for You

As the chief executive officer of your company you can make management by objectives (MBO) work for you. You'll find its strategy and tactics follow the behavioral recommendations made in Chapter 14 for managing the people who work for you.

You gain a great advantage when you use MBO for managing your new company right from the very start. That's because you won't have to undo less effective, more traditional ways of management that have become ingrown, as happens in so many companies that have operated in the old ways.

The new way is to sit down with those who report directly to you and work out with them the major objectives for your company. When you start your company there may be only one or two people who work for you; as your company grows and adds managers, you'll want to go through the same procedure with a larger group.

Then you'll work with each of your subordinates in helping them set their personal objectives. Since they now know what the major objectives of the company are, they can fit their plans in with yours. You may assign the authority for carrying out one or two of the company objectives to each of the people who report to you. They will then develop the plans for the activities they will engage in to accomplish these major objectives. The result will be a network of plans aimed at achieving the overall objectives of the company.

All personnel will know how their efforts fit in with the total effort of the company. The network of plans compose a productivity improvement program for your business, and each member will have had something to say about his or her contribution to the total.

All plans will be written down informally in memos from subordinate to boss. In essence these memos will be a record of agreement between the two. They become a confirmation of a psychological contract of work. The subordinate says in essence: "We've agreed to what I'm supposed to accomplish during the next six months or year, and I understand how my efforts will contribute to the productivity of the business. You've done your part by coaching me in the discussion we've had. In one or two instances you've shown me that I'm reaching too high; in others I set too low a target. But now we're agreed, and I'm willing to be judged by how well I do in reaching those targets. Of course we both understand that if I fail to achieve an objective because of circumstances beyond my control, you'll take that into consideration in assessing my performance."

In putting MBO to work for you the process should result in plans and objectives that contribute to the input and output aspects of productivity improvement. Be sure that plans contain an appropriate *balance* between efficiency-type objectives and effectiveness-type objectives.

Kinds of Plans

It's wise to limit the number of terms used in planning to a tested few. Here are our suggestions:

- *Objectives* are overall purposes or positions to be reached. They are relatively long-range, perhaps a year or so for practical managerial purposes. Larger companies in the United States often consider objectives as five-year plans. The requirements of the business will set the length of an objective. Small companies usually find a period of one year most practical in planning objectives.

- *Subobjectives* are end results desired by a specific time. Subobjectives tend to be more concrete, more limited in scope and time, than objectives. Generally, several subobjectives will have to be achieved and put together, or integrated, to reach an objective.

- *Action plans* are steps, activities, tasks, projects, or programs, which when put together accomplish subobjectives. Action plans are the ultimate step that make MBO work. Action plans imply activities—people doing things, working and interacting with others inside and outside the company.

Guides to Writing Plans

Here are some well-tested guides that will help you and your managers write the plans used in MBO:

- No company, division, department, or individual management position should have more than six or seven major objectives in work at any time. Management by objectives avoids spelling out in step-by-step detail how people should do their jobs. Planning in MBO affords guides that are specified as *results,* which may be thought of as standards of performance. Therefore, managers are free to do their jobs in ways they feel comfortable with. The ultimate criteria of performance are: Do they do a good job—that meets the specifications, on time, and within the budget of money and resources allocated?

- Plans should be written informally, not on standard forms developed for the purpose. Use of standard forms tends to move the system toward bureaucracy, in which filling out the forms becomes the important part of the MBO process. Means become ends and the whole purpose of gaining enthusiastic commitment to achievement is thwarted.

- Each plan should contain only one idea. The point is to keep the procedure simple. If you want to deal with two ideas, write two plans.

- Plans should be stated in simple, clear language. A clear crisply stated plan says what is intended without being hard to interpret or causing confusion.

- Each plan should start with an active verb, which says *do something*, don't just sit there. Verbs show action. Here are typical active verbs that might start a plan: *Reduce* scrap, *increase* net profit from . . ., *hire* two people for . . ., *buy* a new site for. . . .

- Each plan should have an end date by the calendar. This means a specific date such as June 15, 1979, or November 10, 1980. A specific date sharpens the focus of timeliness of achievement. Take advantage of it.

- Each plan should specify a way of measuring achievement toward its accomplishment. Wherever possible numbers should be used, for example, dollars of profit, pounds of scrap, or percentage of turnover. Some plans aim at goals that can't be put in numbers. If so, use a scale of some kind, for example, ranging from poor through fair, good, and excellent.

- The final suggestion: In addition to a means for measuring progress toward a goal, there should be a statement of how often feedback on progress should be checked. Looking at performance too often tends to be disruptive. Looking at performance at too long an interval may cause trouble by allowing performance that's too much at variance from that desired; it may be impossible to correct in the time left. The appropriate interval for checking progress must be set by sound managerial judgment.

Planning Should Be Practicable

Planning in MBO should be practicable. It should be within the capacity of the company and the individual. It should not be blue sky. But planning should stimulate growth of the company and the people who make up the company. Plans should be set at high enough levels to stimulate growth but not so high as to be clearly out of reach. By encouraging growth, individuals become more competent and the company becomes more effective.

An Example of Plans in MBO

Figure 15-2 shows typical plans in MBO for a small company. Plans should be set in areas of major importance to the company or position, such as innovation, marketing, profit, growth, and management succession.

Advantages of MBO

The system of managing by objectives carries certain distinct advantages over more traditional ways of managing. Most important, MBO will assure that efforts are directed toward specified results in achieving high productivity. When introduced

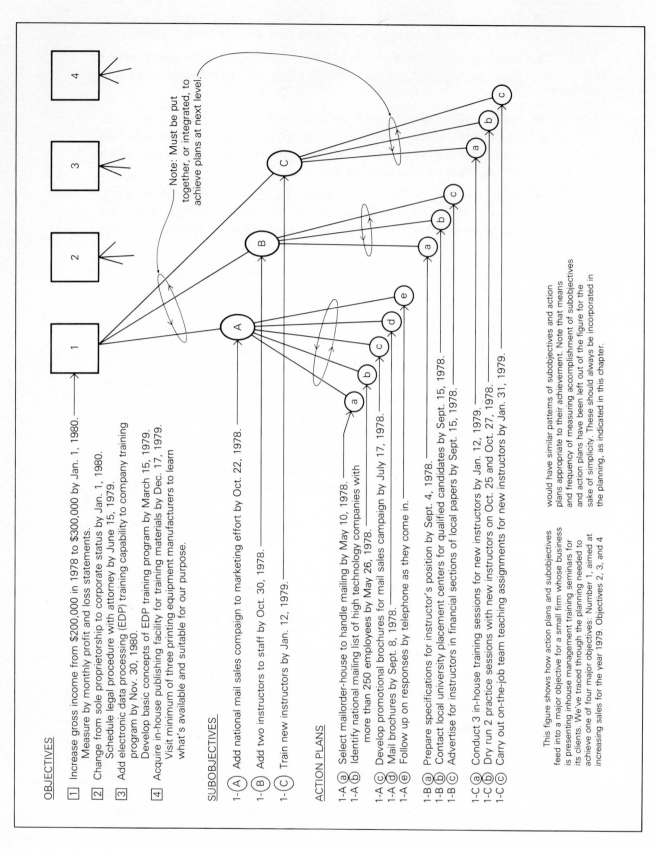

OBJECTIVES

1 Increase gross income from $200,000 in 1978 to $300,000 by Jan. 1, 1980.
   Measure by monthly profit and loss statements.
2 Change from sole proprietorship to corporate status by Jan. 1, 1980.
   Schedule legal procedure with attorney by June 15, 1979.
3 Add electronic data processing (EDP) training capability to company training
   program by Nov. 30, 1980.
   Develop basic concepts of EDP training program by March 15, 1979.
4 Acquire in-house publishing facility for training materials by Dec. 17, 1979.
   Visit minimum of three printing equipment manufacturers to learn
   what's available and suitable for our purpose.

SUBOBJECTIVES

1-(A) Add national mail sales compaign to marketing effort by Oct. 22, 1978.

1-(B) Add two instructors to staff by Oct. 30, 1978.

1-(C) Train new instructors by Jan. 12, 1979.

ACTION PLANS

1-A (a) Select mailorder-house to handle mailing by May 10, 1978.
1-A (b) Identify national mailing list of high technology companies with
        more than 250 employees by May 26, 1978.
1-A (c) Develop promotional brochures for mail sales campaign by July 17, 1978.
1-A (d) Mail brochures by Sept. 8, 1978.
1-A (e) Follow up on responses by telephone as they come in.

1-B (a) Prepare specifications for instructor's position by Sept. 4, 1978.
1-B (b) Contact local university placement centers for qualified candidates by Sept. 15, 1978.
1-B (c) Advertise for instructors in financial sections of local papers by Sept. 15, 1978.

1-C (a) Conduct 3 in-house training sessions for new instructors by Jan. 12, 1979.
1-C (b) Dry run 2 practice sessions with new instructors on Oct. 25 and Oct. 27, 1978.
1-C (c) Carry out on-the-job team teaching assignments for new instructors by Jan. 31, 1979.

This figure shows how action plans and subobjectives feed into a major objective for a small firm whose business is presenting inhouse management training seminars for its clients. We've traced through the planning needed to achieve one of four major objectives: Number 1, aimed at increasing sales for the year 1979. Objectives 2, 3, and 4 would have similar patterns of subobjectives and action plans appropriate to their achievement. Note that means and frequency of measuring accomplishment of subobjectives and action plans have been left out of the figure for the sake of simplicity. These should always be incorporated in the planning, as indicated in this chapter.

Note: Must be put together, or integrated, to achieve plans at next level.

Figure 15-2 How Objectives, Subobjectives, and Action Plans Tie Together

into your company, it promotes individual commitment to work. Once the ideas for planning in the fundamental business requirements have taken hold, the system of MBO can later include features such as appraising individual performance, gaining insight into individual strengths and weaknesses, adjusting salaries and other compensation, and developing a management succession program.

Cautions in Introducing MBO

We should point out that these various uses of MBO should never be introduced all at once. They should follow one another gradually over a long period, perhaps two or three years, as the company grows and management gains experience in the use of MBO. If all these features were introduced as a package the learning needed to make the MBO system operate well would be too complicated, confusing, and self-defeating.

MBO, a Human Strategy

Management by objectives offers the means for fusing individual and company effort. Its strategy supports individual differences. Members of the firm can do things in their own way. Individual style or method are not of concern; what is important is the achievement of the results needed to contribute to the accomplishment of the company's overall productivity objectives. The only constraint on members of the firm is that they behave in a legal and ethical way. In a word, the strategy of MBO permits individual freedom in a disciplined approach to organizational achievement.

Although focusing on individual needs and performance, MBO ensures the development of teamwork through the need to consult with others and to arrive at mutually acceptable planning in the process. The consultative procedures inherent in MBO support the emergence of an open climate of management. This in turn supports the teaching, learning environment from which innovative and powerful proactive management develops.

ASSESSING YOUR PRODUCTIVITY PERFORMANCE

After the business gets going, how can you determine its performance in achieving a high level of productivity? The crucial, key test is, of course, profit. But changes occur so rapidly, you can't wait until the end of the year or even until the end of the quarter to find out about the health of your business. You must continually ask the key productivity questions we raised earlier: Are we doing things right? Are we doing the right things? In using MBO as your system of management you employ a powerful tool for guiding your efforts and the efforts of those who work for you toward the highest possible level of productivity performance.

You've solved half of the productivity assessment problem if you're asking the right questions. We'll cover here the crucial areas in which to assess productivity performance and supply you with some probing questions you'll need to answer.

The Internal Component

You

The health of your business will depend on how well you're managing. The discussion in this chapter should help you to assess yourself in this role. You must learn and grow as a manager if your business is to grow and prosper. Your own personal growth will be reflected in the continually increasing productivity of your venture. Here are some questions to test the quality of your personal growth:

- Do you know more about managing your business well now than you did a month ago?

- Are you able to see more relationships in knowledge than you did before? Are you developing wisdom by being able to correlate and apply different kinds of knowledge purposefully for achievement?

- Are you more creative, more innovative than you were, through combining what you know in newer, better, more effective ways?

- Do you tolerate and deal with ambiguity and uncertainty more effectively than in the past?

- Are you able to work cooperatively with others while preserving your unique qualities?

- Are you showing real growth through the acquisition of increasingly higher levels of competence?

The first five criteria center in assessing specific skills; the sixth, in judging overall personal growth.

Your Employees

Productivity increases with satisfying working conditions, as does morale. Your employees' morale may be judged by their attitudes toward work and their cooperation in trying to achieve the objectives of your business; high morale is a key test of a well-managed organization. You'll have satisfied workers and the desirability of high morale if you possess and demonstrate the characteristics of the ideal manager we have described. As your business expands, you might ask yourself these kinds of questions about factors that influence morale:

- Do I let my employees know what's expected of them?

- Am I sensitive to their needs?

- Am I open and honest in dealing with them?

- Do I encourage them to come forward with their ideas?

- Do I communicate clearly with them and listen actively to what they have to say?

- Do I let them have some control and let them alone to do it their way?

- Are they paid adequately compared with other businesses?

- Do they feel a sense of participation, pride in the business, and believe they're doing something worthwhile?

High morale doesn't necessarily guarantee high productivity. Employee attitudes toward the job and your business will also be affected by outside conditions beyond your control. But high morale indicates a strong predisposition toward increased productivity and presents clear evidence of sound management of people.

The External Component

Your business will have important relationships with the community, suppliers, government, and creditors as well as with customers. These relationships affect both the input and output sides of productivity.

Your Customers

Developing and maintaining a consumer orientation has been a persistent theme of this book. Your business will thrive or fail depending on how consumers cast or withhold their dollar votes. That is why we've devoted so much attention to marketing. Favorable consumer response to your marketing strategies is, of course, the principal output or result you want. Some questions to guide you in assessing productivity of your marketing efforts are:

- Am I maintaining or improving the quality of my products or services?

- Is the right quantity of my products or services available at the right place, at the right time?

- Am I maintaining expertise and improving my technical knowledge of my product or service?

- Am I constantly gathering new information about the market my business serves? Am I alert for changes in consumers' needs?

- Is my promotion strategy reaching potential customers with an effective message and conveying the image I want for my business?

- Am I keeping track of competition and staying ahead of it?

- Do I have new products or services in development to satisfy present customers better or to tap new market segments?

- Are my marketing expenditures related to specific marketing objectives?

These questions and others like them will have to be raised to guide your business toward its ultimate goal—consumer satisfaction that produces profit. Remember, the consumer is now your boss in the market you serve.

Your Community

Your business must pay its civic rent. This requires your active participation in local affairs and local clubs or organizations to gain community goodwill. Your business should become part of the social as well as the commercial fabric of the community.

In addition to the personal satisfaction of making social contributions, civic involvement benefits both the input and the output sides of productivity. From informal relationships with community business leaders, you'll learn about changes in the local market, new business techniques, new sources of supplies or business services. You may even pick up hints for new products or services your business might offer or economical ways you haven't tried before to reach potential customers.

The questions here are straightforward:

- Am I an active member in appropriate civic organizations?

- Have I assumed or can I attain leadership in any local clubs, committees, or civic groups?

- Have I contributed to or has my business sponsored any local drives, charities, or fund-raising activities?

Your Suppliers

Suppliers are a major input, but they can also affect the output side of productivity. The businesses that supply your firm with operating materials, equipment, or inventory can become an extension of your business. Establish and nurture good working relationships and they will become assets that supply much more than physical goods. Industrial sales people are usually much more than order takers. They are professionals who keep abreast of trends and state-of-the-art techniques in their field. They'll be able to give you advice on technical matters and keep you informed of what other companies in your industry are doing. Your business will reap dividends far beyond acquisition of needed supplies if you treat them right. Some questions to test your responsiveness follow:

- Am I prompt in paying my accounts?

- Am I fair in negotiating transactions?

- Do I take full but fair advantage of purchase discounts offered?

- Am I receptive to suggestions made?

- Do I display and promote the suppliers' inventory as I assured them I would?

- Do I allow enough lead time for the supplier with my reorders?

- Do I thoroughly and fairly analyze cost and service before switching to a new supplier?

Your Government

Your relations with the federal, state, and local governments affect productivity too—both positively and negatively. Taxes reduce the financial results or outputs of your business. But the services of government available for small business, as we've described previously, can be major inputs in the form of capital or technical and management assistance. You should take full advantage of these services since you'll be helping to pay for them with the taxes your business pays. Ask yourself:

- Do I fill out business forms properly and am I paying taxes on time to avoid reprimands, censures, or penalties?

- Am I exploiting the governmental resources available, both financial and human, to help make my business successful?

Your Creditors

Commercial banks or other institutions will be lending you working capital as inputs to enable you to purchase tangible resources. Like suppliers and some government agencies, creditors can also give sound business advice that helps achieve greater outputs. For example, the loan officer you deal with at the bank will know your financial condition and may be able to suggest ways to economize on purchases or minimize loan carrying charges. Having financial dealings with other small businesses, the banker will know first-hand some of the pitfalls to avoid. In addition, the loan officer may be able to steer you to advisers to help you resolve unique problems, to individuals with ready cash to invest, or to suppliers of special business services you may need. Some questions to help you assess your relations with creditors are:

- Am I meeting my loan repayment commitments on time?

- Am I planning far enough ahead to get working capital when I need it?

- Am I keeping my banker informed of the progress of my venture?

- Have I let my banker know enough about my business and my problems to be able to help me?

You should establish the same confidential and professional relationship with your banker as you would with your accountant and attorney. All three of them will want you to be successful and can help you along the way.

SURVIVING THE CRITICAL FIRST YEARS SUMMARY

Your success in getting your business off the ground will depend on your ability to get things done through and with other people. Your entrepreneurial talents and the detailed planning you've accomplished with the help of this book will serve you well in getting your business started. However, shortly after you launch your business, you'll need additional managerial skills. You will need to make the transition from entrepreneur to manager.

We've outlined the three kinds of competence you'll seek to achieve to make this transition: technical competence, system competence, and interpersonal competence. Technical and system competence concern your skills in manipulating and integrating things in an innovative way. Interpersonal competence measures your ability to work effectively with people: your employees, customers, business associates, creditors, and suppliers.

Your success in surviving the first years in your business will depend on how well you fill the basic roles of the professional manager as we've described them in

317

this chapter. Your performance in these roles will, in turn, depend upon the levels of your technical, system, and interpersonal competencies.

You will aim for the highest possible productivity in every aspect of your business. To do this you'll use the best managerial judgment you're capable of to strike a proper balance between efficiency and effectiveness. You'll reach this balance by answering the two key questions: Are we doing things right? Are we doing the right things? These questions will challenge you continually in your position of chief executive officer of your company.

Management by objectives is a tested and accepted management system for improving productivity in your business. During your first year or two in business, with the need to take care of myriad tasks, you should be wary of being caught in the "activity trap." If you are trapped, you can readily find yourself swamped in detail, ignoring the forward-looking planning and doing mandatory to the survival of your business.

Management by objectives gives you the way to avoid the activity trap. Its systematic approach to management makes it easy for you to set objectives for increasing productivity in every aspect of your business, for assigning accountabilities for results, and for gaining commitment for achievement from all members of your company. MBO offers a methodology for attaining unified organizational effort. By using it you will build teamwork and high morale in your workforce. You'll build an achieving firm.

You'll want to keep an eye on the internal and external elements of your business and the internal and external forces that develop pressure for change. By asking and answering the right questions you'll be able to plan appropriately for improving productivity—for doing things right and for doing the right things. We've suggested a number of questions that should help you get started in deciding where the payoff is in your planning. By continually adjusting your plans to take care of anticipated change you'll practice proactive management—and you'll control the destiny of your company.

CHAPTER 15/FOOTNOTES

[1]Peter Drucker, *The Practice of Management*, Harper & Row, New York, 1954. Ch. 11.
[2]Douglas McGregor, *The Human Side of Enterprise*, McGraw-Hill, New York, 1960, Ch. 5.

Managing for Survival and Growth

1. Study the list of attributes expected of an ideal manager. Comments associated with each of these attributes are given in this chapter. Evaluate yourself: Rank your attributes on the lines below, from the strongest, in which you feel most proficient, to the weakest, in which you feel the least proficient.

   a. _____

   b. _____

   c. _____

   d. _____

   e. _____

   f. _____

2. Review your list. In the space below make notes to yourself about the implications of your strong and weak points. Answer this question: How can I use my strong points to advantage and how can I overcome my weak points? Add notes about your strengths and weaknesses as shown in exercise 1 above.

   _____

   _____

   _____

   _____

   _____

   _____

   _____

   _____

   _____

   _____

   _____

3. Develop major objectives for your first year of business operation. Key your objectives to levels of productivity, including consideration of both efficiency and effectiveness. Before you begin, review the section on MBO in this chapter. Pay special attention to the definition of *objective* and to the guidelines for writing plans.

   a. _____

   _____

   _____

b. _____
_____
_____

c. _____
_____
_____

d. _____
_____
_____

e. _____
_____
_____

f. _____
_____
_____

4. In what ways will you evaluate productivity performance in your business? Using the questions we presented in this chapter as guides, under each section below list at least three of the most important questions you should ask and answer about productivity in your business.

   a. Internal—activities or operations inside the company:

      (1) _____
_____
_____

      (2) _____
_____
_____

      (3) _____
_____
_____

   b. External—activities or operations outside the company:

      (1) _____
_____
_____

(2) _____

_____

_____

(3) _____

_____

_____

There are not many references available on the subjects taken up in this chapter, with the exception of management by objectives. You will find some material in the following books:

Peter Drucker, *The Practice of Management*, Harper & Brothers, New York, 1954. You'll find the original description of management by objectives in Chapter 11 of this book; the chapter is titled "Management by Objectives and Self-Control." Drucker here laid down the fundamental concepts of MBO as a strategy and practice of management. These basic ideas have been developed and elaborated by many others since.

Arthur H. Kuriloff, *Organizational Development for Survival*, American Management Association, New York, 1972. Chapters 9 and 10 of this reference give the behavioral research background and the practical management methodology for using MBO. If you want to delve a bit more deeply into both theory and practice than we do in Chapter 13, you'll find the material in this book suitable.

Paul Mali, *Improving Total Productivity*, Wiley-Interscience, Somerset, N.J., in press. Showing specifically how to deal with productivity problems, the author explores what productivity is, how it operates in an organization, and how it can be improved. Step-by-step operating procedures are included on how MBO can be used to guide the organization toward higher productivity. Although the book isn't designed specifically for the small business, the concepts and guidelines can be easily adapted by entrepreneurs for their own organizations.

Appendix A

Outline for Developing Your Basic Business Plan (Prospectus)

Appendix B

Examples of Basic Planning for the Small Business

Outline for Developing Your Basic Business Plan (Prospectus)

1 Executive Summary

A. Description of your proposed business
  (1) Describe your product or service
  (2) Support with diagrams, illustrations, or pictures (if available)
B. Summary of your proposed marketing method
  (1) Describe the market segment (submarket) you're aiming to reach
  (2) Outline the channel you plan to use to reach this market segment (retail, wholesale, distributors, mail order, or other)
C. Summary of your financial estimates
  (1) State the dollars in sales you aim for in each of the first three years
  (2) State the estimated profit for each of the first three years
  (3) State the estimated starting capital you'll need

2 Statement of Objectives

A. Statement of the desirability of your product or service
  (1) Describe the advantages your product or service has, its improvements over existing products or services
  (2) State the long-range objectives and the short-range subobjectives of your proposed business
  (3) Describe your qualifications to run the business
  (4) Describe the "character" you want for your business, the image you'd like your customers to see

3 Background of Proposed Business

A. Brief summary of existing conditions in the business you're intending to enter (the "state of the art" as it is now)
  (1) *Where* the product or service is now being used
  (2) *How* the product or service is now being used
B. Detailed explanation of your place in the state of the art
  (1) Describe the projections and trends for the industry or business field
  (2) Describe competition you face (place competitors' advertisements and brochures in the appendix at the end of your prospectus)
  (3) State your intended strategy for meeting competition
  (4) Describe the special qualities of your product or service that make it unique

4 Technical Description of Product or Service

A. A complete technical description of product or service

    (1) Describe in a technically accurate way how the product works or how the service is used

    (2) Outline the tests that have been made and give the test data and results

    (3) Outline the tests that are to be made and describe the test objectives

    (4) State briefly your concepts for follow-on (next generation) products or services

5 Marketing Strategy

A. A comprehensive description of marketing strategy

    (1) Describe the segment of the market you plan to reach

    (2) Describe in full detail the distribution channel you plan to use to reach your market segment: retail, jobbers, wholesalers, brokers, door to door, mail order, party plan, or other

    (3) Describe the share of the market you expect to capture versus time

6 Selling Tactics

A. An outline of the activities to be used in selling the product or service

    (1) State the methods you expect to use to promote your product or service: direct calling, telephone, advertising, mail, radio, television, or other

    (2) Include a sample brochure or dummy, advertisements, announcements, or other promotional literature

    (3) Present data supporting your ability to meet your sales goals: actual orders, personally known prospective key accounts, and potential customers

    (4) Explain the margins of safety you've allowed in your sales forecasts

7 Plan of Operation

A. Description of the proposed organization

    (1) Show an organization chart describing the needed business functions and relationships

    (2) Describe the key positions and identify the persons to fill them

    (3) Give resumés of the key persons

    (4) List equipment or facilities and the space and location required

    (5) Describe the research and development facilities you'll need

    (6) If manufacturing, outline the kind of production you'll do in-house and that to be subcontracted

8 Supporting Data

A. Information required to support the major points in the business plan

    (1) Include a set of drawings of the product to be manufactured or a detailed description of the service to be offered

    (2) Show a list of the tooling you'll require for production and estimated costs of the tooling

    (3) List the capital equipment you'll need and its estimated cost

    (4) Provide a layout of your proposed plant, supported by a manufacturing flow chart (include the estimated cost of manufacturing your product)

    (5) Give a packaging and shipping analysis

(6) List a price schedule for your product line or service

(7) Include your detailed market survey data

(8) Supply the following financial data:

    (a) Projected Profit and Loss Statement and Balance Sheet for the first two years by the month and for the third year by the quarter

    (b) Income Statement for two years by the month

    (c) Cash Flow Projection for two years by the month

    (d) Break-even Chart for two years, by the year

    (e) Fixed Asset Acquisition Schedule by the month, showing each item you expect to buy and its cost

9 Conclusions and Summary

A. A statement of proposed approach in starting the new organization

    (1) State the total capital you'll need and the safety factor you've used

    (2) State how much profit you expect and when you expect to show it

    (3) Tell what percentage of ownership you want for yourself and your partners

    (4) Indicate the total capital you need and how it's to be made up:

        (a) Your share of the starting investment

        (b) How much more you'll need from others and when you'll need the money

        (c) State what share of the business you'll give to the investors or lenders for this additional capital

    (5) State your planned schedule for starting your business

Examples of Basic Planning for the Small Business

In appendix B we have included examples of planning for a retail bookstore, a small manufacturing concern, a complete prospectus for a retail waterbed store, and planning assumptions and important parts of a business plan for a service firm. You can use these examples as guides for your projections and planning in developing a prospectus for your own business.

Financial Projections for a Bookstore

The following financial projections were prepared for a mythical bookstore. They are presented as a sample of the package of financial plans that should be made on an ongoing basis by all entrepreneurs. Although the bookstore, Tobias Booksellers, is fictional, the assumptions upon which these financial projections are based were drawn from real data graciously furnished us by the American Booksellers Association. In addition, we took some fundamental concepts and financial ratios from *A Manual on Book-Selling,* 2nd edition, published by the American Booksellers Association, New York, 1974.

We've included here complete financial projections for the first year of operation of Tobias Booksellers, 1978. You'll also find a projection of planned sales for the years 1979 and 1980. These estimated sales are keyed to the business growth desired by the proprietor in those years.

These data will give you the opportunity to practice making financial projections. We suggest that, on the basis of the planned sales, you work up balance sheets, cash flow projections, monthly income statements, and yearly income statements for 1979 and 1980. If you do this before you start the financial projections for your business, you'll be well prepared to accomplish your planning readily and efficiently.

Two suggestions may help you in this learning process: (1) We've drawn some direction arrows on the cash flow analysis to show how key numbers are derived and how they are moved from column to column. (2) When you have a question about where a number comes from, go back to the assumptions. The assumptions will tell you the procedure for arriving at a specific quantity.

Assumptions

The financial projections given here for a new bookstore were derived from the following assumptions:

1. The store opens for business on January 2, 1978.

2. The owner, an experienced bookseller, aims for a $30,000 gross income (before—tax income) from sales in the third year.

3. Sales volume is expected to increase 20 percent in each of the second and third years; thereafter the growth of the business will slow down gradually over a period of three years to 5 percent.

4. The business will generate $150,000 in sales the first year; with sound management this volume can be achieved in a store of 1500 square feet area. Rent costs 6 percent of this gross volume, or $9000 per year.

5. The inventory of stock will turn three times during the first year. Books for inventory are bought at 40 percent discount from the retail price. The *average* inventory at cost for the first year of business is therefore: 60 percent of $150,000 divided by 3, which equals $30,000.

6. Fixtures for the store cost $4000 and are to be depreciated at 1 percent a month.

7. Deposits and advance payments will require $3000.

8. A cushion for unexpected costs or setbacks will be included, in addition, at about $1000.

9. Estimated cash required to open the store:

Inventory (average per month)	$30,000
Three months' rent, at $750	2,250
Fixtures	4,000
Advance payments	3,000
Cushion for unexpected costs, at least	1,000
Total	$40,250

10. The proprietor plans to start with $25,000 cash investment with an inventory smaller than the average required for the year. The inventory will be built up rapidly as sales grow and the holiday season at the end of the year approaches. The proprietor invests $15,000 from personal savings and borrows $10,000 at the bank against a collateral of blue chip stocks worth $35,000 on the current market. Money will be borrowed against this collateral as the business shows the need for cash. Interest will be paid monthly on borrowings at the rate of ¾ percent per month.

11. The stock of inventory on hand at the beginning of any month will not exceed the total of planned sales for the next three months. Inventory level is therefore set at 75 percent of cost of books sold for the next three months. This working rule gives a reasonable way, on the basis of experience, for estimating the dollars' worth of books to be bought each month.

12. Exhibit 2 shows the sales forecasted for three years ahead. These figures are based on the proprietor's experience plus analysis of the marketing data for the segment of the market expected to be reached.

13. Three-fourths of sales are for cash. One-fourth of sales are for credit, with collection in thirty days.

14. Three-fourths of purchases are for cash. One-fourth are to be paid in thirty days.

15. Beginning cash balance for any month should be at least one-half of sales for that month. The beginning cash on hand at the start of the business, January 2, 1978, is $3000.

16. On the basis of a reasonably profitable first year, income taxes are projected at 40 percent of gross profit.

EXHIBIT 1

BALANCE SHEET

2 January 1978

Assets		Liabilities	
Cash (beginning cash balance)	$ 3,000	Bank loan	$10,000
Inventory	10,575	Proprietor's Capital	15,000
Fixtures	4,000	TOTAL	$25,000
Two months' rent	1,500		
Other advance payments	3,000		
Cushion for unexpected costs	2,925		
TOTAL	$25,000		

EXHIBIT 2

PLANNED SALES

	1978	1979	1980
Jan	$ 6,000	$ 7,200	$ 8,640
Feb	8,500	10,200	12,240
Mar	9,000	10,800	12,960
Apr	11,000	13,200	15,840
May	13,000	15,600	18,720
Jun	10,500	12,600	15,120
Jul	6,500	7,800	9,360
Aug	6,500	7,800	9,360
Sep	10,000	12,000	14,400
Oct	13,500	16,200	19,440
Nov	16,500	19,800	23,760
Dec	39,000	46,800	56,160
	$150,000	$180,000	$216,000

NOTE: The book business tends to be highly seasonal, with much of the sales volume for the year occurring in the year-end holiday season. The planned, or forecasted, sales figures are therefore shown as building up heavily toward the end of the year.

EXHIBIT 3

CASH FLOW ANALYSIS FOR TOBIAS BOOKSELLERS—1978

	Jan	Feb	Mar	Apr
1. Planned sales (retail)	$ 6,000	$ 8,500	$ 9,000	$11,000
2. Cash sales (75%)	4,500	6,375	6,750	8,250
3. + Credit sales (25 %)	0	1,500	2,125	2,250
4. Total cash receipts (2 + 3)	4,500	7,875	8,875	10,500
5. Cost of goods sold (60%)	3,600	5,100	5,400	6,600
6. + Ending inventory required @ 75% of these values	17,100	19,800	20,700	18,000
	12,825	14,850	15,525	13,500
7. Total required (5 + 6)	16,425	19,950	20,925	20,100
8. − Beginning inventory	10,575	12,825	14,850	15,525
9. Purchases required (7 − 8)	5,850	7,125	6,075	4,575
10. Cash payment (75%)	4,387	5,344	4,556	3,431
11. Credit payment (25 %)	0	1,463	1,781	1,519
12. Total payment (10 + 11)	4,387	6,807	6,337	4,950
13. Salary—proprietor	0	0	0	0
14. Salaries—other (W-2)	378	378	546	546
15. Total salaries (13 + 14)	378	378	546	546
16. Rent	750	750	750	750
17. Advertising & promotion	500	150	100	100
18. Delivery charges (0.6%)	36	51	54	66
19. Supplies & postage (1.2%)	200	80	100	130
20. Taxes (payroll, state, etc., 1.4%)	84	119	126	154
21. Insurance (0.8%)	100	100	100	100
22. Travel & entertainment (0.4%)	50	50	50	50
23. Bad debts (0.1%)	0	8	9	11
24. Professional fees (0.3%)	150	0	0	100
25. Telephone (0.6%)	36	51	54	66
26. Other operating expenses (1.8%)	108	153	162	198
27. Total payments (15 to 26)	2,392	1,884	2,045	2,265
28. Beginning cash balance	3,000	5,846	6,110	7,074
29. + Cash receipts (4)	4,500	7,875	8,875	10,500
30. Total cash available	7,500	13,721	14,985	17,574
31. − Cash outlays (12 + 27)	6,779	8,691	8,382	7,215
32. − Interest expenses	75	114	123	127
33. Cash balance before borrowing	646	4,910	6,474	10,226
34. Additional borrowing	5,200	1,200	600	0
35. Cumulative borrowing	15,200	16,400	17,000	17,000
36. Cash balance after borrowing (33 + 34)	5,846	6,110	7,074	10,226

332

May	Jun	Jul	Aug	Sep	Oct	Nov	Dec
$13,000	$10,500	$ 6,500	$ 6,500	$10,000	$13,500	$16,500	$39,000
9,750	7,875	4,875	4,875	7,500	10,125	12,375	29,250
2,750	3,250	2,625	1,625	1,625	2,500	3,375	4,125
12,500	11,125	7,500	6,500	9,125	12,625	15,750	33,375
7,800	6,300	3,900	3,900	6,000	8,100	9,900	23,400
14,100	13,800	18,000	24,000	41,000	37,620	33,840	16,920
10,575	10,350	13,500	18,000	31,050	28,215	25,380	12,690
18,375	16,650	17,400	21,900	37,050	36,315	35,280	36,090
13,500	10,575	10,350	13,500	18,000	31,050	28,215	25,380
4,875	6,075	7,050	8,400	19,050	5,265	7,065	10,710
3,656	4,556	5,287	6,300	14,287	3,949	5,299	8,032
1,144	1,219	1,519	1,762	2,100	4,762	1,316	1,766
4,800	5,775	6,806	8,062	16,387	8,711	6,615	9,798
0	0	200	200	400	400	600	800
546	546	378	378	546	1,050	1,400	1,600
546	546	578	578	946	1,450	2,000	2,400
750	750	750	750	750	750	750	750
100	100	100	300	200	250	400	500
78	63	39	39	60	81	99	234
150	100	70	70	100	150	200	450
182	147	91	91	140	189	231	546
100	100	100	100	100	100	100	100
50	50	50	50	50	50	50	50
13	10	7	7	10	13	16	39
0	0	100	0	0	100	0	0
78	63	39	39	60	81	99	234
234	189	117	117	180	243	297	702
2,275	2,112	2,035	2,135	2,590	3,451	4,252	5,999
10,226	15,518	11,623	10,201	6,423	8,480	9,772	21,077
12,500	11,125	7,500	6,500	9,125	12,625	15,750	33,375
22,726	26,643	19,123	16,701	15,538	21,105	25,522	54,452
7,075	7,887	8,841	10,197	18,976	12,162	10,867	15,797
127	127	75	75	75	165	172	222
15,518	18,623	10,201	6,423	(3,520)	8,772	14,477	38,426
0	(7,000)	0	0	12,000	1,000	6,600	(29,600)
17,000	10,000	10,000	10,000	22,000	23,000	29,600	0
15,518	11,623	10,201	6,423	8,480	9,772	21,077	8,826

EXHIBIT 4

INCOME STATEMENT BY MONTH

	Jan	Feb	Mar	Apr	May	Jun
Sales	$ 6,000	$ 8,500	$ 9,000	$11,000	$13,000	$10,500
— Cost of sales	3,600	5,100	5,400	6,600	7,800	6,300
Gross margin	2,400	3,400	3,600	4,400	5,200	4,200
— Cash payments	2,392	1,884	2,045	2,265	2,275	2,112
— Interest	75	114	123	127	127	127
— Depreciation	40	40	40	40	40	40
Total	2,507	2,038	2,208	2,432	2,442	2,279
Before—tax profit	(107)	1,362	1,392	1,968	2,758	1,921

	Jul	Aug	Sep	Oct	Nov	Dec
Sales	$ 6,500	$ 6,500	$10,000	$13,500	$16,500	$39,000
— Cost of sales	3,900	3,900	6,000	8,100	9,900	23,400
Gross margin	2,600	2,600	4,000	5,400	6,600	15,600
— Cash payments	2,035	2,135	2,590	3,451	4,252	5,999
— Interest	75	75	75	165	172	222
— Depreciation	40	40	40	40	40	40
Total	2,110	2,250	2,705	3,656	4,464	6,266
Before—tax profit	490	350	1,295	1,744	2,136	9,339

EXHIBIT 5

YEARLY INCOME STATEMENT—1978

Sales		$150,000
Cost of sales		90,000
Gross margin		60,000
Salaries	$10,892	
Rent	9,000	
Advertising & promotion	2,800	
Delivery charges	900	
Supplies & postage	1,800	
Taxes (payroll, state, etc.)	2,100	
Insurance	1,200	
Travel & entertainment	600	
Bad debts	143	
Professional fees	450	
Telephone	900	
Other operating expenses	2,700	
Interest	1,477	
Depreciation	480	
	35,442	
Total expenses		35,442
Before-tax profit		24,546
Taxes (40% per IRS table for sole proprietorship*)		9,818
After-tax profit		14,728
Proprietor's capital (2 Jan 1978)		15,000
Proprietor's capital (31 Dec 1978)		$ 29,728

*40% income tax rate assumes that this profit figure represents clear profit above deductible personal expenses.

EXHIBIT 6

BALANCE SHEET—31 DECEMBER 1978

Assets			Liabilities & Equity	
Cash		$ 8,826	Accounts payable	$ 2,678
Accounts receivable		9,750	Taxes payable	9,818
Inventory, ending		12,690	Bank loan	0
Fixtures	$4,000		Proprietor's capital	29,731
— Depreciation	480		TOTAL	$42,200
	3,520	3,520		
Two months' rent deposit		1,500		
Other advance payments		3,000		
Cushion for unexpected costs		2,925		
TOTAL		$42,200		

(NOTE: Totals rounded to 3 figures)

BREAK-EVEN CHART FOR TOBIAS BOOKSELLERS, 1980

The break-even chart for Tobias Booksellers for the year 1980 was prepared on the basis of data representative of average practice in the trade.

The assumptions upon which the various figures for the chart were developed are as follows:

1. Planned sales for the year = $216,000

2. Cost of books sold = 60% of 216,000 =

Cost of books sold = 60% of 216,000 =	$129,000 (V)
Direct labor @ 11.9% =	25,074 (V)
Rent @ 4.2% =	9,000 (F)
Advertising and promotion @ 1.9% =	4,104 (F)
Delivery charges @ 0.6% =	1,296 (V)
Supplies @ 1.2% =	2,592 (V)
Taxes, payroll, state and local @ 1.4% =	3,024 (V)
Insurance @ 0.8% =	1,728 (F)
Travel @ 0.4% =	864 (F)
Bad debts @ 0.1% =	216 (V)
Professional fees @ 0.3% =	648 (F)
Telephone @ 0.6% =	1,296 (F)
Other operating expenses @ 1.8% =	3,888 (F)
Owner's salary @ $800 per month =	9,600 (F)

Items that increase with sales (variable items) are identified by the symbol (V); items that stay essentially the same regardless of sales volume (fixed items) are identified by the symbol (F). Judgment must often be applied in deciding whether an item should be classified as variable or fixed. Since the items that might be questioned tend to be small, classifying them one way or the other has little effect on the significance of the break-even chart.

You will recall from Chapter 8 that the break-even chart is a tool of proactive management. It need not be minutely accurate to serve the purposes of management choice and decision making.

3. The owner draws a salary of $800 a month. Gross income will therefore be figured as salary plus gross profit for income tax purposes, as the owner will be taxed on both combined. The owner estimates combined gross income will be about $30,000 for 1980. Therefore, income taxes will be at the 40 percent level or about $12,000 on the assumption that allowable personal deductions are not here considered.

4. The break-even chart, as shown in Exhibit 7, is made by combining the fixed and variable numbers as shown below and plotting them in the way described in Chapter 8.

Assumptions

1. Planned sales for 1980 = $216,000

2. Fixed costs:
   a. Owner's salary, $800 per month = 9,600
   b. Rent, $750 per month = 9,000

   $18,600

   c. Advertising and promotion, 1.9% = 4,104
   Insurance, 0.8% = 1,728
   Travel, 0.4% = 864
   Professional fees, 0.3% = 648
   Telephone, 0.6% = 1,296
   Misc. operating expenses, 1.8% = 3,888

   $ 12,528

3. Variable costs:
   a. Cost of goods sold, 60% = $129,600
   b. Direct labor, 11.9% = $ 25,704
   c. Delivery charges, 0.6% = 1,296
   Supplies, 1.2% = 2,592
   Taxes, payroll, state, local, 1.4% = 3,024
   Bad debts, 0.1% = 216

   $ 7,128

Uses of the Break-Even Chart

The break-even chart may be used for many purposes of proactive management. Some typical data that can be drawn from the chart are:

EXHIBIT 7

BREAK-EVEN CHART TOBIAS BOOKSELLERS-1980

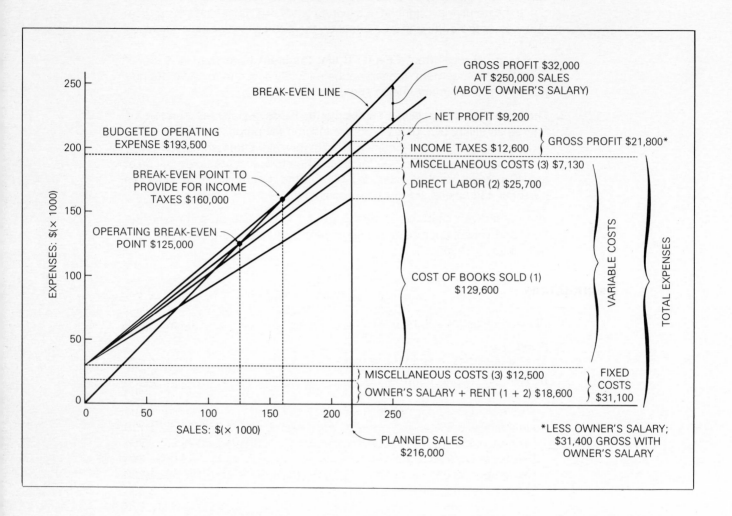

1. What is the break-even point in gross sales? The chart shows this figure to be $125,000. At this value of sales, Tobias Booksellers neither makes nor loses money for the year.

2. What is the break-even point to provide for the estimated income taxes of $12,000? This value shows as $160,000 on the chart.

3. What would the gross profit be if sales could be increased by $34,000 for the year without increasing fixed costs? The new gross sales would be $250,000. At this value, gross profit would rise to $41,600 for the year ($32,000 + $9,600 salary).

4. What is the effect of decreasing or increasing the cost of direct labor for the year? Direct labor is the largest single variable cost. Decreasing this cost a small amount may be seen to move the break-even point down significantly. The amount of change may be found by redrawing the variable cost

lines after lowering the direct labor point at the planned sales vertical. The effect of increased direct labor cost may be found in the same way.

5. The break-even chart offers a graphic way of showing the possibilities for making money in the business. It's easier to see the effect of changing costs in fixed and variable items than it is to analyze columns of figures. Therefore, the break-even chart makes an effective communication and sales tool.

Financial Projections for a Small Manufacturing Plant

Prepared by Keith V. Smith

BACKGROUND AND ASSUMPTIONS

1. The product to be produced is a bench-size laboratory temperature test chamber. It is used to test the performance of electronic and electromechanical components under programmable temperature conditions from $-300°$ F to $+800°$ F.

2. Units (chambers) are produced on assembly lines. Each line has a capacity of forty units per month. Each line requires production equipment costing $20,000.

3. Two partners set up a corporation and invest a total of $50,000 to launch the business. They purchase equipment for one line for $20,000 cash. They buy raw stock and components for eighty units for $24,000; they pay out for this material $12,000 in cash; the remainder of $12,000 is due in thirty days.

4. The business begins at the end of December 1976.

5. The beginning Balance Sheet is as follows:

BALANCE SHEET

December 31, 1976

Cash	$18,000	Accounts Payable	$12,000
Inventory	24,000		
Equipment	20,000	Common Stock	50,000
	$62,000		$62,000

6. Each unit is sold for $1000. Collections for sales are expected to be 50 percent in thirty days, and 50 percent in sixty days.

7. For each unit produced:

Materials cost	$300	Purchases to be paid for in thirty days
Direct labor	180	Paid in cash
Manufacturing expense	80	Paid in cash
Cost of goods sold	$560	

8. Equipment to be depreciated at the rate of 1 percent per month.

9. Rent, utilities, marketing expense, and maintenance expense as shown in Monthly Cash Projections (Exhibit 1).

10. As additional financing is needed, it is to be borrowed by the corporation in $5000 increments. Interest on this financing is to be paid monthly at the rate of 0.8 percent.

11. Taxes are estimated at the rate of 45 percent, due at the end of the calendar year.

12. No dividends are to be paid to the shareholder partners; all earnings are to be retained.

340

EXHIBIT 2

INCOME STATEMENTS FOR 1977 AND 1978

	1977	1978
Sales	483,000	1,460,000
− CGS	270,480	817,600
Gross profit	212,520	642,400
− Operating expenses	221,800	465,700
EBIT	(9,280)	176,700
− Interest	17,840	35,680
Earnings before taxes	(27,120)	141,020
− Taxes	0	63,460
Earnings after taxes	(27,120)	77,560
+ Beginning retained earnings	0	(27,120)
Ending retained earnings	(27,120)	50,440

EXHIBIT 3

BALANCE SHEETS

AT END OF YEARS 1977 AND 1978

	1977		1978	
Assets				
Cash		74,160		139,580
A/R		115,000		230,000
Inventory				
Raw material		48,000		96,000
Finished goods		87,920		76,720
Equipment	40,000		80,000	
—Accumulated				
Depreciation	3,200	36,800	10,400	69,600
		361,880		611,900
Liabilities & Equity				
A/P		24,000		48,000
Needed financing		315,000		400,000
Taxes payable		0		63,460
Common stock		50,000		50,000
Retained earnings		(27,120)		50,440
TOTAL		361,880		611,900

Prospectus
Waterbeds East—A Retail Store

Prepared by Douglas Markley

THE STORE CONCEPT

This proposal aims at the establishment of a retail store specializing in waterbeds and related furniture and accessories. The store is to be located in South Portland, Maine in the Maine Mall, the major shopping center for the Portland area; this would enhance the credibility of the product and the company and ensure maximum exposure to shoppers.

The store will be well appointed to project a substantial image as a quality furniture store and will carry a wide selection of waterbeds—from the modest to the luxurious. It will display a variety of frame designs, arranged in a homelike setting, with accompanying furniture. Bedspreads, sheets, and other accessory items will be stocked, as well as a line of contemporary "beanbag" and foam-filled chairs and lounges. Waterbeds with frames, ranging in price from $75 to $500 will be on hand for cash-and-carry sales. A more complete selection will be available to order.

The new Portland store will complement an existing retail outlet in Brunswick, Maine, thirty miles up the coast, and will use the same name: Waterbeds East. The Brunswick store includes a facility for manufacturing waterbed frames and accompanying furniture. It will supply these items to the Portland store.

The Brunswick store will oversee the operations of the Portland store and will coordinate and combine purchases and advertising. Significant economies of scale are envisioned, particularly in advertising and, to a lesser extent, in purchasing and production. With the opening of the Portland store, television advertising, which is expected to increase traffic and sales dramatically, should become feasible. More promotion and sales should result from present radio schedules, because the same stations serve both areas.

The modern waterbed industry is still in its infancy nationwide, but in Maine the market is almost untapped. Indications from the small Brunswick store have been quite favorable. On the basis of sales in Brunswick, estimates show that the proposed new store should gross about $200,000 per year within three years. It should net approximately $35,000 per year on an initial investment of less than $10,000.

THE PRODUCT

The modern waterbed system is an attractive and serious alternative to conventional bedding. It offers flotation support, which distributes body weight nearly uniformly, applying an almost equal pressure at every point on the body. Consequently, it reduces pressure points at shoulders and hips, and increases support to back, neck, and knees. The mattress accommodates to any position of the sleeper, increasing comfort. (For these reasons, waterbeds have found significant use in hospitals in the treatment of burns and bedsores.) With the advent of modern frames and heating devices, waterbeds have become a viable consumer product with a strong market potential.

The waterbed is much more than just a bag of water. The water mattress, roughly the same size as a conventional mattress, fits inside a vinyl safety liner to preclude any possibility of water escaping. The liner is mounted in a sturdy frame, usually of wood, which encloses and supports the water laterally to eliminate stress on the mattress surface. With no tension on the surface of the water mattress, a free-floating surface is created that makes possible the uniform lower pressure of flotation support. Beneath the safety liner a waterproofed UL-certified waterbed heater regulates water temperature from 60° F to 105° F, according to the preference of the user. A supporting pedestal raises the waterbed to the normal bed height.

The waterbed is safe. Waterbed mattresses will not burst; they have withstood exhaustive testing, including loading with the weight of many people, and even having trucks driven over them. If punctured they are easily repaired, usually without the need to drain them. Any leaked water is caught by the safety liner. They can be easily installed by anyone. They are drained and filled with a common garden hose, and are simpler to transport than a conventional box spring and mattress. A fully filled waterbed weighs approximately forty pounds per square foot, which is less than the design load for even most upper floors; consequently, a waterbed can be installed with confidence in all but the most deteriorated structures. There is no record of a waterbed having crashed through a floor anywhere.

The waterbed does not induce seasickness. Motion sickness usually results from an incessant, repetitive motion or from unaccustomed G-forces; these do not occur in waterbeds. The bed responds to the motion of the sleeper with gentle undulations that die out within sixty seconds. Interestingly, it has been found that people tend to toss and turn less when sleeping on a waterbed, often waking in the same position in which they fell asleep.

Waterbeds are available in twin, full, queen, and king sizes; the king and queen sizes are by far the most popular. They come in a great variety of styles, from colonial to contemporary, with rich furniture-quality wood finishes or upholstered in fur or synthetic leather. Some have elaborate bookcase headboards or canopies. Matching high and low chests and night tables are usually available.

THE INDUSTRY

The waterbed is a product that has high consumer recognition but that so far has been severely undermarketed. This is especially true on the East Coast, and particularly so in Maine. Its introduction in 1969–1970 was followed by sudden "fad" production and distribution of inferior products by inexperienced people drawing on inadequate knowledge and research. These shortcomings were compounded by insufficient knowledge on the part of the users, who often installed and used the beds improperly. The fad image and a great body of misconceptions about waterbeds have endured, especially in Maine and similar locations where no significant marketing of modern waterbed systems has taken place.

Today the industry has begun to coalesce. A trade magazine has been widely distributed for nearly three years. Manufacturing and retailing associations have begun to discuss common problems and to establish standards and goals. An industry advertising group has begun to address that critical area. Retail outlets are benefitting from this activity. They are also becoming more sophisticated marketers as more well-qualified managers enter the industry.

California has been the cradle of the waterbed industry, and waterbeds are still far more evident there than they are in the rest of the nation, although in many other areas of the country the business is growing at a faster rate than in California. Most major cities now have at least several first-rate waterbed stores, but in California they seem to rival gas stations in frequency. There, 8 percent of the people now sleep on waterbeds, as compared with about 3 percent nationally.[1] Almost all true waterbed stores are located in densely populated areas; in small towns waterbeds are available only through "head shops," where they are sold incidentally and inexpertly as a novelty item. Not surprisingly, the progress in the waterbed industry has not reached Maine. Substantially rural in character, the state has seen only two real attempts (in addition to the Brunswick store) to establish waterbed stores. One, in Bangor, has failed after two years. The other, in downtown Portland, has been in business over four years and so predates the Brunswick store. However, it seems to be unprofessionally run and suffers badly from poor management and from the competition of the Brunswick store. It is still hanging on but has been operating without a telephone for about five months. It is not viewed as significant competition.

THE OWNER

The owner holds bachelor of science and bachelor of business administration degrees granted by the University of Wisconsin in 1969 and is currently working toward an M.B.A. at UCLA. In the interim he spent six years in the Navy as an officer and a pilot of multiengine patrol aircraft. While stationed in Maine during his naval service, he conceived and opened the Brunswick waterbed store.

MARKET ANALYSIS

People are curious about waterbeds. Product recognition is generally high, but marketing experience in Maine has shown that potential buyers require extensive consumer education. This education should include a thorough description of the waterbed system, an explanation of its safety, and a clear demonstration of its construction.

West Coast retailers have found that a high-density traffic location is essential. The failure of East Coast retailers to develop a significant marketing and distribution system outside major metropolitan areas is traceable directly to inadequately traveled loca-

[1]Estimate given by Rowanne Haley, Editor of *Industry Magazine,* February, 1977.

tions.[2] Although there are a fair number of outlets from which waterbeds may be purchased, they are generally: small specialty shops that have low traffic, often in out-of-the way spots; shops whose image fails to attract the serious furniture shopper; shops that do not advertise or do not advertise waterbeds; and shops that tend to sell inferior products and to promote them, if at all, improperly.

The Portland location offers a superb opportunity for staking a claim to the undeveloped waterbed market. The ambience of the Maine Mall is ideal for attracting browsers and for increasing the general level of familiarization with the product. The proposed location on the main concourse of the mall should attract a high volume of traffic. In short, a high visibility, high-traffic location that prominently displays attractive modern waterbed systems, that employs a competent staff, and that advertises adequately will draw well and will cultivate a substantial market unhindered by significant competitive drain.

Brunswick experience has shown that a substantial low-end market exists, with sales averaging in the $150 to $200 range. This market will not necessarily predominate in Portland because the more elaborate and complete store should encourage higher-priced sales. Nevertheless, particularly in the current economic climate, considerable demand exists for less expensive bedding. And the least expensive waterbeds are of better quality and of significantly lower price than inexpensive conventional beds. The store will be prepared to handle both elaborate and modest systems, as well as individual components such as mattresses and heaters.

This broad-based approach is consistent with data from sales in Brunswick, which indicate that waterbed customers are difficult to categorize beyond their being predominantly in the 18 to 35 age group. No correlation could be established with respect to sex, race, marital status, employment, education, or income.

SELLING

Selling strategy is based on three interdependent aims: attracting customers to the store, projecting an image of professionalism and competence, and educating the customer about the product.

Every effort will be made to induce people to visit the store. Although the novelty of the waterbeds will draw many shoppers in for a quick look, the experience of the Brunswick store shows that radio advertising will draw customers from all over the southern part of the state, and even from out of state. Television advertising will also be used to increase store traffic.

Good salesmanship will be a major goal; it will focus on educating the customer to the advantages of the waterbed, to understand and accept the facts about the product. The sales technique will focus on a helpful and informative posture aimed at earning the confidence of the customer—an essential prerequisite to doing business successfully in Maine. Emphasis will be on the safety and comfort of flotation sleeping, and on the integrity of the company and its product. Experience shows that if browsers leave the store feeling goodwill and carrying literature about waterbeds, sales will follow.

[2]This conclusion comes from informal discussions with manufacturers and retailers at Chicago Trade Show, April, 1976.

Contrary to popular belief, waterbed customers are not easily categorized but, instead, are quite diverse, and no pat profile can be established. Consequently, it is not productive to direct advertising at a narrow segment of the market; this may alienate more potential customers than it attracts. In particular, a focus on the youth culture will be avoided, as this stereotype is considered counterproductive.

Advertising is recognized as an essential element in the development of the business. It will not present a financial problem to the new Portland store because there will be no additional cost at first. Present advertising for the Brunswick store will simply be amended to include Portland. Once sales volume is sufficient to permit television advertising (planned for the fourth month of operation), Portland will be able to assume its share of this expense.

PLAN OF OPERATION

The owner will act as manager of the store. Initially, one salesperson will be hired; this person will be trained at the Brunswick store prior to the opening of the new location. Because of limited warehousing space and for simplicity in managing it, the Portland store will operate as a satellite of the Brunswick store. Brunswick will do all purchasing, warehousing, and manufacturing and will supply the Portland store as required. Accounts of the two stores will be kept separate, but goods will be transferred at cost. Portland will maintain only a minimum inventory, mostly in display stock, and will incur no advertising or administrative expense initially, simplifying management of the cash flow.

Experience at the Brunswick site has been quite favorable despite its small size and its relatively poor location. With the excellent mall location near the population center of Portland, with the goodwill already attached to the store name, and with the lack of effective competition, it is expected that Portland sales should double those of the Brunswick store within three months of opening, and triple within a year. Because of the simplicity of the operation and the help of the Brunswick store, the Portland venture should show a profit from the first month of operation.

EXHIBIT 1

BALANCE SHEET

1 July 1978

Assets		Liabilities & Equity	
Cash	$ 500	Bank loan	$6,400
Inventory	3,000	Proprietor's	
Fixtures	1,900	capital	3,000
Truck	4,000	TOTAL	$9,400
TOTAL	$9,400		

EXHIBIT 2

FORECASTED MONTHLY SALES

	1978	1979	1980
Jan		$ 8,000	$ 10,000
Feb		10,000	12,000
Mar		15,000	18,000
Apr		12,000	15,000
May		15,000	18,000
Jun		14,000	16,000
Jul	$ 5,000	14,000	16,000
Aug	6,000	15,000	18,000
Sep	10,000	18,000	20,000
Oct	12,000	15,000	18,000
Nov	12,000	15,000	18,000
Dec	12,000	15,000	18,000
TOTAL	$ 57,000	$166,000	$197,000

EXHIBIT 3

CASH FLOW ANALYSIS FOR 1978

	Jul	Aug	Sep	Oct	Nov	Dec
1. Sales (cash)	$5,000	$6,000	$10,000	$12,000	$12,000	$12,000
2. Cost of sales	2,500	3,000	5,000	6,000	6,000	6,000
3. Ending inventory	3,500	3,500	3,500	4,000	4,000	4,000
4. Goods available	6,000	6,500	8,500	10,000	10,000	10,000
5. Beginning inventory	3,000	3,500	3,500	3,500	4,000	4,000
6. PURCHASES	3,000	3,000	5,000	6,500	6,000	6,000
7. Salary—proprietor	0	0	0	1,000	1,000	1,000
8. Salary—salespersons	500	600	1,000	1,200	1,200	1,200
9. Rent	600	600	600	600	600	600
10. Advertising	0	0	0	500	500	500
11. Supplies	100	20	20	30	30	30
12. Telephone	35	20	20	25	25	25
13. Utilities	25	25	25	25	25	25
14. Insurance	60	60	60	60	60	60
15. Truck operation	80	80	80	100	100	100
16. Taxes and misc.	100	100	100	100	100	100
17. EXPENSES	1,500	1,505	1,905	3,640	3,640	3,640
18. Beginning cash	500	936	1,367	3,408	3,724	4,055
19. Cash receipts	5,000	6,000	10,000	12,000	12,000	12,000
20. Cash available	5,500	7,036	11,567	15,708	16,124	16,555
21. Purchases	3,000	3,000	5,000	6,500	6,000	6,000
22. Expenses	1,500	1,505	1,905	3,640	3,640	3,640
23. Interest	64	64	54	44	29	9
24. Loan amortization	0	1,000	1,000	1,500	2,000	900
25. Loan balance	6,400	5,400	4,400	2,900	900	0
26. CASH BALANCE	936	1,367	3,408	3,724	4,055	5,506

Notes:
1. All sales are cash (or credit card).
2. Purchases will all be from the Brunswick store. Normally there will be an immediate cash exchange, but, of course, this will be as flexibile as necessary.
3. Cash-on-hand figures are higher than required to show the comfortable margin allowed.
4. Loan will be arranged as balance due in six months. Schedule allows for probable prepayment.

EXHIBIT 4

INCOME STATEMENTS FOR 1978

	Jul	Aug	Sep	Oct	Nov	Dec	Total
Sales	$5,000	$6,000	$10,000	$12,000	$12,000	$12,000	$57,000
Cost of sales	2,500	3,000	5,000	6,000	6,000	6,000	28,500
Gross margin	2,500	3,000	5,000	6,000	6,000	6,000	28,500
Operating expense	1,500	1,505	1,905	3,640	3,640	3,640	15,830
Interest expense	64	64	54	44	29	9	264
Depreciation (truck & fixtures)	164	164	164	164	164	164	984
Total deduction	1,728	1,733	2,123	3,848	3,833	3,813	17,078
NET PROFIT	772	1,267	2,877	2,152	2,167	2,187	11,422

EXHIBIT 5

YEARLY INCOME STATEMENT, 1978

Sales		$57,000
Cost of sales		28,500
		28,500
Salaries	$ 8,700	
Rent	3,600	
Advertising	1,500	
Supplies	230	
Telephone	150	
Utilities	150	
Insurance	360	
Interest expense	264	
Truck operation	540	
Taxes and misc.	600	
Depreciation	984	
Total expenses	$17,078	17,078
Net profit		11,422
Proprietor's capital		3,000
Net profit 1978		11,422
TOTAL		$14,422

349

EXHIBIT 6

BALANCE SHEET

31 December 1978

	Assets		Liabilities & Equity	
Cash		$ 5,506	Proprietor's capital	$ 3,000
Inventory		4,000	Add net profit	
Fixtures	$1,900		1978	11,422
Depreciation	317	1,583	TOTAL	$14,422
Truck	4,000			
Depreciation	667	3,333		
TOTAL		$14,422		

EXHIBIT 7

MISCELLANEOUS DATA

Cost of Fixtures

Carpet—90 yds @ $10/yd	$ 900
Partitions and interior finishing	N/C
Sales counter	100
Cash register	300
Sign	600
TOTAL COST OF FIXTURES	$1,900

Straight line depreciation over 36 months
52.78/mo × 6 mo = 316.67

Purchase of delivery van (used) $4,000
Straight line depreciation over 36 months
111.11/mo. × 6 mo. = 666.67

Initial Inventory

5 display beds @ $200	$1,000
Accompanying furniture	500
Bedspreads	400
Sheets	300
Beanbag chairs	300
Accessories	100
Mattresses	200
Heaters	200
TOTAL INITIAL INVENTORY	$3,000

Store Rental Fee
Dimensions—15' wide × 60' deep
900 sq ft @ $7.50/sq ft/yr = 6,750/yr = 598.75/mo

EXHIBIT 8

CASH FLOW ANALYSIS FOR 1979

	Jan	Feb	Mar	Apr	May
1. Sales (cash)	$ 8,000	$10,000	$15,000	$12,000	$15,000
2. Cost of sales	4,000	5,000	7,500	6,000	7,500
3. Ending inventory	4,500	5,000	4,500	6,500	6,500
4. Goods available	8,500	10,000	12,000	12,500	14,000
5. Beginning inventory	4,000	4,500	5,000	4,500	6,500
6. PURCHASES	4,500	5,500	7,000	8,000	7,500
7. Salary—proprietor	1,500	1,500	1,500	1,500	1,500
8. Salary—salespersons	800	1,000	1,500	1,200	1,500
9. Rent	700	700	700	700	700
10. Advertising	700	700	700	700	700
11. Supplies	30	30	30	30	30
12. Telephone	30	30	30	30	30
13. Utilities	30	30	30	30	30
14. Insurance	60	60	60	60	60
15. Truck operation	80	100	150	120	150
16. Taxes and misc.	300	300	300	300	300
17. EXPENSES	4,230	4,450	5,000	4,670	5,000
18. Beginning cash	5,506	4,776	4,826	7,826	7,156
19. Cash receipts	8,000	10,000	15,000	12,000	15,000
20. Cash available	13,506	14,776	19,826	19,826	22,156
21. Purchases	4,500	5,500	7,000	8,000	7,500
22. Expenses	4,230	4,450	5,000	4,670	5,000
23. Interest	0	0	0	0	0
24. Loan amortization	0	0	0	0	0
25. Loan balance	0	0	0	0	0
26. CASH BALANCE	4,776	4,826	7,826	7,156	9,656

	Jun	Jul	Aug	Sep	Oct	Nov	Dec
	$14,000	$14,000	$15,000	$18,000	$15,000	$15,000	$15,000
	7,000	7,000	7,500	9,000	7,500	7,500	7,500
	6,500	6,500	7,000	7,500	7,500	7,500	6,500
	13,500	13,500	14,500	16,500	15,000	15,000	14,000
	6,500	6,500	6,500	7,000	7,500	7,500	7,500
	7,000	7,000	8,000	9,500	7,500	7,500	6,500
	1,500	1,500	1,500	1,500	1,500	1,500	1,500
	1,400	1,400	1,500	1,800	1,500	1,500	1,500
	700	700	700	700	700	700	700
	700	700	700	700	700	700	700
	30	35	35	35	35	35	35
	30	35	35	35	35	35	35
	30	30	30	30	30	30	30
	60	60	60	60	60	60	60
	140	140	150	150	150	150	150
	300	300	300	300	300	300	300
	4,890	4,900	5,010	5,310	5,010	5,010	5,010
	9,656	11,766	13,866	15,856	19,046	21,536	24,026
	14,000	14,000	15,000	18,000	15,000	15,000	15,000
	23,656	25,766	28,866	33,856	34,046	36,536	39,026
	7,000	7,000	8,000	9,500	7,500	7,500	6,500
	4,890	4,900	5,010	5,310	5,010	5,010	5,010
	0	0	0	0	0	0	0
	0	0	0	0	0	0	0
	0	0	0	0	0	0	0
	11,766	13,866	15,856	19,046	21,536	24,026	27,516

EXHIBIT 9

INCOME STATEMENTS FOR 1979

	Jan	Feb	Mar	Apr	May	Jun
Sales	$8,000	$10,000	$15,000	$12,000	$15,000	$14,000
Cost of sales	4,000	5,000	7,500	6,000	7,500	7,000
Gross margin	4,000	5,000	7,500	6,000	7,500	7,000
Operating expenses	4,230	4,450	5,000	4,670	5,000	4,890
Depreciation (truck & fixtures)	164	164	164	164	164	164
Total deductions	4,394	4,614	5,164	4,834	5,164	5,054
NET PROFIT	(394)	386	2,336	1,166	2,336	1,946

	Jul	Aug	Sep	Oct	Nov	Dec	Total
	$14,000	$15,000	$18,000	$15,000	$15,000	$15,000	$166,000
	7,000	7,500	9,000	7,500	7,500	7,500	83,000
	7,000	7,500	9,000	7,500	7,500	7,500	83,000
	4,900	5,010	5,310	5,010	5,010	5,010	58,490
	164	164	164	164	164	164	1,968
	5,064	5,174	5,474	5,174	5,174	5,174	60,458
	1,936	2,326	3,526	2,326	2,326	2,326	22,542

EXHIBIT 10

YEARLY INCOME STATEMENT, 1979

Sales		$166,000
Cost of sales		83,000
Gross margin		83,000
Salaries	$34,600	
Rent	8,400	
Advertising	8,400	
Supplies	390	
Telephone	390	
Utilities	360	
Insurance	720	
Truck operation	1,630	
Taxes and misc.	3,600	
Depreciation	1,968	
Total expenses	60,458	60,458
Net profit		22,542
Proprietor's capital 1978		3,000
Net profit 1978		11,422
Net profit 1979		22,542
TOTAL		$36,964

EXHIBIT 11

BALANCE SHEET

31 December 1979

Assets			Liabilities & Equity	
Cash		$27,516		
Inventory		6,500	Proprietor's Capital	$36,964
Fixtures and truck	5,900			
—Depreciation	2,952 =	2,948		
TOTAL		$36,964		

355

Pacific Clear Writing Clinics:
A Prospectus

This prospectus outlines a plan for a venture aimed at teaching adults in business, government, and not-for-profit organizations how to write clear, concise memos, letters, and reports. The venture stems from the founder's experience in teaching professionals and managers the craft of clear writing.

Pacific Clear Writing Clinics recognizes the need for clear writing that exists at all management, administrative, and supervisory levels in most organizations today. Pacific offers a training service designed to fill this need.

We conduct in-house clear writing clinics for adults whose jobs require writing of a professional quality: executives, managers, administrators, engineers, scientists, technical writers, supervisors, secretaries—all persons who need or wish to improve their writing skills.

PLANNED MARKET SEGMENTS

Pacific addresses three market segments; each of our clinics is designed for a special market:

1. *Overcoming Fear of Writing* keys its contents to individuals who must write or want to write and who experience difficulty in getting started. This clinic is psychologically oriented and teaches techniques for unblocking, for liberating creativity.

2. *The Craft of Clear Writing* is skills-oriented. It is designed for people in industrial, business, government, and not-for-profit organizations who must write clear reports, letters, and memos. This clinic presents techniques for writing clear, concise, expository prose.

3. *The Technique of Proposal Writing* fits a market segment consisting of organizations that get some or much of their business through bidding by proposal. Bidding is usually highly competitive. Proposals must be prepared skillfully to win business. This clinic offers methods and techniques for acquiring the skills to prepare successful proposals.

REACHING OUR MARKETS

Our programs for *Overcoming Fear of Writing* and *The Craft of Clear Writing* have been tested, modified, and strengthened over the past seven years in many university-sponsored continuing education seminars for adults. During this time we gathered information about our participants.

The audience for *Overcoming Fear of Writing* consists mainly of mature professionals, administrators, writers of all kinds who write but who have many difficulties associated with their writing.

The Craft of Clear Writing attracts mainly people in business, managers, technical professionals, secretaries and supervisors whose jobs require them to write for themselves and for their bosses.

The Technique of Proposal Writing attracts as clients technically oriented companies for the most part.

Our experience to date shows that the most effective way to reach our audience for *Overcoming Fear of Writing* is through limited local advertising and direct mail advertising, and through word-of-mouth referral from previous clients.

Promotion for *The Craft of Clear Writing* and *The Technique of Proposal Writing* gets the best results with least expense through telephone contacts and referrals from one satisfied client organization to another. Successful contacts result in clinics conducted on the client's premises. *The Craft of Clear Writing* may well respond to a mail order and limited advertising campaign; we plan to experiment with this approach this year.

FINANCIAL ESTIMATES

We estimate gross sales for the next three years as follows:

1978	$68,750
1979	$157,000
1980	$206,000

On the basis of these annual gross sales, we expect to produce a gross profit before taxes of:

1978	0
1979	$27,000
1980	$33,000

We estimate the starting capital we will need to found Pacific at $7000.

PACIFIC'S OBJECTIVES

We have tested our market in the past two years by conducting clear writing clinics for the general public under university sponsorship and in-house for several companies. We have seen substantial and rapid improvement in the writing of participants in our seminars. This has been evidenced by feedback from both individuals and the companies for which they work. As a result of these experiences we are able to state that our clinics promote clear, concise writing. They serve the purposes of the organization in achieving clarity in internal and external written communications, and they therefore help individuals achieve their career goals.

The teaching approach Pacific uses in its clinics offers unique advantages. It is designed for adults. The instructors present principles of clear writing in short talks. The participants engage in exercises tailored to reinforce the learning of the basic principles of clear writing to which they have been exposed. Exercises are practiced individually and in small groups.

This method of teaching has been developed by the founder of Pacific over a twenty-three-year period. Pacific's director, and instructors have been consistently gratified to see quick, positive, and permanent results from our seminars. Our participants experience immediate and substantial improvement in their writing.

QUALIFICATIONS OF THE MANAGING DIRECTOR

The managing director of Pacific, Anthony Herald, B.S.M.E., M.B.A., brings to his position as chief executive an extensive background in both business and management and in teaching clear writing. Mr. Herald has had over twenty-five years of line management experience in small and large business organizations.

Herald experienced the need for clear writing in the reports submitted to him for his signature by senior engineers who worked for him in the research and development division of a large corporation in 1954. At that time he asked the management training group to teach his engineers how to write clear, well-organized, concise reports. The training group countered with the suggestion that he do this himself. Herald agreed to take on the teaching chore with management training assisting in the preparation of a course syllabus.

At the end of the first training sessions, which took fifteen instruction hours, Herald saw a clear improvement in the writing that came from his group. At the request of the chief engineer of the company, Herald took on the task of training 5000 other technical people in the company in the craft of clear writing.

Anthony Herald has taught this subject ever since, both for educational institutions and for private organizations.

CHARACTER OF THE BUSINESS

Pacific wishes to project a professional image as a highly qualified company capable of fulfilling its promise to help its clients gain significant improvement in the subject areas of our clinics. Our selling approach will be low key, without fanfare and hoopla. We aim for a careful presentation of professional competence in all aspects and details.

All promotional materials, including logo, letterheads, memos, reports, telephone manners, and advertising will be tailored to support the image of professional competence we wish to portray.

358

DEALING WITH COMPETITION

A limited number of individuals and companies now offer the kind of service we have described. In this county not more than a dozen individual consultants present seminars in writing. Half of these concentrate on writing from a literary point of view. The others gear their work primarily to business writing. As far as our research shows, no firm in the county offers the specific programs we offer. Nor do they use the advanced pedagogical techniques we have adopted and continue to perfect. Most of our competition comes from university professors or ex-English teachers.

Our strategy for meeting competition centers in our unique approach to instruction and on reference to satisfied clients. We use three avenues for substantiating our claims: letters from satisfied clients, phone checks to former clients by prospective clients, and written appraisals of our clinics by the participants.

Features of our teaching methods include using modern applied psychology to help clients unblock; presentations carefully prepared in the language of the organization; specific tools for achieving clear, concrete, concise writing; exercises in writing developed from the client organization's own examples of bad writing; and a carefully developed, lively, and supportive climate that makes learning a joyful occasion.

DESCRIPTION OF OUR SERVICE

Overcoming Fear of Writing presents a workshop-clinic designed especially for those who want or need to write but who have trouble getting words on paper. This clinic helps participants gain self-confidence and unlearn the psychological obstacles to writing easily and well. Techniques derived from current research in brain hemisphere function and from holistic learning theory are used in an innovative approach to writing with minimum anxiety and maximum competence.

Overcoming Fear of Writing, conducted in a supportive environment, is an introduction to the process and psychology of writing and to practical strategies for unblocking, for discovering one's personal voice, and for becoming one's own teacher.

Participants are given the opportunity to explore the process of composition, to share their experience and insights, to discover meaning in resistance, and to practice specific techniques and strategies that reduce anxiety and enhance the writer's natural fluency and skill.

The Craft of Clear Writing offers a workshop-clinic in written communication skills for executives and professionals. The goal of this clinic is to enable each participant to write clear, simple, direct, and persuasive expository prose and to do so with a minimum of anxiety and a maximum of competence. Most business writing is bad writing. It fails to communicate. It is often unclear, badly organized, and dull. It is hard to read (and harder to write). Most people have been taught to fear and hate writing. This clinic is conducted in a lively and supportive environment; it is designed to help participants improve the ease and competence with which they write.

Topics include:

- Analysis of individual writing problems

- Writing for the boss, associates, customers

- How to get started when you can't

- Writing for readers

- Testing for your obscurity quotient

- Building a blacklist of words you won't use

- Beginnings and organizing

- Being persuasive but honest

- Language as power

Individual and small group exercises in the special language of the organization allow opportunities for practice and feedback. Our instructors welcome discussion. Participants are encouraged to share their experiences and insights.

The Technique of Proposal Writing is for those who have to prepare proposals for government procurements, internal company or agency purposes, grants, or commercial purposes. It is designed as a workshop-clinic in which the participants are given the opportunity to practice the kind of writing that makes for a good proposal.

Major topics covered in this clinic are:

- What makes a good proposal?

- What makes a bad proposal?

- Fixing a faulty proposal

- Why are so many proposals bad?

- Avoiding pitfalls

- Proposal format and structure

- Exercise in proposal writing

- Controlling the cost of the proposal

- Organizing to write the proposal

- Techniques and procedures for proposal writing

- Elements of clear writing

This clinic was designed on the basis of eighteen years' experience in writing proposals in industry. The principles and procedures offered have been used by the instructors in actuality to produce proposals that resulted in many millions of dollars worth of business.

COST OF PACIFIC CLEAR WRITING CLINICS

We usually recommend a series of three five-hour workshop-clinics for in-house programs. Groups are limited to twenty-five people for best teaching results. Our fee for

360

this program is $2750, plus out-of-pocket expenses, as is customary, at cost. A reference book and complete course outline are given to each participant.

MARKETING STRATEGY AND SELLING TACTICS

In the beginning, the marketing strategy for *Overcoming Fear of Writing* requires a somewhat different approach from *The Craft of Clear Writing* and *The Technique of Proposal Writing.*

Data collected about the attendees in university-sponsored *Overcoming Fear of Writing* seminars show that the typical audience is composed of women and men predominantly in the twenty-five- to thirty-five-year-old bracket. Women make up about two-thirds of any seminar group. The typical participant is well-educated, articulate, and has an annual income in the range of $15,000 to $30,000. A specialized mail campaign appears the most logical method for developing business for this clinic.

As clinics are put on through mail campaigns, data will be gathered from the participants. This information will be converted into a mailing list that will be expanded with time and used for future promotional purposes.

The other two clinics, *The Craft of Clear Writing* and *The Technique of Proposal Writing,* will be promoted through personal selling. First contacts will be made by telephone. These will be followed by personal meetings with executives who have the power to authorize the clinics. As an aid to campaigning for business, satisfied clients will be asked to give the names of friends in other organizations that might be developed into clients. Referrals of this kind make calling easier and more productive than cold calling.

Clients Served Recently

Anthony Herald has tested the market and the material presented at the clinics by conducting actual workshop-seminars for a number of different organizations. In the past several years he has conducted clear writing clinics for adults in the Industrial Relations Center at Caltech, for continuing education programs through the University of California, for Michigan State University, and for many business, industrial, and government clients. Among his clients have been the key executive groups of:

- Forest Lawn
- Southern California Gas Company
- Automobile Club of Southern California
- Pertec
- Logicon Corporation
- Perkin-Elmer
- City of Inglewood
- City of Garden Grove

- Orange County Transit District
- Pioneer Hospital of Norwalk

On the basis of this experience, the programs we offer have a tested foundation upon which to build the Pacific Clear Writing Clinics' future.

PLAN OF OPERATION

The Pacific organization consists of a small central staff employing external consultants who have been specially trained to conduct our seminars. The central staff includes:

Anthony Herald, Managing Director
Lucille Romand, Associate Director
Marie Enciso, Secretary

Consultants trained and available to instruct in the workshop-clinics are:

Alathena Kennert, M.A., M.L.S.
Robert J. Langloise, D.B.A.
Karen Johnson, Ph.D.
Anne I. Grayson, Ph.D.

Resumes of Key Personnel

Anthony Herald, Managing Director brings to Pacific over twenty years in line management and much experience in writing successful proposals for both private industry and government contracts. He has started and run three successful small businesses and keeps his hand in now by running his own consulting firm.

Herald has conducted educational seminars for executives at many universities and colleges. He was at Yale University as Visiting Fellow in Industrial Administration for the academic year 1965–1966. He served as lecturer in administration in the Graduate School of Administration, University of California, Irvine, from 1969 to 1971. He currently teaches in the Graduate School of Management, UCLA. And he is the author of four books on management subjects as well as numerous articles on management principles and practice.

Mr. Herald has taught the craft of clear writing in university-sponsored programs and in in-house clinics for business organizations for the past twenty-three years.

Anne I. Grayson, Ph.D., consultant-instructor, has taught writing at UCLA, Berkeley, and other campuses of the University of California as well as at Golden Gate University and the Industrial Relations Center of the California Institute of Technology. Her doctoral studies at the University of California, Berkeley, were in higher education, with a concentration in learning psychology and creativity.

Ms. Grayson's special clinic, *Overcoming Fear of Writing,* is the direct result of her dissatisfaction with traditional approaches to teaching composition, of her concern about the epidemic among adults of the "battered writer" syndrome, and of her research in therapeutic learning.

Herself a writer, Anne Grayson's poetry has appeared in *Atlantic, Chicago Review, Yankee,* and *Ploughshares,* among others.

Ms. Grayson serves as consultant to business and government and works extensively with private clients.

Alathena Kennert, M.A., M.L.S., consultant-instructor, has worked for the past five years as an independent consultant to technologically based firms, helping them to improve their report writing. Her background includes eight years of teaching English composition at the college level. Ms. Kennert then spent seven years at a large aerospace company, first as a technical writer, then as a trainer in report writing for engineers and scientists in that company. She brings a solid background of principle and practice to her teaching in our clinic-workshops.

Karen H. Johnson, Ph.D., taught creative writing at the university level for six years. She then devoted two years to writing articles and short stories for various journals and magazines. More recently she consults with television and movie script writers, helping them to solve their writing problems. Ms. Johnson brings her special competence in this area to our staff of Pacific's consultant-instructors.

Robert J. Langloise, D.B.A., worked as a staff specialist in organized development for Mille International Corporation for seven years before setting up his own management consulting office in Chicago. During his assignments, he became aware of the difficulty his client firms had with written communications. He noticed particularly the need for training in technical and business proposal writing and decided to develop a specialty in this area. His work came to the attention of many technically oriented firms including Orion Research & Development Corporation. This company and other West Coast companies have used his consulting help in the preparation of various kinds of reports for the past eighteen years.

Mr. Langloise's affiliation with our firm adds great strength in teaching the techniques of proposal writing.

LOCATION AND FACILITIES

Pacific's operations require only a modest office. A central location is not important because business is conducted by telephone, mail, and in person at the client's office. Therefore, an office of about two hundred square feet is adequate for our purpose; it can be located in a low-rent area.

Facilities required are also modest and include the following: desk, conference and work table, six chairs, three three-drawer file cabinets, two typewriters (one IBM or other correcting machine and one regulation electric machine), copying machine, and miscellaneous small office equipment.

STARTING CAPITAL, EXPENSES, AND PROFIT

The starting capital for Pacific is estimated to be $7000 and the estimated expenses for the first year of operation are $18,000. Breakdowns of these figures are given in the tables that follow.

On the basis of the forecasted sales for the first three years, the estimates of fees to be paid to consultant-instructors, and the estimated expenses for each year, the funds available for salaries to staff and draw to the proprietor are shown at the end of these tables. Profit that may be reinvested is also shown.

The fundamental characteristic of the business permits a high contributed value once the first stages of investment, development of the programs, training of consultants in the instructional techniques, and growth has taken place. Simply stated, Pacific has a high potential for producing profit.

EXHIBIT 1

ESTIMATED STARTING CAPITAL REQUIRED AND EXPENSES

1. Rent, three months advance @ $250/month: $ 750

2. Office equipment and supplies:

2 desks	$ 500	
2 3-drawer file cabinets	150	
1 executive typewriter	900	
1 office electric typewriter	400	
Secretary's chair	90	
6 office chairs	390	
Conference table	400	
Miscellaneous small equipment	100	
Stationery and supplies, including graphic art work	600	
Miscellaneous advance payments	750	
Cushion for unexpected costs	2,000	
Total	6,280	
	7,030	
Estimated starting capital, say,	$7,000	

3. Estimated expenses per month, first year:

Rent	$ 250
Telephone	150
Utilities	100
Promotion	150
Supplies	100
Postage	75
Insurance	75
Fees	50
Miscellaneous	250
Taxes	300
	1,500

Total for the year = $18,000

4. Forecasted sales

	1979	1980	1981
Jan	$ 2,750	$ 11,000	$ 16,500
Feb	2,750	11,000	16,500
Mar	2,750	11,000	16,500
Apr	5,500	13,750	16,500
May	8,250	13,750	19,250
Jun	5,500	13,750	19,250
Jul	2,750	11,000	16,500
Aug	2,750	11,000	13,750
Sep	5,500	13,750	16,500
Oct	8,250	13,750	16,500
Nov	11,000	16,500	19,250
Dec	11,000	16,500	19,250
	$68,750	$156,750	$206,250
	25	57	75	client assignments

5. Estimated fees to consultants:

Year	Fees
1979	25 × $750 per 15-hour work-shop = $18,750
1980	57 × 825 per 15-hour work-shop = 47,025
1981	75 × 900 per 15-hour work-shop = 67,500

6. Estimated funds available for salaries,
   draw for proprietor, reinvestment in the
   business, and taxes:

1979

Gross income		$ 68,750
Expenses	$18,000	
Fees	18,750	
		36,750
Available funds		$ 32,000

1980

Gross income		$156,750
Expenses (increased 15%)	$20,700	
Fees	47,025	
		67,725
Available funds		$ 89,025

1981

Gross income		$206,250
Expenses (increased 25%)	$25,875	
Fees	67,500	
		93,375
Available funds		$112,875

7. *Note:* If the owner draws the amounts shown each year, the amounts available for profit and reinvestment in the business would be as follows:

	1979	1980	1981
Available funds	$32,000	$89,000	$113,000
Owner's draw	16,000	32,000	45,000
For profit and reinvestment	$16,000	$57,000	$ 68,000
Assume reinvestment of	16,000	30,000	35,000
Gross profit before taxes	0	$27,000	$ 33,000

EXHIBIT 2

Typical announcement for promotional brochure

PACIFIC CLEAR WRITING CLINICS

The Craft of Clear Writing

The goal of this program is to enable each participant to write clear, simple, direct, and persuasive expository prose and to do so with a minimum of anxiety.

Most business writing is bad writing. It fails to communicate. It is often unclear, badly organized—and dull. It is hard to read (and hell to write). THIS IS NOT YOUR FAULT. Most people have been TAUGHT to fear and hate writing. This program is a clinic for adults, specifically tailored to the requirements of executives, managers, administrators, administrative and staff assistants, and engineers and other professionals whose work requires them to write well.

Writing Without Tears

The format of the program includes:

Specific principles of effective writing—we will NOT concern ourselves with the traditional emphasis on mechanics of "grammar" and "composition" to which you may have been subjected as a student.

Class and small group exercises in the techniques and skills relating to these principles.

Minimum of lecturing by the instructor.

Two texts and a notebook containing detailed outlines and notes will be given to each registrant.

Specific Topics to Be Covered

- What you should know about your readers; improving readability.
- Using outlines and file cards.
- Methods for organizing a logical structure.
- Writing like you talk—approximately.
- How to judge when your writing is clear and effective, and what to do about it when it isn't.
- How to write when you can't: techniques for overcoming blocks to writing.
- Formats for memos, letters, and short and long reports.
- How to influence your boss—and make him or her like it.

More practical help for managing your own business.

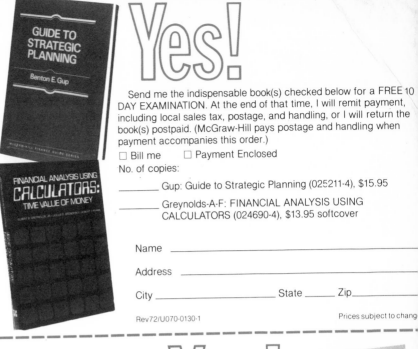

GUIDE TO STRATEGIC PLAN-NING Benton E. Gup, University of Tulsa

Learn the techniques of successful strategic planning with Gup's outstanding new guide. You'll find valuable advice on such issues as portfolio theory, financial decision making, portfolio strategies, managing dividend policies and leverage for growth, methods of valuation, and many more.
1980, 239 pages

FINANCIAL ANALYSIS USING CALCULATORS: Time Value of Money
Elbert B. Greynolds, Jr., Julius S. Aronofsky, and Robert J. Frame, all of Southern Methodist University

This valuable new book shows how to use hand-held calculators to solve a wide variety of financial analysis problems. Among the important topics covered are the analysis of investments, mortgages, leases, and sinking funds.
1980, 472 pages

LEADERSHIP: What Effective Managers Really Do . . . And How They Do It
Leonard R. Sayles, Columbia University

This insightful book shows what successful managers *really* do to motivate subordinates, introduce change, influence their bosses, and maintain and improve their resource and political base. Full of how-to-do-it advice and vivid examples, it provides a highly realistic account of managerial in-fighting and the impact of personality differences on managerial styles.
1979, 288 pages

EFFECTIVE LETTERS: A Program for Self-Instruction 3/e
James M. Reid, Jr., James M. Reid Company, and Robert M. Wendlinger, Bank of America

Here's a tested, easy-to-follow guide for improving an essential business skill: writing successful business letters. Based on a program developed jointly by McGraw-Hill and the New York Life Insurance Company, its unique programmed format allows you to practice writing letters as you learn new techniques.
1978, 304 pages

Want additional copies of *How to Start Your Own Business . . . and Succeed?* (It makes a great gift, as well as an indispensable addition to your professional library!) Just fill out and mail the attached postpaid card.

More practical help for managing your own business.

GUIDE TO
STRATEGIC
PLANNING

Benton E. Gup